Tax Systems and Tax Reforms in Europe

The last decade has seen important changes taking place in the tax regimes of many European countries. A comprehensive picture of what is happening in European fiscal systems has not been easy to find – until now.

This comprehensive volume provides impressive analyses of tax systems and tax reforms in various European countries including France, Germany, Italy and the United Kingdom. With a Preface from Vito Tanzi and a large range of contributions, the book identifies and analyzes the main common forces that drive fiscal reforms such as globalization, European reunification and fiscal federalism.

This book will be of great interest not only to academics interested in international finance and fiscal studies but also to those professionals involved in the financial sectors across the world.

Luigi Bernardi is Professor of Public Finance at the University of Pavia, Italy. **Paola Profeta** is Assistant Professor of Public Economics at the University of Pavia, Italy.

Routledge studies in the modern world economy

Tax Systems and Tax Reforms in Europe

Edited by
Luigi Bernardi and Paola Profeta

Foreword by Vito Tanzi

LONDON AND NEW YORK

First published 2004
by Routledge
11 New Fetter Lane, London EC4P 4EE

Simultaneously published in the USA and Canada
by Routledge
29 West 35th Street, New York, NY 10001

Transferred to Digital Printing 2004

Routledge is an imprint of the Taylor & Francis Group

Typeset in Baskerville by Wearset Ltd, Boldon, Tyne and Wear
Printed and bound in Great Britain by TJI Digital, Padstow, Cornwall

British Library Cataloguing in Publication Data
A catalogue record for this book is available from the British Library

Library of Congress Cataloging in Publication Data
A catalog record for this book has been requested

ISBN 0-415-32251-0

Contents

viii   *Contents*

Figures

Tables

Contributors

Graziano Abrate, Ph.D. student. University of Pavia and University College of London. Dipartimento di Economia Pubblica e Territoriale. Università di Pavia. Strada Nuova 65. 27100 Pavia, Italy.

Luigi Bernardi, Professor of Public Finance. University of Pavia. Dipartimento di Economia Pubblica e Territoriale. Università di Pavia. Strada Nuova 65. 27100 Pavia, Italy.

Fedele de Novellis, Senior Economist, Ref-Research on Economics and Finance. Via Gioberti 5. 20123 Milano, Italy.

Luca Gandullia, Professor of Public Economics. University of Genoa and OECD. Dipartimento di Scienze Economiche e Finanziarie-DISEFIN. Largo Zecca 8–14. 16124 Genova, Italy.

Giorgia Chiara Maffini, Ph.D. student. University of Pavia and University College of London. Dipartimento di Economia Pubblica e Territoriale. Università di Pavia. Strada Nuova 65. 27100 Pavia, Italy.

Giuseppe Migali, Ph.D. student. University of Pavia and University College of London. Dipartimento di Economia Pubblica e Territoriale. Università di Pavia. Strada Nuova 65. 27100 Pavia, Italy.

Salvatore Parlato, Senior Economist. Ref-Research on Economics and Finance. Via Gioberti 5. 20123 Milano, Italy.

Paola Profeta, Assistant Professor of Public Economics and Lecturer of Economics. Università di Pavia and Università Bocconi. Dipartimento di Economia Pubblica e Territoriale. Università di Pavia. Strada Nuova 65. 27100 Pavia, Italy.

Alessandro Sommacal, Ph.D. student. University of Pavia and Catholic University of Louvain. Dipartimento di Economia Pubblica e Territoriale. Università di Pavia. Strada Nuova 65. 27100 Pavia, Italy.

Simona Scabrosetti, Ph.D. student. University of Pavia. Dipartimento di Economia Pubblica e Territoriale. Università di Pavia. Strada Nuova 65. 27100 Pavia, Italy.

Vito Tanzi, Former Deputy Secretary of State for Economy and Finance, Italian Government. Via XX Settembre 75. 00100 Roma, Italy.

Davide Tondani, Ph.D. student, University of Pavia and University of Leuven. Dipartimento di Economia Pubblica e Territoriale. Università di Pavia. Strada Nuova 65. 27100 Pavia, Italy.

Foreword

Common pressures to reform European tax systems

Vito Tanzi

Introduction

In recent years, taxation has been a lively area of economic policy as many countries have proceeded to reform their tax systems to achieve either revenue or other objectives. This book is a contribution to the large literature on tax systems and tax reforms. Its main aim is to provide a comparative and economically oriented description of the tax systems of seven European countries. At the same time the book provides useful information on how these systems have changed in recent decades. The countries covered by this survey were chosen to include the four largest European countries, plus Spain, the Netherlands and Ireland, countries that for different reasons were deemed to warrant inclusion.

The authors of the chapters looking at each individual country were asked to cover similar aspects of taxation so as to make it possible for the reader to draw general conclusions. The chapters have been given a broadly similar structure that should make the book particularly useful to scholars interested in comparative tax analysis. The chapters cover a period of about three decades, starting in 1970. The chapters looking at individual countries are preceded by three general chapters that discuss issues which are not country-specific, plus a comparative survey of the country studies. These include: (a) a comparative view of recent changes and reforms in the selected European tax systems; (b) the opportunities for more radical reforms than those recently adopted or at present under way; (c) the political economy of tax reform; and (d) the relation between tax reform and fiscal consolidation in the European Union.

The present chapter provides a general introduction to the book. It does not summarize its content and does not focus on any single aspect. Rather, it presents a few general reflections that the reader may wish to keep in mind as he or she reads the book. It also provides a few observations on the tax reforms of recent years.

Tax reforms are rarely made in a vacuum. They normally reflect needs or concerns of a particular country, or react to particular domestic or external pressures. These needs or pressures are not likely to be the same for different countries. At the same time, especially for countries from a given region, it is realistic to assume that there is some commonality in the pressure they experience and that these, at given times, induce the policy makers to enact tax reforms in their countries.

For the European countries, the common pressures experienced in recent years are likely to have come from: (a) the globalization of the world economies and the impact of this phenomenon on the tax revenue of specific countries; (b) the constraints imposed on Member Countries by the process of European unification; (c) the perceived need to reduce the high taxes on labor; (d) the process of fiscal decentralization going on in several countries; (e) possibly the links that may exist between the level and structure of public expenditure and the level and structure of taxation; and (f) the need for tax simplification.

A brief discussion of these common pressures may be worthwhile, but it must be understood that some of these effects have gone in directions that have tended to neutralize others in terms of impact on revenue. In other words, while some tended to reduce the level of taxation, others tended to raise it.

Globalization

Particularly in recent years, the intensification or the deepening of the process of integration of the world economies, combined with the liberalization of capital movements on the part of many countries, has started to have a growing impact on the tax revenue and on the structure of tax systems (see Tanzi 1995). The finance ministers of, for example, France and Germany, have at times complained about the negative impact that, in their opinion, globalization and tax competition were having on the tax revenue of their countries. As a consequence there have been progressively more insistent requests on the part of some political figures to harmonize the tax systems in order to reduce tax competition.

Globalization has: (a) stimulated tax competition among countries. In other words it has encouraged some countries to take advantage of the globalization process to attempt to export some of their tax burden; (b) increased the elasticity and the mobility of some tax bases with respect to the effective tax rates; and (c) made tax administrators and policy makers begin to worry about the impact of these developments on the tax system of their country. Some countries have began to take measures aimed at neutralizing or, at least, at reducing some of the unwanted effects of globalization. Several countries have reformed their systems of income taxation to give preferential treatment to income from capital to discourage its emigration to other countries. The introduction of dual income taxes in the countries of Northern Europe or the reduction of tax rates on financial income in other countries are examples of attempts to respond in some systematic way to the challenge posed by globalization (see

Sorensen 1994). These changes not only tend to reduce the progressivity of the income tax but they change this tax in a more fundamental way.

For much of the past 50 years, many experts on taxation have followed Henry Simons' view that individuals should be taxed on their total or *global* income with *progressive* rates (see Simons 1938). This view was strongly endorsed by influential economists such as Richard Musgrave, Joseph Pechman, Richard Goode and others, and had much influence in shaping the tax systems of many (though not all) countries in the period after World War II. A global income tax requires the pooling (in a conceptual basket) of all the incomes of a person, regardless of their source, before the "global" income is subjected to the progressive tax rates.

For the majority of individuals who receive most of their income from work but, additionally, have some income from capital sources, this approach implies that the income from capital sources becomes the marginal income. As such, the latter is taxed at the highest tax rate to which the taxpayers are subject. Because these rates were at times very high, the incentive to evade the high taxes, by taking the financial capital out of the country, was great. Globalization has made it easy for capital to emigrate to places where it is taxed at low rates or is not taxed at all. Some of the reforms described in this book were a reaction to these concerns. It remains to be seen whether globalization will eventually kill completely the global income tax while giving more intellectual respectability to the old-fashioned schedular taxes that existed in Latin countries and that were much maligned by scholars from Anglo-Saxon countries.

European unification and the Maastricht criterion

In order to be admitted to the exclusive club that is the European Monetary Union (EMU), countries were required to satisfy certain economic criteria, among which were those related to the public accounts. In particular, the fiscal deficit of a country, defined according to specific Eurostat definition, had to be less than 3 percent of GDP and was supposed to be progressively reduced to zero under normal cyclical conditions after the country joined the EMU. Countries that found it difficult to reduce primary public spending were forced to raise more tax revenue in order to be able to cut the deficit to the required level. This was the case of Italy. Thus, some of the changes in the tax systems introduced in the 1990s were a reflection of the need to meet one of the Maastricht criteria. The need to raise the tax burden at times contrasted with the policy makers' desire to reduce the countries' fiscal burdens or with their electoral promises.

The perceived need to reduce taxes on labor

In recent years there has been a growing preoccupation to reduce the high taxes levied on labor income. In fact a large share of the countries' total taxes comes from this source. The chapters in this book that deal with country-specific experiences show that the tax wedge on labor income tends to be very high, in some countries more than others. There is a widespread view that this high wedge contributes to high unemployment so that its reduction would lead to more employment. At international meetings, the policy makers of European countries have stated their commitments to reduce these high wedges on labor income. Some countries (Italy, for example) have started to move in this direction. It is, however, an open question as to how far these tax wedges can be reduced, especially in the short term.

First, since labor is a less elastic tax base than capital, or even than some consumption, taxes on labor can be cut substantially *only* if total taxes can be reduced. But the financial stability of a country and the European Union's Growth and Stability Pact require that total taxes be reduced only if public spending falls in a permanent manner as a share of GDP. It is unlikely that the tax wedge on labor income can fall significantly in those countries that are not able to reduce the share of public spending into GDP. The hope that a modest tax reduction will lead, by itself, to a significant acceleration of the rate of growth of the country, which in turn would lead to a reduction in the fiscal deficit, while possible, must prudently be considered a hope not certain to be realized. Of course, major tax reductions over the long term will lead to a faster growth of the economy if they do not lead to macroeconomic imbalances.

The reduction in public spending requires major structural reforms in sensitive areas such as pensions, health, education, public sector employment and so on. In other words, it requires a different conception of what the role of the state must be in the economy and especially of the role played through public spending and not through regulations. The country chapters show that some countries have succeeded in recent years in reducing tax revenue by reducing public spending, while others have not been able to do so. But in all European countries, primary public spending remains higher than it could be so that it will continue to restrain the size of the tax reduction that becomes feasible.

Second, in most European countries pensions tend to be public and to be financed on a pay-as-you-go fashion by social security taxes paid by the workers or by their employers and earmarked for the pension expenditure.[1] Generally the higher the pension benefits and the number of pensioners, the higher the taxes paid by the working generation must be. In spite of relatively friendly demographic developments in past years, pension expenditures are already very high as shares of GDPs in many European countries. Because of less fiscally-friendly demographic changes in future years, that will lead to fast aging of the population, the weight of the pension expenditure under current policies is expected to grow in the future. Various official and non-official country studies, or studies carried out by international institutions, have estimated this likely growth of pension spending in European countries in the future. In some countries, this growth will be very large. Unless major reforms that reduce the size of pensions benefits or significantly raise the retirement age, it is difficult to see how taxes on labor incomes can be significantly reduced in future years. But, of course, the structure of existing taxes can be changed. Furthermore, it must be kept in mind that globalization will tend to put downward pressure on taxes on capital incomes and, to some extent, on taxes on easily transportable consumer goods. So a reduction in taxes on labor income could not be financed by an increase in these other taxes.

We may add here some comments on the progressivity of the taxes on personal incomes and their possible impact on the international mobility of some taxpayers. It has already been said that the facility with which financial capital can migrate from high-tax countries toward low-tax countries in an increasingly integrated world has created the necessity to reduce the effective tax rates on income from financial capital. However, similar arguments can be advanced vis-à-vis the incomes of highly skilled individuals.[2] These individuals may be a small proportion of the total workforce but they are important for their contribution to the total income tax payments and to the economic growth of countries. Individuals with exceptional or rare skills generally earn large incomes that place them in the income brackets subject to the highest tax rates. But highly skilled individuals are also the most mobile internationally. These are the taxpayers that can change their fiscal residence with the greatest facility. It is, therefore, likely that globalization will increase the pressures on countries to reduce the highest (marginal) tax rates on regular incomes in order to prevent, or reduce, the potential exodus of these individuals. The chapters in this book relating to individual countries do, in fact, indicate that the highest marginal tax rates on labor income have been coming down in most countries. This trend is likely to continue as the process of globalization intensifies.

For all the reasons indicated above, it is unlikely that the total income taxes on labor income, including social security taxes, can be reduced much in future years unless major reductions in public spending become possible.

Fiscal decentralization

The expansion of public sector activities that took place in the period between 1950 and 1980 in most European countries was largely concentrated at the central government level. It was the central government that led the way in the growth of expenditure for pensions, health, education and other social programs. The local governments played hardly any role in that expansion. During those decades, fiscal decentralization and fiscal federalism were not important objectives of economic policy and most policy makers and economists paid little attention to them. Normally taxes were set and collected at the national level and when necessary some of these revenues were transferred to sub-national administrations. Of course, countries that were born as federations (such as the United States, Germany, Canada and Switzerland) had specific tax provisions and larger spending responsibilities for the local governments.

The past two decades, however, have witnessed a great awakening of political and academic interest in fiscal decentralization, and the pressures for fiscal federalism have intensified in many countries. As the chapters on individual countries indicate, these pressures have been strong in Italy, Spain, the United Kingdom, and even France. Federalism has definitely become popular in today's world and, as the chapters indicate, in most countries we witness a progressive increase of the share of total taxes collected at, or at least transferred to, local government. Federalism will inevitably have a major impact on the structure of the tax systems. It is likely to change the importance of some taxes, because only particular taxes can be efficiently assigned to local governments. It will also have major implications for the cost of tax administration if a central tax administration comes to be replaced in part by many local administrations, at least for some taxes. The question of mobility of tax bases, already discussed with respect to globalization at the international level, becomes relevant with respect to federalism because some tax bases could move from region to region in the search for the lowest tax burden. Some taxes, such as those on real property and perhaps environmental taxes, become preferred choices for assignment to local governments, while the need for coordination of some taxes between national and local authorities becomes very important. It is also evident that federalism increases the complexity of tax coordination at the international level.[3]

The country studies in this book provide useful information of the extent to which fiscal federalism is already influencing the structure of tax systems. A good guess is that, over future years, this influence will grow, leading to changes in tax structures and tax levels. These changes are not easy to predict at this time. This is an area that will require the full attention of economists and other tax specialists. It is an area where it is easy to make major mistakes.

Links between taxes and spending

Particularly in the decades following World War II, tax specialists put a lot of importance to the objective of progressivity of the tax system. This objective was recognized by some constitutions as, for example, that of Italy. Personal income taxes became the focal point of tax systems because they could more easily be structured to pursue this objective. They came to be considered as the fairest taxes in several surveys conducted in the United States in the 1960s and 1970s. The marginal rates with which these taxes were levied reached very high levels, at times exceeding 80 percent.

Obviously at that time the objective of vertical equity was considered much more important than that of efficiency.

Starting in the second half of the 1970s, however, attitudes started to change, in part because of the growing influence of more conservative, or market-oriented economists; in part as a consequence of the results of major analyses as, for example, that conducted by the Meade Commission in the United Kingdom; and in part because of the slowdowns of economic growth in many countries that took place in that decade. Income taxes came to be subject to attacks on analytical as well as political fronts. Some economists pointed to their capacity to generate significant disincentives, and econometric research found these disincentives to be more significant than they had been considered in the past. Some pointed to their short-comings in terms of horizontal inequity when high marginal tax rates were accompanied by widespread "tax expenditures," given for many reasons, or by significant tax evasion. Some economists pointed to the superior qual-ities, in terms of economic efficiency, of general sales or expenditure taxes.

Over this period, the value added tax, which was a recent important technological development in the tax area, gained ground and became a tax of preference in many countries.[4] The supply-side "revolution" of the early 1980s, which was partly an intellectual movement and partly a polit-ical movement, can be considered in some way a frontal attack on the traditional structure of the personal income tax. In this period, in the United States, the marginal tax rate for individual income tax was reduced from 70 percent in 1980 to 28 percent in 1986! Within a few years, however, this low marginal tax rate had to be raised again to almost 40 percent to deal with a growing fiscal deficit.

There is no question that the great, earlier interest in the redistributive capacity of the tax system has become attenuated in today's world. Some now argue that equity concerns could be better pursued through the expenditure side of the budget so that the tax system could become less of an obstacle to the growth of the economy. As the descriptions of the changes in tax systems in this book show, the European countries have not been immune to these changes in attitudes even though they have been much more strongly held in Anglo-Saxon countries.

The objective of simplification

An area where the gap between declared intentions and reality has remained wide is in the objective of simplification. Many of the tax reforms promoted in recent years have included this objective. There is a widespread view among taxpayers, tax experts and tax administrators that the tax systems have become too complex and in great need of simplification. In their present form, the tax systems impose high administrative and compliance costs on society. However, the objective of simplification does not seem to have been achieved to any great extent in any of the recent reforms. Perhaps, the reason is that, in the process of formulation and implementation of these reforms, their objectives generally grow in number. What may have started as a simple scheme to achieve a specific objective soon becomes a highly complex one. Part of the problem is that policy makers continue to wish to have tax systems that are tailor-made for many taxpayers, that take into account many different situations. Another is that lobbies continue to have much influence on policy makers and, through them, on tax systems. This results in tax systems that remain much too complex.

Concluding remarks

A conclusion that emerges from the analysis and description of the tax systems of the seven countries covered in this book is that the tax systems of the European countries are still widely different from one another. There seems to have been relatively little movement toward tax harmonization except in a few areas. Furthermore, there is no obvious, ideal, or theoretical system that is acting as a reference point for tax reforms. In some way the situation has changed for the worse in recent decades. While three or four decades ago there was some convergence of views among tax experts on how a good tax system should look, there in now no system that gets the approval of the majority of tax specialists. This explains why tax systems continue to be so widely different among countries and reduces the chance that tax competition will spontaneously generate a convergence of these systems.

Perhaps leading international organizations should invest substantial resources to see whether they could develop an "ideal" tax system that could be supported by a majority of tax experts. If this were possible, it could provide the needed reference point for future tax reforms. But perhaps this is a Utopian objective.

Notes

1 Economic theory often assumes that the incidence of these taxes is always on the worker, regardless of who pays the tax. But this long-term conclusion may need to be amended, especially in the short term when labor unions on minimum wage reduce the (short term) possibility of wage adjustments.
2 On this, see Tanzi (1995), especially Chapter 4.
3 Many of these issues are discussed in Ahmad and Tanzi (eds) (2002).
4 From a revenue point of view, the introduction of value added tax was very important because it contributed up to 10 percent in GDP in revenue for some countries.

References

Ahmad, E. and Tanzi, V. (eds) (2002) *Managing Fiscal Decentralization: London and New York*, London: Routledge.

Simons, H. (1938) *Personal Income Taxation: The Definition of Income as a Problem of Fiscal Policy*, Berkeley: University of Chicago Press.

Sorensen, P.B. (1994) "From the global income tax to the dual income tax: recent tax reforms in the Nordic countries," *International Tax and Public Finance*, 1: 57–79.

Tanzi, V. (1995) *Taxation in an Integrating World*, Washington, DC: The Brookings Institution.

Preface

During the 1990s, almost all European countries introduced important changes in their tax systems, and they have planned many others. This fiscal revolution, which, so far, has not been deeply evaluated across European countries, has been driven by many easily identifiable forces, which, interestingly, often conflict with each other. Tanzi's Foreword lists and discusses many of them. As a starting point, Tanzi reminds us that tax reforms are rarely made in a vacuum. They normally reflect particular country needs or concerns, or react to particular domestic or external pressures. For the European countries, the common pressures experienced in recent years are likely to have come from: (a) the globalization of the world economies and the impact of this phenomenon on the tax revenue of specific countries; (b) the constraints imposed on Member Countries by the process of European unification; (c) the perceived need to reduce the high taxes on labor; (d) the process of fiscal decentralization going on in several countries; (e) the links that may exist between the level and structure of public expenditure and the level and structure of taxation; and (f) the need for tax simplification.

A comprehensive picture of what has happened and is happening in European fiscal systems is not at all easy to find. Information is dispersed among various sources, both at national and at international level, and often it is not directly comparable. Thus it is difficult to get, in a user-friendly format, a clear and updated idea of the present state of European fiscal systems. The first aim of this book is to fill this gap. Many data are collected from different sources, together with relevant institutional features and sophisticated indicators of equity and efficiency on the distribution of fiscal burden. The book focuses on seven national cases (France, Germany, Ireland, Italy, Spain, the Netherlands and the UK). These countries have been selected since they are the main European countries and/or those which have introduced more relevant fiscal reforms.

After building an updated picture of the current status of many European tax systems and reforms, the book analyzes the main common trends of recent or planned reforms and their ability to cope with the different pressures under the reforms of the fiscal systems, following the lines shown by Tanzi. The analysis starts from the recent European experience, but is extended to cover wider topics of tax reforms. The general interest of this analysis represents the second contribution of the book to the literature and the debate of tax policy.

The European experiences (see Chapter 1) may be briefly summarized as follows. Looking at the structure and evolution of the European tax systems over the past 30 years, the EU area confirms its peculiarities compared with the main international experiences outside Europe (US and Japan) and, more generally, compared with the OECD area. In the EU area, the tax burden is, on average, higher than in the OECD area. European countries rely more on social security contributions and less on consumption taxes; a higher share of tax revenues is allocated to the social security sector and a lower share to sub-national governments; taxes on labor and their contribution to total tax revenues are higher in Europe than in the OECD area. However, the European averages show marked differences across individual countries. Tax ratios, tax structure by legal and economic categories and the allocation of revenues across levels of government differ markedly between the seven selected countries, even if some evidences show that more recently a process of slow convergence is ongoing. Up to the mid-1980s, country divergences increased considerably, while over the last 15 years the separation between individual countries has largely been reversed, most likely as a consequence of some common pressures. It follows that some common trends in the recent evolution of tax systems and policies may be identified, essentially a traditional rate-cutting, base-broadening reform. No radical tax reforms occurred, but some common issues have arisen in the discussion of tax design in the selected European experiences: i) *Equity*. Recent reforms have addressed the issue of equity, which has been rather neglected during the 1980s' season of reforms. In this respect, new tax measures tried to introduce limited horizontal equity objectives and reinforce progressivity. However, they have mainly concerned tax rate cuts not only for the bottom income levels, but also for the top levels. ii) *Competitiveness*. Competitiveness is one of the main objectives of many planned reforms, which aim at introducing tax measures specifically targeted to increase national competitiveness with respect to financial capital, real capital and other production factors (mainly labor). iii) *Innovation*. Tax bases have been broadened in order to introduce tax incentives to selectively stimulate innovation and growth in four areas (small firms, R&D investments, venture capital and stock options). iv) *Fiscal relations across government levels*. The structure of fiscal relations across government levels is changing in all the analyzed countries, though the distribution of tax powers remains to be defined; recent evidence predicts a lower redistributive impact of the whole tax system in the future.

Are these really the most appropriate fiscal reforms to the current fundamental needs of European countries? Bernardi's chapter (Chapter 2) shows that these reforms have introduced some useful simplifications and more rationality to the existing systems. It notices, however, that almost all the reforms have been narrow in size and limited in scope. They seem, therefore, unable to successfully cope with three fundamental features required of tax systems in Europe:

i   tax competition and harmonization efforts should set up a common and necessarily harmonized framework of a "European" tax system, as required by an efficient working of the single market;

ii   there exists a pressing need to promote the declining economic growth, and welfare by increasing fiscal fairness;

iii   a European institutional setting and the EU Constitution should guarantee the satisfaction of basic social needs.

Tax reforms capable of addressing these features are then discussed in their general aspects. Taxes on labor and corporations should be lowered. Due to the constraints of the Stability Pact, and the difficulty of cutting public expenditure by a relevant amount in the short-to-medium term, charging the lost yield to rents, environment and consumption levies is unavoidable. Vertical and horizontal equities should be strengthened to improve overall welfare through an increase of fiscal and social fairness. A central European tax authority should be created, and some present nations' functions will be shifted to the highest tier of Union government. A common characteristic of these reforms is that they are all somewhat "radical" in their size and scope, compared to those implemented during the 1990s. Their effective implementation thus leaves opened more than one specific question.

Profeta's chapter (Chapter 3) addresses, with new issues, the traditional points of the literature on taxation reforms using the recent political economy approach. The growing literature on political economics suggests that the complex (multidimensional) tax structure that we observe in the countries under discussion in this book depends on political elements and factors, such as political instability and political influence. The chapter predicts that major tax reforms will be adopted and sustained if political support exists for them. After a brief review of the alternative frameworks provided by the political economy literature to address the multidimensionality of tax systems and tax reforms, the focus is on probabilistic voting. This turns out to be appropriate to analyze the current structure of the tax systems and their evolution over time. Following this approach, some specific issues raised by the country studies are analyzed: tax neutrality, horizontal equity, complexity and progressivity of the income tax, competition and decentralization versus harmonization. To understand the role of these issues in the political economy context, consider the following. The structure of income taxation that we observe can be seen as a result of a political process where politicians try to maximize their expected number of favorable votes. To maximize voters' support, each party is induced to carefully discriminate among heterogeneous voters. However, when the system becomes well developed, this requires an increase of complexity of regimes and raises the administration costs, which forces the government to simplify again, reducing complexity and grouping the individuals together. At this point, special provisions arise as a way to reintroduce differentiation, as required by political optimality, in a broadly defined, simplified tax structure. Therefore, the common trend toward a reduction of complexity and a reduction of the degree of progressivity that we observe in our countries has not only economic determinants, mainly efficiency reasons, but also political determinants, such as the need to reduce high administration and information costs in order to increase political support, or to meet the preferences of groups of voters who exert more influence. As a consequence, horizontal equity turns out to play a secondary role. Moreover, competition, along with decentralization and globalization, have a strong impact on fiscal policies, as shown by the recent experiences of the countries under consideration in this book. In an internationally integrated world, we see countries competing among each other on tax rates and on tax incentives affecting the tax base. Decentralization might also arise as an alternative solution to high administration and information costs. Both competition and decentralization create information.

These selected issues show that, in democracies, political factors may represent a constraint to the feasibility of tax reforms, in addition to that suggested by the optimal taxation literature. On the other hand, the feasibility of tax reforms that reduce revenues depends on the availability of considerable funds within national budgets.

De Novellis and Parlato address this point in Chapter 4 by evaluating the budget positions of European countries. The purpose is to show the room for fiscal reforms left after accounting for the constraints imposed by the Stability and Growth Pact. A crucial role in the identification of these resources is played by economic policies (Stability and Growth Pact, single European currency) and by the persistent differences between output growth and inflation among the countries of the euro area, which tend to be inconsistent with the objective of reducing taxation, at least in the transition phase. If, as it is at present, inflation differentials and therefore real interest rates do not reflect the different growth rates of the various economies, this would have particular consequences for government finances. In fact, for Germany in particular, at the present time, real interest rates exceed growth in real GDP by a broad margin and this results in inconsistencies between development objectives and balancing the national budget, under the assumption that fiscal stance may stimulate growth, at least in the short term.

The chapter shows that the "close to balance" principle would allow only (a few) particularly virtuous countries to pursue expansionary fiscal policies (tax cuts). A shift of public finance targets from deficits to debt would free resources to reduce the tax burdens of precisely those countries that most need to stimulate GDP growth. Since the overall standing of European public finances is quite sound from the viewpoint of stabilizing public debt, it would be wise to recommend a revision of the Stability Pact along those lines. This recommendation is particularly strong in the case of Germany, that not only has a low rate of inflation but also the lowest economic growth rate.

On the contrary, the current provisions of the Stability Pact ensure that only those countries close to potential growth are able to reduce taxation, while those with weaker economies are obliged to delay the launch of tax reduction programs. In fact, neither the Stability Pact nor ECB inflation target allow the full mitigation of cyclical downturns for those countries which are well below the potential output.

However, in the long run, a large reduction of fiscal pressure may require some socially acceptable structural reduction of public expenditure. Past relevant experiences, like Japan, suggest that additional caution is necessary in promoting fiscal expansion, when the supply elasticity is low. Deficits can increase, the economy remains stagnant and the public debt increases significantly.

To conclude, this book makes clear that tax reforms are a crucial topic in the current policy debate. The current design of European tax systems is not able to cope with the increasing economic and political pressures of the last decade and the future. Comprehensive reforms are needed, and the situation calls for immediate provisions. However, political and budgetary constraints make it difficult to perform "radical" and immediate reforms, as would be required. The question of how to shape policy interventions which, though partial and subsequent, can really make the tax systems suitable to the current European needs remains open. To this respect, a superior institution, with tax policy decisions taken at European rather than country level, may play a role in allowing solutions to many open questions. We encourage future research on these policy issues.

Luigi Bernardi and Paola Profeta

Acknowledgment

This book is the result of research on "The European System of Public Finance," fostered by Italian Ministry of Education, University and Scientific Research, "Scientific research programs of national interest – financial year 2002." Operating Unit, "The European tax systems: trends and issues," directed by L. Bernardi: Department of Public and Environmental Economics, University of Pavia (Italy). Additional financing from the Fondazione Cassa di Risparmio delle Provincie Lombarde and the Fondazione Banca del Monte di Lombardia are gratefully acknowledged.

We are grateful to S. Scabrosetti, who, in addition to her own chapter, provided excellent research assistance during the whole project. We also thank A. Piazza who contributed with a careful update, to March 2003, of the economic outlook and budget situations of the main European Member Countries.

Part I

Main topics in European tax systems and tax reforms

1 A comparative view of selected European countries

Luca Gandullia[1]

Introduction and main conclusions

The structure and evolution of the European tax systems over the past 30 years confirms the peculiarities of the EU area compared with the main international experiences outside Europe (US and Japan) and more generally compared with the OECD area (Joumard 2001; van den Noord and Heady 2001; Cnossen 2002). In the EU area the tax burden is, on average, higher than in the OECD area; European countries rely more on social security contributions and less on consumption taxes; a higher share of tax revenues is allocated to the social security sector and a lower share to sub-national governments; taxes on labor and their contribution to total tax revenues are higher in Europe than in the OECD area. However the European averages conceal marked differences across individual countries. Tax ratios, tax structure by legal and economic categories and the allocation of revenues across levels of government differ markedly between the seven selected countries, even if some evidence shows that, more recently, a process of slow convergence is ongoing.

Up to the mid-1980s, country divergences within Europe increased considerably, while, over the last 15 years, the isolationism of individual countries has been largely reversed (Messere 1998), most likely as a consequence of some common pressures (growing globalization, international tax competition, the influence of the European Union at both macro and micro level). Looking at the seven selected European countries (France, Germany, Ireland, Italy, the Netherlands, Spain and the UK), some common trends in the recent evolution of tax systems or in reforms currently under way may be identified: a traditional rate-cutting, base-broadening reform both in the personal and corporate income taxes; efforts to strengthen the horizontal and vertical equity of the tax system at the lower end of the income scale; efforts to reduce the tax burden on lower-paid labor and to foster work incentives; the growing use of tax systems to deliver social benefits; the reorientation of business tax incentives to selective objectives and the use of the tax system to correct market failures (for instance R&D and environment).

No radical tax reforms occurred during the 1990s. Changes enacted were made mainly through continuous updates of the tax codes. The main non-marginal tax reforms occurred in Spain in 1998 (OECD 2000b), in Italy in 1997 (OECD 2000d) and in Germany in 2000 (Keen 2002a), but just the Italian reform can be seen as innovative, especially in the sector of capital income taxation (Guerra 1998; Bordignon, Giannini and Panteghini 2001; Chapter 8, this volume).

Some common issues have arisen in the recent discussion of tax design. (i) *Tax equity.* After a period where tax reforms placed more emphasis on efficiency than on equity, in the recent years a number of tax measures have been introduced to achieve horizontal equity objectives and to strengthen progressivity at the lower end of the income scale. (ii) *Competitiveness.* A number of countries have planned reforms where competitiveness is one of the main motivations; tax measures specifically targeted to increase national competitiveness have been introduced with regard to financial capital, real capital and other production factors (mainly labor). (iii) *Innovation.* The broadening of tax bases have been followed by the reorientation of tax incentives to selectively stimulate innovation and growth, mainly in four areas (small firms, R&D investments, venture capital and stock options). (iv) *Fiscal relations across levels of governments.* The structure of fiscal relations across levels of government is changing in all the selected experiences, but the distribution of tax powers is still not definite; some recent evidences prefigure a lower redistribution pattern of the whole tax system in the future.

This chapter is organized as follows. First, some indicators of the macro structure and evolution of the selected tax systems over the period 1970–2000 are presented, focusing on tax ratios by legal and economic categories and on the allocation of revenues across sectors of government. Second, some common features of the current tax systems (personal and corporate income taxes and consumption-based taxes) are illustrated, presenting some indicators to measure and compare their equity and efficiency. Finally, some common micro-policy issues that have arisen recently in the discussion of tax design in the selected European experiences are discussed.

Tax systems: structure and developments

Even if it's only a rough indicator of the tax burden across time and countries, the ratio of taxes to GDP is a useful scaling factor and a signal of the country's preference for the size of the public sector (OECD 2000a). According to OECD (2002a)[2] in the past 30 years (1970–2000, see Table 1.1) tax ratios generally increased in OECD countries (by 9.1 percentage points) and 15 EU countries (by 11.2 percentage points). For the selected EU countries, the rise has been lower (about eight percentage points). More recent developments (2001) suggest the trend increase in the

Table 1.1 Total tax revenue as a percentage of GDP

	1970	1975	1980	1985	1990	1995	1999	2000	2001 Provisional
Ireland	28.8	29.1	31.4	35.0	33.5	32.7	31.3	31.1	29.2
Spain	16.3	18.8	23.1	27.8	33.2	32.8	35.0	35.2	35.2
Germany	32.3	35.3	37.5	37.2	35.7	38.2	37.8	37.9	36.4
United Kingdom	37.0	35.3	35.2	37.7	36.8	34.8	36.4	37.4	37.4
The Netherlands	35.8	41.6	43.6	42.6	43.0	41.9	41.2	41.4	39.9
Italy	26.1	26.1	30.4	34.4	38.9	41.2	43.3	42.0	41.8
France	34.1	35.9	40.6	43.8	43.0	44.0	45.7	45.3	45.4
OECD total	28.3	30.5	32.1	33.9	35.1	36.1	37.1	37.4	n.a.
EU 15	30.4	33.2	36.0	38.8	39.5	40.0	41.5	41.6	n.a.
EU selected	30.1	31.7	34.5	36.9	37.7	37.9	38.7	38.6	37.9

Source: OECD (2002a).

OECD area may be ending. Apart from France, the provisional data for 2001 show light decreases (Ireland, Germany, the Netherlands and Italy) or constant trends (Spain and the UK).

The trends have been different over time and between countries. In the period 1970–2000, the ratio increased in six countries (Spain, Germany, UK, Italy, the Netherlands and France) and stayed constant in Ireland. The figures for Italy and Spain are the highest (respectively, 61 and 116 percent); in these countries, the 1970 ratios were the lowest. On average, both in the OECD countries and in the 15 EU countries, the main portion of these changes occurred during the 1970s and, to a lesser extent, during the 1980s. The pattern of individual countries has been different. For instance, in Italy, the increase in the tax-to-GDP ratio was higher during the 1980s than in the previous decade. In the 1990s, up to 2000, while the ratios decreased markedly in Ireland and the Netherlands, in France, Germany and Spain they increased at an average rate of about 0.24 percentage points per annum. In the same decade Italy registered the highest increase in the tax-to-GDP ratio (from 38.9 percent to 42 percent).

At the end of the period (2001) the difference between the highest ratio (France) and the lowest (Ireland) still remains significant (16.2 percentage points), even if the figures suggest that the tax ratios of individual states moved closer to the average. The latest available data (2000) confirm that, in the EU area, the tax burden is on average higher than in the OECD area and the difference during the period 1970–2000 has increased from 2.1 to 4.2 percentage points.

As the total tax ratio has risen sharply, the tax structure by legal tax categories, measured as the distribution of tax revenue among major taxes (income taxes, taxes on goods and services, social security contributions and property taxes), has changed over time (see Table 1.2). Currently, the tax structure of the OECD area differs from that of the European area mainly in respect of two items: social security contributions (higher in the EU countries) and taxes on goods and services (lower in the EU countries). But in the last two decades, the differences between the two areas decreased. For instance, the difference between the relative importance of social security contributions in the OECD area and in the EU area has decreased from about seven percentage points (1980) to 2.7 percentage points (2000). This is the effect of two opposite trends registered in the two areas: while the ratio has risen on average in the OECD countries, it has decreased in the 15 EU states. Within Europe the main share of this reduction comes from the seven selected countries.

In Europe the current tax mix is composed of taxes on goods and services (30 percent), social security contributions (28.4 percent), personal income tax (25.6 percent), followed by corporate income tax (9.2 percent) and property taxes (5 percent). In the last two decades a shift has occurred from the personal income tax and social security contributions to the corporate income tax and the property tax.

The seven selected countries vary considerably in the relative importance of these main revenue sources. Table 1.2 shows clearly the peculiarities of the "Anglo-Saxon model" compared to the other countries. In the UK and Ireland, income taxes and consumption taxes account for a much higher share of total tax revenues, while social security contributions account for approximately half of the European average. Italy reflects exactly the average European model of taxation, while the remaining countries are all characterized by the fact that they rely heavily on social security contributions and less on the personal income tax (France, Spain and the Netherlands) or on corporate income tax and property taxes (Germany).

Table 1.2 also gives explanations about the different incidence of taxes on GDP between the OECD and the EU areas and between different countries within Europe. On average the higher tax burden on GDP in the European area (about four percentage points in 2000) is explained by the higher incidence of social security contributions and payroll taxes (1.9 percentage points), followed by the personal income tax (0.9) and taxes on goods and services (0.7). Both the corporate income tax and the property taxes are in line with the OECD average.

In 2000, within the EU some countries (Table 1.1) show higher tax burden than the European average (France, for example), while others are in the opposite situation (Germany, Ireland, Spain and the UK, for example). In France this is explained by the relatively higher incidence of social security contributions and property taxation, while both income and corporate taxes are under the European average. The lower tax burden in the Anglo-Saxon countries is mainly due to the incidence of

Table 1.2 Tax structure: tax revenue of major taxes as a percentage of total tax revenue and GDP

	Personal income			Corporate income			Social security and payroll			Property			Goods and service		
	1980	1990	2000	1980	1990	2000	1980	1990	2000	1980	1990	2000	1980	1990	2000
France	11.6	11.8	18.0	5.1	5.3	7.0	44.9	46.0	38.4	4.8	5.1	6.8	30.4	28.4	25.8
	4.7	*5.1*	*8.2*	*2.1*	*2.3*	*3.2*	*18.3*	*19.7*	*17.5*	*2.0*	*2.2*	*3.1*	*12.4*	*12.2*	*11.7*
Germany	29.6	27.6	25.3	5.5	4.8	4.8	34.5	39.4	39.0	3.3	3.4	2.3	27.1	26.7	28.1
	11.1	*9.8*	*9.6*	*2.0*	*1.7*	*1.8*	*13.0*	*13.4*	*14.8*	*1.2*	*1.2*	*0.9*	*10.2*	*9.5*	*10.6*
Ireland	32.0	31.9	30.8	4.5	5.0	12.1	14.5	16.1	13.6	5.3	4.7	5.6	43.7	42.3	37.2
	10.0	*10.7*	*9.6*	*1.4*	*1.7*	*3.8*	*4.6*	*5.4*	*4.2*	*1.7*	*1.6*	*1.8*	*13.7*	*14.2*	*11.6*
Italy	23.1	26.3	25.7	7.8	10.0	7.5	38.6	33.2	28.5	3.7	2.3	4.3	26.5	28.0	28.4
	7.0	*10.2*	*10.8*	*2.4*	*3.9*	*3.2*	*11.8*	*12.9*	*11.9*	*1.1*	*0.9*	*1.8*	*8.1*	*10.9*	*11.9*
The Netherlands	26.3	24.7	14.9	6.6	7.5	10.1	38.1	37.4	38.9	3.6	3.7	5.4	25.2	26.4	29.0
	11.5	*10.6*	*6.2*	*2.9*	*3.2*	*4.2*	*16.6*	*16.6*	*16.1*	*1.6*	*1.6*	*2.2*	*11.0*	*11.3*	*12.0*
Spain	20.4	21.7	18.7	5.1	8.8	8.6	48.6	35.4	35.1	4.6	5.5	6.4	20.7	28.4	29.8
	4.7	*7.2*	*6.6*	*1.2*	*2.9*	*3.0*	*11.2*	*11.8*	*12.4*	*1.1*	*1.8*	*2.3*	*4.8*	*9.4*	*10.5*
United Kingdom	29.4	27.1	29.2	8.4	11.2	9.8	21.0	16.7	16.4	12.0	10.3	11.9	29.2	30.5	32.3
	10.3	*10.0*	*10.9*	*2.9*	*4.1*	*3.7*	*7.4*	*6.1*	*6.1*	*4.2*	*3.8*	*4.4*	*10.3*	*11.2*	*12.1*
Unweighted average:															
OECD Total	31.3	29.4	26.0	7.6	7.9	9.7	23.5	23.7	25.7	5.3	5.7	5.4	32.3	31.8	31.6
	10.5	*10.7*	*10.0*	*2.4*	*2.7*	*3.6*	*7.8*	*8.6*	*9.9*	*1.6*	*1.6*	*1.9*	*10.1*	*10.9*	*11.6*
EU 15	29.0	27.2	25.6	5.8	6.8	9.2	30.4	29.0	28.4	4.2	4.4	5.0	31.0	31.5	30.0
	11.1	*11.1*	*10.9*	*2.1*	*2.7*	*3.8*	*10.7*	*11.4*	*11.8*	*1.5*	*1.7*	*2.0*	*11.0*	*12.2*	*12.3*
Selected EU countries	24.6	24.4	23.2	6.1	7.5	8.6	34.3	32.0	30.0	5.3	5.0	6.1	29.0	30.1	30.1
	8.5	*9.1*	*8.8*	*2.1*	*2.8*	*3.3*	*11.8*	*12.3*	*11.9*	*1.8*	*1.9*	*2.4*	*10.1*	*11.2*	*11.5*

Source: OECD (2002a).

social security contributions, while in Germany and Spain direct taxes and taxes on goods and services are under the European average.

In the countries that registered an increase in tax-to-GDP ratios during the 1990s (France, Germany, Italy and Spain), the largest part of the increases has taken the form of higher personal and corporate income taxes (France), social security contributions and consumption taxes (Germany and Spain), while Italy used a mix of increases in the personal income tax, property and consumption taxes.

Selected countries also differ in prevailing fiscal arrangements between the central and the sub-central levels of government. In particular, Table 1.3 illustrates the attribution of tax revenues to the three sub-sectors of general government (central, local and social security sectors).[3] Taking into account only unitary countries, the tax allocation structure, that was different in the 1970s, currently appears to be very similar between OECD and EU unitary countries, with the largest part of tax revenues (63 percent) attributed to the central government, about one-quarter to the social security funds and just 12 percent to local governments.

Within the EU (excluding Germany) the selected countries show, on average, a higher share of revenues allocated to the security sector and a lower share to local governments. But this is the result of extremely different patterns of individual countries. The combined share of sub-central governments in total tax revenues in 2000 shows a wide variation from 1.8 percent in Ireland and 3.4 percent in the Netherlands to 11.4 percent and 16.9 percent in Italy and Spain respectively. In the last 25 years, two clear

Table 1.3 Attribution of tax revenues to sub-sectors of general government

	Central government			Sub-central government			Social security funds		
	1975	1985	2000	1975	1985	2000	1975	1985	2000
France	51.2	47.2	42.4	7.6	8.7	9.6	40.6	43.5	46.9
Germany	33.5	31.6	30.8	31.3	30.9	30.0	34.0	36.5	39.2
Ireland	77.4	82.1	86.6	7.3	2.3	1.8	13.1	13.6	11.6
Italy	53.2	62.3	60.0	0.9	2.3	11.4	45.9	34.7	28.6
The Netherlands	58.9	51.9	57.1	1.2	2.4	3.4	38.4	44.3	39.3
Spain	48.2	47.8	48.2	4.3	11.2	16.9	47.5	41.0	34.9
United Kingdom	70.5	69.4	78.2	11.1	10.2	4.0	17.5	17.8	15.5
OECD unitary countries	64.2	64.2	62.7	12.3	12.3	12.7	23.1	22.9	24.2
EU 12 unitary countries	61.0	61.4	62.8	10.4	10.8	12.0	28.0	26.8	24.7
EU selected countries	59.9	60.1	62.1	5.4	6.2	7.9	33.8	32.5	29.5

Source: OECD (2002a).

trends can be identified: a move to fiscal centralization in the UK and Ireland and an opposite move in Italy and Spain.

A variety of taxes are used by sub-national authorities in the EU. The pattern of taxes is illustrated by Table 1.4, that reports the percentage contribution to each country's total sub-national tax revenue accounted for in four main sets of taxes used in OECD classifications. Figures don't allow the drawing of general conclusions about the choice of taxes by local governments. On one side Ireland and the UK rely exclusively on property taxation; on the other side, Germany, Italy, Spain, the Netherlands and, to a lesser extent, France seem to use a composite mix of local taxes; apart from France, these countries make use of local income and profits taxes, even if a decreasing trend can be found in Germany, Italy and Spain.

Moreover it should be mentioned that two countries (France and Italy) have "other taxes" with significant yields. In each case this is explained by the presence of two local business taxes (the French "*taxe professionnelle*" and the Italian regional tax on productive activities – *IRAP*), whose tax base is some mixture of two or more different components (profits, payrolls, interest and property). Finally, looking at the structure of local tax systems over time, the only clear evidence (with the exception of Germany) seems to be the growing relevance of local property taxation.

A closer look at the incidence of individual tax revenues by economic categories (labor, capital and consumption) gives a more useful explanation about the structure of the European tax systems and their evolution.[4] The economic structure of European tax systems, measured as the share of individual taxes in total tax revenue by economic category, shows that, on average, taxes on labor contribute for more than half the total tax revenue, consumption taxes for about one-third and taxes on capital for just about 15 percentage points (Cnossen 2002). This tax mix has remained quite stable during the 1990s.

But a full picture of where the macro-tax burden falls can be obtained by looking at the implicit tax rates, measured as individual tax revenues expressed as a percentage of their respective tax base (Table 1.5). As shown in Table 1.1, the last 30 years have been characterized in Europe by the rise of tax-to-GDP ratios; at the same time, the incidence of different tax bases relative to GDP has changed over time, with the labor tax base declining and the capital and consumption tax bases increasing. As a consequence, the implicit tax rates on production factors and consumption changed significantly. In the EU at the beginning of 1970s, the incidence of taxation on capital and consumption was about the same (19–20 percent), while the incidence on labor was higher (25.5 percent). During the last three decades (up to 1999) the implicit tax rates on consumption grew slightly; the increase has been much higher for capital (about 24 percent) and especially for labor (47 percent). This is the result of increases that occurred during the 1970s and 1980s, while, during the last decade, the rise in capital and consumption taxation has been higher

Table 1.4 Sub-central tax structure: tax revenue from the main local taxes as a percentage of total tax revenues of sub-central governments

	Income and profits			Property			Goods and services			Other taxes		
	1975	1985	2000	1975	1985	2000	1975	1985	2000	1975	1985	2000
France				46.0	47.2	48.2	7.9	13.1	11.5	46.0	39.7	40.4
Germany												
State	62.8	62.9	51.7	6.2	5.4	4.9	31.0	31.7	43.4			
Local	78.4	80.9	78.0	20.3	18.1	15.8	0.9	0.8	6.0	0.4	0.2	0.2
Ireland				100.0	100.0	100.0						
Italy	80.0	66.7	12.2	17.5	–	18.6	2.5	10.5	8.6	0.0	22.7	60.6
The Netherlands	15.4			54.2	75.1	56.0	30.4	24.9	44.0			
Spain	57.3	26.9	25.2	8.5	16.8	37.3	34.2	52.8	36.1		3.5	1.4
United Kingdom				100.0	100.0	99.8						0.2
OECD unitary countries	45.0	47.0	38.0	35.0	29.9	31.6	14.0	14.4	16.8	5.4	8.6	9.1

Source: OECD (2002a).

Table 1.5 Implicit tax rates on production factors and consumption

	Consumption					Labor					Capital				
	1970	1990	1999	1970–99	1990–9	1970	1990	1999	1970–99	1990–9	1970	1990	1999	1970–99	1990–9
France	23.6	23.1	24.5	3.81	6.06	26.6	39.7	42.4	59.40	6.80	15.5	17.9	22.6	45.81	26.26
Germany	19.2	17.8	17.9	–6.77	0.56	29.4	38.3	44.0	49.66	14.88	18.3	16.2	15.9	–13.11	–1.85
Ireland	20.6	22.1	24.8	20.39	12.22	9.8	24.6	24.2	146.94	–1.63	26.9	18.9	20.8	–22.68	10.05
Italy	16.4	16.9	22.9	39.63	35.50	20.7	35.9	35.8	72.95	–0.28	11.9	22.7	26.2	120.17	15.42
The Netherlands	15.9	16.7	19.5	22.64	16.77	29.9	38.5	36.9	23.41	–4.16	19.5	21.5	25.1	28.72	16.74
Spain	11.6	15.2	17.7	52.59	16.45	12.1	27.9	29.9	147.11	7.17	8.9	19.9	18.5	107.87	–7.04
UK	15.2	15.6	18.2	19.74	16.67	25.0	24.8	25.2	0.80	1.61	35.2	34.4	35.1	–0.28	2.03
EU 15	20.0	19.4	20.8	4.00	7.22	25.5	35.7	37.6	47.45	5.32	19.0	21.3	23.6	24.21	10.80
Selected EU countries	17.5	18.2	20.8	18.78	14.21	21.9	32.8	34.1	55.31	3.79	19.5	21.6	23.5	20.56	8.38

Source: Eurostat (2000); EU Commission (2000).

(10.8 percent and 7.2 percent respectively) than that on labor (5.3 percent). At the end of the period under review, labor still bears a tax burden (37.6 percent) much higher than capital (23.6 percent) and consumption (20.8 percent).

Even in this issue the European averages conceal marked differences across individual countries. Looking at the structure of implicit tax rates in 1999, tax rates on labor are significantly below the average in Spain and even more in the UK and Ireland, while they are above the average in France and Germany. Marked differences still exist in the implicit tax rates on consumption and on capital. For instance the incidence of taxes on capital in Germany (15.9 percent) is less than half of the UK figure (35.1 percent). Between the selected countries, the variance of tax rates is generally higher for labor and capital than for consumption, but some evidence shows that a process of slow convergence is ongoing.

Common features of current tax systems

Personal income tax

The fundamental structure of personal income taxes is highly similar across the OECD countries, but differences can be found in the tax rates and base structures. Table 1.6 (combined with Table 1.7) gives some basic information about the structure of personal income tax in the seven selected countries.

All the countries turn from the model of the pure comprehensive personal income tax in favor of some hybrid taxation models where elements of expenditure tax are present. Large differences still exist in the treatment of the tax base (taxable incomes and tax expenditures). Diversities are mainly due to the different use of the tax systems to pay social benefit, for instance tax breaks for private pensions (Adema 2001). Moreover not all income from capital is included in the personal income tax base. As a general trend, a growing number of countries introduced lower, flat rates for certain types of capital income (interest, dividends and capital gains). This is the case in those countries (France and Italy) where interest is subject to flat withholding taxes. As far as the integration of personal and corporate income taxes is concerned, the full imputation system is absent both for dividends (with the exception of Italy, but at the option of the taxpayer) and capital gains. Even if this result can be interpreted as a response to growing pressure from international tax competition, or part of a more general strategy designed to lower the efficiency costs of taxation in open economies, the taxation of capital income outside personal income tax can reduce the overall progressivity of the tax system and compromise its redistributive impact.

Family status is taken into account in the selected countries in three major ways (OECD 2003): (i) through the application of a tax schedule

Table 1.6 Main components of the personal income tax's structure

	Zero rate band	Zero rate band as proportion of APW (%)	Basic allowances	Tax relief as proportion of APW (%)	Basic tax credit	Tax credit as proportion of APW (%)	Lowest standard rate	Highest standard rate	Number of brackets	Highest rate starts at[1]
France	Y	18.8	Y	20.0	–		7.5	52.75	7	2.12
Germany	Y	21.8	–	–	–		Formula based	48.5	Formula based	1.66
Ireland	–	–	–	–	Y	6.0	20.0	42.0	2, different according to family status	1.11
Italy	–	–	–	–	Y[2]	1.8	18.0	45.0	5	3.25
The Netherlands	–	–	–	–	Y	5.3	2.95	52.0	4	1.54
Spain	–	–	Y	17.7	–	–	15.0	39.6	6	3.60
United Kingdom	–	–	Y	23.4	–	–	10.0	40.0	3	1.52

Source: own calculations from OECD (2003) data.

Notes
1 proportion of APW wage.
2 In Italy the basic tax credit is only applied on dependent workers.

Table 1.7 The taxation of capital income

	Resident				Non-resident	
	Dividends	Capital gains	Interest[1]		Dividends	Interest[1]
France	PIT and tax credit (50%)	Separate taxation (26%)	Final withholding tax (15%)		Final withholding tax (25%)	Not taxable
Germany	PIT on half income	Exemption	PIT		Final withholding tax (25%)	Not taxable
Ireland	PIT	Separate taxation (20%)	PIT		Not taxable	Not taxable
Italy	Final withholding tax (12.5%). Option for PIT and tax credit (56.25%)	Separate taxation (12.5%)	Final withholding tax (12.5%)		Final withholding tax (27%) (4/9 recoverable)	Not taxable
The Netherlands	Exemption	Exemption	PIT		Final withholding tax (25%)	Not taxable
Spain	PIT and tax credit (variable)	Separate taxation (18%)	PIT		Final withholding tax (18%)	Not taxable
United Kingdom	Separate taxation (10%–32.5%) and tax credit (11.11%)	Separate taxation (6%–24%)	PIT		Not taxable	Not taxable

Source: REF (different years).

Note
1 From public bonds.

that varies according to family status. In this respect the tax unit is the individual in Italy, the Netherlands and the UK, while it is the family in France, Germany, Ireland and (by option) in Spain; (ii) by providing tax credits and allowances related to marital status and the presence of dependent children. For instance, a tax credit is provided for children in Germany, Italy, the Netherlands and the UK; (iii) by supplying cash transfers or benefit outside the tax system. Cash transfers for dependent children are present in all the selected countries, with the exception of Germany.

Looking at the structure of personal income tax, countries differ in the way they give relief to low-income individuals. As shown by Table 1.6, a certain amount of income may be exempted from tax (France, Spain and the UK) or taxed at 0 percent (France and Germany). In other countries, basic tax relief is granted through tax credits (Ireland and the Netherlands), which in Italy are reserved only for employment income. To evaluate how much these basic reliefs may reduce the personal tax burden, they can be expressed as a percentage of the gross wage of an average production worker (APW). On this measure, Spain exempts 17.7 percent of the APW, Germany 21.8 percent and the UK 23.4 percent; in France the exempt amount is higher as a result of zero rate band and basic allowances. Even if not directly comparable, the value of tax credits as percentage of APW is lower in Italy (1.8 percent) than in the Netherlands (5.3 percent) and Ireland (6 percent).

Apart from Germany, which applies several tax formulae, in the other countries, income is sliced into brackets, ranging from two (Ireland) to seven (France). Income in the first bracket is taxed at a low rate in the Netherlands (2.95 percent), while Ireland and Italy apply higher tax rates (20 percent and 18 percent). Top marginal tax rates range from 39.6 percent (Spain) to 52.75 percent (France). More significantly, in Ireland taxpayers at the income level of an APW are already exposed to the top marginal rate of 42 percent, while in Italy and Spain workers must earn more than three times as much the average before they start paying the top rate. Looking at the evolution of the top marginal tax rate, a clear trend toward its reduction can be observed (Bernardi 2000), mainly explained in the grounds of efficiency. Since 1996 (OECD 1997, 2003) top marginal tax rates have been reduced from 54 percent to 52.75 percent in France, from 53 percent to 42 percent (2005) in Germany, from 48 percent to 42 percent in Ireland, from 51 percent to 45 percent in Italy, from 60 percent to 52 percent in the Netherlands and from 56 percent to 39.6 percent in Spain. In Italy the new plan of tax reform reduces the top rate by a provocatively high amount (from 45 percent to 33 percent).

Equity of the personal income tax

Even if the concept can be ambiguous and subject to different interpretations, some recent changes in tax systems can be seen as directed to
achieve greater horizontal equity. A number of features of tax systems can
be seen as instruments directed to this objective. But, fundamentally, tax
systems differ in the way they consider the number of children that people
have and their marital status as elements to evaluate the "similar economic
position" for tax purposes (OECD 2003).

Specific measures of horizontal tax equity, even if imperfect, are shown
in Table 1.8, where both the personal income tax and social security contributions are considered. The table compares the average effective tax
rates of two different categories of taxpayers: a single individual without
children and a one-earner married couple with two children, both
earning the same income level (APW). In each country differences in the
effective tax rates represent how the tax system treats different economic
positions of taxpayers. Looking only at the personal income tax, horizontal equity seems to be pursued more in some countries (France, Germany,
Ireland and Spain) and less in other (Italy, the Netherlands and the UK).
Apart from the Netherlands, social security contributions are not directed
at horizontal tax equity purposes. However, a more comprehensive
picture can be obtained from the last column, where average effective tax
rates are determined, taking into account both the tax system (personal
income tax and social security contributions) and the benefit system (cash
transfers). Ireland, Germany, and to a lesser extent, Italy appear to be the
countries which give more emphasis to horizontal tax (and benefit)
equity.

Measures of statutory vertical equity can be constructed by comparing
the share of income paid in tax by taxpayers at different income levels
(van den Noord and Heady 2001). Table 1.9 reports measures of statutory
tax progressivity for low-wage (67 percent of the APW) and high-wage
(167 percent of APW) people, taking into account only personal income
tax or the social security contributions. Personal income taxes are progressive in all selected countries, even if at varying degrees. Germany shows a
pronounced tax structure across different income levels, while the progressivity is more concentrated at below-average income levels in France,
Spain and the UK, and at above-average income levels in Ireland, Italy and
the Netherlands.

Statutory social security contributions are neutral or progressive for
most countries, with two main exceptions: the structure is regressive across
different income levels in the Netherlands and just at higher income
levels in France.

Table 1.8 Measures of horizontal tax equity

	Average effective tax rate (income tax)		SSC		Average effective tax rate (income tax + SSC − cash transfers)	
	Single individual without children (APW) (%)	One-earner married couple with two children (APW) (%)	Single individual without children (APW) (%)	One-earner married couple with two children (APW) (%)	Single individual without children (APW) (%)	One-earner married couple with two children (APW) (%)
France	13.3	6.9	13.3	13.3	26.5	14.2
Germany	20.5	−2.0	20.7	20.7	41.2	18.6
Ireland	11.4	2.4	5.0	5.0	16.4	−0.8
Italy	18.9	11.8	9.2	9.2	28.1	12.2
The Netherlands	7.2	6.6	21.5	16.0	28.7	18.2
Spain	12.9	4.0	6.4	6.4	19.2	10.4
United Kingdom	15.7	10.1	7.7	7.7	23.3	10.8

Source: own calculations from OECD (2003) data.

Table 1.9 Statutory income tax progressivity

Countries	Low-wage progressivity		High-wage progressivity	
	Income tax	*Total*	*Income tax*	*Total*
France	6.81	8.03	5.59	5.47
Germany	8.06	10.89	10.89	12.61
Ireland	4.86	8.16	13.96	15.13
Italy	5.47	6.17	6.92	7.88
The Netherlands	3.84	2.29	17.73	9.85
Spain	6.43	6.94	6.00	6.50
United Kingdom	3.75	5.65	3.09	3.69

Source: own calculations from OECD (2003) data.

The taxation of labor

The average effective tax rate on labor in the EU area appears to be higher than in the OECD area, even if during the 1990s many EU countries introduced measures to lower the tax burden (Joumard 2001), mainly financed through the shifting of the tax burden from labor to capital or to broader tax bases (as in the case of the Italian *IRAP*) and to activities that cause pollution (Germany, Italy and the UK).

Looking at the total tax wedge on labor in the selected EU countries (100 percent APW, Table 1.10a) and its evolution during the last seven years (where homogeneous data are available), the tax burden has decreased in France, Italy and the UK and more markedly in Ireland and the Netherlands, while it has remained constant in Germany and Spain. Currently, labor is most heavily taxed in Germany, France and Italy, while in the UK, Ireland, the Netherlands and Spain, labor is taxed less than the European average.

If, in general, labor is taxed more heavily in Europe than in the OECD

Table 1.10a Tax wedges on labor: Income tax plus employee and employer contributions (as % of labor costs), 1996–2002 single individual without children (APW)

	1996	*1997*	*1998*	*1999*	*2000*	*2001*	*2002*
France	49.7	48.7	47.6	48.1	48.2	48.3	47.9
Germany	51.2	52.3	52.2	51.9	51.8	50.8	51.3
Ireland	36.1	33.9	33.0	32.4	28.9	25.8	24.5
Italy	50.8	51.5	47.5	47.2	46.7	46.1	46.0
The Netherlands	43.8	43.6	43.5	44.3	45.1	42.3	35.6
Spain	38.8	39.0	39.0	37.5	37.6	37.9	38.2
United Kingdom	32.6	32.0	32.0	30.8	30.1	29.5	29.7

Source: OECD (2003).

area, the issue appears to be most relevant for lower-paid labor. Concerns about high tax burdens on lower-paid labor and possible substitution of (low-skill) labor with other production factors or relocation abroad of productive activities prompted initiatives in several EU countries (France, the Netherlands, Spain and the UK) to reduce effective tax wedges on low-paid workers. Such initiatives aimed both at enhancing the vertical equity of the tax and benefit system and at increasing job opportunities. Table 1.10b compares the evolution of effective tax rates on low-incomes in the selected countries. With the exception of the Netherlands, all the surveyed countries apply lower tax wedges on low-income (67 percent APW). In a period where, on average, the EU countries have tried to reduce tax wedges on labor, the reduction appears to be more marked for low-income workers.

The corporate income tax

As explained in more detail in the chapters on specific countries, a number of approaches to taking company profits may be observed, especially in the determination of taxable income and integration of the corporate and personal income taxes. Table 1.11 simply compares the nominal rate structure ("all-in") applied to taxable profits across time and countries.

Two general trends have characterized the last decade: the reduction in statutory tax rates, resulting mainly from international tax competition between countries (Devereux, Lockwood and Redoano 2002) and (with the exception of Ireland) their convergence to the European average. The case of Ireland, as a small open economy, is not comparable to the others, with regard both to the amount of the reduction and the low level of the current tax rate (12.5 percent).

Between the selected countries, after the recent abolition of the local business tax (*taxe professionnelle*) in France, currently only Italy and Germany levy sub-central taxes on corporate income. Even if arguments in

Table 1.10b Tax wedges on labor: Income tax plus employee and employer contributions (as % of labor costs), 1996–2002 single individual without children (67% APW)

	1996	1997	1998	1999	2000	2001	2002
France	44.3	41.6	39.4	40.3	39.6	38.4	37.8
Germany	46.5	47.7	47.5	47.0	46.5	45.5	45.9
Ireland	26.5	24.9	23.4	21.5	18.1	17.4	16.6
Italy	48.3	48.8	44.4	44.1	43.3	42.8	42.7
The Netherlands	39.3	38.8	39.2	40.2	40.6	36.8	37.2
Spain	34.4	34.8	35.1	32.6	32.8	33.4	33.9
United Kingdom	26.8	28.4	28.5	25.8	25.3	24.5	24.7

Source: OECD (2003).

Table 1.11 Statutory corporate "all-in" tax rates

	1993	1998	2003		
	"All-in" tax rate	"All-in" tax rate	"All-in" tax rate	of which local rate	preferential rate
France	33.33	41.6	35.43	–	15.45
Germany	52.15	54.3	39.72	12.0–20.0	–
Ireland	40.0	32.0	12.5	–	10.0
Italy	52.2	41.25	34.25–38.25	4.25	–
The Netherlands	40.0	35.0	34.5	–	29.0
Spain	35.0	35.0	35.0	–	30.0
United Kingdom	33.0	31.0	30.0	–	0–19
15 EU average	37.85	36.76	32.62	–	–

Source: REF (different years).

favor of the sub-central taxation of productive activities may be identified (Alworth, Boffano and Gandullia 1996), both in Germany and especially in Italy, the reform or abolition of the local business tax is currently under discussion.

Apart from the UK and Italy, all the countries studied have adopted a flat corporate income tax; the UK has a graduated tax structure in place, with the low bracket rate (currently 0 percent) often coined the "small business" tax rate; Italy applies two different tax rates under the dual income tax system. Special corporate tax rates apply to small enterprises in some other countries (France, the Netherlands and Spain). Generally these measures are targeted to stimulate entrepreneurship and to correct financial market failures that can create obstacles to SMEs in raising new capital (Chen, Lee and Mintz 2002).

Excluding the innovative Italian system of the dual income tax and the local business tax (*IRAP*), all the countries adopt a traditional model of corporate income taxation that, combined with the taxation of capital income at the personal level, makes the tax systems in the surveyed countries structurally not neutral on a firm's organization, investment, funding and location decisions. Table 1.12 illustrates three sets of effective tax rates' measures on enterprises: forward-looking marginal and average tax rates on investments (EU Commission 2001b; Giannini and Maggiulli 2001); forward-looking effective tax rates on production marginal costs in the presence of multiple inputs, fundamentally capital together with labor (Gandullia 2002, following the methodology developed by McKenzie, Mintz and Scharf 1997); and, finally, backward-looking effective average tax rates (Nicodeme 2001).

The comparison of METRs between the selected countries shows the different structure of incentives and disincentives given by the different tax systems to undertake a standard investment (given a certain location).

Table 1.12 Effective tax rates on enterprises

Country	METRs (2001)	Forward EATRs (2001)			ETRs on production marginal costs (2002)	Backward EATRs (1999)
		Overall	Equity	Debt		
France	31.80	34.7	39.0	26.8	34.19	17.6
Germany	26.10	34.9	38.7	27.7	33.47	21.8
Ireland	11.70	10.5	11.7	8.2	18.17	n.a.
Italy	−15.90	27.6	28.7	25.5	27.31	26.4
The Netherlands	22.70	31.0	35.2	23.3	30.17	17.9
Spain	22.80	31.0	35.2	23.3	27.77	16.2
UK	24.80	28.3	31.8	21.7	25.91	n.a.
EU average	18.32	28.54	32.0	22.0	28.7	17.9
Standard deviation	*10.8*	*6.0*	*6.9*	*4.7*	*3.9*	*4.2*

Source: EU Commission (2001b); Nicodeme (2001); Gandullia (2002).

As a consequence of accelerated depreciation allowances and of the equity allowance introduced in 1997, in Italy marginal investments received (up to 2001) a subsidy by the tax system (METR was negative). Between the other countries the structure of incentives/disincentives varies markedly, ranging from Ireland (11.7 percent) to France (31.8 percent).

The variance is lower looking at the forward overall EATRs that measure the relative competitiveness of a country as a location for intra-marginal investments. Ireland appears to be, on average, more attractive than France or Germany. But the differences between countries decrease significantly if, assuming financial flexibility (Sinn 1987), investments are financed by debt. This shows that generally "real" distortions induced by the tax system can be attenuated through the optimization of the company financial policy.

Following a different forward approach, ETRs on production marginal costs show the effects of both capital and labor taxation on marginal costs of production. Differences in ETRs modify the production efficiency and thus the competitive position of firms coming from different locations and competing in the same international market; international trade may be distorted. Following this approach, large differences between countries still exist (in Ireland, ETR is 18.2 percent, while in France it is 34.2 percent), but, not surprisingly, the variance between countries seems to be much lower.

Finally, backward ETRs, based on data of corporate profits drawn from financial statements, give some information about the distribution of the tax burden and also about the ability of firms coming from different countries to use tax-planning techniques to reduce the tax burden

(Cnossen 2002). Following this approach, firms located in Italy and Germany appear to bear a higher tax burden than those located in France, the Netherlands and Spain.

Consumption-based taxes

As illustrated on page 7 (Table 1.2), countries rely heavily on consumption-based taxes that account for about 30 percent of total tax revenue and 11–12 percent in terms of GDP. Taxes on general consumption cover the main share (18.2 percent of total tax revenue, and 7.5 percent in terms of GDP). Moreover, taxes on general consumption as a percentage of GDP appear to be more similar across the selected countries than taxes on specific goods and service (OECD 2002a). In particular VAT revenues, as a percentage of GDP, never vary more than one percentage point between the selected countries.

Despite this picture, countries apply different VAT tax rates structures (Table 1.13): a dual-rate structure (Germany, the Netherlands and the UK) and a multiple-rate structure (France, Italy, Ireland and Spain). The standard rates range from 16 percent (Germany) to 20 percent (Italy and Ireland). With the exception of Ireland, in the last 20 years all the countries have increased the standard tax rates; on average, at the EU level, the standard rate increased from 17.5 percent to 19.4 percent.

All the countries maintain rate differentiation and exemptions, motivated by historical and social factors, by concerns over distributional effects of indirect taxation or by industrial policy objectives. On aggregate the effects of rate differentiation and exemptions, and thus the effectiveness of VAT, can be measured through the ratio between the effective and the statutory rate of VAT (van den Noord and Heady 2001), where the first is

Table 1.13 VAT structure and effectiveness

	Statutory tax rates			Preferential tax rates 2002	Effective VAT rates 1998	Effective VAT rates as percentage of standard rates
	1980	*1993*	*2002*			
France	17.6	18.6	19.6	2.1/5.5	10.9	53.0
Germany	13.0	15.0	16.0	7.0	9.4	59.0
Ireland	25.0	21.0	20.0	0.0/12.5	12.2	58.2
Italy	14.0	19.0	20.0	4.0/10.0	8.5	42.7
The Netherlands	18.0	17.5	19.0	6.0	10.5	60.1
Spain	n.a.	15.0	16.0	4.0/7.0	8.0	49.7
United Kingdom	15.0	17.5	17.5	0.0	8.8	50.1
EU average	17.5	19.4	19.4	–	10.5	54.2

Source: Cnossen (2002); van den Noord and Heady (2001).

VAT revenues divided by the potential VAT base. On average the effectiveness of VAT in Europe is still slightly over 50 percent, meaning that rate differentiation and exemptions are pervasive and that base erosion is significant. Between the selected countries only Germany, Ireland and the Netherlands are placed above the European average. Italy appears to be the country where the VAT system is less neutral and efficient mainly as a consequence of tax erosion and evasion. These non-neutralities across Europe signal that national VAT systems could be improved in order to reduce distortions that affect competition within EU countries and also on digital and cross-border shopping in boundary areas (Keen 2002b).

Compared to VAT, the contribution of the other consumption taxes to total taxation and their incidence on GDP is less homogeneous (OECD 2002a). These taxes raise revenues in the range of 8.2 percent of the total tax revenue (France) to 14.1 percent (Ireland). A substantial share is levied on energy consumption in order to achieve both fiscal and environmental policy goals. Apart from the Netherlands (where environmental levies were introduced in 1988), France, Germany, Italy and the UK have initiated green tax reforms more recently (Barde and Braathen 2002): France introduced a general tax on pollution activities in 2000; Germany initiated a green tax reform in 1999, through a new tax on electricity and an increased taxation of mineral oil; in Italy a green tax reform is being implemented over the period 1999–2005 through the introduction of a carbon tax; in the UK a "climate change levy" on energy use by business and the public sector was introduced in 2001. According to the last available data (OECD 2001a), revenues from environmental taxes range from 4.7 percent of the total tax revenue (France) to 8.7 percent (the Netherlands) as a consequence of the different emphasis that individual countries place on fiscal and extra-fiscal objectives and on concerns about distribution effects of taxation and international competitiveness of national firms.

Table 1.14 illustrates a somewhat emblematic case of the variance of

Table 1.14 Selected environmentally related taxes: the case of electricity consumption

	VAT rate	*Excise rate*	*Effective tax rates (2000)*
France	19.6	0.0073	21.1
Germany	16.0	0.0128	13.8
Ireland	12.5	exempt	11.1
Italy	10.0	0.0201	22.9
The Netherlands	19.0	0.0601	34.0
Spain	16.0	0.0056	18.0
United Kingdom	5.0	exempt	4.8

Source: own calculations from OECD environmentally related taxes database and IEA (2002).

effective tax rates on the final price of household electricity consumption. As an effect of the presence of different country structures of indirect taxation (VAT and excise taxes), the incidence of taxes as a percentage of the market prices appears to vary markedly, ranging from 4.8 percent (the UK) to 34 percent (the Netherlands). Similar disparities can also be found in industrial electricity consumptions (IEA 2002), meaning that, when the destination principle can't be applied, competition in the internal market can be distorted.

Tax reforms and selected policy issues

As a result of tax changes and reforms made during the 1990s, or reforms currently on the policy agenda, illustrated in more detail in the chapter on specific countries, some issues have arisen in the recent discussion of tax design in the selected European experiences: (i) tax equity; (ii) competitiveness; (iii) innovation and growth; (iv) fiscal design across levels of government.

(i) *Tax equity.* During the 1990s, tax changes or reforms in the European countries structurally reduced the progressivity path of the personal income tax. This was the result of two different policies: the flattening of the tax schedule and the exclusion of (part of) capital income from the PIT base. Both the policies have been motivated mainly on the grounds of efficiency. Looking at the late 1990s (OECD 1997 and 2003) the main changes in personal income tax have been the sequenced cut in marginal tax rates, the increase in the basic allowances (or tax credits) and the reduction in the level at which the top marginal tax rate applies.

The emphasis that tax reforms placed on efficiency has been only partly matched by tax equity considerations. To this end, in more recent years, a number of tax measures have been introduced or are planned in some countries to achieve horizontal equity objectives (mainly through child and family tax relief) and to strengthen the progressivity of the tax system at the lower end of the income scale (through basic allowances and tax credits). A number of these measures have replaced pre-existing cash transfers, reinforcing the trend toward the use of tax systems to deliver benefits. This is the case, for instance, of the German child tax credit (that, in 1996, replaced the former cash child allowance) or the new child tax credit in the UK.

Since the mid-1990s, some countries have introduced measures targeted to reduce the tax burden on lower-paid labor and at the same time to foster work incentives (EU Commission 2001a). Within personal income tax, cuts in marginal rates on labor income have been targeted to lower income groups in France and Italy. Tax relief to make work more attractive for targeted groups (in most cases spouses and low-paid workers) have been introduced, for instance, in the UK (working earned income tax credit) and in France (*prime pour l'emploi*).

(ii) *Competitiveness.* The growing integration of economic activities in the EU is exerting pressures on national tax systems. The location of financial and real capital appears to be becoming increasingly sensitive to tax regime differences between competing countries. Many EU countries have instituted (Germany, France and the UK) or are currently considering (Italy) reforms where competitiveness is one of the main motivations.

Tax measures specifically targeted to increase national competitiveness have involved three main areas: financial capital; real capital; production factors other than capital.

Concerns about competitiveness was the motivation in the 1990s for the generalized reduction in withholding taxes on capital income paid to non-residents. Currently, no country levies taxes on interest and on capital gains as a mean to attract foreign capital in a world where the resident principle de facto can't be applied. The same reason justified the lowering of capital income taxation for resident investors as an instrument to protect against the coming out of capital. More recently, Italy adopted (and Germany is still considering) a tax amnesty for illegally exported capital.

In the business sector, especially after the adoption of the European Code of Conduct and thus the prohibition of "harmful tax practices," countries have began to compete mainly over corporate tax rates in order to attract greater volume of foreign direct investment (Keen 2001). Deep corporate tax cuts occurred in Ireland, Italy, France and Germany. A number of other micro tax measures have been introduced with the same aim; for instance, the adoption of the tax participation exemption regime (or similar regimes) is seen as an instrument intended to favor the location of multinational headquarters in the Netherlands, the UK and in Italy (according to the new tax reform).

More generally, comprehensive approaches to the competitiveness issue have been followed in a number of countries. Many countries (France, Italy, the Netherlands, Spain and the UK) have cut payroll taxes since the mid-1990s in order to both stimulate the demand for labor and the location of production activities inside the country. In deciding if and how to institute green tax reforms or environment-related taxes, concerns about possible competitiveness losses have been one of the main arguments in Italy, Germany and the UK (Barde and Braathen 2002).

(iii) *Innovation and growth.* The structure and design of business taxation and personal taxes have implications for growth performance. Across the EU countries, there has been a broad reduction of both personal income taxes and corporate income taxes in the view that high tax rates can distort economic activity. There has also been a trend toward broadening the tax base and changing the structure of business investment incentives. With the exception of Italy, where tax incentives in the business sector still appear to be general (even if sometimes reinforced when directed to underdeveloped areas), in the other selected countries the broadening of tax bases has been followed by the reorientation of tax incentives to selectively stimulate innovation and growth. Tax measures that EU countries have targeted to stimulate innovation and growth can be grouped into four main areas: SMEs, venture capital, intangibles investments (R&D) and stock options.

Specific tax incentives targeted to SMEs have been motivated by the idea that innovative start-ups and small firms can play an important role in spurring productivity growth. To this end some countries (France, Ireland, the Netherlands, Spain and the UK) have lowered corporate taxes on small firms (emblematic is the case of the UK where, since 2002, the zero starting rate has been applied to small firms); to address the problem of operating losses, that may discriminate against smaller enterprises, some countries (Germany, Ireland and the Netherlands) allow losses to be carried forward indefinitely; more generally, as a consequence of the European discipline against state aids, all the selected countries have more generous or targeted tax incentives on investments conduced by SMEs.

Several countries have introduced specific tax incentives in favor of venture capital as a means to correct market failures that prevent innovative start-ups and SMEs from accessing the stock market. Tax incentives take two broad forms: front-end incentives whereby investors receive tax credits on income tax for qualifying investments; back-end incentives whereby investors receive reductions on capital gains tax. Schemes of front-end incentives have been introduced in France (in favor of *Fonds Commun de Placement dans l'innovation*), Ireland (Business Expansion Scheme), the Netherlands (Tax Compensation Scheme) and the UK (Enterprise Investment Scheme and Venture Capital Trust). Schemes of back-end incentives are present in France (in favor of *Fonds Commun de Placement a Risques* and *Sociétés de Capital Risque*), the Netherlands (Tax Compensation Scheme), Spain (*Fondos de Capital Riesgo*) and the UK (Enterprise Investment Scheme and Venture Capital Trust).

Preferential tax measures (compared to ordinary salary compensation) targeted to stock options were introduced during the 1990s as an instrument to promote entrepreneurship and innovative small firms. Different approaches have been followed, but generally tax schemes used in the UK and Ireland appear to be more favorable for employers and employees than those adopted, for instance, in France or Spain.

Finally, due to positive externalities, several countries have introduced tax incentives to stimulate intangible investments (R&D). Countries offer tax credits applied to the level of (Italy, the Netherlands) or an increase on (Spain) R&D investments or they offer tax allowances (the UK and Ireland). According to one indicator of the relative generosity of R&D tax measures (Warda 2001), Spain and the Netherlands have the most generous fiscal incentives for large manufacturing firms, while Italy and the UK are the most generous for R&D investments conduced by small firms.

(iv) *Fiscal design across levels of government.* The structure of fiscal relations across different levels of government is far from stable in most of the selected countries. For some years, Germany has been considering the reform of intergovernmental fiscal relations toward a more efficient public sector (OECD 1998). As a response to desires by different parts of the nation with strong identities for regional assemblies that allow a measure of self-determination, Spain introduced "strong" regional assemblies (Basque region, Catalonia) and is currently strengthening the "weak" regions to become equally as strong, while the UK introduced new regional assemblies for Scotland and Wales and is considering the possibility of introducing regional assemblies in England. After the 2001 constitutional reform, Italy has markedly decentralized the structure of fiscal relations between central and sub-central governments (Giarda 2001) and is currently considering more radical processes of devolution. In the most centralized country in Europe (France) the reform of the constitution toward more decentralized structures is currently on the policy agenda.

Although there are many changes in the institutional settings that prefigure higher degrees of decentralization of the public sectors in the future, the distribution of taxing powers across levels of governments is still not definite.

In recent years, the structure of sub-national taxation has been mainly characterized by (OECD 1999, 2002a, 2002b): growing use of property taxes; increased relevance of non-tax revenues (user charges), based on the benefit principle; progressive desertion of local business taxes; use of environmentally related taxes; and, finally, growing use of tax revenue sharing sources. What has been seen as the most innovative experience of local tax (the Italian *IRAP*) is going to be abolished according to the tax reform plan under discussion in Italy.

All these trends seem to be consistent with the theory, but together with the increased degree of decentralization, they prefigure in the future a lower redistribution pattern of the whole tax system.

Notes

1 Thanks are due for comments and suggestions received from L. Bernardi, C. Heady, T. McGirr, N. Iacobone and A. Tiraferri.
2 In this chapter, data on tax revenues are mainly drawn from the OECD that allows comparative analysis between the EU area and the OECD area. As known tax data collected by the OECD differ in some respects from those collected by other organizations (for instance in Europe by Eurostat). Sometimes the differences for individual countries in the tax-to-GDP ratios are significant. For instance, the 2000 tax-to-GDP ratio accounted for Germany by the OECD is about four percentage points less than that from Eurostat; in this case, as in others, the difference can be explained in the accounting of tax credits, of voluntary/compulsory social security contributions and of figurative public social security contributions.
3 Obviously this is just an imperfect measure of fiscal decentralization as it

neglects the share of sub-national revenues on total government revenue (or on GDP). For more accurate measures of fiscal decentralization, composition of sub-national revenues (tax, non-tax revenues and grants) and degree of local taxing powers, see OECD 1999 and 2002b.

4 On the significance of the use of economic categories and legal categories see Martinez-Mongay 2000. Tax burdens by economic categories are shown by Eurostat 2000, EU Commission 2000 and Cnossen 2002.

References

Adema, W. (2001) "Net social expenditure," 2nd Edition, Labour Market and Social Policy Occasional Papers 52, Paris: OECD.

Alworth, J., Boffano, S. and Gandullia, L. (1996) "Le imposte locali sulle attivita' produttive: confronti internazionali," *Economia pubblica*, 5: 61–94.

Barde, J.P. and Braathen, N.A. (2002) "Environmentally related levies," paper prepared for the Conference on Excise Taxation, 11–12 April, The Hague.

Bernardi, L. (2000) "Note sull'evoluzione recente e sulle prospettive future dei sistemi tributari," *Studi e Note di Economia*, 1: 25–50.

Bordignon, M., Giannini, S. and Panteghini, P. (2001) "Reforming business taxation: lessons from Italy?," *International Tax and Public Finance*, 8: 191–210.

Chen, D., Lee, F. and Mintz, J. (2002) "Taxation, SMEs and entrepreneurship," OECD–STI Working Paper 2002/9, August.

Cnossen, S. (2002) "Tax policy in the European Union: a review of issues and options," CESIFO Working Paper 758, Munich, August.

Devereux, M., Lockwood, B. and Redoano, M. (2002) "Do countries compete over Corporate Tax rate?," Working Paper, University of Warwick, April.

EU Commission (2000) "Public finances in EMU," *European Economy*, 3: 69–92.

—— (2001a) "Public finances in EMU," *European Economy*, 3: 85–95.

—— (2001b) *Company Taxation in the Internal Market*, SEC(2001) 1681, Brussels: EU Commission.

Eurostat (2000) *Structures of the Taxation Systems in the European Union, 1970–1997*, Brussels: European Commission.

Gandullia, L. (2002) "Imposte e competitività delle imprese in Europa: una nota," in Praussello, F. (ed.) *Euro Circulation and the Economic and Monetary Union*, Milano: Franco Angeli.

Giannini, S. and Maggiulli, C. (2001) *The Effective Tax Rates in the EU Commission Study on Corporate Taxation: Methodological Aspects, Main Results and Policy Implications*, CAPP, Università di Modena e Reggio Emilia.

Giarda, P. (2001) *Fiscal Federalism in the Italian Constitution: the Aftermath of the October 7th referendum*, mimeo.

Guerra, M.C. (1998) "La riforma tributaria: attuazione e prospettive," in Bernardi, L. (ed.) *La Finanza pubblica italiana. Rapporto 1998*, Bologna, Il Mulino: 159–82.

IEA (2002) *Energy Prices and Taxes*, Fourth Quarter, IEA Statistics.

Joumard, I. (2001) "Tax systems in European Union countries," Economic Department Working Paper 301, Paris: OECD.

Keen, M. (2001) "Preferential regimes can make tax competition less harmful," *National Tax Journal*, 54: 757–62.

—— (2002a) "The German tax reform of 2000," *International Tax and Public Finance*, 9: 603–21.

—— (2002b) "Some international issues in commodity taxation," IMF Working Paper, July.

Martinez-Mongay, C. (2000) "The ECFIN effective taxation databank. Properties and comparisons with other databanks," European Commission Economic Paper 146, Brussels: EU Commission.

McKenzie, K.J., Mintz, N.M. and Scharf, K.A. (1997) "Measuring effective tax rates in the presence of multiple inputs," *International Tax and Public Finance*, 4, 3: 332–59.

Messere, K. (ed.) (1998) *The Tax System in Industrialized Countries*, Oxford: Oxford University Press.

Nicodeme, G. (2001) "Computing effective corporate tax rates: comparison and results," European Commission Economic Paper 153, Brussels: EU Commission.

OECD (1997) *The Tax/Benefit Position of Employees*, Paris: OECD.

—— (1998) *Economic Surveys – Germany*, Paris: OECD.

—— (1999) "Taxing powers of state and local government," *Tax Policy Studies*, 1, Paris: OECD.

—— (2000a) "Tax burdens. Alternative measures," *Tax Policy Studies*, 2, Paris: OECD.

—— (2000b) *Economic Surveys – Spain*, Paris: OECD.

—— (2000c) *Economic Surveys – The United Kingdom*, Paris: OECD.

—— (2000d) *Economic Surveys – Italy*, Paris: OECD.

—— (2001) *Environmentally Related Taxes in OECD Countries. Issues and Strategies*, Paris: OECD.

—— (2002a) *Revenue Statistics 1965–2001*, Paris: OECD.

—— (2002b) *Fiscal Decentralization in EU Applicant States and Selected EU Member States*, Paris: OECD.

—— (2003) *Taxing Wages 2001–2002*, Paris: OECD.

REF (1990–2003) *Osservatorio fiscale REF. Imposte sui redditi da capitale in Europa*, Milano.

Sinn, H.W. (1987) *Capital Income Taxation and Resource Allocation*, Amsterdam: North Holland.

van den Noord, P. and Heady, C. (2001) "Surveillance of tax policies: a synthesis of findings in economic surveys," Economic Department Working Paper 303, Paris: OECD.

Warda, J. (2001) "Measuring the value of R&D tax treatment in OECD Countries," *OECD STI Review*, 27.

2 Rationale and open issues of more radical reforms

Luigi Bernardi[1]

Introduction

From the early 1990s, most of the tax systems in Europe were subject to significant changes. Many others are currently under way or in the planning stages (for the details see Chapter 1 and chapters relating to specific countries, and also Joumard 2001). The forces which shaped the reforms were several (see Foreword) and often conflicting. Fiscal systems were requested to raise revenue, in order to fulfill the Maastricht requirements and then those of the Stability Pact (see Chapter 4). A reduction of fiscal pressure was also called for to boost declining growth and employment. To sustain this proposal, a recurring argument was the comparison with the USA, whose growth was higher but taxes much lower. Fiscal competition in an increasingly integrated world affected tax rates and structures of the most mobile bases. Common opinion called for more efficiency, thus stressing the need for making taxes more simple and neutral. Political factors, however, such as the pressure of lobby groups (see Chapter 3), prevented this process from going very far.

The same constraints were at odds with the most radical proposals of fiscal reforms. These proposals were thus fated from the outset, possibly lacking electoral support (but also budget means). As usually happens, a greater degree of fairness was invoked but, on the contrary, income tax top rates were reduced virtually everywhere. The unavoidable result so far has been a difficult mix of tax cuts and tax increases, continuous shifts from one tax to another and continuous minor tax codes updates. A further consequence could not be avoided. In the 1990s, European countries' tax changes were narrow in size and limited in scope, i.e. "marginal" in optimal taxation (OT) language.

Are these really the most suitable fiscal reforms for the fundamental, present needs of European countries? My answer is quite negative. The most authoritative views, including the main international organizations (e.g. EU Commission 2000; Joumard 2001) stress the urgent need to make taxation more supply-friendly, by taking off labor and productive capital to some extent. The burden should be shifted onto consumption, immovable properties and environment externalities, and heavy losses on revenues from capital incomes should be avoided. The basic features of main national taxes should be brought closer, to make the overall "European" tax system more neutral and efficient. The working of the single market would thus be improved.

These suggestions are well founded on qualitative grounds, but the true questions simply and suddenly arise: how much and how far? Such questions come from three current key factors which heavily impinge on European tax systems and any future changes hoped for.

(i) Several years of tax competition and harmonization efforts have, up to now, failed to set out a basic common framework for a "European" tax system. We mean a system suitable for the present mixed "Confederation"-to-"Federation" EU institutional setting, and really enabling a mobility of people, goods and capitals, within the single market and free from fiscal distortions.

(ii) The European economy's growth rate decrease seems at this point almost endless. Prospects for future recovery are continuously postponed. The outlook of economic decline cannot be excluded, even amongst the more established countries. Could fiscal reforms really contribute to enhancing economic growth? Furthermore, how should the tax system be shaped in order to keep up the level of welfare of the Pigouvian "national dividend," by matching the decreasing growth rate with increased levels of fairness?

(iii) The rebuilding of the European institutional setting is just beginning. Common historical heritage of the federal states leads to a prediction of profound changes in the allocation of government tiers' taxing and spending powers. Constitutional guarantees for the satisfaction of basic needs are likely to be strengthened.

The following part of the chapter is devoted to opening an intuitive discussion of how tax reforms should be shaped in order to be consistent with the environment depicted. I am well aware that my remarks may appear general and vague. I look at this as the due price to pay in order to take account of the large and fundamental topics we have to cope with and to avoid the endless debates of minute (if not irrelevant at all) issues. Thus, I end with my preliminary main conclusions, but I also stress the need for further research efforts devoted to pinpointing the fiscal reforms best suited to the essential needs of Europe.

The missing common basic framework of the European tax systems

The survival of countries' tax-clusters

In the early part of the 1970s, European[2] countries were almost all mid-to-high fiscal pressure countries. The total figure (taxes and social contributions) was about 33 percent of GDP,[3] and was already over that of both the US (about 27 percent) and Japan (still at about 22 percent) (EU Commission 2000; Eurostat 2000; OECD 2001). This book's selected countries were more or less close to the continental average, the only relevant exceptions being the low-taxing Italy (27.5 percent) and, even more, Spain (25.6 percent). The picture looks quite different by splitting overall pressure into its main headings. A wide dispersion emerges among direct taxes and social contributions from country to country (see Table 2.1). Countries' indirect taxes (then prevailing on direct taxes) were closer to the average figure. By combining these differences, four countries' tax-clusters[4] come out, originating from their different historical, economic and institutional roots.

(i) *Nordic countries*:[5] the fiscal pressure was very high. It was made up in large amount by direct and (at a smaller size) indirect taxes, to pay for a comprehensive and advanced welfare state.

(ii) *Rhine countries*: the fiscal pressure was somewhat higher than the European average. Direct taxes prevailed in some countries, indirect ones' elsewhere. Throughout the area, however, social contributions raised to a high level, in order to finance a generous Bismarckian welfare state.

(iii) *Anglo-Saxon countries*: the fiscal pressure was still close to the European average. Taxes' share was far larger than the share of social contributions. The public health service was paid out from general tax revenues. The public Beveridgean pension schemes were tightened to only dispense low-amount social security treatments.

(iv) *Mediterranean countries*: the development's delay kept total fiscal pressure at a low level. Tax systems had social contributions close to the European average. Taxes (especially direct ones) still stood well below European standards.

Throughout Europe, fiscal pressure increased from the early 1970s to the late 1990s (see Table 2.1), apart from in Ireland and in the United Kingdom.[6] It was pulled up (six points) by a growing social expenditure essentially during the 1970s (Eurostat 2000; van den Noord and Heady 2001) and a final increase due to the accomplishment of Maastricht Treaty's requirements (1.8 percent in the 1990s). The total average figure rose to more than 42 percent of GDP in 2000, thus leaving well behind both that of Japan (increased to 27.9 percent) and the USA (remained virtually the same at 28.3 percent). After the mythic peak of 1997, only minor and scattered tax cuts were adopted.[7] The questionable forces of the "Stability Pact" were and continue to be at work, forcing European Member countries to keep up fiscal pressure (see Chapter 4).

The wide dispersion of tax levels among countries, already apparent at the beginning of the 1970s, essentially continued to hold firm. The growth of direct taxes and social contributions was, however, very fast, whereas the profile of indirect taxes on the contrary was almost flat. The main features of tax-clusters did not generally undergo dramatic changes.

Table 2.1 Structure and development of fiscal revenues in European countries as a percentage of GDP, 1970–97

	1970								1997							
	D	E	F	IRL	IT	NL	UK	EU	D	E	F	IRL	IT	NL	UK	EU
Direct taxes	10.9	7.1	7.3	9.4	5.3	12.9	17.4	8.9	10.1	11.9	11.3	14.7	16.5	13.4	15.6	13.7
personal income	8.2	4.8	4.4	7.0	0.1	9.7	11.1	5.5	7.8	8.3	8.1	10.4	9.6	6.8	9.3	9.3
corporation income	1.7	1.2	2.1	1.5	2.4	3.0	2.9	2.2	1.9	2.1	2.2	3.7	4.3	4.6	4.3	3.0
Indirect taxes	13.2	6.6	15.0	19.4	10.5	10.9	14.2	13.0	12.7	10.9	15.8	14.8	12.7	13.5	14.6	13.9
VAT	5.9	0.0	8.9	0.0	0.0	5.4	0.0	5.1	6.6	5.8	7.9	7.3	5.7	7.0	7.1	7.0
excise duties	3.4	1.5	2.9	10.2	4.9	3.0	6.6	3.5	2.9	3.0	3.0	5.1	4.0	3.4	4.0	3.5
Total taxes	24.1	13.7	22.3	28.8	15.8	23.8	31.6	21.9	22.8	22.8	27.1	29.5	29.2	26.9	30.2	27.6
Social contributions	11.6	11.8	12.7	2.8	11.7	13.5	5.6	11.7	19.0	12.8	19.2	4.5	14.9	18.9	7.0	15.0
employers	5.4	9.3	9.3	1.4	7.9	6.1	2.8	7.2	8.2	8.9	12.2	2.8	10.3	3.6	3.7	8.2
employees	4.9	1.9	2.4	1.3	1.7	5.7	2.6	3.5	7.2	2.2	5.6	1.5	2.9	11.9	3.1	5.0
self-employed	1.4	0.7	1.0	0.0	0.4	16.5	0.2	1.0	3.6	1.7	1.6	0.2	1.7	3.7	0.2	1.9
Total revenues	35.7	25.6	35.1	34.7	27.5	36.0	36.9	33.5	41.8	35.5	46.6	34.0	44.1	45.8	37.2	42.1
Administrative level																
Central government	95.9	94.9	96.5	96.0	97.8	99.4	95.5	96.4	94.7	89.3	94.6	95.2	94.4	96.5	98.2	95.8
Local government	4.1	5.1	3.5	4.0	2.2	0.6	4.5	3.6	5.3	10.7	5.4	4.8	5.6	3.5	1.8	4.2

Source: Eurostat (2000).

Notes
Minor items are omitted. EU 9 up to 1979, EU 15 thereafter. Local revenues do not include sharing to state taxes. Data stop at 1997 to be consistent with those of Table 2.2, not available for subsequent years. See chapters relating to specific countries for an update of this information.

The shift to the "dual income tax system" (Soerensen 1994) did not significantly change the fiscal structure of Nordic countries. In the Rhine area, fiscal pressure grew yet more. Personal income tax jumped up and social contributions effected a further upward turn. The Anglo-Saxon countries were left at the starting post: fiscal pressure did not increase, nor was its structure dramatically changed. Mediterranean countries marked the main change. The total fiscal pressure of the European development newcomers[8] increased by about 10–15 points. Tax structure changed markedly in favor of direct (in Spain, also indirect) taxes.

Not enough convergence and narrow reforms: macro and micro issues

Table 2.2 shows a set of macro-indicators pertaining to the convergence of tax systems in our selected countries, from 1970 to 1997. As to the simple ratios to GDP, the convergence processes (by competition or harmonization) seem to have impinged on direct[9] and still more indirect taxes.[10] Neither total taxes nor social contributions show clear signals of convergence. What about the tax burden? An analysis by economic functions (i.e. main aggregates of internal resources or employments, Eurostat 2000) as ratio to their overall value (more or less the GDP), shows strong evidence of convergence for consumption and far lower for capital (be aware that "capital" here means all the heterogeneous incomes which constitute operating surplus in national accounting). Convergence for labor and total fiscal burden seem to have almost not existed.

However, different degrees of tax base buoyancy rather muddy such evidence, thus requiring a closer look at the movement of tax structure as depicted by the implicit rates (i.e. the revenues on single factor or employment as a ratio of a national accounts potential tax basis: see Martinez-Mongay 2000). Taxation on labor increased by almost 50 percent and at the same time diverged; heterogeneous capital was affected by a stable rate converging taxation, while for consumption it remained much the same story as before.

It looks to me quite impossible to claim that, today, the EU[11] is working well and pursuing its declared aims, those being the status and the trends of its Member Countries' fiscal systems. Is it really possible to strengthen the single market, particularly as to the free movement of goods, people and capitals without fiscal interference, when maximum-to-minimum values of fiscal pressure, sorted by type of tax or their burden, diverge by two-digit figures? Notice further that the only process of convergence under way to this day seems have been due to the growth of the income tax, the harmonization of VAT and some tax competition on the most mobile capital. Again, the main and bad final result has been an increase of nearly 50 percent in the labor average tax wedge during long years of declining growth and increasing unemployment.

The unavoidable flipside of the coin is that only wide reforms can

Table 2.2 Descriptive statistics of fiscal systems in selected European countries, 1970–97

1970

	% of GDP 1970				Economic functions 1970				Implicit rates 1970		
	Total	Direct	Indirect	Contrib.	Labor	Capital	Consum.	Total	Labor	Capital	Consum.
Max. value	36.9	17.4	19.4	13.5	18.9	11.8	16.0	37.2	34.2	55.4	21.1
Min. value	25.6	5.3	6.6	2.8	8.4	4.7	5.3	25.6	16.1	16.6	7.3
Mean	33.3	10.0	12.8	10.0	13.9	6.3	10.7	32.6	26.6	29.2	16.1
St. dev.	4.7	4.0	4.1	4.1	3.6	2.5	3.2	5.1	6.2	13.4	4.6
(Max–min)/mean %	33.9	121.0	100.0	107.0	75.4	112.4	100.3	35.5	68.0	132.9	85.9
SD/mean %	14.1	40.0	32.0	41.0	26.0	39.5	30.4	15.6	23.1	45.8	28.4

1997

	% of GDP 1997				Economic functions 1997				Implicit rates 1997		
	Total	Direct	Indirect	Contrib.	Labor	Capital	Consum.	Total	Labor	Capital	Consum.
Max. value	46.6	16.5	15.8	19.0	23.9	10.0	12.9	46.4	50.7	42.1	23.7
Min. value	34.0	10.1	10.9	4.5	12.9	4.0	9.8	34.0	26.5	20.5	15.7
Mean	40.6	13.4	13.6	13.8	19.4	7.9	11.3	40.7	39.7	30.7	18.8
St. dev.	5.3	2.4	1.6	6.0	4.6	2.0	1.1	5.1	9.3	7.4	3.5
(Max–min)/mean %	31.0	47.8	36.0	105.1	56.6	75.9	27.4	30.5	61.0	70.3	42.6
SD/mean %	13.1	17.9	11.8	43.5	23.5	25.9	9.9	12.5	30.2	18.6	18.6

Sources: data and our computations from Eurostat, 2000. Countries as in Table 2.1.

correct such widely varying tax systems and structural differences, and to substitute inefficient existing processes of tax competition and harmonization. These were not, however, the reforms pursued by many European countries during the 1990s, which essentially brought about some simplifying and rationalizing effects of the existing systems, together with a lot of other minor changes (see Chapter 1), but sometimes did not improve many already critical situations at all. Let us explore some of the main cases.

(i) *Corporate tax.* It is commonly recognized that, from the 1980s onwards, corporations' statutory "all-in" tax rates decreased markedly, by about 15 points (from less than 47 percent to nearly 32 percent in the EU average during the years 1980–2003 (forecast figure) (Cnossen 2002). This has been commonly attributed to a greater fiscal competition, which, in turn, would be highly correlated with the increasing degree of globalization and capital mobility (Bretschger and Hettich 2002). The tax burden decrease was empirically confirmed for the *ex ante* but not the *ex post* effective rates. This trend of implicit (=effective *ex post*) rates is also due to the broadening of the bases that usually matched rates cuts (Devereux, Griffith and Klemm 2001). The final result might have been of no-incentive-investments reforms, as is suspected by Keen (2002) for the much vaunted German case and its planned Italian mirror opposite (see Chapter 8). If I am right, Keen's fine analysis of the German 2000 tax reform (see Chapter 6) also hints, between the lines, at the fact that at least one reason for the alleged simplification adopted (participation exemption and the end of the imputation system) has also been a reaction to the difficulties in coping with elusive practices and harmful competition.

(ii) *Financial capital incomes.* The original Razin and Sadka prophecy (1991) of this tax basis progressively vanishing has proved to be untrue without full mobility of assets and within imperfect capital markets. Inside EU countries, tax rates on interest unambiguously decreased during the last decade by about ten points (from nearly 46 percent in 1990 to slightly less than 37 percent in 2000), but this has been mainly due to the substitution of final withholdings for the inclusion in the income tax basis. The reduction of dividend rates was far less and statistically insignificant. The whole system of income capital taxation has diverged and become less neutral (Gorter and de Mooij 2001). Inside the large majority of countries, the shift to low-rate withholdings on interest enlarged a distortional spread with dividends taxation.[12] National models of interest taxation became more uneven (Joumard 2001; van de Noord and Heady 2001). Partial (Luxembourg, the UK, the Netherlands) or total (Denmark, Germany, Spain, Ireland) inclusion in the income tax basis at marginal rates of up to 60 percent are in force as well as final withholdings (Austria, Belgium, France, Finland, Greece, Italy, Portugal, Sweden) at rates going from 12.5 percent (Italy) to 30 percent (Finland and Sweden). Up to mid-

January 2003, non-residents were generally exempt even if this was not for-mally the case in Greece and Portugal. The EU agreement of 21 January 2003 is based mainly on monitoring and information exchanges to allow taxation in the country of residence (except for Austria, Belgium and Lux-embourg). The adopted solution is well informed to the better residence principle (compared to that of origin). Its results, however, are somewhat reduced by the increasing exclusion of total interest income from progres-sive income tax base as previously discussed. Further, one must hope that monitoring and information exchanges will be effective and really cooper-ative. Needless to say, tax regimes for dividends and capital gains are still more fragmented than for interests. The same claimed "general" shift away from the imputation system (whatever its very doubtful merits) up to now has been realized by a minority of European countries (van de Noord and Heady 2001). For income capital taxation, these are the poor results of tax competition on the most mobile bases.

(iii) *Social contributions and income tax.* In the early 1990s, the European average tax wedge on labor was already at about 50 percent. The implicit rate was at 35 percent, some ten points above the US level (EU Commis-sion 2000; Cnossen 2002). Inescapable was the conjecture that this had something to do with the different pattern of growth and employment then observed in the two areas. The suggestion to remove tax on labor, particularly non-skilled labor, was obvious. It was first put forward by the authoritative voices of Drèze and Malinvaud (1994) and thereafter repeat-edly raised both by the OECD and the UE Commission: it became manda-tory for the Union Member States at the Lisbon Council of 2000.

What has really been achieved? From 1990 to 2000, the implicit rate increased by about two further points, equally distributed between social contributions and income tax (Martinez-Mongay 2000). As to social con-tributions, just small cuts were introduced, by no more than a few points, generally only at the lower end of the wage scale and not in all European countries (Chapter 1 and EU Commission 2000).

Tax cuts of the income tax were similar (see Chapter 1 and chapters relating to individual countries), but usually they were extended also to the top rate, sometimes in quite a reasonable way (Germany and France, for example), in other cases they were planned for a provocatively heavy amount (Italy). The burden for the (most dense) central income classes usually remained relatively unchanged. The total redistributive[13] effect thus has not generally been particularly relevant. The enlargement of the no-tax area was certainly welcome, mostly as much as producing higher equity, incentives on the labor supply being instead so minute as to be, in fact, uncertain (see Chapter 1 and page 39). Unfortunately the price paid to implement this cut[14] was a large increase of marginal rates over the no-tax area. To (partially) correct this effect, new decreasing deductions had to be introduced, complicating further a tax structure that any committed country would seek to simplify. Furthermore the no-tax area should have been enlarged up to a threshold able to cover the equivalent household level of poverty; this has rarely been achieved, especially for the households with many dependents, i.e. by adopting a poor equivalence scale.

The reduction of top rates, very difficult to explain on the grounds of efficiency (the mobility of the highly skilled and their tax "dissatisfaction" have been alleged), is not easily understood on political economy grounds either (see Chapter 3). The beneficiaries are few (usually not more than 10 percent of voters) and supposedly already in favor of the right-wing governments which usually introduced top rate cuts. One is thus forced to see this change as an ideological signal consistent with the various currents of thought which, for example, from Locke to Nozik and Buchanan, allege the existing of some "natural" or "implicit constitutional" limits to the power to tax. This stream of thinking about fiscal and social justice is however very questionable (e.g. Bernardi 2002) and certainly not new. It has been revived by the recent diffusion of right-wing ideas and governments. As usual, some economists tried to refresh an old idea, whose essence dates back to Aristotle (fifth century BC).[15]

Horizontal equity was, as ever, largely forgotten and usually did not cross the traditional border of adjustments in fiscal treatment of household or of different kinds of workers (see Chapter 1 and chapters relating to specific countries). Within these boundaries a widespread innovation was, however, the more favorable regime granted to the aged and disabled people. The allowances for dependent parents were also widely augmented, but the increase was substantial only in very few countries. Elsewhere they were dispersed among a largest number of minute benefits. The excess burden on single worker households remained undercorrected almost everywhere, the exception being the well-known case of France.

Reforms to enhance growth and to strengthen fairness within European countries

Reforms to enhance growth

When the fiscal burden began to increase, academics studying public finance became worried about its possible negative effects on growth. The first pioneering inquiry by the Colwyn Committee, in 1927 (Steve 1976), was reassuring, at least regarding to labor supply. In the 1950s and 1960s, the Western countries' fast growth and declining unemployment rate pushed the topic to one side. In 1959, the seminal Musgrave's "Theory of public finance" reflected this attitude. "Supply-siders" and OT theorists in the 1970s brought the topic to light once more. Making tax systems supply friendly, by reducing rates and broadening bases, became thus the "buzz idea" of the tax reformers of the 1980s, but the results were not as positive as expected (see, for example, Bosworth and Burtless 1992, for the paramount US case). The taxation-to-growth link then became a topic of endless discussion, with perhaps just one evident robust conclusion being reached up to now. The story could be briefly summarized as follows.

(i) *Supply and demand of labor.* Today the consensus of opinion is that elasticity figures differ from zero, but in the mid-range remain relatively small, albeit with some differences between labor market core or marginal areas (particularly between men and married women, see, for example, Blundell 1992). A gross average estimate in the US case has been set at around 0.15[16] for total supply and 0.25 for demand. Sure enough, the more unionized European labor markets[17] allow for a somewhat higher supply value, but how much is not clear at all (Leibfritz *et al.* 1997).

(ii) *Economic theory.* Neoclassical economic growth aggregate models *à la* Solow do not say very much about taxation effects, if not about the same post-Keynesian and plain common sense advice to promoting capital accumulation, i.e. taking off taxes as much as possible from investments and savings (at least as to their short-to-medium-term effects). Endogenous growth models claimed to be able to provide much more robust and targeted prescriptions (Myles 2000). However, empirical checks showed once again that the general level of average and marginal fiscal burden is of minimal relevance (Cassou and Lansing 2000; Myles 2000). Specific allowances should be allowed for physical and human capital accumulation (Tanzi and Zee 1997), but once more the linking figure does not seem clear-cut (Besley 2001). Last, the so-called "new theory of economic growth" stresses the need for taxes (e.g. Jones 2002; Tanzi 2002) and institutions (going back to North 1990) not hindering or meddling with economic transactions induced by the market. Up to now the list of specific prescriptions is still short and selective (for taxes) or somewhat vague (for institutions).

(iii) *Statistical inference.* The simple checks of statistical correlation (a very poor, although still popular tool of analysis) between taxes and growth dates back some 30 years. During all this time and throughout a long list of exercises, the hypothesis of such negative (positive) correlation existing has been proved alternatively to be true, false and spurious, and finally indeterminate (Agell *et al.* 1997). Looking at present data, one cannot however deny that some low taxes (especially labor and corporations) countries seem to perform better, such as Ireland and the United Kingdom among the Europeans.

As I have stated, the story has only one relatively robust conclusion. Negative relationships between taxes and growth seem to exist, but their size is small and they can be caught up just by looking at selective channels. As a consequence, growth-enhancing tax reforms should be huge in amount and strictly targeted, i.e. the opposite from the prevailing ones mostly adopted by the European countries in the 1990s. The difficulty in finding enough budget backing suddenly arises. The analysis provided by De Novellis and Parlato (Chapter 4) makes it clear that abiding also by the present "soft" rules of the Stability Pact prevents most European countries from having the room to reduce fiscal pressure, without compensating for this.[18] Expenditure cuts are commonly suggested (see the Foreword in this book, and Tanzi and Schuknecht 1997) and may be useful in the long term, under the condition that the welfare state is not dismantled together with its contribution to economic growth, social cohesion and fairness (Atkinson 1999a). De Novellis and Parlato warn us, however, that expenditure cuts, workable in the short to medium term, must already be devoted to fulfilling the Stability Pact requirements.

Wide and selective tax shifts thus become the last option to consider. The candidates are labor and corporate taxes to be reduced by a relevant extent. To have more than just a marginal effect, the reduction of their amounts must roughly reach one-third for both the burdens.[19] This means, in the EU average, more or less one point of GDP for "all in" corporation taxes and nearly five points of GDP in (mainly employers') social contributions (Eurostat data, see Table 2.1). Income tax on labor should instead not be dramatically changed – to lower contributions and to raise taxes in funding social security, and because of vertical equity. On the contrary, tax burdens on consumption, rents and externalities (that is, environment) should become substantially heavier. These latter two may produce a higher yield of about two-to-three points of GDP.[20] Thus, an increase in consumption taxes of the size of three-to-four points of GDP should be required at the end. It must come from VAT and not excise duties which have more narrow bases and higher rates. Further, notice that inflationary effects have not to be overestimated. Higher consumption taxes should substitute social contributions, that is, an item of cost of labor at least in part passed on prices.[21]

The main open question is, instead, if it is really effective to reduce the tax burden on labor by increasing consumption taxes. The topic is controversial and highly debated in multi-faceted literature. Hereafter we report just three main points which, together, lead to the (tentative) conclusion that more consumption taxes may allow the alleviation of those which are burdens on labor, the two being imperfect substitutes.

(i) *Theory.* The traditional textbook equivalence of taxation on labor income and consumption obviously still has some good arguments (e.g. Cnossen 2002), but it is increasingly open to question, due to its lack of an empirical frame (Carone and Salomaki 2001).[22] Further, the old proposition that heavier taxes on consumption may increase savings and investments still holds. Finally two central OT arguments should be reminded: first, consumption taxes do not change the inter-temporal consumption allocation and therefore its growth rate (Milesi-Ferretti and Roubini 1998); second, efficiency losses would be reduced if taxation was shifted at a lesser rate to a wider basis.

(ii) *Econometric estimates.* The last and more robust estimate has been performed using the EU Commission's Quest II model. As to its main result, a 1 percent shift in GDP from corporate to consumption tax would move GDP by 1.6 points and wages by 2.1 points from the average European baseline levels. The same amount of shift but from labor to consumption taxes should increase employment by 0.6 points and GDP by 0.7 points (Leibfritz *et al.* 1997).[23]

(iii) *Political feasibility*. Chapter 3 introduces more than one caveat concerning the political feasibility of a tax shift by an amount of about six point of GDP. This is probably particularly so if the shift almost entirely goes from dependent workers to all the consumers (and producers). Some parts of the workers' contributions to their PAYG pension schemes is charged on other taxpayers-voters. In my mind, just one way can make this politically feasible. It could be done by charging on general taxes the financing of a universal social security safety net, that must also include minimum pensions, whose share on the total treatments can thus be subtracted from the funding through workers' social contributions.

Looking to strengthen fiscal and social fairness

From its very beginning, the "old" welfare economics (Pigou 1929) clearly stated that the level of social welfare is given not just by the amount but also by the even distribution of the social "dividend" (GDP), due to the principle of decreasing marginal utility. Thus it seems worthwhile to look for an increase in fiscal and social fairness to sustain welfare and compensate for the current decrease of the growth rate. Something like a Rawlsian society (Rawls 2001) is outlined in the background, i.e. the well-ordered society of equal opportunities, highly endowed with freedom and social justice, particularly for the less advantaged. How to link tax reforms to fiscal and social fairness? The main way obviously requires the improvement of tax equity; some other features of tax systems are involved, keeping in mind that some final and maybe far more important traits of social fairness have little to do with fiscal systems. Looking, of course, only at these latter examples, here I limit myself to briefly speculating on three main points, and just in an intuitive way.

(i) *Political process and fiscal exchange*. Rawls (2001) stated some normative conditions, which can allow the political process to generate fair social outcomes. These however seem unlikely to occur, according to Profeta's findings (Chapter 3). Is this always the case? In the literature it has been stressed that interest groups' pressure may decrease during emergency times (for example, Drazen and Grilli 1993).[24] Second, the "traditional" "Public choice" frequently argued that radical reforms, which deeply redistribute property rights, can go further than the piecemeal and uncompensated cutting of single rents (e.g. Buchanan 1980).

The political process on taxation should not just be legitimated but also perfectly transparent. I stress this apparently obvious point (the real and not only formal implementation of the principle "no taxation without representation") because we saw that some recent European tax reforms were not exactly transparent. Avoiding fiscal illusion is truly important to allow citizens to properly evaluate the fairness of fiscal exchange, being rational and well-informed (further simplification of the tax system may help), and also, if possible, somewhat altruistic.

(ii) *Taxing rules and social behavior.* The structure of tax rules has wide effects on social behavior, not just on tax compliance. The latter should obviously be empowered in order to make taxation reliable and sure, amnesties should be avoided, evasion and corruption should be heavily fought against, tax administration should be efficient and correct for tax-payers. Once more I recall obvious textbook features just because they are, in fact, largely absent in European countries, especially the Mediterranean ones (Bovi 2002). The social effects of taxing rules are, however, deeper and far reaching. These rules intervene in the most sensible relationship between the state and the citizens. Being well-behaved and observed, they induce a higher degree of Kantian public ethics which, in turn, stimulates better-educated behaviors, more social cohesion, more sound and altruistic preferences. All this is also welfare and it might trigger a virtuous chain reaction with growth rates.

(iii) *Tax equity.* Vertical equity (see pp. 37–8) was not strengthened but, if anything, weakened by recent European tax reforms. Tax progressivity has been largely contrasted by alleging both efficiency and ideological arguments. This theoretical and political stance is pretty questionable and seems not to compare favorably with the following three arguments. Taken together, these arguments favor the empowering and not the dismantling of the degree of vertical equity, i.e. of the redistributive purpose of the tax system.

Argument 1. It is commonly alleged that redistributive targets can be reached more effectively through the expenditure rather than through the revenue side of the budget (for instance, EU Commission 2002). But can we credit the underlying calculations? Ultimate demonstrations have been given (for example, Goodin and Le Grand 1987) according to which welfare and other public services are mostly captured by the middle class. The redistributive impact should then be due mainly to social protection and particularly to public pensions, thanks to their predominant size. However, the unavoidable suspicion is that these estimates are single-generation ones, without considering together the effects of PAYG social contributions, which are usually proportional if lower net wages but regressive when passed on prices in non-competitive markets.

Argument 2. In a world and at a time in which inequality of *ex ante* incomes evidence is rapidly (and worryingly) increasing (Atkinson 1999b), not to weaken the redistributive effects of taxation seems like a suitable and reasonable policy choice.

Argument 3. Under the light shed by the most recent theoretical and empirical literature, it turns out that standard theory arguments against redistributive policies (i.e. their supposed incentive-reducing effects with respect to growth) do not seem to hold and perhaps need to be reversed.[25] Be careful, of course, not to mistake the general taxation-to-growth effect (see p. 39) for the differential impact of redistributive taxation.[26]

Vertical equity has also been eroded by the decreased burden on capital incomes due to fiscal competition. The Nordic "dual income tax system" has then been viewed as a good compromise between equity and contrasting capital flights (Cnossen 2002). In reality, it is only so under the condition that income and wealth are evenly distributed and highly correlated. This may be the case in some countries, but not in all. For the early 1990s, Wagstaff *et al.* (1999) report Gini coefficients on *ex ante* incomes ranging from 0.25 (Germany) to 0.41 (the United Kingdom). Also, an even level of capital income tax rate is required and this the case in many European countries (see pp. 36–7). Just as one example, for the mid-1990s, Joumard (2001) reports rates on interests ranging from 12.5 percent (Italy) to 30 percent (Sweden, not surprisingly).

Horizontal equity does not seem to be at the center of political action. We have already discussed a widespread lack of equity in the fiscal treatment of households, with reference to the number of both earners and dependents. As to the latter, the modern "welfare view," restricting the need of allowances only to low-income families, is now contrasted by a renewal of the old "optimum size view," induced by the worries of a European declining population. According to this view, allowances should also be extended to the middle-to-high incomes and should reach a huge amount in order to work effectively.

True fairness should further extend the concept of horizontal equity at least in two directions. First, the tax system should contribute to make the social justice principle of equal opportunities effective. For instance, taxing human capital formation is not only inefficient, but also unfair. Similarly, inheritance taxes should be empowered and not written off, as is largely occurring. Second, the old-fashioned qualitative discrimination among incomes (traditionally in favor of dependent work) should be enlarged and extended to encompass more features, for instance those that can differentiate the social merit of some income and wealth levels.[27] Thus the market distortions at the individual income levels (due to rents, information failures and under-evaluation of social value of some activities) should be compensated by the fiscal system. For instance, lawyers and football players should be taxed more, whereas less taxes should be charged on teachers and long-term care nurses. The same could be said, looking also at efficiency targets, by considering the high difference which generally exists between labor supply elasticity of men and married women (e.g. Blundell 1992).

Tax reforms and the incoming changes within the European institutional and policy setting

Structure and functions of government tiers

The EU is now taking relevant steps toward becoming a full fledged "Federation," leaving the "Confederation" model behind. The process may be slow-moving but eventual arrival is almost certain. This at least has been the common historical experience of existing federal states. The outlining of tax reforms should then show awareness of EU institutional trends and not conflict with them, difficult as they are to be precisely foreseen.[28] Due to this uncertainty, here we will not go beyond a brief discussion of some (personal) broad guesses. This somewhat daring attitude is, however, necessary to pinpoint a first (rough and uncertain) framework which might serve as a starting reference to begin (and not evade) a discussion of such relevant questions, commonly skirted and left to the speculations of a few amateurs of European issues.

The present institutional setting of the EU is made up of no less than five tiers of government: union, national countries, regions, local governments; the last usually split into counties and municipalities. It is very doubtful whether this arrangement could ultimately function, due to its huge transactions costs and the large room for overlaps between upper and lower tiers.[29] Widespread opinion suggests that national governments will not disappear at all but will be the losers in the process, overwhelmed by the need to enlarge union powers and the enforcement of the subsidiarity principle at the lower (regional and local) tier.

With few exceptions, the prevailing literature seems to favor an enlargement of powers for the EU from time to time, provided that Europe government has been made democratically accountable. Stabilization function has begun a long, difficult and piecemeal shift from the states to the Union, but by common consent its present stage of transition is still quite unsatisfactory. Allocation function should go beyond current regulatory activities and the strengthening of the internal market. A largely shared proposal is to gradually extend its role in its area of intervention, so as to encompass defense, research and development and a European transport network.

The main open question relates to the distribution function, on top of the already existing programs of regional development, which, however, should continue to be in force. A particular emphasis must indeed be devoted to the recurrent proposal of making the EU declared aims of social protection really effective, whereas up to now they merely consisted of high-sounding statements of rights.[30] New pressures to change may arrive with the incoming European Constitution, which will most likely adopt the Tobin's principle of "Specific Egalitarianism" as endorsed by the Nice 2000 "Charter of European Union's fundamental rights."[31]

The reason to put also social protection programs in operation at the EU the level is twofold (Atkinson 1992). Member Countries' programs suffer from a severe weakness which is made evident by the approximately 70 million people (18 percent of the total) at risk of poverty who still live in the core of Europe. Social benefits reduce the risk but to very different degrees, ranging from only about 10 percent (Greece and Italy) to more than 70 percent (Finland); 31 percent is the European average (Eurostat 2002). Further and connected to this, differences in GDP level and in budget conditions may discriminate one country from the other as to their ability to cope with social protection needs. The proposal of a "European safety net" targeted to specific countries' lines of poverty might overcome the otherwise not easily solvable dilemma between countries' or individuals' targeted plans (Atkinson 1992).[32] Such a proposal should be strongly welcomed in order to implement our suggestion of a tax shift from social contributions to consumption tax, particularly VAT. This means that, in any European country, the "safety net" should also cover the social security minimum pensions that in this way should be paid out from general taxation.

The sharing of the remaining functions between national and local governments will probably depend on the preferences of individual countries, traditions, institutions and de facto conditions. Once progressively deprived from a stabilization function, national governments will probably concentrate on regional and personal distribution, higher educations, law and order, national infrastructures, general administration and, obviously, debt service. Education, health, local transport and other services will probably implement the subsidiarity principle at the level of local governments, but one should always bear in mind that overlaps, with constraints from (and monitoring by) higher tiers will be widespread, and not easily managed or disentangled.

The financing of the EU and of lower levels of government

At the moment the EU budget (Laffan 1997) is not (and must not be) higher than 1.27 percent of its GDP, i.e. around 85 billion euro. This plentiful amount of money comes from custom duties on extra Union imports (about 15 percent of total resources), a sharing of Member Countries' VAT (about 35 percent), and, for the residual amount (about 50 percent), from countries' contributions in accordance with their GDP. About half of these resources are absorbed by agricultural policy alone. One-third goes to the so-called "structural actions," that is, to regional development and other cohesion initiatives. The small amount left is dispersed among some minor items. Repeatedly during recent years, both Parliament and Commission proposed some (marginal) budget increases and intra-resources shifts, taking into account the arrival of the candidate countries, with an estimated cost of about ten billion euro (e.g. Gretschmann 1998). At the

1999 Berlin Council, any proposal of this kind was rejected, including the budget enlargement for new members. National *premiers* remained stuck in the strange puzzles of the EU budget.[33]

This essential information about the EU budget allows us to go back to the discussion of tax reforms, and integrating this discussion with the previously outlined proposal about the allocation of functions between government tiers. When (and if) fully implemented, such proposals would require resources near to 10 percent of GDP at the EU level,[34] something less than 25 percent at the nation level, and near to 15 percent for local tiers, provided that the total amount of public resources would more or less remain at present levels.

Going on with this parable, we can now speculate that the EU's current resources should be increased up to nearly three points of GDP. The GDP contribution will cease to be in force but it might be more than compensated by attributing to EU level the total revenue accruing from VAT on imports from outside the Union itself, together with the yields from the (increased) environmental levies. The new additional financial tools should be outlined according to sound criteria of tax design and fiscal federalism. Our choice is twofold, and seriously takes into account the previously outlined requirements about tax reforms being an enhancement to both growth and fairness. First, for the working of a government that appears to be so distant from its citizens, a part of new revenues should be highly visible and keep politicians for their use. This task may be better performed by an EU VAT rate, that is made explicit to consumers, than by a sharing of income tax revenues, which on the contrary is hidden in the withholdings on labor incomes. At the moment such withholdings account for three-quarters of total tax yield. The VAT rate should be set at a level that is sufficient to pay out for the "safety net," thus giving further visibility to EU social protection and must add to present national rates. We know that this would mean three-to-four points in GDP terms. The second leading principle should be to directly attribute to the EU level those taxes that most require highly puzzling (see Keen 1996; Haufler 1999) coordination, i.e. corporations and income capital taxes. Taking into account the need to alleviate corporation tax, altogether they could amount to about 4 percent of GDP and should be set around an even rate[35] (20 percent to 25 percent). This rate should be applied to any kind of capital incomes (interests, dividends, capital gains) to be perceived through final withholdings. It could realize an acceptable "dual income tax system." In fact, among European countries, income tax mean rates (Wagstaff *et al.* (1999)) range from 9 percent (France) to 33 percent (Sweden), and an average European un-weighted rate is at about 15 percent.

We must then conclude that an even, progressive income tax, as well as social contributions, should be left at the national level. This is the tier where personal distribution function is concentrated. It would be appropriate to add excise duties: their cross border shopping distortions might be relevant at the local level, which does not seem to happen in the VAT case (Cnossen 2002). The circle would thus be closed by allocating to the conglomerate of local tiers present VAT, benefit taxes and tariffs (including in the category those on making a business) and on immovable property, the last to be substantially augmented in accord with our reform scheme. Notice that VAT can be a relatively good tool (at least compared to the possible alternatives) of financing local (that is, regional) tiers, to which it may be apportioned on the basis of easy statistical clearings in accordance with the amount of within-boundaries private consumption. Its wide basis further allows the collection of higher or lower yields through minor rate changes. Finally the basis is evenly enough distributed among regions and thus the need for equalizing transfers is lower with respect to other eventual resources (for example, the German case, see Chapter 6). To conclude, notice that this structure of lower tiers financing would also be in line with a long theoretical tradition and the main examples of well established federal states.

Some conclusions and the need for further research

A work like this raises many questions, gives some answers and opens many further issues which deserve further research efforts. In my firm opinion, European countries' tax reforms adopted from the 1990s introduced some improvements, mainly by streamlining existing systems, but they have been mostly narrow both in terms of size and aims. Sound fiscal choices that are targeted at Europe should instead be more radical and intended to cope with our continent's great events and fundamental needs. This, I admit, is not an easy way, nor is it well defined.

Many years of common market, the single market, and monetary union, together with the harmonization efforts of the (weak) European government, did not consequently realize a high degree of tax system convergence, which is required for the EU's single market efficiency. Reducing remaining differences raises wide political, institutional and national-identity costs. It is not clear to which institutions and procedures the task of driving further convergence processes is to be assigning.

Before any further analysis, basic common sense suggests that (average) tax wedges on labor at around 45 percent and implicit rates over 30 percent for corporations have something to do with the European declining growth rate and increasing unemployment. Theoretical hints and empirical data suggest that tax reforms could help, but only if the burden taken from labor and corporate capital can be pushed to a relevant extent if it is to give some sizeable advantages. How to finance such huge tax-cuts is the subsequent puzzle.

The Stability Pact prevents the reduction of fiscal pressure and takes in any workable expenditure cuts, if not those which would heavily roll back the welfare state. Thus the escape route necessarily involves shifting the tax burden, from labor (social contributions, mainly those of employers) and corporations to rents, environmental externalities and, mainly, consumption (VAT). Theory and evidence are, in fact, not thoroughly reassuring about this policy, while political economy predictions warn us to beware of its electoral feasibility. To climb over this last obstacle, I propose that the heavier consumption taxes should fund a universal social security safety net, which also encompasses minimum pension treatments.

In a world where growth rates decline, one is forced to find an additional source of welfare by increasing social fairness, to which fiscal fairness may contribute. First, through a legitimated and transparent political process of tax voting; second by establishing an equitable fiscal exchange and well behaved tax rules between state and citizens, finally through the most familiar channels of vertical and horizontal equity. Each has to be empowered and enlarged to better contribute to the society of pair opportunities. This direction of reform should get general approval, but in fact it might raise a long list of ideological and vested interest oppositions.

European countries should be aware that present tax reforms are to be applied in dramatically changing institutional settings. We can (and must) speculate on the main (and uncertain) consequences. It is indeed necessary to have a tentative framework within which one can discuss such relevant issues, being however aware that the overall effective scenario might be largely different and its moves could come very slowly in time.

The EU's central functions will probably increase: here it is suggested that financing should come partly from a transparent tax such as an (additional in our scheme) EU VAT rate which is visible to consumers (and better than a sharing of income tax revenues, which on the contrary is largely hidden in the withholdings on labor incomes). The remaining amount of financing can be found by attributing to the Union level both environmental levies and the two taxes which need more coordination, this, however, being particularly difficult (that is, taxation on corporate and income capital at about the same, even rate).

National tiers should be the center of the distributional function and herein the financing should be assured particularly by a progressive income tax and the remaining social contributions, plus excise duties, due to their relevant cross-border shopping distortion, when applied to lower tiers. In accordance with the subsidiarity principles, many services may be scaled down to the conglomerate of local governments, where the best eligible candidates to build the tax systems are the present VAT system, increased taxes on immovable property, benefit and the creation of a business tax. Such choice is consistent with traditional theory of taxation and closely resembles the principal examples coming from the most established federal states.

Notes

1 M.C. Guerra, together with M. Bernasconi, R. Puglisi and A. Zanardi, provided me with the invaluable contribution of careful reading, sharp comments and stimulating suggestions. I have also to thank the co-authors of the research, G. Arachi, C. Bronchi, I. Joumard, A. Majocchi, F. Osculati and W. Oates for suggestions in a number of areas.
2 EU 9 up to 1979 and EU 15 thereafter.
3 Chapter 1 gives more details on the structures of European tax systems during the last few decades.
4 Such clusters aren't just a convenient paradigm. The estimated correlation coefficients (country data sets of Table 2.1) generally are in line with the values expected according to the tax-clusters hypothesis both for 1970 and 1997 (data not reported here and available from the author).
5 Nordic countries have not been considered in this book, both for their marginality with respect to the Euro-area and for their economic and social peculiarities.
6 Care must be taken when comparing international fiscal data sets, mainly when welfare provisions and financing show different institutional arrangements. One should take account, *inter alia*, of the spread between gross and net social expenditure and of the reduction of fiscal pressure due to existing tax expenditures (Adema 2001). Eurostat 2002 data suggest that total (public + private) welfare demand and supply is very close to a common figure within European countries.
7 Among our selected countries, Italy, the Netherlands and, to a very low extent, Germany and Ireland, reduced total fiscal pressure up to 2001, the remaining three did not cut or increase their taxes (OECD 2002a).
8 Italy adopted a fundamental tax reform in 1972, Spain followed not many years after (see Chapters 8 and 9).
9 This has been mainly due to the income tax, which is largely the prevailing amount in this category. See pages 36–7 for corporate and capital incomes taxes.
10 Do not forget that, in 1970, a true income tax was still not in existence in many European countries and VAT was only in force in France.
11 The EU may now be seen as an institution which falls between a "confederation" and a "federation." According to the common language of political philosophy, "federation" means that the center and the states are coordinate and independent. The center is instead subordinate to the states in a "confederation" (from Cnossen 2002).
12 This bad result somehow could be avoided by adopting a "true" "dual income tax system" which should tax any kind of capital income at the same rate. As to 1998 this solution was, however, not yet adopted by all the same Nordic countries (van de Noord and Heady 2001).
13 Usually measured by the difference between the Gini's index of pre- and post-tax incomes.
14 Through an enlargement of deduction at the bottom scale, combined with reducing and flattening the rates. With respect to a more graduated rates schedule, this technique has the political advantage of an apparent greater visibility, but it implies the (not easy to be perceived) distortion in the equity and efficiency mentioned in the text. There is a clear case of tax laws being unfair (see pp. 41–2).
15 Here we are making reference to the diffuse "entitlement-based view" criterion of social justice, particularly when the latter is combined with social mobility, also referred to as equality of opportunity. In such a case some even argue that

inequality in income, due to differences in ability, talent and hard work, might not only be considered as a factor not to be compensated for, but may also be viewed as a positive good (see e.g. Johnson and Reed 1996), among other things implying that the support for redistribution should be lower (Benabou and Ok 2001).

16 This, for instance, means that a tax cut which can raise net wages by 10 percent will increase labor supply just by 1.5 percent.

17 According to a diffused opinion, labor market institutional setting might play a greater role than the level of tax wedge to explain the degree of unemployment, particularly in a comparison between Europe and the USA (e.g. Blanchard 1999).

18 Making the Pact more rational and less binding is also suggested, by substituting debt to deficit as the target for budget consolidation.

19 This comes for labor from the quoted elasticity figures and for corporations from international past experiences (e.g. Ireland) and planned reforms (e.g. Germany).

20 They could arrive from an increase of present European average to the level of the countries taxing immovable property more (United Kingdom, 3.5 percent) and environment externalities (the Netherlands, 1.7 percent) (Eurostat data).

21 In 2000, private consumption in the euro area amounted to 3,674 billion euro at current price and to 3,383 billion euro at constant (1995) prices. The current GDP was in the order of 3,380 billion euro (ECB Bulletin, 1, 2003). Consequently, consumption deflator was 1.086. It rises to 1.10 if charged by 0.7 GDP points of VAT increase, by assuming a five-year planning period. The apparent large inflationary impulse of 1.4 points decreases to one half if one assumes that social contributions are already embodied in labor cost by at least 50 percent and decreases further to something more than 0.4 points, by limiting VAT shifting to 75 percent. Consider further that both the hypotheses adopted in the previous calculations are rather conservative.

22 EU taxes on consumption have a basis one-third higher than labor income taxes. Tax basis for capital is half that for labor.

23 The two sets of results may seem asymmetric, but one must take account of the non-linearities and the substitution effects embodied in the model.

24 One may, however, doubt if this is really the state of affairs that (rational and well informed?) European citizens at present do perceive.

25 The conventional OT idea concerning the unavoidable trade-off between equity and efficiency has recently been heavily challenged by a large number of empirical analyses. A negative correlation was repeatedly found between inequality and growth. Still more surprisingly, growth rates seem positively influenced by redistributive policies, also if performed by increasing tax progressivity. The most convincing theoretical root of these evidences has been found with reference to economies in which wealth and human capital endowments are heterogeneous across individuals and capital markets are imperfect. The negative effects of inequality on growth might thus depend on: a) the reduction of investment opportunities; b) the worsening of borrowers' incentives; c) more macro-economic volatility (Aghion and Caroli 1999).

26 The standard competitive analysis of labor markets usually considers labor tax progressivity (i.e. the degree of substitution effect) conflicting with employment. This result is, however, generally reversed by unionized markets analysis (e.g. Pissarides 1998).

27 Notice some similarity with Atkinson's (1996) "Participation Income Scheme."

28 This is also true for the widespread processes of fiscal decentralization which are occurring in many European countries (see Chapter 1 and chapters relating to specific countries).

29 The figures are far from being reassuring. By considering only present EU Member Countries', regional governments are in the order of about 150, counties, provinces and departments are about 400, municipalities stay well over 100,000, of which the most have less than 10,000 inhabitants (OECD 2002c). It is obvious that some restructuring will take place, but it is also hard to precisely envisage possible future solutions.

30 During the 1970s and 1980s the EC's Acts basically took up the 1945 UN "Charter of human rights." In 1989 the "Charter of fundamental social rights" was adopted by the Community (although with the UK dissenting). Its aims were confirmed by the Social Protocol annexed to the Maastricht Treaty (UK still dissenting). The central idea was to extend social protection to wider cohorts of beneficiaries and specifically target it to fight against poverty. A Social Fund was effectively adopted but it was always made up of not more than some dozens of ECU/euro millions and mainly devoted to improve workers' mobility.

31 Specific guarantees are stated regarding the right to: free mandatory education (art. 14); satisfactory, regular employment (art. 15); securing a high standard of healthcare (art. 35); being admitted to social protection and services, "in case of motherhood, sickness, labor accidents, dependency and old age, besides that in case of losing the job, *according to Union's and national laws*" (our italics).

32 A policy which redistributes among countries should be preferred if inequality does exist, especially among countries. A redistributive action among individuals should, however, be taken if inequality is mainly an infra-country phenomenon. Available data show a mixed picture not easily disentangled. We saw that, in the early 1990s, Gini on gross incomes ranged from about 25 percent (Germany) to about 41 percent (the UK). Per capita income at PPPs in 2000 is relatively close to an average of something more than 100 (mean figure for the EU and USA) albeit if with some outliers. But the poor Mediterranean countries (Spain, Portugal and Greece) have an average figure of near 80 (computations of Cnossen 2002). Number and distance of diverging countries will obviously dramatically increase with the arrival of current EU applicants. GDP per head at PPPs ranges from 24 (Bulgaria) to 82 (Cyprus), 100 being the EU level and about 45 the candidate countries, weighted average figure (Eurostat 2002).

33 The words are by themselves amusing and enlightening: "British correction," "Rotterdam or gateway effect," "VAT frozen rate," and so forth.

34 This amount is quite close to both US and Canadian figures and could make the EU budget an adequately exogenous macro-shock absorber.

35 The proposal to shift corporation tax at the EU level is certainly not new (e.g. Albi *et al.* 1997) and has recently been authoritatively brought in again (Cnossen 2002).

References

Adema, W. (2001) "Net social expenditure," 2nd Edition, Labour Market and Social Policy Occasional Papers, 52, Paris: OECD.

Agell, J., Lindh, T. and Ohlsson, H. (1997) "Growth and the public sector: a critical review essay," *European Journal of Political Economy*, 3: 33–52.

Aghion, P. and Caroli, E. (1999) "Inequality and economic growth: the perspective of the new growth theories," *Journal of Economic Literature*, 37, 4: 1615–71.

Albi, E., Paredes, R. and Corona, E. (1997) *Corporate Tax as a Possible Fifth Own*

Community Resource: How Much Harmonization is Necessary?, study XIX/BI/9602 prepared for the DG-XIX, Brussels: EU Commission, June.

Atkinson, A.B. (1992) "Toward a European social safety net?," *Fiscal Studies*, 13, 3: 41–53.

—— (1996) *Incomes and the Welfare State*, Cambridge: Cambridge University Press.

—— (1999a) *The Economic Consequences of Rolling Back the Welfare State*, Cambridge, MA: The MIT Press.

—— (1999b) "Equity issues in a globalizing world: the experience," in Tanzi, V., Chu, K. and Gupta, S. (eds) *Economic Policy & Equity*, Washington, DC, International Monetary Fund: 63–80.

Benabou, R. and Ok, E.A. (2001) "Social mobility and the demand for redistribution: the POUM hypothesis," *Quarterly Journal of Economics*, 116: 447–87.

Bernardi, L. (2002) "Imposte giuste, giuste giustizie e riforme impossibili," *Politica economica*, 3: 585–96.

Besley, T. (2001) "From micro to macro: public policies and aggregate economic performance," *Fiscal Studies*, 4: 357–74.

Blanchard, O. (1999) "European unemployment: the role of shocks and institutions," *Bank of Italy Lezioni Paolo Baffi di moneta e finanza*, Roma: Edizioni dell'elefante.

Blundell, R. (1992) "Labour supply and taxation: a survey," *Fiscal Studies*, 3: 15–40.

Bosworth, B. and Burtless, G. (1992) "Effects of tax reform on labour supply, investment and saving," *Journal of Economic Perspectives*, 6: 3–25.

Bovi, M. (2002) "The nature of underground economy, some evidence from OECD countries," Documento di lavoro, 26/02, Roma: ISAE.

Bretschger, L. and Hettich, F. (2002) "Globalization, capital mobility and tax competition: theory and evidence for OECD countries," *European Journal of Political Economy*, 18: 695–716.

Buchanan, J.M. (1980) "Reform in the rent-seeking society," in Buchanan, J.M., Tollison, R.D. and Tullock, G. (eds) *Toward a Theory of the Rent-Seeking Society*, College Station, TX: A&M Press.

Carone, G. and Salomaki, A. (2001) *Reforms in Tax–Benefit System in Order to Increase Employment Incentives in EU*, EU EC/160, Brussels: EU Commission.

Cassou, S.P. and Lansing, K.J. (2000) *Growth Effect of a Flat Tax*, mimeo of Kansas State University and the Federal Reserve Bank of San Francisco.

Cnossen, S. (2002) "Tax policy in the European union: a review of issues and options," *FinanzArchiv*, 4: 1–93.

Devereux, M.P., Griffith, R. and Klemm, A. (2001) *Have Taxes on Mobile Capital Declined?*, London: mimeo IFS.

Drèze, J.H. and Malinvaud, E. (1994) "Growth and employment: the scope for a European initiative," *European Economy – Reports and Studies*, 1: 75–106.

Drazen, A. and Grilli, V. (1993) "The benefit of crises for economic reforms," *American Economic Review*, 3: 598–607.

EU Commission (2000) "Public finances in EMU," *European Economy*, 3: 69–92.

—— (2002) *The Social Situation in the European Union*, Brussels: EU Commission and Eurostat.

Eurostat (2000) *Structures of the Taxation Systems in the European Union, 1970–1997*, Brussels: European Commission.

Goodin, R. and Le Grand, J. (1987) *Not Only the Poor: the Middle Class and the Welfare State*, London: Allen & Unwin.

Gorter, J. and de Mooij, R.A. (2001) *Capital Income Taxation in Europe. Trends and Trade Offs*, CPB Netherlands bureau for economic policy analysis, Special publication 30, Den Haag: SDU Uitgevers & Centraal Planbureau.

Gretschmann, K. (1998) *Own-Resources Reform and Net Position in the EU Budget, Study for the European Parliament*, D.G. Research. PE 228.586/RES, Brussels: European Parliament, October.

Haufler, A. (1999) "Prospect for co-ordination of corporate taxation and the taxation of interest incomes in the EU," *Fiscal Studies*, 2: 133–54.

Johnson, P. and Reed, H. (1996) "Two nations? The inheritance of poverty and affluence," *IFS Commentary*, 53, London: Institute for Fiscal Studies.

Jones, C.I. (2002) *Introduction to Economic Growth*, 2nd Edition, New York and London: W.W. Norton Company.

Joumard, I. (2001) "Tax Systems in European Union Countries," Economic Department Working Paper 301, Paris: OECD.

Keen, M. (1996) "The welfare economics of tax coordination in the European Community," in Devereux, M.P. (ed.) *The Economics of Tax Policy*, Oxford: Oxford University Press, pp. 189–214.

—— (2002) "The German tax reform of 2000," *International Tax and Public Finance*, 9: 603–21.

Laffan, B. (1997) *The Finances of the European Union*, European Union Series, London: Macmillan.

Leibfritz, W., Thornton, J. and Bibbee, A. (1997) "Taxation and Economic Performance," Economic Department Working Paper 136, Paris: OECD.

Martinez-Mongay, C. (2000) "The ECFIN effective taxation databank. Properties and comparisons with other databanks," European Commission Economic Paper 146, Brussels: EU Commission.

Milesi-Ferretti, G. and Roubini, N. (1998) "Growth effects of income and consumption taxes," *Journal of Money, Credit and Banking*, 340: 721–44.

Myles, G. (2000) "Taxation and economic growth," *Fiscal Studies*, 1: 141–68.

North, D.C. (1990) *Institution, Institutional Change and Economic Performance*, Cambridge: Cambridge University Press.

OECD (2001) *Revenue Statistics 1965–2000*, Paris: OECD.

—— (2002) *Revenue Statistics 1965–2001*, Paris: OECD.

Pigou, A.C. (1929) *The Economics of Welfare*, London: Macmillan.

Pissarides, C.A. (1998) "The impact of employment tax cuts on unemployment and wages: the role of unemployment benefit and tax structures," *European Economic Review*, 42: 155–83.

Rawls, J. (2001) *Justice as Fairness: A Restatement*, Cambridge, MA: Harvard University Press.

Razin, A. and Sadka, E. (1991) "International tax competition and the gains from harmonization," *Economic Letters*, 1: 69–76.

Soerensen, P.B. (1994) "From the global income tax to the dual income tax: recent tax reforms in Nordic countries," *International Tax and Public Finance*, 1: 57–80.

Steve, S. (1976) *Lezioni di Scienza delle Finanze*, Padova: CEDAM.

Tanzi, V. and Schuknecht, L. (1997) "Reforming government: an overview of recent experience," *European Journal of Political Economy*, 13: 395–417.

Tanzi, V. (2002) "Transazioni, imposte e sviluppo economico," *Ezio Vanoni Lecture*, University of Pavia: December.

Tanzi, V. and Zee, H.L. (1997) *Fiscal Policy and Long-run Growth*, Washington, DC: IMF Staff Papers, 44, 2.

van den Noord, P. and Heady, C. (2001) "Surveillance of tax policies: a synthesis of findings in economic surveys," Economic Department Working Paper 303, Paris: OECD.

Wagstaff, A. *et al.* (1999) "Redistributive effect, progressivity and differential tax treatment: personal income taxes in twelve OECD countries," *Journal of Public Economics*, 72: 73–98.

3 Public finance and political economics in tax design and reforms

Paola Profeta[1]

Introduction

The theory of taxation and tax reforms has been largely studied in the literature of public finance. To finance its goal of both providing public goods and services and operating changes in the distribution of income generated by the market, the government uses taxes. The positive analysis of taxation has concerned the different taxes that are used by the government, their features, their distribution and their impact on the economic system. The normative analysis has focused on how the government should minimize the "excess burden," that is, welfare losses from taxation. The literature suggests that this would require taxation to be imposed as a lump-sum, so that taxpayers could not avoid taxation by changes in their behavior. However, since public goods have a different nature than private goods, and due to the limited information of the government, which makes it impossible to identify individual characteristics that taxpayers cannot change to avoid their tax payments, taxes are usually compulsory and not of a lump-sum nature. In this context, the well-known trade-off between efficiency and equity may arise (Fair 1971; Stern 1976; Ahmad and Stern 1984): a tax system is efficient if it minimizes the total excess burden of raising revenues, while this rule turns out to be in contrast with the purpose of redistribution. The more general literature on optimal taxation (OT) (Ramsey 1927; Mirrlees 1971, 1972, 1976) includes redistributive purposes, but at the expense of practicality. The New New Welfare economics, reviewed by Stiglitz (1987), makes clear the nature of these equity–efficiency trade-offs, inherent in redistributive tax policies. The government is assumed to start with imperfect information, as a limit to its ability to impose taxes, and it tries to identify the Pareto efficient tax structures, i.e. the tax structures which get the economies to the utilities possibilities schedule. It turns out that in this "second best" world, a self-selection, or a partial pooling equilibrium, is required for Pareto efficiency, with the marginal tax rate on the highest income individuals being equal to zero. The trade-off derives from the fact that the self-selection constraint generates distortions from redistributing resources from the more able to the less able individuals, and this distortion is larger if a larger revenue has to be raised.

An alternative approach to the normative analysis of taxation is the equitable taxation theory (ET), derived primarily from the work of Simons (1938): the public sector has the important role of providing services that the private sector cannot supply and to redistribute. Taxation has to be developed according to the principles of fairness and has to limit interference of the political process in the market economy. This idea leads to the concept of comprehensive income and comprehensive tax base, which, however, turns out to involve many measurement problems and administrative difficulties.

However, efficiency and redistributive issues may not exhaust the theory of taxation and tax reforms. A crucial role is played by collective choice and political institutions, and thus a political economy approach (Persson and Tabellini 2000a) should be included. Collective choice mechanisms and their functioning are central both at the allocative level (how to pay for the service to provide, how much, etc.) and at the redistributive level (the degree of redistribution and how to finance it). From a positive point of view, in democratic countries, voting and the competitive political process (rather than a social planner) determine tax policies and tax systems and shape the equity and efficiency effects of taxation. From a normative point of view, in democracies, economic reforms, such as tax reforms, may be adopted and sustained if they enjoy enough political support. The action of pressure and interest groups may also play a significant role in shaping fiscal policies and fiscal reforms (Becker 1983).

Wicksell (1896) and Lindahl (1919), and later Buchanan (1976) and Brennan and Buchanan (1980), open this strand of the literature, which has been defined as the normative fiscal exchange (FE) approach to taxation. The central problem addressed in the early literature was how to design institutions of government appropriate to the electorate's preferences and how to avoid the action of organized interest groups having an impact on the functioning and outcome of the electoral processes. Later, the analysis of Brennan and Buchanan (1980) has focused on the role of the electoral process as a constraint to limit the government's power to tax (the Leviathan) and on the design of the most desirable electoral process. Tax design is a question of constitutional design, and tax reform is a matter for constituent assemblies or other groups of taxpayers, not for the government itself.

Since then, there have been few relevant contributions trying to include political economy issues into the traditional optimal taxation theory (see Atkinson 1995). A relevant exception is the work of Hettich and Winer (1988, 1997, 1998, 1999, 2000), which I will refer to extensively in this chapter.

This chapter proposes a theoretical introduction to the case studies analyzed in the second part of the book. Following the above considerations, I adopt a comprehensive theoretical perspective to include efficiency, redistributive and political considerations. This chapter interprets several issues raised by the analysis of tax systems and tax reforms in European countries in the perspective of the results of both the traditional taxation theory and the political economy approach. It is thus intended as a link between what we actually observe in the countries and how this can be explained by the theory. The theory may help us to stress what are the determinants[2] (the interrelation between economic and political factors) of the current systems and the main forces behind the proposed reforms, and it may suggest directions for future economically and politically feasible reforms.

The chapter is organized as follows: first, it presents some results of major contributions of the political economy literature concerning taxation and tax reforms and links them to the rules of the traditional public finance literature on taxation. Second, it identifies specific issues at the center of the current debate on taxation and tax reforms in the selected countries and interprets them from a theoretical perspective. This is followed by a conclusion.

Theories of taxation and tax reforms

In this section, I review some of the theoretical issues raised by the political economy literature concerning taxation and tax reforms. First, I examine different approaches in the political economy literature to analyze the complex tax structure that we observe in our democratic countries. Second, I focus on the role of political influence and political instability on taxation.

Political economy and taxation

In democratic societies the political process plays a crucial role in shaping the complex tax systems that we observe. Many authors have explained how the interaction of the private economy and the political process determines the current structure of the tax systems (see Hettich and Winer 1999 for a review). They have adopted different frameworks. First, a median voter approach has been used to study which single proportional tax rate imposed to finance a public good will emerge in equilibrium, when individuals have preferences for both the public good and the output of the private economy, and the tax rate is chosen by majority rule (Roberts 1977). The standard result applies: if all preferences are single-peaked, the equilibrium tax rate is the one which maximizes the welfare of the median voter. However, tax structure is inherently multidimensional, including tax bases, rate structures and several special provisions. Thus, a multidimensional policy space arises. It is well-known that, in a multidimensional issue space, Nash equilibrium of a majoritarian voting game may not exist. The literature provides alternative solutions: structure-induced equilibrium, probabilistic voting, the Leviathan model, the bargaining game, interest groups, factional conflict.

The structure-induced equilibrium considers an institutional structure where the dimensions of the tax policy space are separated, and each of them is decided upon in a separate legislative committee. In each committee the median voter theorem applies, given the median choices of other committees. This approach has proved to be more useful to study specific features of a tax structure than the formation of an entire tax system, as in Inman and Fitts (1990). However, this approach requires a separation of decisions on different aspects of tax systems, which is difficult to identify.

The probabilistic voting model assumes that voters choose between parties on the basis of the policies proposed by the parties, while parties propose their platforms without knowing with certainty how voters will vote, but maximizing their expected number of votes. This approach implies that a small change in a policy platform will not lead to a total change of the support from the incumbent to the opposition (or vice versa, according to which party proposes a more favorable outcome), like happens in deterministic voting, but it only leads to a change in the probability of support. Therefore, an equilibrium exists even if the tax system is multidimensional. The equilibrium is a balance of opposing interests in the electorate, with some interests being more politically influential than others. The tax structure which emerges as an equilibrium from this approach is quite realistic (see Warksett, Winer and Hettich 1998), as a simple example based on this approach shows in the next subsection.

The Leviathan model (Brennan and Buchanan 1980) assumes that there are no constraints to the power of taxation of the state, which has the objective of maximizing total revenues. This assumption is quite unrealistic, since public policies are normally influenced by many opposing interests. The tax structure chosen by the Leviathan is multidimensional (bases, rate structures, special provisions). However, the results are quite unrealistic: broad bases should be preferred to minimize tax evasion and regressive tax rates accompanied with special provisions to maximize revenues.

The cooperative game model delivers the formation of tax structures from coalitions, where voters play a cooperative bargaining game with threats. Aumann and Kurz (1977) find interesting results using this approach and introducing the attitude of voters toward risk. They find that marginal tax rates are above 50 percent for all voters and are equal to 50 percent if utility functions are linear. Additionally, marginal tax rates turn out to be higher for voters with higher absolute risk aversion.

The interest groups model assumes that the political process is affected by the resources (money, information or time) given by special interests to the political parties in exchange for favorable policies (Downs 1957; Stigler 1970; Breton 1974; Becker 1983). However, the role of such special-interest groups does not appear crucial to explain the tax structures or the complexity of taxation in the real world, in addition to economic and political elements.

A new alternative approach has been recently formulated by Roemer (1999), who develops a new equilibrium concept for political games, based on factional conflicts within parties. There are two parties. Each party is assumed to consist of three factions: reformists, militants and opportunists. Each faction has a complete preference order on the policy space, but together they can only agree on a partial order. In this context, the author shows the existence of Nash equilibria of the two-party game, where the policy space consists of all quadratic income tax functions (bidimensional). The author also shows that, in these equilibria, both parties propose progressive income taxation, which is a realistic prediction.

This brief description of the different models suggests that the probabilistic voting approach is quite appropriate, in terms of technicality and empirical implications, to explain the economic and political factors which determine the complex tax systems in our democratic societies, and I thus choose to focus on this approach next.

Political influence: a probabilistic voting model

Following Winer (2003), I formalize a simple probabilistic voting model to show that the political influence of different groups of voters may have a crucial role to determine the tax structure, on top of equity and efficiency considerations. Formally, this means that if political influence is distributed unequally among voters, it may be an optimal reallocation along the Pareto-utility frontier. This result belongs to the positive analysis of taxation.

I assume that the fiscal system consists in a government providing one public good, G, and imposing H proportional tax rates, t_h, one for each voter, applied to the voter's tax base, B_h. Each individual h solves his or her economic problem by maximizing his or her utility function, which depends positively on the public good, G, and negatively on its tax rate, t_h. The maximization problem delivers the indirect utility function of the individual h: $v_h(t_h, G)$.

There are two parties, or candidates: the incumbent, i, and the opponent, o. Before the election takes place, parties commit to a policy platform, $(t_{1i}, t_{2i}, \ldots t_{Hi}, G_i)$ and $(t_{1o}, t_{2o}, \ldots t_{Ho}, G_o)$. They act simultaneously and do not cooperate. Each party chooses the platform which maximizes its expected number of votes. Platforms are chosen when the election outcome is still uncertain. Voters vote for a party according to a probability function, which depends on the policy platforms proposed by the opposite parties. The probability that voter h votes for the government is a function of the difference in the voter's indirect utility under the government's policies and those of the opposition:

$$\pi_h = f_h(v_{hi} - v_{ho}) \tag{3.1}$$

where v_{hi} is the indirect utility of voter h, under the policies implemented by the incumbent government i and v_{ho} is the indirect utility of voter h, under the policies implemented by the opponent government, o. The function, f_h, is a generic function of this difference, which may include an ideological term.[3]

The total expected vote for the government i can be written as:

$$EV_i = \sum_{h=1}^{H} \pi_h = \sum_{h=1}^{H} f_h(v_{hi} - v_{ho}) \tag{3.2}$$

and similarly for the opposition. There is common knowledge to competing parties of the probability density functions and the structure of the private economy.

In the absence of administrative costs, the government chooses the tax rates $t_1, t_2, \ldots t_H$ and the level of public good, G, to maximize the expected total support, given the platform of the opposition and subject to the budget constraint:

$$G = \sum_{h=1}^{H} t_h B_h \tag{3.3}$$

where B_h is the tax base of tax on individual h, $h = 1, \ldots H$ and it thus depends on t_h.

The first-order conditions are the following ($h = 1, \ldots H$):

$$\frac{(\partial f_h / \partial v_h) * (\partial v_h / \partial t_h)}{B_h(1 + \epsilon_h)} = \lambda$$

$$\sum_{h=1}^{H} \frac{\partial f_h}{\partial v_h} \frac{\partial v_h}{\partial G} = \lambda \tag{3.4}$$

where $\epsilon_h = \partial B_h / \partial t_h * t_h / B_h$ is the elasticity of base, B_h, with respect to t_h, and λ is the Lagrange multiplier associated with the government budget constraint.

The first order conditions make clear that the government chooses the tax rates among voters that equalize across taxpayers the marginal political cost or reduction in expected votes of raising an additional unit of money. For a given level of revenues the total political cost has to be minimized. As a result, the tax structure is complex, with a different tax rate for any different individual. Additionally, the government chooses the level of public good so that the marginal political benefit of spending an additional unit of money is equal to the marginal political cost (λ).

It is a standard result that, since they solve a symmetric problem, in equilibrium (if it exists) the two parties will choose the same policies. Let us assume that an equilibrium exists and define θ_h as the particular value of the partial derivative $\partial f_h/\partial v_h$ with $h = 1, \ldots H$ at a Nash equilibrium of the electoral game. Then, the first order conditions for politically optimal equilibrium strategies can be written as follows:

$$\frac{\theta_h * \partial v_h/\partial t_h}{B_h(1+\epsilon_h)} = \lambda \tag{3.5}$$

This condition is the same as the one that will be derived by maximizing the political support function, $S = \Sigma \theta_h v_h$, subject to the government budget constraint, and it is thus consistent with Pareto efficiency. The weights, θ_h, represent the responsiveness of the voting behavior to a change in the individual welfare, as perceived by the party, and thus they are a measure of the effective influence exerted by different voters on policy outcomes.

From equation 3.5 it can be noted that if these weights, θ_h, are equal for all voters, the tax system equalizes the marginal efficiency cost of the tax for all individuals and minimizes the excess burden of taxation, while, if the political influence is distributed unequally because θ_h are different, it is politically optimal to impose a lower tax rate on the more politically influential individual (with a higher θ_h) and thus impose on him or her a smaller loss of utility (lower $\partial v_h/\partial t_h$) with a larger marginal efficiency cost (higher $B_h(1+\epsilon_h)$). Notice that this means that parties trade-off the welfare and support from different voters, even though Pareto-efficiency is achieved. This implies that political elements play their own role on top of efficiency/equity considerations.

If the function f is specified, including the propensity of voters to move from one party to the other as the policy change, as opposed to their ideological attachment to the party, an additional policy implication arises: governments, who take preferences and ideology of the voters into account, may be willing to implement reforms which favor the more "mobile" groups, i.e. groups that are ready to reward them with their votes in case of a reform which favors them (swing voters). This is in line with a more general result of the political economy literature: reforms are implemented only if they are politically feasible and sustainable, i.e. if they enjoy enough support from the voters (in the field of social security, see Galasso and Profeta 2002 for a review).

The simple model developed here highlights the role of political influence on the determination of the income tax structure. Later in this chapter (pp. 62–73) these results will be compared with the experience of the selected countries, and additional relevant factors, which are not included in this simple mode, such as administration and information costs, will be discussed.

Political instability

The structure of tax systems, as well as their evolution, depend on the economic structure of the country and on its political system. Cuckierman, Edwards and Tabellini (1992) show that two features of a political system are important: the instability, represented by the probability of losing office, and the degree of polarization between the alternating governments. The equilibrium efficiency of the tax system depends on these two features. At any given moment of time, the existing tax system represents a constraint on the fiscal policy (i.e. the choice of tax rates and the level and composition of government spending) of the current government. This constraint may be welcome by politicians who oppose the current governments. This implies that tax reforms may be determined by strategic considerations, i.e. by taking into account how they will constrain fiscal policies of future governments. For example, previous governments may deliberately choose to maintain an inefficient tax system, in order to constrain the choices of future governments with which they might disagree. The authors show that this is more likely to happen in countries with more unstable and polarized political systems. In other words, political instability and political polarization are associated with an inefficient tax system, which facilitates tax evasion and imposes high collection costs, since it induces government to behave myopically, or strategically, in order to create a "constituency for re-election." As a consequence, the following empirical prediction is tested across countries: more unstable and polarized countries collect a larger fraction of their revenues through seignorage, which reflects inefficiency, i.e. high tax administration and collection costs. According to the authors' data, the ranking of the countries analyzed in this book is as follows: Italy has been characterized by the highest political instability and highest tax inefficiency, followed in order by Spain, Ireland, Germany, France and the United Kingdom.

Issues of taxation and tax reforms: theory and practice

This section is devoted to the analysis of specific issues raised by the studies of specific countries in this book, which I examine taking into account both the factors raised by traditional public finance theory and the political determinants. I select the following issues: tax neutrality, horizontal equity, complexity of the income tax, progressivity of the income tax, competition and decentralization versus harmonization (including the role of local taxes and the impact of globalization).

Tax neutrality

According to the rule of tax neutrality, all taxable activities from different sources (labor, capital) should be treated equally by the tax system (taxed at the same effective marginal rate). Similarly, different capital incomes should be taxed equally. Traditional normative theories of public finance do not agree on this rule.

The optimal taxation (OT) literature proceeds through a constrained optimization of a social welfare function by the social planner, given the revenue constraint, available tax instruments and their influence on private behavior. A trade-off between equity goals and the deadweight costs of taxation arises. A tax on consumption is preferred to a tax on income to avoid distortion in the intertemporal allocation of resources. Capital taxation plays a minor role. Broad-based taxes are preferred since, given the total revenue, they distort the relative prices less, avoiding inducing substitution among activities that are taxed at different rates. If other bases are present, a general result (Ramsey 1927) is that differentiation is required to efficiency, according to the inverse elasticity rule, i.e. heavier taxation on more inelastic bases.

The theory of equitable taxation (ET) considers comprehensive income the more appropriate measure of ability to pay, and therefore the appropriate tax basis of a single, broad tax. This implies complete tax neutrality: any source of income, including capital, should be taxed equally.

The fiscal exchange approach (FE) instead prefers the adoption of narrow, multiple bases, that limit Leviathan to a desirable level of total tax revenues. Taxes on labor income or consumption are better than taxes on capital, since labor and consumption are more elastic bases and thus increases in tax rates induce large economic responses, which are desirable.

Political economy considerations suggest that tax differentiation should be preferred to tax neutrality, as required by the nature of the political competition. For instance, grouping different activities into the same tax base in order to achieve neutrality leads to an increase in political opposition, since it raises a taxpayer's deadweight loss associated with the tax payment. However, administration and information costs play a role in the opposite direction. By grouping, for instance, income from different labor activities in the same tax base, the government can save on administrative costs and use the resources saved to provide public goods which may lead to additional political support. Information problems also arise, if in a differentiated context taxpayers are induced to substitute more heavily taxed with more lightly taxed activities, and thus tax neutrality can be justified. In a political economy framework this kind of information problem is even worse, since it has to take into account not only the effect of taxation on the economic behavior of the individuals, but also on their voting behavior. This argument is again in favor of tax neutrality.

Political economy considerations about the rule of tax neutrality have played a crucial role in several common trends which can be identified from the analysis of the reforms recently implemented in the European countries considered in this book. I focus and explain two of them.

We observe a general trend toward the shift away from labor taxation

This shift away from labor taxation may be achieved in a number of alternative ways (or a combination of ways), as happened in the countries under discussion in this book:

- a trend from direct to indirect taxation (the Netherlands);
- a reduction of the personal income tax (the UK, the Netherlands, Italy);
- a reduction of the social contributions (the UK, Ireland, the Netherlands, France);
- an increase of the tax on property (the UK, France);
- an increase in environmental taxes (the Netherlands).

The general justification for this shift is that it will improve the market performance and the efficiency of the system (according to the OT rules) and will enhance growth. However, I argue that these alternative ways are implemented under political constraints. The decrease of direct taxation, especially personal income taxation, with the details that I will specify below (p. 67), and increase of indirect taxation also derive from political competition. The low rate of social contributions in the UK or Ireland responds to a "Beveridgean" social security system, which is highly redistributive and characterized by a small public PAYG system completed by a large second private pillar. In a political economy framework, it can be shown that countries with larger inequality and better performance of the capital markets are more likely to have this kind of system, which not only redistribute in favor of the poor, but, implying lower contributions, allows the richer to invest more in alternative and more profitable assets. Also, consistently with the approach of interest and pressure groups in the political economy literature, environmental taxes may arise under pressure from interest groups (such as the environmentalist), i.e. these taxes tend to be higher in countries where the pressure of these groups are larger (like the Netherlands, and not, for instance, in Italy).

There is a trend toward neutrality in capital income taxation

The common and uniform treatment of all capital income is a declared objective of the OECD, and many governments have adopted it. This is justified for efficiency reasons, as a way to reduce tax evasion and erosion of the tax base, due to the shift from more heavily taxed capital income sources to less taxed ones. However, on political grounds, it seems very difficult to be pursued, due to the need for differentiation to reach a political support. Competition among countries also plays a crucial role in capital income taxation (see pp. 68–9).

Horizontal equity

Another rule established by the traditional public finance theories of taxation, on the basis of the equitable taxation (ET) approach, is horizontal equity. The concept of horizontal equity is based on the definition of a comprehensive income tax base, as proposed by Simons in the 1930s and 1940s. Individuals with equal ability to pay taxes, as measured by comprehensively defined incomes, should pay equal taxes. However, this idea has never been implemented, because of practical (measurement) and theoretical (is the correct base for comprehensive income the income or the consumption?) reasons. On the political level, one might expect that this idea would receive the support of the taxpayers, who would perceive such a tax system as fair. But in practice, difficulties also arise on political grounds. There is no political reason for a government to tax only, or to a larger extent, comprehensive income. Political costs associated with different components of comprehensive income vary a lot, and thus income from these different sources should also be treated differently for political reasons (see the discussion on tax neutrality, pp. 63–5). In fact, political competition requires appropriate differentiation to gain the support of taxpayers, since individuals and groups exert a different effective political influence in the political process. Therefore, horizontal equity may not be an objective for a party, since it has to maximize its support by taking into account the effective political influence of different groups.

The recent experience of the countries considered in this book can be read in this perspective: planned reforms are stressing the vertical equity much more than the horizontal equity, by mainly focusing on the degree of progressivity and the complexity of income tax, as I explain later in the chapter (pp. 66–7). The rule of horizontal equity has generally been neglected, with the justification that it will remain a minor problem, when the income tax is simplified. However, as is clear from the case of Italy, many distortions regarding horizontal equity may arise since the system planned by the reform combines an apparent simplification with several special provisions. Therefore, it can be argued that horizontal equity is not discussed, not because it is not a serious problem, but because it is politically optimal to differentiate according to the political influence that the different groups of earners exert as voters.

Complexity of income tax

In the analyzed countries we observe a general common declared inten-
tion of increasing simplicity of income tax, mainly through a reduction of
the number of brackets (the UK, Italy). However, de facto, the implemented changes do not really seem to reach this objective of simplicity,
since deductions, exemptions and special cases multiply. I argue that this
inconsistency is due mainly to political factors.

Traditional theories of taxation are not able to explain the income tax
structures that we observe and the trends of planned reforms. The
optimal taxation literature (OT) predicts that each individual should be
taxed at a different rate, depending on its marginal utility and its weight
in the social welfare function, which delivers the maximum complexity of
the income tax. However, regarding special provisions, the predictions are
not clear: exceptions, deductions and tax credits are considered appropriate depending on the government's objectives, restrictions and the screen-
ing problems faced by policy makers. This explains only a part of what we
observe, mainly the complexity, but cannot account for the fact that the
countries are currently planning to introduce more simplicity as an objective of their reforms. The equitable taxation (ET) approach instead does
not care about the vertical complexity of the income tax structure (the
number of brackets as an instrument to reach vertical equity), while it
argues strongly against the existence of special provisions. It thus cannot
explain why we observe so many special provisions. The fiscal exchange
(FE) approach argues for complexity of the tax structure, also in terms of
special provisions, to limit tax discrimination exerted by the Leviathan.
Again, how to explain the trend toward more simplicity remains unsolved.

Following a political economy approach, economic and political considerations are interrelated in explaining the complexity of income tax
that we observe in our countries and the trend toward a simplified structure, with an important role for special provisions. As shown in the simple
model presented in the previous paragraph, in a democracy the political
competition requires complexity, i.e. many tax rates which allow careful
discrimination among heterogeneous voters (Warskett, Winer and Hettich
1998) and thus to maximize the support that each party expects to receive
in the next election. The extreme result of this reasoning would be that
each person should be taxed with a different tax rate, to better respond to
its preference. This result is similar to that obtained in the OT literature.
However, this is not the end of the story. When the system becomes well
developed, public expenditures and taxation rise and this requires an
increase of complexity of regimes and raises the administration costs,
which make such a complicated tax structure too expensive, and force a
reduction of complexity and a grouping together of individuals. Thus, the
government decides to create rate brackets to group individuals. Then, it
has to decide how to establish the politically optimal number of brackets,

how to assign individuals to these brackets in a manner consistent with its political objectives and how to choose the rate of taxation applied to each group. A trade-off is implicit in the choice of the number of brackets: on one side, decreasing the number of brackets implies a larger loss in expected support, since it is no longer possible to equalize marginal political costs or oppositions to taxation across individuals. On the other side, decreasing the number of brackets implies lower administration costs, and thus higher revenue and the possibility of spending more on public goods, which can be converted into additional support. In the presence of administration costs, information costs may induce an even stronger simplification, if taxpayers self-select and choose to earn a reduced income in order to be eligible for a lower tax rate (if their increase in leisure more than compensates the loss in after-tax earnings). Therefore, a well-developed system may be at a point where costs are so high that the need to simplify is predominant. At this point, special provisions arise as a way to reintroduce differentiation, as required by political optimality, in a broadly defined simplified tax structure.

So, how can we explain the recent experience of the European countries?

1   With high administrative and information costs, the structure which emerges is less complex. In fact, the flat-rate or broad-based tax is becoming very popular (the UK, Italy).
2   However, in a democracy, we need to combine a flat-tax rate (or broad-based) with special provisions (exemptions, deductions, exclusions) which are another way to differentiate, as necessary, because of the political competition (see Italy and the UK).
3   The political influence of the poor increases the degree of complexity, because the rich oppose an increase of the tax rate on them less, as required by the poor, if there is more differentiation. Therefore, governments which take the interests of the poor into account more tend to increase the number of brackets, special regimes and complexity in general.

Progressivity of income tax

Related to the general issue of the complexity of income tax, there is the important and more specific issue of the degree of progressivity of personal income tax. Less complex income taxes, closer to a flat rate tax, imply in general a lower degree of progressivity, though if these systems provide larger special provisions (deductions, exemptions, and so on) the impact on the degree of progressivity is unclear.

The optimal taxation theory (OT) suggests a hump-shaped progression of marginal rates: the optimal tax rate is zero for the poorest, to respond to equity considerations, and zero for the richest to reduce their huge distortion, in order to reach efficiency. The equivalent taxation (ET) theory leaves vertical equity indeterminate but insists that persons with the same comprehensive income must pay the same amount of taxes regardless of the sources of their income. The fiscal exchange (FE) approach argues for progressive or proportional taxation to oppose Leviathan's taste for regressivity.

The degree of progressivity depends on economic factors, such as the income inequality, and on political factors, such as the political competition, or the degree of information of the voters.

Recent evidence shows that the degree of progressivity in OECD countries is related to political factors, such as the number of parties and political instability, or to interest groups factors, such as the unionized labor force and the number of elderly (Galli 2002).

The experience of the countries considered in this book show a common trend toward both a reduction of the top marginal tax rates and a reduction of the bottom marginal tax rates. Political constraints may play a role behind these facts. First, the reduction of the top marginal tax rates, as a measure of the reduction of progressivity,[4] depends on political elements, as in Galli (2002): the ideology of the government (left-wing governments tend to favor progressive taxation), the degree of political instability (unstable governments are not able to cut expenditures or increase taxes and thus they favor tax progressivity) and the power dispersion in the government (competition among parties in a coalition government results in higher spending and higher progressivity than a single-party majoritarian government or a minority government).

Moreover, the reduction of the bottom rates may respond not only to efficiency motivations for the low-skilled, but also to political motivations, if the competing parties assume "Rawlsian"-oriented objective functions and seek the support of the low-skilled groups.

Competition and decentralization versus harmonization

Another crucial issue in the policy debate is the combined trend toward more competitive and decentralized tax systems and the effects of globalization and harmonization in the European Union.

On one side there is a general trend toward more competitive tax systems, in particular a trend to reduce the tax on financial and corporate capital with the purpose of attracting investments. This has already been done in Ireland and the Netherlands and it was one of the main objectives of German reform in 2001, as well as Italian reform. At the same time, we observe a general trend toward decentralization of the tax policy process (Italy, Spain). Similar political reasons may explain this combination of competition and decentralization: competitive political process may generate information in a decentralized system. Decentralization is required by the complexity of current systems, and may be a solution of the information problems and the high administrative costs explained in the chapter thus far. Decentralization, in fact, allows information collection and processing costs to be economized and to benefit from specialization of knowledge required for the use of particular tax instruments. Efficiency reasons also play a role in the process of decentralization: an economically efficient tax system in a modern economy is necessarily too complicated and one can choose either to reach a compromise by adopting simplified rules, which may reduce welfare, or to decentralize. At a local level, politicians may better reflect voters' preferences about taxation. This implies that political reasons play a crucial role in decentralization. Political reasons behind decentralization have been tested by Ashworth and Heyndels (1997) for the Flemish case. Politicians, who have the objective of maximizing expected votes, decide the tax rates taking into account their beliefs about the political cost (in term of loss of votes) associated with the tax rate and their attitudes toward taxation in general. The authors show that, at a local level, both these factors depend closely on the voters' preferences and oppositions.

However, decentralization also has several problems. Tax competition among jurisdictions in a decentralized world may have a detrimental impact on the efficiency of public goods' supply and redistribution. Following Tiebout (1956), fiscal autonomy is necessary for achieving a Pareto-efficient allocation of local public goods when there exist different competing local communities. Citizens are expected to "vote with their feet," i.e. choose their residence in a community which provides them with their personally optimal combination of fiscal burden and public goods. Communities are therefore competing and in equilibrium they will result in different quantities and types of public goods according to citizens' preferences. However, if skilled labor and capital are not perfectly mobile, different tax rates emerge which may represent detrimental effects for the citizens. Feld (1997) argues that participation in the political process, elections, political parties, demonstrations, i.e. "voice," may be another mechanism, alternative to the Tiebout one of "exit," for the voters to express their opposition to the government in a democracy, and may have an effect on allocative and distributional outcomes, such as tax competition.[5] Moreover, at a decentralized level, pressure groups may be more powerful in exerting their influence and politicians are induced to favor them without taking into account the implications for all voters. This creates a political market failure with the government creating actions that deviate from Pareto efficiency. This case has been characterized by Rodrik (1992) as "subordinate government." Subordinate government may also use information in a biased manner, disregarding the incentive effects of its tax policy for the activity of special interests and the consequences of these effects for the welfare of individual voters. In the end, the choice of government may not coincide with the optimal allocation.

On the other side, globalization and international integration also affect the tax structure. These effects are explained by the so-called "efficiency hypothesis" (governments compete for mobile factors and goods) and "compensation hypothesis" (governments expand the welfare state to ensure citizens against the increased economic risk related to globalization). The basic results of the tax competition literature show that capital taxation is negatively related to the degree of international capital mobility (though this relation is much less clear when effective tax rates are considered rather than official tax rates), while labor taxation is positively related to international integration of national economies. Also, larger countries levy higher capital tax rates than smaller countries, because the erosion of their tax base is smaller in per capita terms. These predictions are tested by Bretschger and Hettich (2002) in a panel of 14 OECD countries. A general result of the literature of tax competition (as originated by Zodrow and Mieszkowski (1986) and Wilson (1986) and recently surveyed by Wilson (1999)) is that capital tax competition generates a fiscal externality which delivers too low tax rates and underprovision of public goods in equilibrium, and it may thus be detrimental. However, this underprovision of public good may be not so bad if it corresponds to a reduction of improductive expenditures. In this respect, political elements play a crucial role (Petretto 2002). In the FE approach, fiscal competition has a positive role in limiting the power of the Leviathan which aims at enlarging the public sector and taxation, in spite of inefficiencies. Local government are assumed to be interested at maximizing their budget and they are only partly motivated by re-elections. If a non-distortionary taxation is unfeasible, fiscal competition induces a reduction of the improductive expenditures (Edwards and Keen 1996). A general principle is that tax competition is preferred, even if it creates distortions, since these distortions are small compared to the large inefficiency due to the improductive public expenditures which would emerge in the absence of competition (Wellisch 2000; Eggert 2001). In the political economy approach, focusing on capital income taxation, Persson and Tabellini (1992) show that, if governments choose their fiscal policies according to the electoral mechanism, i.e. taking into account the voting behavior of the citizens, the competition across countries does not lead to an extreme reduction of the equilibrium tax rates on capital income. This is because voters know that an increase of the tax rate in their country will be partly compensated by a correspondent increase in the "foreign" country (as the optimal strategies of the governments in two competing countries are strategic complement), while the governments over-estimate the amount of capital that would be induced to migrate due to a change in their fiscal policy. As a consequence, in a symmetric equilibrium, the median voter in each country votes for a government with a capital endowment lower than its own capital, and thus the tax rates on capital are higher than would be obtained without considering the voting mechanism.

In a recent paper, Janeba and Schjelderup (2002) aim at conciliating the tax competition literature and the "public choice" approach in a single framework. They examine the effect of increasing capital mobility (or globalization) both in terms of fiscal externalities and political distortions arising from selfish policy makers. They show that increasing competition is likely to improve voter utility. Moreover, they analyze the different political response to increasing tax competition between Europe and the USA: while in Europe there is a long-debated issue of coordination or harmonization of tax policies (not really achieved, but at least pursued by rules and agreements), in the USA competition among states is positively considered as a key element of the federal system. According to the authors, these different political responses may be explained by the different political and budgetary institutions of Europe and the USA (Persson and Tabellini 2000b): parliamentary democracies, which are common in Europe, provide a more cohesive government responsible for the entire government budget, which turns out to be associated with higher taxes, higher public goods provision and higher government waste than presidential–congressional democracies, like the USA, where the budget-making process is made by committee with separated powers. Following this comparative public finance approach, and generalizing by introducing multiple countries whose governments compete for mobile capital, they study tax competition in a base version of the model with politicians seeking re-election. In a closed economy, a general result is that voters must allow politicians to obtain some rents for them to seek re-election. As a consequence, in both regimes, the closed economy is not efficient, since taxes are too high. Interesting results are found when the authors compare the equilibrium in an open economy (consisting of an arbitrary number of identical countries that have the same political system) and in a closed one. In the base version of the model, opening the economy reduces tax rates on mobile capital under both political regimes (parliamentary democracies or presidential–congressional) and reduces the rents to politicians. This is due to the fact that tax rates in the rest of the world decrease, making it difficult to raise revenues for politicians foregoing re-election, and to the fact that when more countries compete to attract capital, the capital stock falls in a country where politicians do not seek re-election. Since politicians' rents also fall, the reduction of tax rates does not imply necessarily a loss in voter utilities (opposite to the traditional view of tax competition). Also, the fall in rents of the politicians does not guarantee an increase in voter utility (opposite to the FE approach). In parliamentary democracies, opening implies that the public good level falls and the effect on voters' utility is thus ambiguous, while in presidential–congressional regimes the public good level is unaffected, and thus voters' utility increase. A more intensive competition over capital (i.e. if more countries compete) yields similar results. Voter utility may increase in parliamentary regimes if the marginal product of capital is a positive constant, while it always increases in presidential–congressional systems. The authors also formulate a second version of the model, where politicians only want to extract government resources for themselves. The results are similar to the ones described for the base version, though in this second version it is more likely that tax competition is harmful under both political regimes.

Tax systems and tax reforms in Europe between public finance and political economy theories

This section summarizes the main results of the chapter and provides a conclusive interpretation of the experience of the European countries according to the suggestions of the theory, taking into account efficiency, equity and political determinants of the tax systems and tax reforms.

The experience of European countries, which is described in this book, shows that economic and political determinants interact to shape the current tax system and the planned tax reforms. The structure of income taxation that we observe can be seen as the result of a political process where politicians maximize their expected number of votes. To gain political support, respecting the constraint of administrative costs, a complex tax structure emerges, grouping individuals in brackets and grouping activity into tax bases and special provisions. The common trend toward a reduction of complexity and a reduction of the degree of progressivity that we observe in the countries under consideration has not only economic determinants, mainly efficiency reasons, but also political determinants, such as the need to reduce high administration and information costs in order to increase political support, or to meet the preferences of groups of voters who exert more influence. Competition, as well as decentralization and globalization, have strong impacts on fiscal policies, as shown by the recent experiences of the countries studied in this book. In an international, integrated world, we see countries competing between each other on tax rates. Also, decentralization arises as an alternative solution to the high administration and information costs. Both competition and decentralization create information.

What conclusive interpretations of the experience of the selected European countries emerge from this analysis?

At the first stage of our modern economies, public expenditures and taxes are low, and thus complexity and differentiation are not required, inefficiency costs and losses are small. Then, public expenditures rise and this requires an increase in differentiation and complexity, both for the traditional optimal taxation objectives (in order to minimize the excess burden and inefficiency) and because of the political economy constraints (in order to maximize political support). But when the system is too complex and information, administration and monitoring costs are too high, a political oriented approach may require simplified solutions (flat rate). The reforms currently planned or recently implemented in the

European countries propose such simplified solutions. Having this simplification as their main objective, these reforms have been marginal and parametric adjustments rather than structural changes, while more radical changes were required for economic reasons (see Chapter 2). This is because structural reforms hit the interests of many groups of current voters. Thus, as in other fields of policy reforms (see, for example, pensions, as explained in Galasso and Profeta 2002), in spite of being economically desirable, structural reforms may be politically unfeasible, and thus they fail to be implemented.

Notes

1 I would like to thank Giampaolo Arachi, Luigi Bernardi, Agnar Sandmo and four anonymous referees for helpful comments. I am grateful to Vincenzo Galasso for his comments and continuous support. All remaining errors are mine.
2 In this chapter I stress the economic and political determinants of the evolution of the fiscal systems. However, administration costs, the revenue budget, tax evasions, etc. are also relevant. For these issues see Musgrave (1969).
3 The probability that a voter votes for a party also depends on ideological elements, see Persson and Tabellini (2000a).
4 The top marginal tax rate may be a measure of progressivity, as in Galli (2002), though it is generally considered quite a poor measure. The Kakwani index or the distance between top and bottom rates is generally preferred.
5 The author also provides an empirical analysis of the impact of referenda, which represent the possibility of participating in the political process by voters, on tax competition between the cantons in Switzerland.

References

Ahmad, E. and Stern, N.H. (1984) "The theory of reform and Indian indirect taxes," *Journal of Public Economics*, 25: 259–98.
Ashworth, J. and Heyndels, B. (1997) "Politicians' preferences on local tax rates: an empirical analysis," *European Journal of Political Economy*, 13: 479–502.
Atkinson, A.B. (1995) *Public Economics in Action*, Oxford: Clarendon Press.
Aumann, R. and Kurz, M. (1977) "Power and taxes," *Econometrica*, 45: 1137–61.
Becker, G.S. (1983) "A theory of competition among pressure groups for political influence," *The Quarterly Journal of Economics*, 3: 371–400.
Brennan, G. and Buchanan, J.M. (1980) *The Power to Tax: Analytical Foundations of a Fiscal Constitution*, Cambridge: Cambridge University Press.
Breton, A. (1974) *The Economic Theory of Representative Government*, Chicago: Aldine.
Bretschger, L. and Hettich, F. (2002) "Globalisation, capital mobility and tax competition: theory and evidence for OECD countries," *European Journal of Political Economy*, 18: 695–716.
Buchanan, J. (1976) "Taxation in fiscal exchange," *Journal of Public Economics*, 6: 17–29.
Cuckierman, A., Edwards, S. and Tabellini, G. (1992) "Seignorage and political instability," *American Economic Review*, 82: 537–55.
Downs, A. (1957) *An Economic Theory of Democracy*, New York: Harper and Row.

Edwards, J. and Keen, M. (1996) "Tax competition and Leviathan," *European Economic Review*, 40: 113–34.

Eggert, W. (2001) "Capital tax competition with socially wasteful government consumption," *European Journal of Political Economy*, 17: 517–29.

Fair, R. (1971) "The optimal distribution of income," *Quarterly Journal of Economics*, 85: 551–79.

Feld, L. (1997) "Exit, voice and income taxes: the loyalty of voters," *European Journal of Political Economy*, 13: 455–78.

Galasso, V. and Profeta, P. (2002) "The political economy of social security: a survey," *European Journal of Political Economy*, 18: 1–29.

Galli, E. (2002) *Tax Progressivity and Economic and Political Determinants: an Empirical Analysis for the OECD Countries*, mimeo, Università di Roma "La Sapienza."

Hettich, W. and Winer, S. (1988) "Economic and political foundations of tax structure," *American Economic Review*, 78: 701–12.

—— (1997) "The political economy of taxation," in Mueller, D. (ed.) *Perspectives on Public Choice: A Handbook*, Cambridge: Cambridge University Press.

—— (1998) *Information, Coordination and Tax Policy Making*, mimeo.

—— (1999) *Democratic Choice and Taxation*, Cambridge: Cambridge University Press.

—— (2000) *Rules, Politics and the Normative Analysis of Taxation*, mimeo.

Inman, R. and Fitts, M. (1990) "Political institutions and fiscal policy: evidence from the US historical record," *Journal of Law, Economics and Organization*, 6: 79–132.

Janeba, E. and Schjelderup, G. (2002) "Why Europe should love tax competition – and the US even more so," NBER Working Paper 9334.

Lindahl, E. (1919) "Positive losung, die gerechtigkeit der besteuerung," Lund, reprinted as "Just taxation – a positive solution," in Musgrave, R.A. and Peacock, A.T. (eds) *Classics in the Theory of Public Finance*, London: Macmillan.

Mirrlees, J.A. (1971) "An exploration in the theory of optimum income taxation," *Review of Economic Studies*, 38: 175–208.

—— (1972) "On producer taxation," *Review of Economic Studies*, 39: 105–11.

—— (1976) "Optimal tax theory: a synthesis," *Journal of Public Economics*, 6: 327–58.

Musgrave, R.A. (1969) *Fiscal Systems*, New Haven: Yale University Press.

Persson, T. and Tabellini, G. (1992) "The politics of 1992: fiscal policy and European integration," *Review of Economic Studies*, 59: 689–701.

—— (2000a) *Political Economics. Explaining Economic Policy*, Cambridge, MA: MIT Press.

—— (2000b) "Comparative politics and public finance," *Journal of Political Economy*, 6: 1121–61.

Petretto, A. (2002) *Unità Europea e Economia Pubblica*, Bologna: Il Mulino.

Ramsey, F.P. (1927) "A contribution to the theory of taxation," *Economic Journal*, 37: 47–61.

Roberts, K. (1977) "Voting over income tax schedules," *Journal of Public Economics*, 8: 329–40.

Roemer, J. (1999) "The democratic political economy of progressive income taxation," *Econometrica*, 67: 1–19.

Rodrik, D. (1992) "Political economy and development policies," *European Economic Review*, 36: 329–36.

Simons, H. (1938) *Personal Income Taxation: The Definition of Income as a Problem of Fiscal Policy*, Chicago: Chicago University Press.

Stern, N. (1976) "On the specification of models of optimum income taxation," *Journal of Public Economics*, 6: 123–62.

Stigler, G. (1970) "Director's law of public income redistribution," *Journal of Law and Economics*, 13: 1–10.

Stiglitz, J. (1987) "Pareto efficient and optimal taxation and the New New Welfare economics," in Auerbach, A. and Feldstein, M. (eds) *Handbook of Public Economics*, vol. II, New York: North-Holland.

Tiebout, C.M. (1956) "A pure theory of local expenditures," *Journal of Political Economy*, 65: 416–24.

Warskett, G., Winer, S. and Hettich, W. (1998) "The complexity of the tax structure in competitive political systems," *International Tax and Public Finance*, 5: 123–51.

Wellisch, D. (2000) *Theory of Public Finance in a Federal State*, Cambridge: Cambridge University Press.

Wicksell, K. (1896) "A new principle of just taxation," Musgrave, R.A. and Peacock, A.T. (eds) (1958) *Classics in the Theory of Public Finance*, London: Macmillan.

Wilson, J.D. (1986) "A theory of interregional tax competition," *Journal of Urban Economics*, 19: 296–315.

—— (1999) "Theories of tax competition," *National Tax Journal*, 52: 269–304.

Winer, S. (2003) "Rules, politics and the normative analysis of taxation" (with Walter Hettich). Forthcoming in Backhaus, J. and Wagner, R. (eds) *Handbook of Public Economics*, Norwell, MA: Kluwer Academic.

Zodrow, G. and Mieszkowski, P. (1986) "Pigou, Tiebout, property taxation and the underprovision of local public goods," *Journal of Urban Economics*, 19: 356–70.

4 Reducing fiscal pressure under the Stability Pact

Fedele De Novellis and Salvatore Parlato[1]

Introduction

Most European countries have recently undertaken reforms designed to reduce tax burdens. Tax reductions occurred in the second half of the 1990s and they should accelerate over the next five years (see chapters relating to specific countries in this book).

The objective is to reduce total taxation as a proportion of GDP, to reduce it on factors of production and on the employment tax wedge in particular. According to a large part of the literature (see Chapter 2), these changes to the tax system must be quantitatively substantial if they are to have significant effects on economic growth.

This assumes the availability of considerable funds within national budgets and these are difficult to carve out of expenditure because cuts in spending are socially undesirable (retreat of the welfare state) or politically unfeasible. On the other hand, although big changes to the composition of total revenue are effective on the supply side, they could not generate any significant effects on the demand side.

In order to assess the consistency of the plans drawn up by many European countries to reduce tax burdens, one must first consider how much room is reasonably available for maneuver over the next few years. A crucial role is played in the identification of these resources by economic policies (Stability and Growth Pact, single European currency) and by the persistent differences between output growth and inflation in the euro area as these tend to generate inconsistencies with respect to the objectives of reducing taxation, at least in the transition phase.

In this respect the "close to balance" principle would allow only (a few) particularly virtuous countries to pursue expansionary fiscal policies (tax cuts). This produces, on aggregate, a mix of restrictive policies for the euro area. A shift of public finance targets from deficits to debt would, de facto, free resources to reduce the tax burdens of precisely those countries that most need to stimulate GDP growth. Paradoxically, the current provisions of the Stability Pact ensure that only those countries close to potential growth are able to reduce taxation, while those with weaker economies are obliged to delay the launch of programs to reduce taxation.

The main result of this type of analysis is also the most critical for the prospects of economic growth in the euro area: the lack of flexibility in the Pact during the transition phase (or until all countries have balanced their budgets and inflation differentials have been eliminated) precludes the use of fiscal policies to counter adverse economic situations for Germany and Italy in particular, which together account for more than 50 percent of the GDP of the entire area. For Italy, inflation and government debt are, in any case, higher than the average and expansionary fiscal policies may not be desirable. For Germany, on the other hand, with the lowest inflation in the area and low national debt, the policy mix is heavily restrictive and unjustifiably penalizing. There are, in fact, clear risks that the German economy may worsen, assisted for the most part by the economic policy stance, and these risks could be reduced if exceptions were made to the Stability Pact.

This chapter is organized as follows. First it focuses on the wide inflation differentials experienced among the European countries during recent years. Second, it examines the consequences on the monetary policies and the coherence between the level of real interest rates and GDP growth rates of the European countries. Four alternative scenarios are shown in order to evaluate the effects on public budgets of the lack of coordination between the monetary and fiscal policy rules. Third, it examines the consistency between the tax reduction plans and the Stability Pact constraints. An assessment on the room for maneuver for tax reductions is proposed next. Finally, some conclusions and policy prescriptions are drafted.

The origin of inflation differences between European countries

The launch of the euro was characterized by large and persistent differences in inflation between single currency Member Countries. Diverging inflation rates do not necessarily constitute a problem within a single currency area. In fact, in some cases, they may have a positive effect to the extent that they demonstrate the capacity of relative prices to respond to shocks that have asymmetric effects on different areas (Alberola *et al.*, 1998). The growing number of inflation rate differences between countries in the euro area gives more grounds for concern when one considers that these differences have persisted since the EMS parity exchange rates were set in 1996. A limited group of countries has consistently recorded higher rates of inflation than others.

This trend may be interpreted in terms of the convergence of prices to a common level, which would have induced higher prices in countries where they were originally lower and lower rates of inflation where prices were higher. It is difficult to establish whether there has been symmetry in this process. It is more probable that downward price rigidity has resulted in convergence occurring mainly through greater inflation in those economies where prices were lower. Nevertheless, OECD statistics on relative price levels in different countries do show interesting trends, at least at a general level.

Price convergence can be illustrated by comparing cumulative inflation differentials over the last five years with differences between price levels in 1997. Germany was used as the benchmark country. Figure 4.1 shows a close correlation between price differences at the start of the euro and cumulative inflation rates in recent years. The Netherlands is not in line with the other countries in the graph, probably because domestic inflation was stimulated by indirect taxation. Finland and Ireland constitute exceptions. Their price levels tend to converge toward those of the economies that are geographically closest, Sweden, Denmark, Norway and the UK respectively.

The persistence of inflation differences shown above does not necessarily imply changes in infra-European price competitiveness. It may be a phenomenon described by the traditional "Balassa effect": when productivity growth in "tradable" sectors of the economy is high, as the result, for example, of a country catching up with more advanced economies, competitiveness measured by real "aggregate" exchange rate indices, based for

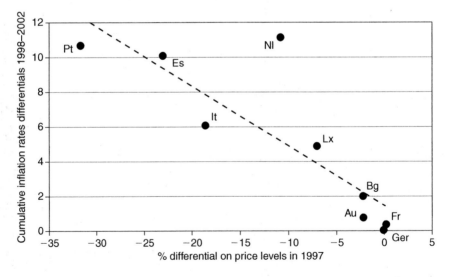

Figure 4.1 Consumer prices: differentials on price levels and inflation rates.[1]

Source: our calculation based on OECD and Eurostat data.

Note
1 against Germany.

example on consumer prices, tends to deteriorate, while competitiveness in the tradable sector alone does not show an analogous deterioration.

Changes in price levels do not therefore necessarily condition the competitiveness of firms, even if some effect in this direction is probable in the short term. What would then occur would be a process of price convergence by low-income countries toward the price levels of high-income countries. It must also be considered that price convergence processes may arise from the presence of imbalances at the time when EMS exchange rates were fixed. Some countries could have joined the system at too high (or too low) a rate, because the exchange rate compared to other currencies was set at a level that was too strong (or too weak). The Balassa effect mechanism could be overlaid by other phenomena, such as simple arbitrage or even the effects of progress made with market integration.

Obviously the price levels of the different countries in the single currency do not have to converge completely. Differences between economies using the same currency are possible as a result of different economic characteristics. It is in any case plausible that differences that existed when the EMS exchange rates were fixed, were to a certain extent excessive. The persistence of inflation differences themselves confirms this hypothesis. The hypothesis of price convergence "on levels" tends to exclude the possibility that inflation differences reflect analogous differences in real economic growth. It is also possible that, in the medium term, participation in the same currency area will strengthen mechanisms which attract prices to common levels that are too high for the less-developed countries of the European Union. Should this phenomenon actually occur, it would have a negative effect on the more underdeveloped economic areas and would polarize development (Canzoneri *et al.*, 2002).

The consequences on the budgetary policies of countries belonging to the EMU

The persistence of inflation differentials between European countries has an effect on their budgetary policies. Countries with low inflation rates have higher interest rates in real terms. Countries with high inflation enjoy exceptionally convenient monetary conditions. This phenomenon is illustrated in Figure 4.2.

If, as in the present case, inflation differentials and therefore real interest rates do not reflect the different growth rates of the various economies, this would have particular consequences for government finances. In fact, for Germany in particular, real interest rates exceed growth in real GDP by a broad margin and this results in inconsistencies between development objectives and balancing the national budget, a situation similar to that experienced by other economies in the 1990s such as Italy and Spain.

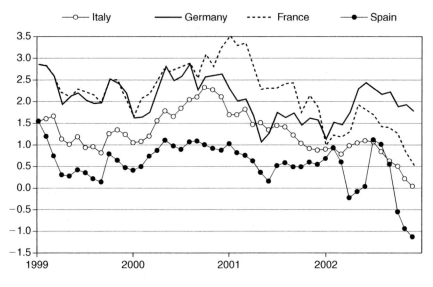

Figure 4.2 Ex post real short-term interest rates.
Source: Thomson Financial, National Statistics Offices.

Countries with higher inflation, on the other hand, experience particularly favorable conditions (Table 4.1). For example, growth in the Spanish economy between 1999 and 2002 was higher than real interest rates by a good three percentage points. For Ireland, this difference was as large as 9 percent.

The first conclusion that can be drawn, as demonstrated below (p. 86), is that Germany, whose economy is afflicted by various problems that limit economic growth, is subject to interest rates that are too high. These are having an adverse effect on the national budget due to the direct impact of higher interest payments and to the indirect effect of lower growth rates resulting from interest rates that are too high. Lower growth rates affect the government budget, and the Stability Pact objective requires budgetary adjustments which further dampen German domestic demand.

Four theoretical scenarios

The launch of the euro determined conditions that were exceptionally unfavorable for some economies and particularly favorable for others. These conditions are exceptional because the process of converging price levels is a transitory phenomenon even if it may require many years to complete. That is why it is plausible to believe that the trends that occurred in the 1999–2002 period could continue for the next four or five

Table 4.1 Coherence indicators between interest rates and GDP growth rates

	GDP (annual average % change)		Nominal interest rate (short term)		GDP deflator (annual average % change)		Real interest rate (short term)		Difference (real interest − GDP)	
	1992–8	1999–2002	1992–8	1999–2002	1992–8	1999–2002	1992–8	1999–2002	1992–8	1999–2002
Germany	1.3	1.5	5.3	3.7	2.3	0.8	2.9	2.9	1.6	1.4
France	1.5	2.5	6.0	3.7	1.6	1.1	4.3	2.6	2.8	0.1
Italy	1.4	1.7	9.1	3.7	3.9	2.2	5.0	1.5	3.6	−0.2
Spain	2.2	3.2	8.5	3.7	4.0	3.5	4.3	0.2	2.0	−3.0
The Netherlands	2.8	2.2	5.1	3.7	1.9	3.6	3.1	0.1	0.3	−2.1
Belgium	1.9	2.0	5.5	3.7	2.1	1.6	3.3	2.1	1.4	0.1
Austria	2.0	1.9	5.2	3.7	2.1	1.3	3.1	2.3	1.1	0.5
Finland	2.7	2.9	6.1	3.7	2.0	1.8	4.0	1.9	1.3	−0.9
Ireland	7.0	8.0	7.5	3.7	3.6	4.4	3.8	−0.6	−3.2	−8.7
Portugal	2.3	2.4	9.6	3.7	5.7	3.5	3.6	0.2	1.3	−2.2

Source: our calculation based on OECD data.

years. This persistence constitutes an element of contradiction with respect to the convergence scenarios of the Stability and Growth Pact. An idea of the quantitative dimension of this inconsistency can be gained from an examination of two benchmark cases that describe the public finance scenarios envisaged under the Stability and Growth Pact both in its current version and if the target is shifted to stability of the debt-to-GDP ratio. It will then be possible, on the basis of these scenarios, to assess the room available for tax cuts. Two theoretical scenarios are also proposed, in which inflation and growth gaps between Member Countries disappear, in order to ascertain the size of the effects that macroeconomic hetero-geneity has on the choice of fiscal policies.

The first scenario ("benchmark I") reflects the current version of the Stability Pact according to which the countries in the monetary union must eliminate their budget deficits by the end of 2005. It must be remem-bered that the interpretation of the Stability Pact has recently been subject to some revisions, first with a preference for the objective of "close to balance" budgets. To avoid excessive discretion in the interpretation of targets, "close to balance" was quantified as a deficit of 0.5 percent, even if this may obviously set a precedent for flexible interpretations. Second, the "close to balance" target has recently been set back to 2006. Here too, a precedent has been set for further future postponements of the target deadline. There is also another element that could, in future, set a precedent for discretionary assessments of the results of the public finances of Member States. The adoption of a target set in structural terms may result in disputes over the methods employed for measuring both output gaps and the output gap elasticity of budget items. Clearly the rigidity of objectives has been impaired by the greater flexibility in the cri-teria for interpreting the pact. The objective of balancing budgets by 2005 assumed in the simulation constitutes therefore a point of reference for assessing policies that result from observance of the Stability Pact rather than an assessment of the policies that will necessarily be adopted by Member States.

Starting with current primary balances, adjusted for the effects of the business cycle, the change in the primary structural balance required to reach the budget balance in structural terms over the next few years is cal-culated. It should be pointed out that the fiscal adjustment required to achieve a balanced budget calculated in this way reflects the budget changes required starting from current levels of revenue and expenditure, but does not involve an assessment of trends in public finances over the next few years. For some countries, spontaneous changes in revenues and spending over the next few years could in fact have already been adjusted by corrective measures adopted in the past. In this sense the size of the adjustment estimated by us is that "which will be made" to achieve object-ives, rather than that which "should be further adopted."

The assumptions for the first hypothesis are as follows.

The hypotheses for growth and interest expenditure made in the OECD forecasts at the end of 2002 are assumed for each country.

The budgetary corrections that may be required are calculated algebraically, given the objective of balancing budgets, starting from the current level of deficit and also taking account of the reduction in interest expenditure generated by increasing the primary surplus. Obviously, it must be remembered that estimates of the structural deficits will differ depending on the method employed to calculate them.

The values presented in Table 4.2 must not therefore be interpreted as absolute and precise snapshots of the situation but as mere indicators of trends.

Starting from the current size of the primary balance, it is clear that practically none of the countries in the euro area except for Finland and Belgium have any room for expansionary type policy maneuvers and a substantial corrective maneuver of almost 3 percent is required by Germany.

The situation presented in the "benchmark I" scenario clearly shows that, as things stand at present, the margins for reducing taxation in Europe are very slender, especially for the larger economies. This is particularly true if account is taken of the considerable efforts already required on the spending side if budgets are to be balanced without increasing fiscal pressure.

A second alternative option can be developed from this first basic scenario.

Table 4.2 Change in structural primary balance required to meet the Pact targets

	Scenario 1[1]	*Scenario 2*[2]	*Scenario 3*[3]	*Scenario 4*[4]
Germany	2.7	0.5	0.1	−0.3
France	2.2	−0.1	−0.2	−0.3
Italy	1.4	0.7	1.0	0.2
Spain	−0.5	−4.1	−3.4	−3.1
The Netherlands	−0.6	−3.6	−3.1	−3.0
Belgium	−1.8	−1.9	−2.3	−2.5
Austria	0.9	−0.7	−1.0	−1.2
Finland	−4.7	−4.8	−4.4	−5.0
Ireland	1.5	−1.3	−0.4	1.7
Portugal	2.1	−2.0	−1.3	−1.1

Source: our calculation based on OECD data.

Notes
1 Target: balanced budget in 2005.
2 Target: stabilization of the debt-to-GDP ratio (reduction by 4 percent of GDP per year for Italy and Belgium), assuming persistent inflation differentials, see the text for the underlying hypotheses.
3 Target: theoretical stabilization of the debt-to-GDP ratio, assuming the same inflation rate for all the countries, see the text for underlying hypotheses.
4 Target: theoretical stabilization of the debt-to-GDP ratio, assuming GDP growth equals the average cost of debt servicing, see the text for underlying hypotheses.

In the second scenario ("benchmark II") the objective is changed to maintenance of a stable debt-to-GDP ratio for all European countries and a drop of 4 percent per year for Italy and Belgium, the countries with the highest levels of debt-to-GDP ratio in the area.

The objective of the second scenario is basically to identify room for maneuver in budget policies and to assess how consistent they are with conditions that would ensure a dynamic stabilization of debt-to-GDP ratio. It constitutes a departure from the logic of setting deficit reduction targets. The purpose is to take into consideration the different levels of government debt before defining deficit targets. The underlying macro-economic situation for this scenario is based on the hypothesis that interest rates and average debt costs converge to the same levels over the next few years, but that the inflation and growth differentials between euro countries observed over the last three years are maintained. It is a useful scenario for projections over a three-to-four-year period.

In this second scenario, almost all euro countries, including those mentioned above (p. 85) are able to reduce their primary surplus. Only Italy and Germany are required to take action to improve their general government primary balances, but the size of the intervention required is much less than in the first scenario. The most interesting aspect of this scenario is that some countries, such as Spain, the Netherlands, Ireland and Portugal, gain room for maneuver to bring in policies that reduce their primary balances. This aspect is very important not just because it makes it possible to introduce policies for the structural reduction of taxation, but also because it quantifies the size of the possible intervention required to stabilize the business cycle. It seems clear that many countries today could pursue policies aimed at reversing the cyclical downturn without damage to the soundness of their public finances. Such room for maneuver was obviously not found in the previous scenario, where the target was set in terms of budget deficit.

Clearly the assessment of the conditions required to stabilize debt proposed in scenario two is affected by the gaps between real interest rates and growth rates discussed previously. Although this phenomenon will reduce over the course of time, it will nevertheless persist for a number of years. It is, however, also true that, although the time horizon of the process is difficult to define, it would seem correct to hypothesize the elimination of inflation differentials within a few years. On the other hand, differences in economic growth rates are destined to last longer.

The third scenario has therefore been constructed as a long-term theoretical scenario. It assumes the same objectives as scenario two, but the assumption of continued inflation differentials has been removed. It therefore gives the new equilibrium, once the process of convergence on common price levels is complete. It removes the anomaly of continued inflation differentials experienced in the start-up phase of the euro, but maintains the assumption of different rates of economic expansion. The average cost of servicing government debt is assumed to be equal to the current level of long-term European interest rates, at a little over 4 percent, with marginal differences between countries. This hypothesis also assumes convergence to a common normal level in the medium term. The average cost of current debt servicing is, in fact, higher at around 6 percent for European countries, a legacy of the higher rates at which debt was issued in the 1990s.

An inflation rate of 1.7 percent is assumed for all countries, consistent with the ECB's target for inflation.

The average real cost of debt servicing is therefore around 2.5 percent, marginally higher than the growth rate for the euro area over the last ten years (2.2 percent between 1994 and 2002). The growth rates assumed for individual countries are the averages observed in the period 1994–2002. This third case basically replicates the results of scenario two, but with smaller differences between countries, affording less room for maneuver to countries which had higher inflation rates in past years. Italy again requires a tightening of fiscal policy amounting to 1 percent of GDP. The room for relaxing Spanish and Dutch restrictive policies reduces, while the position of Germany improves further and would not require further fiscal corrective maneuvers.

To summarize, a comparison of scenario three with scenario two shows that the conditions for the stabilization of government debt-to-GDP ratio for different countries in the euro area differ as a function of the different rates of inflation in individual countries. Furthermore it makes it possible to quantify the relative cost of large differences in inflation rates for countries with low inflation rates. Obviously one last point concerning the differences in growth rates between countries remains to be discussed. If Ireland is excluded, all the euro countries recorded average growth rates of between 1.5 percent (Germany) and 2.9 percent (Finland) in the 1999–2002 period, while average inflation rates for the same period measured by the GDP deflator ranged from 0.8 percent (Germany) to 3.5 percent (Spain, the Netherlands and Portugal).

The problem of growth differentials is, however, also important for Italy and Germany. In fact, while the growth rates of other countries in the euro area have been more or less satisfactory, Italy and Germany have recorded average GDP growth rates of around 1.5 percent. What is more, according to the OECD method (different methods of calculation produce very similar results) growth rates for potential output are at around the same level.

In this case too, it is clear, as with differences in inflation rates, that inconsistencies can emerge between the growth rates of individual economies and interest rates. For example, the average GDP growth rate for the United States over the last four years (1999–2002) was 2.7 percent, while it was 2.3 percent for the euro area without Germany. In the same period, real average short-term interest rates were 1.8 percent in the

United States and 1.4 percent in the euro area without Germany. Germany on the other hand has recorded average growth of 1.5 percent and real short-term interest rates of 2.1 percent.

In this case, too, we can try to quantify the consequences that the presence of GDP growth rate differences has for public finances by repeating the exercise performed for the previous scenario. In the fourth scenario not only is the assumption of different inflation rates removed, but also that of different economic growth rates. The hypothesis is that the average cost of debt servicing is equal to economic growth for all countries. The results obtained are shown in the fourth column of Table 4.2. The aspect to note is the increased room for fiscal policy maneuver acquired by Italy and Germany, the countries with the lowest GDP growth rates.[2] Conditions for the countries with the highest GDP growth rates in recent years, Spain and above all Ireland, worsen.

The theoretical scenario that we have proposed may therefore constitute a point of reference for quantifying how much of the recent economic downturn of some European economies reflects different growth and inflation rates within the area. The most striking case is Germany. There are no specific problems of imbalance in German government finances. Stabilization of the debt-to-GDP ratio would require a restrictive maneuver amounting to approximately 0.5 percent of GDP (scenario two), which is in any case due to European real interest rates being too high with respect to the German GDP growth rate. Similar results are obtained for France and, although to a lesser extent, for Italy (where the objective is not to stabilize but to reduce the debt-to-GDP ratio).

The results also show that the public finances of euro countries are, on average, sound. The conditions for stabilizing debt under the theoretical assumptions of scenario four are basically observed by all countries with the exception of Ireland, which should take corrective fiscal action amounting to 1.7 percent of GDP, but thanks to the current level of interest rates can achieve the same result with a worsening of the primary rate by 1.3 percent of GDP (scenario two).

Tax reduction, growth and Stability Pact constraints

There are many reasons why a reduction in fiscal pressure is desirable both from the viewpoint of equity and efficiency. One of the recurring justifications for policies designed to reduce fiscal pressure is that of growth (see Chapter 2 and the Foreword in this book). It is, in fact, held that high taxation in an economic system causes inefficiency by generating distortions and adverse incentives which prevent a country from growing at its potential rate of development (or from raising this). This assumption is not fully shared in the economic literature in general, but represents one of the cornerstones of supply-side economics. It is true, however, that fiscal policy plays an important role in governing business cycles and that is why countries that have recorded modest GDP growth rates for a period of time should seek to reduce fiscal pressure.

Let us, therefore, leave aside requirements to reduce tax burdens as dictated by structural factors, high fiscal pressure, low growth potential, and concentrate on identifying economies within the European Union which would need to take action to stimulate demand in the next three years. The focus of our analysis here is on room for maneuver within the European Union for reducing taxation without paying for it with spending cuts, which otherwise would have a negative effect on demand, at least in the short term.

One measure of the need to cut taxation for countries in the European Union might be the output gap.[3] A classification of countries most in need of reducing their tax burden can be drawn up from OECD estimates for European countries over the three-year period 2002–4 by simply comparing individual output gaps with the average for all the countries considered.

Table 4.3 shows first of all that, in the period considered, GDP is lower than potential output for all the countries in the euro area and that the average output gap for the European Union is −1.2 percent for each year. In absolute terms, therefore, a reduction in taxation that would stimulate growth with effects on demand would be desirable for all countries. In relative terms, those countries furthest behind with respect to the European average are the Netherlands, Portugal, Finland, Germany, Italy, Austria and, to a lesser extent, Belgium, all with a greater need to reduce taxation. It should also be noted that of these countries, Finland, Austria, Italy and Belgium (together with France) have the highest fiscal pressure in the euro area, leading one to suspect that, for these countries, a high tax burden constitutes at least one of the most important factors (on the supply side) that is holding back potential economic growth. On the other hand, countries like Spain, the UK and Ireland do not seem to require urgent and substantial tax cuts both because of their estimated position in the business cycle in the 2002–4 three-year period, with GDP growth at rates higher than the potential rate (relative to the European average), and because of their current tax levels (they are the countries with the lowest fiscal pressure in the European Union). The positions of France and Portugal are not so clear, the former characterized by high fiscal pressure but also with GDP growth rates higher than the potential rate, while the latter is characterized by the opposite.

Once the countries which require substantial tax cuts have been identified on the basis of the output gap criterion, we can see which of them has sufficient resources to reduce taxation without corresponding cuts in spending, starting from the current budget position and the Stability Pact constraints. As can be seen from Table 4.3, there are very few matches of countries with should reduce fiscal pressure and which have the funds to do so under the conditions of scenario one ("benchmark I"). Basically,

Table 4.3 Room for maneuver

	Germany	France	Italy	Spain	The Netherlands	Belgium	Austria	Finland	Ireland	Portugal	EU
Fiscal adjustment required (as % of GDP)											
Scenario 1	2.7	2.2	1.4	-0.5	-0.6	-1.8	0.9	-4.7	1.5	2.1	
Scenario 2	0.5	-0.1	0.7	-4.1	-3.6	-1.9	-0.7	-4.8	-1.3	-2.0	
Scenario 3	0.1	-0.2	1.0	-3.4	-3.1	-2.3	-1.0	-4.4	-0.4	-1.3	
Scenario 4	-0.3	-0.3	0.2	-3.1	-3.0	-2.5	-1.2	-5.0	1.7	-1.1	
Output gap											
2002	-1.9	-0.6	-1.6	-0.7	-1.9	-1.5	-1.6	-1.8	2.6	-1.3	
2003	-1.8	-0.8	-1.8	-1.0	-2.6	-1.6	-1.6	-1.8	-0.6	-2.4	
2004	-1.0	-0.1	-1.1	-0.8	-2.5	-0.9	-1.2	-1.3	-2.8	-2.5	
2002–4	-1.6	-0.5	-1.5	-0.8	-2.3	-1.3	-1.5	-1.6	-0.3	-2.1	-1.2
Deviation from EU average dispersion	-0.4	0.7	-0.3	0.3	-1.2	-0.2	-0.3	-0.5	0.9	-0.9	0.7
Countries requiring tax cuts	Yes	No	Yes	No	Yes	Yes	Yes	Yes	No	Yes	
Countries which can afford tax cuts											
Scenario 1	No	No	No	Yes	Yes	Yes	No	Yes	No	No	
Scenario 2	No/Yes	Yes	No	Yes	Yes	Yes	Yes	Yes	Yes	Yes	
Scenario 3	No/Yes	Yes	No	Yes	Yes	Yes	Yes	Yes	Yes	Yes	
Scenario 4	Yes	Yes	No/Yes	Yes	Yes	Yes	Yes	Yes	No	Yes	
Matching											
Scenario 1	No	No	No	No	Yes	Yes	No	Yes	No	No	
Scenario 2	No	No	No	No	Yes	Yes	Yes	Yes	No	Yes	
Scenario 3	No/Yes	No	No	No	Yes	Yes	Yes	Yes	No	Yes	
Scenario 4	Yes	No	No/Yes	No	Yes	Yes	Yes	Yes	No	Yes	
Effect on output gap deriving by a shift to Scenario 2											
Output gap	-0.1	1.0	-1.0	1.6	-0.3	-1.2	-0.4	-1.6	1.6	0.6	0.2
Dispersion											1.1

Source: our calculation based on OECD data.

under the terms of the Stability Pact, which requires a structural reduction of budget deficits, only the Netherlands, Belgium and Finland are in a good position to guarantee the necessary stimulus to their economies, with the latter in a particularly good "room for maneuver–output gap" position compared to the other two economies. It should also be noted that the terms of the Stability Pact are so strict that, quite apart from whether there is a need or not, only four countries have any room for maneuver to make a significant reduction in taxation, and the limits imposed by the Stability Pact are extremely penalizing for the two main economies, Italy and Germany, in need of action to put growth back on a path closer to that of potential output. As mentioned previously, changing the targets of the Pact from deficit to debt would loosen its iron grip on the economic policies of European Union countries. With the same action that is planned to structurally balance budgets (current version of the Pact), room for maneuver would be created to cut taxes by an average of 2 percent of the GDP of the economies in question. This would amount to around 0.7 percent of GDP growth per year, a by no means small amount for the purpose of stimulating growth. According to Leibfritz *et al.* (1997), the impact on European GDP of reducing taxes by 1 percent of GDP would range, depending on the taxes in question, from around 1.5 percent (if the reduction was exclusively on consumption taxes) to 3 percent (if only taxation on corporate income was cut), if it was funded from an equal reduction in expenditure or had a neutral effect on the net budget balance. Since under the hypothesis of the "benchmark II" case, additional resources would be created with respect to achieving the objectives, the reduction in the tax burden would not have to be paid for to have the same effects estimated by Leibfritz *et al.* (1997).[4] It follows that the adoption of a Stability Pact based on debt would allow cuts in taxation sufficient to close the output gap, if an elasticity of two is assumed, halfway between the values given above, together with a reduction in the tax burden by 0.7 percentage points per year. Nevertheless, because the change of target from deficit to debt does not give all countries the same uniform advantage, the divergence among countries would be aggravated, since compared to the deficit target, use of the debt target reduces the heterogeneity of the corrective action required. In fact, if it is assumed that the gain resulting from revising the Pact is used to reduce taxation, and that this has the effect of raising GDP with an elasticity of two, what emerges is an increase in the variation of output gaps with respect to the current situation.

To assess the desirability of such a change of policy, account must therefore be taken of the trade-off between raising GDP growth rates in the European Union (and in the euro area in particular) and the importance of convergence between countries. It is in fact found that the achievement of the former objective is tied inevitably to pursuing policies that favor Germany and which could not involve a reduction in existing differentials in the euro area in the short term. The fragility of a fiscal policy with a common set of rules for all countries in the area is therefore evident, both because of its rigidity and of the arbitrary manner in which the constraints that comprise it are set.

Reforms in the making and room for maneuver

The arguments set forth in the preceding pages make a considerable contribution to reducing the credibility of some plans to reduce taxation announced in major European countries. Given the structural constraints of the Stability Pact, what emerges is a substantial lack of resources to fund significant cuts in taxation unless this is done with sharp reductions in spending. Without going into an analysis of what would constitute the best combination of revenue and expenditure, what we wish to point out here is the large gap that exists between the size of plans to cut taxes and the most optimistic forecasts of growth that might provide the resources required to fund those plans. Reasoning in terms of structural balances reduces the possibility of revising estimates of GDP growth rates upwards and of increasing the room for maneuver to reduce tax burdens, because a cyclical rise in GDP growth (and therefore in revenues) would have no effect on structural deficits as calculated by the European Commission. In fact, no strong heterogeneity emerges from the estimates provided by the European Commission (2002) itself with regard to the sensitivity of deficits to cyclical variations, since the range varies from an elasticity of 0.7–0.8 for northern countries to 0.3–0.4 for the smaller countries, with strong convergence on the value of 0.5. Consequently, unless the business cycle performs much better than forecast for some countries, no great changes are to be expected in the estimates made by the OECD concerning structural balances. On the other hand, the potential growth rate of some European countries could be pushed upwards to automatically reduce the need for corrective budgetary action and create room to free resources that could be used to reduce fiscal pressure. In this case too, the size of the revisions would be minimal compared to the plans announced to reduce taxation and to close the gap between current budget situations and the structural deficit. It is implausible to think that changes in potential GDP growth rates would be sufficient, in the cases of Germany and Italy, to fund reductions in budget deficits and cuts in taxation which, for these two countries, amount to approximately 4.2 percent and 3.4 percent of GDP (see the chapters relating to individual chapters in this book). Even under the extremely optimistic hypothesis put forward by some national governments, that tax cuts will fund themselves as a result of rises in potential GDP, Germany and Italy would in any case lack the funds to reach the target of a structurally balanced budget which, as already seen, are considerable, amounting to 2.7 percent and 1.4 percent of GDP respectively. Similar reasoning is also applicable to other European Union countries which need to reduce fiscal pressure but which, as previously shown, lack the resources to fund cuts of this size and, at the same time, observe the constraints of the Stability Pact. In conclusion, it is difficult to imagine significant reductions on fiscal pressure in Europe, at least over the next three years, unless this is balanced by substantial cuts in spending.

Fiscal reforms: the Stability Pact and a single monetary policy

One of the elements highlighted by the analysis conducted in this chapter is the persistence of inflation and GDP growth differentials among countries in the euro area, which would not seem to be offset by the adoption of a common monetary policy.

Furthermore, scenarios three and four presented above (pp. 84–5) show that even if these inflation and GDP growth differentials are eliminated, there would not be sufficient room for maneuver to allow implementation of the plans to cut taxes put forward by individual national governments.

Recognizing that there is a lack of resources, to fund a reduction in fiscal pressure in Europe that is not accompanied by cuts in spending consistent with observance of the Stability Pact, raises the question of what room there is for maneuver, with revenues remaining constant, to generate changes in national fiscal systems. Account must also be taken here of the effects that a single monetary policy could have on deciding which taxes to cut in the presence of significant inflation differences.

According to the estimates of Leibfritz *et al.* (1997), for example, although it is difficult to quantify because of the possible inflationary effects and the uncertainty connected with shifts in taxation, changing the composition of taxes by 1 percent of GDP from tax on labor to tax on consumption could increase GDP by around 0.7 percent on average in Europe, with a greater effect estimated for the Netherlands (0.9 percent), Germany and France (0.8 percent in both cases).

Without going into problems connected with the feasibility of policies that reallocate taxation (see Chapters 2 and 3), one may first deduce that among countries in need of expansionary policies to boost growth in their economies, those subjected to particularly restrictive monetary policies would have more incentive to pursue expansionary fiscal policies or even inflationary policies designed to counter them. Observation of Table 3.3 shows that the Netherlands, Portugal, Finland, Germany, Italy and Austria are countries that might require expansionary fiscal policies. Of these, Germany and Austria experienced restrictive monetary policy in the three-year period 1999–2002, while the other four benefited from particularly favorable monetary conditions, the Netherlands and Portugal especially so. In a similar context, since Germany and Austria did not have the resources to fight fiscal pressure, they could on the other hand be motivated to change the composition of their taxes that, although it would fuel inflation, would stimulate growth and compensate for the restrictive monetary policy. On the other hand, a policy that increased consumption taxes would not be advisable at all for Italy and Portugal and would, in any case, be a difficult course to follow since they already suffer from high inflation.[5]

What therefore emerges, given the architecture of economic policies in Europe (euro area), is the possibility for some countries to change the rates of individual taxes and, as encouraged by the European Commission, to reduce the tax burden on labor in particular, since they are unable to reduce total fiscal pressure in the short term.

The other side of the coin, however, is that if such a phenomenon occurred, it would mean that the institutions and the rules that govern economic policy would show a propensity to encourage greater inflation. Free-riding phenomena might occur together with conflicting tariff policies that could hinder the central bank in its activity of maintaining price stability.

Some policy suggestions

The analysis proposed in this chapter has dwelt on various inconsistencies between the macroeconomic situation and the fiscal and monetary policies of Member States in the euro area. The emphasis has been placed on the divergence between GDP growth rates and real interest rates in different countries. It has been argued that, if this type of divergence is to be considered normal and taken for granted in the euro area, it is also true that the size of the differences has been particularly high as a result of an anomalous divergence of inflation rates. One would suppose that a process of catching up to reach common price levels was in progress. The lack of consistency between fiscal policies and interest rate levels should, in any case, constitute a transitory phenomenon. However it is worth noting that these phenomena could not only last a long time but also occur again when other countries join the euro area. We will now list some possible policy prescriptions for the coming years.

The large differences in inflation rates started with the exchange rate grid, which induced large gaps in price levels when countries first joined the euro. From this viewpoint, one policy prescription is that in future, new countries joining the single currency should preferably decide to fix their exchange rate in line with the euro for a very long period (of at least five or six years) before adopting it. Obviously this indication may result in other types of inconvenience which we will not dwell on here.

It has been found that inflation differences have generated government budget problems for countries with low inflation. One policy prescription is that these countries must not be doubly penalized because the Stability Pact obliges them to take substantial measures to reduce their current deficits, especially for those countries that do not have a high level of debt. In fact given that the overall situation of European public finances is quite sound from the viewpoint of stabilizing public debt, it would be wise to recommend a revision of the Stability Pact along those lines. This recommendation is particularly valid in the case of Germany that not only has a low rate of inflation but also the lowest economic growth rate.

The difficulty in reducing total fiscal pressure under the Stability Pact, together with the presence of inflation and economic growth differentials that are not attenuated by a common monetary policy, indicates the existence of incentives (or requirements) to change the composition of taxes that would lead to greater output growth, but also to increased prices.

The aspects mentioned here apply essentially to Germany, which is, at the moment, the economy most heavily penalized by the gap between its GDP growth rate and its interest rates. One possible alternative for the architecture of economic policies could consist of a special exception being made for Germany with regard to the balanced budget objective.

As a further comment to the results summarized here, it should be noted that none of the policy caveats we have proposed question the final objectives of European policies as described by the current ECB objectives and the Stability Pact. We have simply shown that the start of the euro represents a transitory phase (which may, however, be quite long) during which various one-off adjustments are occurring. These adjustments are modifying behavior patterns and making it more difficult to establish the outcomes of policies. The unusual uncertainty that characterizes the current phase would suggest cautious policies without over-ambitious objectives. Big changes can have unpredictable outcomes. However, setting targets for both public finances (balanced budgets) and for inflation (price stability) was very ambitious. While it is true that redesigning the objectives could have negative consequences in terms of loss of credibility, it must also be considered that wider margins for deviating from those objectives would allow the difficult phase we are going through to be managed with greater flexibility. These proposals have been partly adopted in the most recent policies which opted for maintaining rigid targets but allowing flexible interpretation (the "close to balance" clause; targets expressed in structural terms and to be fulfilled later than previously required). It is a useful compromise between the need to prevent fiscal squeezes in the current phase and to avoid the loss of credibility that would result from explicitly revising the objectives (Buti *et al.* 2003).

To conclude, however, one general result of the analysis conducted in this chapter is that policies to reduce tax burdens are incompatible with trying to achieve parity for general government structural balances over the next three years. Achievement of this dual objective can only be guaranteed by substantial (even if not advisable, from our point of view) cuts in spending, higher than those already planned by many countries in order to observe the constraints of the Stability Pact.

Notes

1 The authors thank Fabrizio Balassone, Luigi Bernardi and Pia Saraceno for their valuable comments without implicating them in any errors that may remain.
2 The figure for Finland should be read with caution since it is determined by its negative net financial liabilities.
3 This approach leaves aside arguments on the cyclical convergence of countries belonging to the European Union to concentrate on the cyclical positions of individual countries with respect to potential output. What results is that, although from a "European viewpoint" countries like the Netherlands, Ireland and Portugal should pursue restrictive economic policies to achieve convergence of GDP growth rates and price levels, from a "national" standpoint, their policies should be expansionary, since these countries are producing below their potential growth rates. This type of analysis therefore makes a far from negligible contribution to criticism of the soundness of the Stability Pact.
4 Basically it is hypothesized that the estimates of Leibfritz *et al.* (1997) continue to be valid in the short term as an impact on demand, if the reduction in taxation is funded with a budget surplus. In this manner the effects on the supply side generated by spending cuts are not considered. However, since they are medium- to long-term phenomena, they are unimportant for the purposes of our analysis.
5 Given the high inflation rates observed in these countries, this prescription holds even if the assumption that higher consumption taxes generate more inflation is not true in general.

References

Alberola, E. and Tyrvainen, T. (1998) "Is there scope for inflation differentials in EMU?," Bank of Finland Discussion Paper 15.
Buti, M., Eijffinger, S.C.W. and Franco, D. (2003) "Revisiting the Stability and Growth Pact: grand design or internal adjustment?," CEPR Discussion Paper 3692.
Canzoneri, M.B., Cumby, R.E., Diba, B. and Eudey, G. (2002) "Productivity trends in Europe: implications for real exchange rates, real interest rates & inflation," *Review of International Economics*, 10, 3: 497–516.
EU Commission (2002) "Public finances in EMU," *European Economy*, 3: 69–92.
Leibfritz, W., Thornton, J. and Bibbee, A. (1997) "Taxation and economic performance," Economic Department Working Paper 176, Paris: OECD.

Part II

National case studies of European tax systems and tax reforms

Luca Gandullia co-editor

5 France

Simona Scabrosetti

Introduction

This chapter aims to discuss the case of France, analyzing the most significant features of its tax system and its more recent changes and reforms.

Inside Europe, one can distinguish four models of tax system (Bernardi 2000): the dual income taxation (DIT) model, that is the system of Nordic countries, the UK (where one observes a reduced level of expenditure, overall tax pressure and social contributions for PAYG pensions), the Mediterranean model (with a low total fiscal pressure and rough welfare) and finally the Rhine model. France is the second European country, behind Germany, to show a very high overall fiscal burden according to this last model, characterized by a different mix of direct and indirect taxes and contributions to finance a very generous Bismarckian welfare state.

Later in this chapter (pp. 100–3), the development of the taxation system from the beginning of the 1970s to the end of the 1990s is considered. The fiscal burden is gradually increased in the long term: the most important changes concern social security contributions, and mainly PIT, whose revenue as a percentage of GDP has more than doubled. The level of tax on income and profits is also significant: thus, it can be predicted that the French tax system is characterized by a relevant tax wedge on labor. All this creates problems and shows the need for reforms since the tax wedge on labor is a concrete obstacle to the French development.

In relation to the main taxes, France is similar to other European countries. However, there are some peculiar elements. The PIT tax base is very narrow in France, the calculation of fiscal liability uses the "family quotient" method, introduced in 1945, and the level of tax progressivity is the highest in comparison with the other OECD countries, showing that PIT acts as a further burden on the highest income levels. There are six classes of income, the minimum rate, according to the Finance Law of 2001, is 7.50 percent whereas the maximum is 52.75 percent.

With reference to corporation tax, France adopts the imputation system and the principle of territoriality. In 2000 the net revenue from this tax was 37.30 billion euro whereas for 2001 it should rise to 42.57 billion euro.

Among direct taxes, France also has the *ISF* (*Impôt de Solidarité sur la Fortune*), a property tax, whereas VAT dominates within indirect taxes.

The state or the regions are the beneficiaries of the employers' contribution to the development of further vocational training, but the most important local taxes are the "*foncier bati*" tax, the "*foncier non bati*" tax, the "*taxe d'habitation*" and the "*taxe professionnelle.*"

Pages 112–15 examine the fiscal burden in France, either through the analysis of the distribution of taxation by economic functions or through the implicit tax rates. The high burden on labor predicted on pp. 99–103 is to be underlined: in fact, in the last 30 years, taxes on labor have increased by over nine percentage points of GDP, whereas the French trend of the implicit tax rate on employed labor has been very similar to the European one. Thus, in 2000, the tax wedge on labor in France occupied fifth place in the OECD list.

The taxes on consumption decreased slightly and, amongst those on capital, taxes on real estate and capital play the most important role. Finally, from the comparison between the effective marginal and average tax rates and the statutory rate, one can understand the wide tax discrimination in favor of debt financing that obviously discourages the firm's capitalization.

The final part of the chapter is devoted to fiscal reforms. The cuts in social security contributions at the lower end of the wage scale, started in 1993, wholly base themselves on the observation of the figures concerning the fiscal burden on labor. Another significant step forward in this direction was taken in 2001 with the introduction of the "employment bonus," a tax credit that will benefit some eight–ten million low-income households. At the moment then, the effects of the shift from labor to consumption or corporate income taxes is being studied with the aim to bring taxation to bear more on scarce resources, such as the environment, than on abundant ones, such as labor supply.

Tax reforms should aim to simplify and modernize the VAT system, whereas for the PIT a further reduction of the top marginal rate to reach 52.5 percent in 2003 should be considered.

When one talks about the changes of the corporate income tax, the need to strengthen the special regime for small enterprises and newly created companies and the neutrality of funding is highlighted. On the one hand, favored tax treatment will be able to compensate for the difficulty in raising finance and for the disproportionate costs stemming from administrative complexities. On the other hand, one will try to wipe out the wide discrimination in favor of the debt financing noted already.

Finally, the reinforcement of the relationship with the taxpayers and the improvement of the efficiency of the tax collection could be two measures not only to free up resources for beneficial uses, such as fighting tax evasion, but also to increase the fiscal revenues of local government.

All in all, after years of economic stagnation and unemployment, from 1997 France started its rapid growth: the efforts made to increase domestic demand and disposable income, to create jobs and reduce the labor costs, to consolidate the budget situation and bring down inflation and, finally, to improve business investments have been repaid.

However, other substantial improvements can and must be realized, also with reference to the structure of taxation in order to continue to grow on a sustainable basis and thus to overcome the slowdown largely caused by world uncertainty, increasingly palpable after the events of 11 September 2001. In particular, in order to continue to reduce taxes, it will be necessary to increase the efforts to control public expenditure, to prevent inflationary effects and to continue fiscal consolidation.

The structure of the system and its development from the 1970s

The current structure of the tax system and social security contributions

In France in 2001, the net borrowing of general government reached the level of 1.4 percent of GDP (EU Commission 2002), whereas in 1993 it was about 6 percent. Naturally this significant reduction was due to the Maastricht Treaty, requiring this value to be reduced to 3 percent, and to subsequent rules of the Stability and Growth Pact, that created a framework in which many EU countries have implemented fiscal consolidation efforts. The primary surplus represented 1.8 percent of GDP whereas the debt amounted to 57.6 percent of GDP, respecting also in this case the Maastricht roof of 60 percent. The total revenues of government in 2001 can be divided into three headings: taxes (27.7 percent of GDP), social contributions (18.1 percent) and other revenues, not of fiscal type (3.7 percent). The level of total expenditures is 52.6 percent of GDP and the primary expenditure amounts to 49.4 percent of GDP, with one of its main items, social monetary transfers, reaching 18.1 percent of the French GDP.

The French structure of taxation in 1999 (the last datum available) is depicted in Table 5.1 (see pp. 100–1 for the analysis of its development). The total fiscal revenue corresponds to 47 percent of GDP: the total tax revenue amounts to 29.5 percent of GDP, whereas the remaining part (17.5 percent of GDP) is represented by social security contributions. In France, like in other OECD countries, social security contributions are the largest single source of general government revenue. The so-called "Bismarckian model" remains the foundation of the social security system in most European countries and it justifies the dominant role of such contributions (Economic Outlook 2001a). According to this model, the government provides social security as a special form of insurance, while benefits and contributions are tied to the wages of workers. Among the chargeable persons, employers play the most important role: their share of the social contributions is 70 percent of the total.

Direct taxes reach 13.9 percent of GDP, almost 30 percent of the total fiscal pressure and they are dominated by the personal income tax, corporation tax being only 2.6 percentage points of GDP.

As concerns indirect taxes, a fast growing revenue source is general consumption tax, especially the value-added tax (VAT). In fact, the substantially increased importance of VAT has served to counteract the diminishing share of specific consumption taxes, such as excises and custom duties. In 1999, French VAT was 0.6 percentage points higher than the European average, whereas the excise duties only totalled 3 percent of GDP.

We can also underline that the share of central government on total tax revenues is higher than the underestimated (because of their various sharing to national taxes) share of local authorities (regions, municipalities) even if the latter has increased over the past 17 years. In 1999 it is 4.7 percent of GDP, a little more than one-fifth of the central government's share.

Within this French fiscal outline, the most important taxes are personal income tax, corporation tax, taxes on financial activities, *ISF*, VAT, excise duties, employers' contribution to the development of further vocational training and the "*taxe professionnelle.*"

We will come back to these subjects in the following paragraphs.

Developments of the system from 1970 to 1999

According to available data and estimates (Table 5.1), in France the share of taxes and social contributions in the GDP increased slightly by 2.2 percentage points to 47 percent between 1995 and 1999. In 1999 the total fiscal revenue was 5.3 percentage points higher than in 1980 and 12 percentage points higher than in 1970. The relatively high tax-to-GDP ratio that we observe today is, to a large extent, due to tax increases in the 1970s, in the 1980s, and, though smaller, in the 1990s: however, recent developments suggest that this trend may be ending.

The share of indirect taxes as a percentage of GDP increased by slightly more than half a point between 1970 (15 percent) and 1999 (15.6 percent), straying under the threshold of 15 percent only at the beginning of the 1990s. The main changes in indirect taxation occurred in the 1970s when the falling of general sales or turnover taxes was only partly balanced by VAT. In particular, the share of VAT in GDP decreased significantly from 1970 (8.9 percent) to 1993 (7.3 percent), reaching 7.9 percent in 1999. Revenues from excise duties remained almost stable at around 3 percent of GDP, whereas other indirect taxes in France still play an important role at the end of 1990s with the growth of their tax burden at 0.4 percentage points from 1993 to 1997.

The share of direct taxes as a percentage of GDP was around 13.9 percent in 1999: there was a big rise of two percentage points between 1975 (7.4 percent) and 1985 (9.4 percent) whereas in the following ten years the increase was more moderate (nearly 0.8 percent). Therefore, the evolution of direct taxes was not smooth. It was affected either by the corporate income tax trend, that stood at about 2.6 percent of GDP in 1999, approximately one percentage point more than in 1993, or by the personal income taxation trend: its revenues, always as a percentage of GDP, are more than doubled compared with 1970. The growth of income tax revenues depended on the significant economic growth during the period. Such growth increased the revenues from most taxes, but had a particularly strong influence on income tax revenue. In the case of personal income taxes, this is because of their progressive rate structure; in the case of corporate income tax, because corporate profits tend to increase more in proportion to output. Direct taxes other than those on personal or corporate income still play a minor role: in 1999 they represented 1 percent of French GDP.

As the tax-to-GDP ratio has risen, the largest part of the increase has taken the form of higher social security contributions: the expanding share of these contributions seems to be directly linked to the upward pressure on aggregate benefit spending arising from higher unemployment, aging population and rising government expenditure on healthcare programs, that is, to the expansion of social insurance systems substantially financed by such contributions. In 1970 they were 12.7 percent of GDP, whereas 25 years later their share increased by 6.7 percentage points to 19.4 percent (Table 5.1). At the end of the 1990s, social contributions represented 17.5 percent of GDP. However, their percentage of total taxation is almost the same as in 1970: as a matter of fact, the most important increase concerns the 1980s and the beginning of the 1990s. Later, there was a weak but continuous reduction, reaching 17.5 percent in 1999.

A comparative view against the European average

The tax burden in the European area, defined as the ratio of government fiscal receipts to GDP is very high as for international standards: in 1999, it was 43.1 percent of GDP. France is generally in line with the European average, and this was especially true in the 1970s. In the 1980s and 1990s, however, the difference becomes more marked: in 1985, for instance, it was 4.6 percentage points. Ten years later, total fiscal revenues in France amounted to 44.8 percent of GDP, whereas in Europe they were around 42 percent. On the other hand, in 1999 French fiscal burden exceeded the European average by four percentage points (Table 5.1).

Differences in the tax burden across Member States are especially due

Table 5.1 Structure and development of fiscal revenue in France and European average as a percentage of GDP, 1970–99

	1970		1975		1980		1985		1990		1995		1999	
	France	Europe	France	Europe	France	Europe	France	Europe	France	Europe	France	Europe	France	Europe
Direct taxes, of which	7.3	8.9	7.4	11.9	8.6	12.7	9.4	13.1	9.4	13.2	10.2	13.3	13.9	14.5
personal income	4.4	5.5	4.6	8.9	5.5	9.3	6.2	9.0	5.8	8.9	7.3	9.6	10.4	9.9
corporation income	2.2	2.2	1.9	1.9	2.1	2.2	2.0	2.8	2.4	2.9	1.9	2.4	2.6	2.8
Indirect taxes, of which	15.0	13.0	14.5	12.2	15.3	13.2	15.8	13.0	15.1	13.0	15.2	15.1	15.6	14.6
VAT	8.9	5.1	8.5	5.7	8.6	6.6	8.6	6.1	8.0	6.6	7.6	6.9	7.9	7.3
excise duties	2.9	3.5	2.6	3.5	2.8	3.2	3.0	3.2	2.8	3.1	3.1	3.4	3.0	3.5
Total tax revenue	22.3	21.9	21.9	24.1	23.9	25.9	25.2	26.1	24.5	26.2	25.4	26.9	29.5	29.1
Social contributions	12.7	11.7	15.0	12.8	17.8	13.4	19.3	13.8	19.3	13.7	19.4	15.0	17.5	14.0
employers	9.3	7.2	10.8	7.7	11.9	7.8	12.5	7.9	11.9	7.8	12.0	8.0	12.3	7.8
employees	2.4	3.5	3.2	3.8	4.6	4.3	5.2	4.5	5.8	4.5	5.9	5.1	4.2	4.5
self-employed	1.0	1.0	1.0	1.3	1.3	1.3	1.5	1.5	1.6	1.4	1.5	1.8	1.1	1.7
Total fiscal revenue	35.0	33.6	36.9	36.9	41.7	39.3	44.5	39.9	43.8	39.9	44.8	41.9	47.0	43.1
Administrative level														
Central government	20.4	19.7	18.9	21.1	20.3	22.3	20.5	22.1	19.5	22.2	20.1	22.5	21.8	23.7
Local government	2.1	2.2	2.8	2.8	3.0	2.9	3.9	3.1	4.1	3.8	4.4	4.0	4.7	4.3

Sources: 1970–95, Eurostat; New Cronos databank 2002 (data equalized with Eurostat, 2000).

Note
Minor items are omitted.

to the weight of the public sector in the economy. There is a close relation between tax receipts and government expenditure as percentage of GDP. The long-term increase in the overall tax burden is closely related to the growing share of the public sector: taxes are upped to finance-increasing levels of spending. The overall tax burden has risen considerably during the past 30 years and, at the same time, the tax structures in Member States have undergone major changes, especially because of increased international tax competition that has played an important role in the convergence of the effective tax rates of the tax systems within the EU.

The most striking feature of these past developments has been the increasing tax burden on labor in order to finance welfare spending, such as pensions, healthcare and other social benefits. For just this reason, France recently followed the example of the USA, the UK, New Zealand and Canada: such schemes aim to increase participation to work of people eligible for unemployment compensation or welfare benefits. This is considered to be effective in encouraging labor supply, particularly if associated with a minimum wage, at a reasonable level, that must be fixed in order to minimize its effects on labor market flexibility.

As concerns direct taxes, France has always been under the European average: from 1995 in France they exceeded 10 percent of GDP, whereas at the European level, they are around 13 percent of GDP (Table 5.1).

Now, we consider indirect taxes: their evolution, compared to that of direct taxes, shows that their share as percentage of GDP has been, from the 1970s, higher than the European average by about two percentage points.

Some quantitative and institutional features of main taxes

*The personal income tax – PIT (*Impôt sur le revenu*)*

This tax is paid by the individual. In the case of partnerships which have not opted to pay corporation tax, the tax is payable by each partner.

The basis of assessment is the total net income, determined according to the formula applicable to each type of income (including income from foreign sources in cases where taxpayers are resident in France), less any legally deductible expenses (such as maintenance payments, cost of accommodating an elderly person and aggregate underpayments from previous years) (EU Commission 2001). In other words, the taxable income is a global income. It includes the totality of net incomes belonging to the following categories: salaries, wages, pensions, private income, life annuity, revenues of movable capital, plus values, land revenues, revenues and along with values of non-salaried professions.

The exemptions (Table 5.2) concern persons whose net income does not exceed the minimum guaranteed of €5,994.55 or the fixed value of €7,250: this threshold rises to €7,920 for people over the age of 65;

Table 5.2 Some measures for the calculation of PIT

Measures	Year 2000	Year 2001
Exemptions		
Minimum guaranteed	up to 38,650 F	up to €5,994.55
Low income (people under the age of 65)	up to 46,800 F	up to €7,250
Low income (people over the age of 65)	up to 51,100 F	up to €7,920
Deductions		
Deduction of 10% of the declared wage or salary	from 2,350 F to 78,950 F	from €364 to €12,229
Abatement of 10% granted for pensions	from 2,080 F to 20,400 F	from €323 to €3,160
Abatement of 20%	up to 722,000 F	up to €111,900
Abatement of €1,590 for elderly or disabled people		up to €9,790
Abatement of €795 for elderly or disabled people		from €9,790 to €15,820

Source: MINEFI (Ministère de l'Économie, des Finances et de l'Industrie) 2002.

interest on certain government loans; certain pensions, benefits and allowances and capital gains. The personal income tax is, however, payable on capital gains realized by individuals when they transfer assets, rights of any kind and securities for a valuable consideration, although there are numerous exemptions from this requirement.

There are then specific deductions (Table 5.2) for all expenses involved in earning or maintaining income. In the case of employees, occupational expenses are fixed, as a general rule, at 10 percent of the declared wage or salary, with a minimum of €364 and a maximum of €12,229 applying to expenses incurred in the 2001 tax year. An allowance of 10 percent is granted for pensions and free life annuities; this allowance may not exceed €3,160 for total pensions received by a household. In the case of salaries, wages, pensions and free life annuities, a personal allowance of 20 percent is granted up to a legally declared income level, after the specific deductions, of €111,900. This treatment also concerns, in certain cases, craftspeople, tradesmen, merchants, industrialists and farmers who have joined registered management centers and persons who have joined registered associations open to members of the professions and to holders of public office. Individuals aged 65 or over and disabled persons qualify for a tax allowance of €1,590 if their total net income is less than €9,790. A reduced allowance of €795 is granted to individuals aged 65 or over or disabled persons whose total net income is between €9,790 and €15,820 (EU Commission 2001).

To mitigate the tax burden of the families, the use of the family quotient has been introduced (law 31 December 1945) in the calculation of fiscal liability: family incomes are aggregated, but the aggregate income is divided by a number of points, awarded on the basis of the taxpayer's family situation (the family quotient). The progressive rate is applied to this resulting income; finally, this partial tax is multiplied by the number of points to determine the recoverable tax. However, the advantage derived from the use of this method is subject to an upper limit.

The Financial Law for 2002 (art. 2, *CGI*,[1] art. 197–I–2°) has brought the roof resulting from the application of the family quotient from 12,440F to €2,017. For single, divorced or separated taxpayers, the roof of the tax allowance joined to the first dependant child goes from 21,930F to €3,490 in 2001. Moreover, the roof of 6,220F granted to single taxpayers who have brought up one or more children, the last aged more than 26, is fixed at €964 for 2001, whereas tax reduction for beneficiaries is €570.

There is also a tax reduction, concerning expenses for (mainly nursery-school) children, of 25 percent of the sum paid in 2001 up to €2,300 per child. On the other hand, €61, €153 and €183 are the tax reductions as a child goes on to a different level of school.

The rates and the income classes for 2001 are indicated in Table 5.3: the Finance Law of this year has reduced the first four rates by 0.75 percent and the last two by 0.5 percent.

Corporation tax – CT (*Impôt sur les sociétés*)

The profits of businesses operating in France are the basis of assessment (principle of territoriality). According to a strict definition (art. 38, 2° sub, *CGI*), these profits comprise the difference between the value of net assets at the end of the financial year and their value at the beginning of the same financial year, plus payments to shareholders less additional injections of capital (Monaco 1999). In practice, a company's profit is determined on the basis of its annual accounts, with adjustments in the

Table 5.3 Personal income tax, 2001

Income classes	Rates (%)
Up to €4,121	0.00
€4,121–€8,104	7.50
€8,104–€14,264	21.00
€14,264–€23,096	31.00
€23,096–€37,579	41.00
€37,579–€46,343	46.75
over €46,343	52.75

Source: MINEFI 2002.

form of statistical deductions and additions to take account of specific fiscal rules.

The bodies exempted from payment, subject to certain conditions, include regions, departments, municipalities, farmers' associations and cooperatives, housing associations, investment companies and societies whose aim is to make goods available to their members.

The standard rate is one-third, but a reduced rate of 19 percent applies to long-term capital gains, except for certain capital gains of a financial nature. A rate of 24 percent or 10 percent applies to income from real estate or farming and to certain types of income from movable property accruing to public institutions engaged in administrative activity, to civic associations and to non-profit organizations (EU Commission 2001). According to the last finance laws, the different effective rates of the corporation tax for 2002 are indicated in Table 5.4.

For companies with a turnover lower than €7,630,000 and capital owned for at least 75 percent by individuals or by similar firms, the rate for the first €38,120 is reduced to 25 percent for 2001 and to 15 percent for 2002.

Dividends that parent companies receive from their French or foreign branches are subtracted from total net profit after a deduction of 5 percent of total dividends, tax credit included. A longstanding issue is that double taxation of distributed profits, first at the corporate level and subsequently at the shareholders' level, can produce a high combined tax rate on equity. Therefore, France, along with some other countries, adopted a system that grants a tax credit to dividend recipients corresponding to the corporate tax on distributed profits.

New companies and those that are installed in sectors needing development can benefit from these temporary exemptions if they satisfy particular requirements. Moreover, in addition to special regimes and allowances, France grants simplified tax filing to small businesses. These measures are designed to offset the disadvantages of new or small enterprises in financing their investment projects, but also to reach equity objectives.

Table 5.4 Corporation tax, 2002

PME[1] exempted from social contribution		*Other than PME (turnover exceeds €7,630,000)*
Up to €38,120	15.45%	profits $34\frac{1}{3}$%–35.43%
over €38,120	$34\frac{1}{3}$%	long-term plus values 19.57%–20.20%
long-term plus values	19.57%	

Source: MINEFI 2002.

Note

1 Petites et moyennes enterprises. This social contribution is calculated with reference to the fiscal liability reduced by an annual abatement that can't exceed €762,245. The rate is 3.3%.

Expenses and charges are deductible on certain conditions:

- they must refer to normal management of the company;
- they must be justified and related to the company's aim;
- they must determine a reduction of the company's net profit;
- their deduction must not be hampered by a particular provision of law.

At the same time, long-term plus-values are deducted from profit and taxed separately at the reduced rate of 19 percent.

The tax credit attached to companies' distributed earnings under the imputation system may be offset in full against tax liability but it is not refundable in principle.

Losses may be either carried forward for a period of five years or, under certain conditions, carried back three years. Depreciation postponed during a loss-making period may be carried forward with no time limit.

All companies also have to pay an annual flat rate according to their turnover, but only if this exceeds €76,000. Furthermore Financial Law of 4 August 1995 has committed corporate bodies to a contribution of 10 percent of corporate income. The rate of this contribution was reduced to 6 percent for 2001 and 3 percent for 2002 (Financial Law for 2001).

Special features are:

- consolidated-group liability: subject to certain conditions, a parent company holding at least 95 percent of the dividends and voting rights of subsidiary companies may assume sole liability for the corporation tax payable by those subsidiaries;
- consolidated-profits regime: when a parent company directly or indirectly holds at least 50 percent of voting rights of other companies in France and abroad, its taxable profit is computed by adding the profits of those other companies;
- worldwide-profits regime: profits and losses, calculated in accordance with French rules, of direct operations abroad are consolidated with the taxable profits of French companies.

Taxation of income from financial capital

As concerns the taxation of financial activities, France applies an imputation system on dividends: they are taxed according to the personal income tax of the shareholders with right to a tax credit (*avoir fiscal*) equal to 50 percent of the dividends. This imputation system does not give any relief to residents who are shareholders in companies established in other countries, with respect to corporate income tax already paid in those countries, while it does for resident companies. However, owing to bilateral tax treaties with certain countries, France grants refundable tax credits to non-residents.

Capital gains deriving from the transfer of shares, bonds and some non-quoted stocks is taxable if the total amount earned (in 2001) exceeded the threshold of €7,623. Therefore only values over this threshold are completely taxable: they are subjected to PIT and the rate is 16 percent plus 10 percent as a social withdrawal.[2] The same treatment is valid for financial profits even if in this case there is not the above-mentioned threshold: so they are always taxable.

The taxation of interest income from government bonds in France only concerns residents and the rate is 15 percent. The withholding tax can be final if the taxpayer so decides. Otherwise, interest income can be included into the taxable income and taxed at the individual's marginal rate.

Certain national savings products are tax-exempt while other short-term products are withheld from 15 percent up to 50 percent when unnamed (Joumard 2001).

ISF (Impôt de Solidarité sur la Fortune)

As concerns property taxation, we consider the institutional structure of the *ISF*. It must be paid by individuals, with fiscal residence in France or abroad owning, on 1 January 2002, a taxable property valued at over €720,000.

The tax is payable on movable goods and real estate, rights and values composing the property, not exempted and belonging to family. The rates and the property classes are indicated in Table 5.5. Total burden is reduced by €150 for dependants.

Finally in the framework of direct taxes we can mention the land tax and the taxes on dwellings.

Value added tax – VAT (TVA)

VAT (*Taxe sur la valeur ajoutée – TVA*) dominates among indirect taxes. The beneficiary is the state, but a levy of 0.7 percent, whose revenue is

Table 5.5 ISF, 2002

Net patrimony value	Rates (%)
Up to €720,000	0.00
€720,000 –€1,160,000	0.55
€1,160,000 –€2,300,000	0.75
€2,300,000 –€3,600,000	1.00
€3,600,000 –€6,900,000	1.30
€6,900,000 –€15,000,000	1.65
over €15,000,000	1.80

Source: MINEFI 2002.

assigned to the special budget for agricultural welfare benefits, is included in each of the VAT rates.

The tax must be paid, in general terms, on the supply of movable goods, the provision of services and other equivalent operations carried out by taxable persons within an economic activity of industrial, commercial, creative, professional, agricultural or civic nature; on the importation of goods; on the acquisitions of movable tangible property made by taxable persons or non-taxable legal persons from taxable persons established in other Member States of the European Union, with certain exceptions and equivalent transactions; on the operations explicitly ordained by law, such as those effected by cooperatives, those connected with real estate, self-supply and purchases of certain products from persons not liable to VAT; on the operations which are not affected by the VAT legislation or are exempt from VAT, but for which the law provides the possibility of opting for this indirect tax, for example certain local authority services.

VAT is collected in connection with the supply of goods or the provision of a service: in this case it's a tax chargeable on receipt of payment. In relation to transfer of ownership, importation, purchase or intra-community acquisition, VAT is chargeable on the fifteenth day of the following month or on the date of the invoice, depending on the nature of the taxable transaction.

The basis of assessment is represented by prices or fees for goods and services, including all applicable charges and taxes other than VAT.

The main exemptions are the following:

- exports and equivalent transactions, but also certain imports;
- certain banking and financial operations;
- activities subject to local entertainments tax such as sporting events, gaming clubs and casinos;
- certain activities carried out by non-profit organizations, government bodies or local authorities;
- certain real-estate operations;
- medical and paramedical activities;
- educational activities.

With some exceptions, VAT paid on the purchase of goods or services for business use is deductible from VAT due in respect of sales. Taxpayers can obtain a quarterly or yearly refund of any overpaid VAT (EU Commission 2001).

The three different rates are (from 1 April 2000):

- standard rate of 19.6 percent;
- reduced rate of 5.5 percent particularly for agricultural products, most foodstuffs, books and theater and cinema tickets;

- minimum rate of 2.1 percent particularly for medicinal products and newspapers.

There are also other rates concerning specific operations in Corsica and in *DOM–TOM* (*Domaines d'outre mer–Territoires d'outre mer*).

Excise duties

The excise duty on mineral-oil and allied products is another example of an important indirect tax payable by the importers, manufacturers and distributors of mineral-oil products who sell these products for consumption. It is levied on mineral-oil and allied products which are used as heating or motor fuels at the point when they are distributed for consumption. Annual rates, as fixed by the Finance Act 1999 (article 26), are indicated in Table 5.6. Article 26V of the Finance Act 1999 established a partial refund of the excise duty on diesel for road haulage vehicles weighing 12 tonnes and over; this refund is granted on the first 40,000 litres per vehicle/year.

Tobacco duty is collected when tobacco products are supplied for consumption. The basis of assessment is the retail price and the standard rates (as percentage of the retail price) referred to different product groups are indicated in Table 5.7.

As concerns the manufactured (Continental France and Corsica) tobaccos, the rate is 0.74 percent of the selling price excluding tax. The beneficiary of this duty is the special budget for agricultural welfare benefits (BAPSA).

Finally, spirits duty is payable on intermediate products and spirits and is levied either per hectolitre of the finished product or on the basis of the pure alcohol content per hectolitre. There is no export duty, whereas, as

Table 5.6 Excise duty on mineral-oil and allied products, 1999

Product designation	1999 rate (in €)	Taxable unit
Leaded petrol		
High-octane leaded petrol	63.36	100 litres
Unleaded petrol		
High-octane unleaded petrol	53.15	100 litres
Diesel	37.83	100 litres
LPG and methane		
as motor fuels	10.02	100 kg net
as heating fuels		
Heavy fuel oil for heating	2.31	100 kg net
Liquid paraffin		
kerosene motor fuel	37.83	100 litres
paraffin oil for heating	7.85	100 litres

Source: art. 26 Finance Act 1999.

Table 5.7 Tobacco duty

Product group	Standard rate (%)
Cigarettes	58.30
Cigars	28.86
Finely-cut tobacco for rolling cigarettes	51.00
Other smoking tobacco	46.74
Snuff	40.20
Chewing tobacco	27.47

Source: Directory of taxes, EU Commission 2001.

regards imports, the tariff applies to all taxable liquids, regardless of their origin. The beneficiary is the old-age solidarity fund (*Fonds de solidarité vieillesse*), but part of the revenue from the duty levied according to the article 403 of the General Tax Code is also allocated to the compulsory health-insurance schemes (EU Commission 2001).

Employers' contribution to the development of further vocational training

Employers have to reserve a minimum percentage of their annual wage bill to the funding of training measures. The beneficiaries are state-registered joint collection bodies and national or regional government training centers; the state or the regions and the state's general budget for the amount resulting from total contributions minus expenditure allocated to training measures. The tax must be paid by all employers, the exemptions concern the state, the local authorities and their public administrative establishments.

The rates, up to 1999, are:

1 1.5 percent of the annual wage bill for employers with an annual average of at least ten employees. For businesses engaged in temporary work, the rate is 2 percent. These rates include a payment of 0.3 percent or 0.4 percent, depending on whether or not the employer is liable for apprenticeship tax, for sandwich-course training and a levy of 0.2 percent (0.3 percent for businesses engaged in temporary work) for individual educational leave;
2 0.15 percent for employers with an annual average of fewer than ten employees, plus a levy of 0.1 percent, which concerns only the employers who are liable for apprenticeship tax.

In addition, all employers must pay a specific contribution of 1 percent of wages and salaries distributed to employees on fixed-term contracts.

The basis of assessment is gross pay, i.e. prior to deduction of national insurance contributions (EU Commission 2001).

Local taxes

The "*taxe professionnelle*" must be paid by individuals and corporate bodies that usually practice a professional non-salaried activity in France. It's an important local tax whose relevance has decreased in recent years.

The basis of assessment is formed by two elements: first, the locative value of immobilizations used to practice the activity; second, either 18 percent of the wages of the executives with an abatement of €152,449.01 (1,000,000F) for 2001 (€914,694.10 for 2002) or one-tenth of the revenues for activities with less than five wage-earners. In 2003 the wage component will be abolished.

According to article 1647E of the *CGI*, companies with a turnover that exceeds €7,622,450.86 (50 million Francs) must pay a "*cotisation minimale*," concerning the annual added value, at a rate of 1.2 percent for 2000 and 1.5 percent from 2001. There is also (*CGI*, art. 1648D) a "*cotisation nationale de péréquation*" to guarantee fiscal uniformity among commons.

Finally, one can observe two kinds of exemptions: permanent and temporary. The first concern the agricultural (*CGI*, art. 63), artisan (*CGI*, art. 1452–5) and some industrial, commercial, non-commercial and social activities. The second can be either geographically limited or applied to the whole territory.

Among local taxes, one can also consider the "*foncier bati*" tax, the "*foncier non bati*" tax and the "*taxe d'habitation*," that is real estate taxes (Liberati 2000). The first and the second are very similar, even if the "*foncier bati*" tax concerns rented built estate whereas the "*foncier non bati*" tax concerns any other kind of rented estate (mines, ponds, etc.). In both cases, the basis of assessment is the opportunely appropriate ratable value, but there is an abatement of 30 percent and 20 percent respectively.

The "*taxe d'habitation*" calculated with reference to the locative ratable value and intended to finance the communities' budgets, is a more "personal" tax: in fact there are basis of assessment abatements linked to the family situation of the taxpayer. The rate can noticeably change; for instance in 2001 for communities it was 10.38 percent whereas for departments it was 5.86 percent. Finally, if the locative value exceeds 30,000F there is also a withdrawal on behalf of the state. In this case, the rates can vary from 0.2 percent to 1.7 percent.

The fiscal burden

The distribution of taxation charge

The distribution of taxation by economic functions (Table 5.8) points out on which economic activity or on which production factor a tax is levied and provides an indicator of the discriminative effects of the tax

Table 5.8 Structure according to the economic function as a percentage of GDP

	1970	1975	1980	1985	1990	1995	1997
Consumption	12.8	11.7	12.1	12.3	11.6	11.4	11.8
Labor	16.4	18.9	22.6	24.3	24.0	25.3	25.7
employed	15.0	17.5	20.8	22.2	21.9	23.2	23.5
self-employed	1.4	1.4	1.8	2.1	2.1	2.1	2.2
Capital, of which	5.8	6.4	7.0	7.8	8.2	8.1	8.9
real estate and capital	2.1	2.6	2.7	3.1	3.1	3.5	3.9
monetary capital	0.4	0.6	0.7	0.8	0.5	0.2	0.2
Environment	2.1	1.8	2.2	2.4	2.4	2.6	2.6
energy	1.8	1.4	1.8	2.0	1.9	2.0	2.0
transport	0.2	0.2	0.3	0.3	0.3	0.3	0.3
pollution	0.1	0.1	0.2	0.2	0.2	0.3	0.3
Total	35.1	36.9	41.7	44.5	43.8	44.8	46.4

Source: Eurostat (2000).

Note
1997 is the last datum available.

system. It can also show the need to shift the French tax burden: for instance, it could be moved away from labor to real capital and environmental taxes.

One can distinguish the following categories: consumption, labor employed, labor self-employed, capital. Environmental taxes, split into taxes on energy, transport, pollution and the use of natural resources, are shown as an "of which" category, since they are usually also consumption or capital taxes.

From 1985 to 1995 in France, the taxation of consumption, measured as a percentage of GDP, decreased by one percentage point, especially because of the fall of revenues from VAT. In the second half of the 1990s, there was an increase up to 11.8 percent of GDP in 1997.

The burden on labor is very high: during the years considered, it increased by 9.3 percentage points up to 25.7 percent of GDP. However the most significant rise happens between 1975 and 1985, when the taxes on labor represent more than 24 percent of GDP.

The share of taxes and contributions belonging to the "employed" category is the most significant: as a matter of fact it always represents 90 percent of taxes on labor even if, in the 1990s, the category "self-employed" exceeded the threshold of 2 percent of GDP. On the other hand, in the long run, the difference between employers and employees, within employed labor, has become less and less significant: only 1.4 percentage points in 1997 against 4.5 in 1975.

From 1970 to 1997 (the last datum available) the taxation on capital as a percentage of GDP also increased, if one does not consider the slight fall in 1992. Despite its name, the category "capital" comprises not only taxes which are directly linked to capital but also taxes which are levied on operating a business, therefore it is even subdivided.

In Table 5.8 we report only the typical kinds of capital: taxes on real estate and taxes on real capital that are all taxes on the ownership, the income from or the transaction in real estate/real capital and taxes on monetary capital that are instead taxes on interests, bank transactions, etc.

The largest part of capital taxation stems, as a matter of fact, from the taxation of real estate and capital: in 1997 it represented 3.9 percent of GDP. The second biggest capital taxes are those on non-allocable incomes. Since 1975 their ratio to GDP has increased from 2.2 percent to 2.6 percent. On the other hand, the tax burdens on monetary capital, wealth and business seem firm, at least in the 1990s.

Finally, between 1980 and 1997, revenues from environmental taxes have increased by 0.4 percentage points up to 2.6 percent. This corresponds to an increase from 5.3 percent to 5.6 percent of total taxation. The growth is almost exclusively the result of higher energy tax revenues which reached the threshold of 2 percent of GDP. The taxation of transport remained constant at around 0.3 percent when measured as a percentage of GDP and the same argument is also valid for taxes on pollution or on the use of natural resources.

A very useful indicator to study the distribution of the fiscal burden in a country is also the implicit tax rate. This is calculated by dividing the revenues from taxes on a special activity or good by an appropriate corresponding aggregate tax base from national account statistics.

The definitions of implicit tax rate to which we refer are those provided by Eurostat. However, the calculation procedure of these tax rates is somewhat controversial and different definitions may provide different values.

The trends of the implicit tax rates in France from 1970 to 1997 relating to labor, consumption and other factors are shown by Figure 5.1.

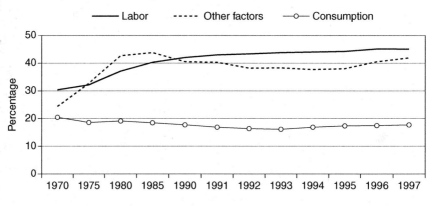

Figure 5.1 France: implicit rates 1970–97.

Source: Eurostat (2000).

At 44.9 percent in 1997, the implicit tax rate on labor is over 14 percentage points higher than at the beginning of the 1970s. However, the evolution of this indicator, that was sustained by income tax and social contributions, is quite stable. From 1973 to 1984, it increased steadily by 0.9 percentage points per year on average, and since then its growth was more moderate: an average of 0.3 percentage points a year.

The implicit tax rate on productive factors other than employed labor has again increased and is more than ten percentage points above the Union's average. This very irregular evolution is mainly the result of a temporary growth in the corporate tax rate.

The most stable is the implicit tax rate on consumption: perhaps the choice of leaving consumption taxation, whose role in France has diminished over recent years, under the threshold of 18 percent as from the 1990s was due to the supposed regressivity of these taxes and to anti-inflationary goals.

We turn now to analyze the equity issue, focusing on the redistributive effects of the PIT in France. Our focus on the PIT, and the consequent exclusion of all other taxes, is obviously somewhat restrictive, especially if one considers that in France social security contributions and indirect taxes are very important in the structure of taxation. However, following this line of argument does not lead to any firm conclusion. Moreover, policy makers seem to accept that income redistribution is a particular policy goal of the PIT, whereas the same cannot be argued for many other taxes.

Usually, the impact of a tax on the distribution of income is measured using the difference between the pre-tax and post-tax Gini coefficients. This measure of redistributive effect depends mainly on two factors: the average tax rate and the progressivity of the tax, calculated with the progressivity index proposed by Kakwany.

Among the OECD countries, according to Wagstaff *et al.* (1999), France shows the lowest difference between Gini coefficients on gross and net incomes (RE = 0.0154), the lowest average tax rate and the highest level of tax progressivity. All this means that, in France, the PIT acts as a further burden on the highest income levels. Therefore income redistribution is an important objective of the French tax system and it is mainly reflected in the highly progressive tax schedule of the personal income tax. However, for low-income working families with children, the French tax system compares poorly with other EU countries, such as Germany and the UK, where there are positive transfers for the most needy, perhaps because the PIT tax base is very narrow in France (Joumard 2001).

Tax wedges on labor and corporate taxation

The tax wedge on labor measures the distortion in the decision of using an additional labor unit. Thus it reveals if the taxation brings differences between marginal labor productivity and net wage.

The French marginal tax wedge on labor is perfectly aligned with the average of the EU area countries, approximately 53 percent (Joumard 2001).

In 2000, the French average tax wedge on labor, after the reduction of five percentage points compared to the beginning of the 1990s, was instead around 48 percent, a little higher than the EU average that reached 44–45 percent. The shares of personal income tax and employees' social security contributions appear very similar, whereas employers' social security contributions count for almost 30 percent by themselves.

Finally the difference with the OECD average is more significant: about 15 percentage points for average tax wedge and 12 percentage points for marginal tax wedge on labor. The high level of the wedge, not only in France but also in the whole of Europe, is one of the main problems faced by European fiscal systems: in fact it depresses employment and growth, either from the side of supply, or from the side of labor demand (Petretto 2002).

We can consider then the distortion on the location and on the choices of investment caused by the taxation system, focusing on the relationship between the effective marginal tax rate, the effective average tax rate (at a probability rate of 20 percent) and the statutory rate (Giannini and Maggiulli 2001). The first is usually lower than the second because of the benefits of tax allowances from the tax base, i.e. for depreciation and interest payments. On the other hand, the statutory rate only gives some information, which can be useful at a first glance, but to have a more precise assessment of the tax burden charged on corporations, one must refer to the effective rates.

These rates may be "backward looking" or "forward looking." The first are useful mainly to compare the distribution of the tax burden among different firms or over time, or with respect to other taxation basis or to changes in tax code (Giannini and Maggiulli 2001). Joumard (2001) reports an estimate according to which, in the middle of the 1990s, the backward effective rate of corporate taxation in France was nearly three points under the "all-in" statutory rate.

According to the Devereux and Griffith methodology (Giannini and Maggiulli 2001), as concerns "forward looking" rates, we can refer either to effective marginal tax rate (EMTR), when the real before-tax return is the minimum rate required to undertake the investment or to the effective average tax rate (EATR) when the investment project generates economic rents.

On the one hand when the source of finance is equity, there was not much difference between the French effective marginal (about 45 percent) and average tax rate (about 42 percent) in 1999: moreover, the first tax rate was very high compared to other European countries and slightly greater than the statutory rate (40 percent), a situation that considerably differs, for instance, from the Italian one.

On the other hand, when investment is financed using debt, the effective marginal tax rate is negative (about −10 percent) because of the interaction between interest payments deducibility and tax allowances. The effective average tax rate is instead positive: it reaches 30 percent and the jump is fairly consistent.

The results show that the potential distortion introduced by the French tax system in the allocation of capital is high and that there is a wide tax discrimination in favor of debt financing.

Taxation by levels of government and fiscal federalism

The share of total tax revenues (excluding social security contributions) that goes to central government is clearly over 50 percent. However, from 1975 to 1999, it fell respectively from 86.3 percent to 74 percent of total tax revenues (Table 5.1).

On the other hand, there has been some rise in the attribution of tax revenues to local government such as the growth of 0.4 point from 1985 to 1999 as a percentage of total tax revenue. In 1999, the local share of fiscal revenues was 4.7 as a percentage of GDP, twice as much compared to 1970.

Communes played the most important role in the process of increasing local tax receipts between 1985 and 1999, whereas regions made only a marginal contribution, although they sharply increased their taxes over the period, perhaps because of their relatively small budgets.

The increase of tax bases explains instead between 80 percent and 90 percent of the total increase in local tax receipts up to 1986, whereas the rise in tax rates only explains the remaining 20 percent.

These figures give an idea of the degree of fiscal decentralization. However, the differences in the share of taxes going to local government are not the only indicator of local political influence.

Even if France is still quoted as an extreme example of a unitary country in the European context, and the capacity of local entities is quite uneven, the map of local jurisdictions is highly fragmented and the fiscal powers of the lower tiers of government remain substantial (Guy 1991). The tax sovereignty is exclusively in the hands of parliament, but communes, departments and regions all benefit from an important taxing power compared with other European countries. The elected assemblies at these lower tiers of government vote on tax rates directly, even if their autonomy in the determination of tax bases is rather limited.

In such a context, intergovernmental fiscal relations in France are often complex, and inter jurisdiction differences in fiscal capacities are sometimes marked. Consequently, the need for fiscal equalization is extremely high and justifies the existence of a wide, efficient system of subsidies for local governments.

However, after a long period of decentralization, in recent years a trend in the opposite direction occurred, as the local authorities' tax autonomy has been reduced (OECD 2002). Own-tax resources of local authorities have been squeezed by the abolition or reduction in local taxes, which have been replaced with grants from central government. In 2002, also with a view to change the current system of financial relations and give more powers to local authorities, the new French government presented a constitutional reform project, actually under discussion.

A comparative view against the European average

In this section we compare the indicators of fiscal burden that we have seen for France with the same figures corresponding to the European average, whose calculation is often characterized by a wide dispersion of national data.

The most general indicators of the incidence of the fiscal burden are certainly the implicit rates. The French trends of implicit tax rates on consumption and labor employed are similar to the European ones, even though in general their levels are higher in France than in Europe. The third kind of implicit tax rate, that is on other factors, appears instead very different from the European average: in 1997 it was 42.1 percent of GDP in France and only 31 percent at the EU level.

From the point of view of efficiency, taxes on labor create a tax wedge in France, which in 2000 occupied fifth place in the OECD list (Joumard 2001). Social contributions paid by the employers play the most important role in the tax wedge determination with the consequence of augmenting labor costs and reducing labor demand. Furthermore, if the system contains some elements of family taxation, high marginal tax wedges on labor may discourage a potential second earner from taking on a job. For most EU countries, high tax wedges on labor largely reflect the important role played by wage-based contributions in financing the transfer system, as well as its broad coverage and public nature. High tax wedges on labor also help to explain the low degree of labor resource utilization since taxes on labor may in turn partly shift forward into labor costs (Daveri and Tabellini 2000).

As regards the taxation of the corporations, we have already noticed that the marginal effective rate is positive and higher than the average of the other countries, considering the case of equity finance, whereas in the case of debt financing it is slightly negative. The effective average tax rate reaches instead the levels of 42 percent and 33.1 percent (equity finance) and 30 percent and 22.3 percent (debt finance) in France and in the EU respectively.

There is not a firm conclusion concerning the comparison of the redistributive impact of PIT between France and the European average. We can only put forward some indications about the share of direct taxes in France, lower than the European average by 0.6 percentage points in

1999. On the contrary, indirect taxes as a percentage of GDP are more important in France, as are social contributions, mainly thanks to the high shares paid by employers.

Finally, the available data does not allow us to compare how taxes are shared out by levels of government between France and other EU countries very well: they only allow us to observe that, in France, something less than 75 percent of total tax revenues (excluding social contributions) goes to central government and more than 15 percent to local authorities, a situation very similar to the European average. The most significant differences are represented by the low revenues of central government in Germany and the high receipts of local authorities in Nordic countries.

Tax reforms in the 1990s and those currently planned

A quick glance at the budget and the general economic environment

After a poor performance during 1990–6, the French economy benefited from rapidly growing activity, low inflation and a rich job market, entering the new millennium with favorable prospects. In fact, the French economy ended 2000 with a strong growth, escaping the production slowdown observed in other OECD countries. Household spending increased under the impulse of robust job creation, lower taxes and strong consumer confidence, whereas companies were enlarging their capacities, strengthening business fixed investments, after years of underachievement in the 1990s and improving export performance together with the competitiveness of French products abroad (OECD economic surveys, France 2000–1). In this favorable landscape, activities related to information and communication technologies have also been particularly important and the unemployment rate declined, reaching less than 9 percent, its lowest level in ten years: one million jobs have been created in the past two years in the business sector and there have been also pro-employment public measures, such as cuts in social security contributions accompanying the weekly working time reduction to 35 hours (Economic Outlook 2001b).

Thus, France benefited from the recovery of world trade – that is, from a positive international environment – and, in spite of tensions on productive capacities surfacing in 2001, was able to control price increases thanks to several factors. First, import as a share of GDP has risen sharply, especially for manufactured products, bridging the gap between demand and output. Second, indirect tax cuts, greater market competition and administrative measures have relaxed consumer price increases. Third, wage moderation has continued to be dominant in an environment of greater labor market flexibility.

These measures have increased the real disposable income and have supported private consumption. Moreover, companies' net earnings have been at a historical high, creating a favorable environment for continuing expansion of the capital stock.

However, progress still needs to be made in invigorating the economy. As a matter of fact, France entered a phase of marked cyclical slowdown at the beginning of 2001. GDP growth relaxed, unemployment rose, business expectations worsened, exports fell back and an increasing inflation reduced the household purchasing power. Moreover, the terrorist attacks on 11 September 2001 in the United States have made matters worse and, consequently, the world slowdown and uncertainty will probably continue in 2003. The impact of this negative situation on public finances is already perceptible. Tax receipts are lower than forecast and the budget deficit will be higher than the projections in the 2002–4 program of public finance. According to the general strategy of public finance adopted from 1997, the level of debt should pass from 57.6 in 2000 to 57.3–57.1 points of GDP in 2003, whereas the GDP growth should settle in a fork from 1.4 percent to 1.6 percent in 2002 and from 2.8 percent to 3.2 percent in 2003. Thus, the next stability program should incorporate a restraint of public expenditure and fiscal policy should continue to target the aim of bringing the structural deficit into balance over the coming years.

Tax reforms in the 1990s

From the mid-1990s, to stimulate the demand of labor, France started to cut social security contributions for the low-paid and/or low-qualified workers: a system of graduated rebates of social charges on low wages was instituted in 1993. Thus, the reduction in non-wage labor costs concerned about one-quarter of wage earners and amounted to about 18 percent for workers at the minimum wage in 1998. The labor cost reduction induced by this system of cuts has three main effects on employment. The substitution effect and the income effect are known, whereas the so-called assessment effect is especially referred to targeted tax cuts. Their interaction can justify the trend break in the employment share of unskilled workers in 1990s, but also the brake on individual wages increases, and can determine an interference with another instrument of structural policy, the minimum wage (L'Horty 2000). If social security contributions are cut, the labor cost of unskilled workers decreases when the minimum wage increases. As a matter of fact, minimum wage and targeted social contributions cuts are two interdependent instruments of structural policy. This interdependence can be seen positively if the targeted social contributions cuts permit the avoidance of the unfavorable consequences of the minimum wage increase on the labor cost and the employment, but without interfering with the minimum wage objective, which is the reduction of the wage differences.

Moreover, from 1999, to make work more attractive for targeted groups of the population, people who qualify for the basic income support can obtain a temporary exemption for the tax on rented flats (*taxe d'habitation*) if they find a job.

With reference to the VAT system, we can consider its evolution up to 1993, that determined the removal of the border controls within the EU and that left to the countries their freedom to use different tax rates, even if an increasing harmonization started in 1991 when the Member States agreed that the standard rate was at least 15 percent. In fact, in 1993, France applied the standard rate of 18.6 percent and two reduced rates of 2.1 percent and 5.5 percent respectively, keeping in line with the European average. At the moment, the VI European Directive regulates the French VAT system and the standard rate, after being raised to 20.6 percent, was set at 19.6 percent, as from 1 April 2000.

During the 1990s, there have been significant changes in the corporate tax rates. In 1990 the tax rate for distributed profits was 42 percent, whereas the tax rate for re-invested profits was 37 percent. This last was reduced by three percentage points in 1991 and it has also been extended to distributed profits in 1992: thus passing from two different tax rates to one. In 1993, this tax rate was once again lowered, reaching the current level of 33.3 percent.

On the other hand, the highest PIT tax rate has been moved from 54 percent to 53.25 percent. In fact, in an environment of increased tax competition, and given the major tax reforms undertaken elsewhere in the European Union, failure to reduce taxes could result in losses of human and financial capital.

Finally, some taxes that were costly to collect and had a low yield, like the road tax, have been abolished; other taxes, for instance the television license fee or quasi-fiscal taxes, might also be done away with.

Tax reforms underway and planned in the light of OECD and EU suggestions

According to two recent OECD studies (Joumard 2001 and OECD 2001c), future tax reforms must above all improve labor market performance; that is, reduce the tax burden on labor.

As we have already noticed, since the mid-1990s, France started to cut social security contributions, but the tax burden on labor still remains high. Thus the digressive reduction of employers' social contributions at the lower end of the wage scale will continue in association with the reduction of the working week, whereas employers' and employees' unemployment insurance contributions will gradually be reduced from 6.18 in 2000 to 5.4 in 2003 (EU Commission 2000). In 2001 social partners have agreed on a new program to help job-seekers return to employment and the authorities have decided that an employment bonus (*prime pour l'emploi*), delivered through the tax system, must be introduced to "make work pay" for low-income families. It is expected to reduce the tax wedge and benefit up to ten million people, mainly full-time workers. Moreover, since 1999, the French government is gradually removing the wage component from the base of the *taxe professionnelle* and extending the tax base to fund contributions for health and family from labor to capital income.

To avoid a situation where the reduction in the tax burden on labor was only paid for by cuts in primary expenditure, the possibility of shifting this burden more onto consumption or capital has been considered. On this subject, econometric simulations based on the European Commission's Quest II model (Leibfritz, Thornton and Bibbee 1997) show that shifting from labor to consumption tax could increase the employment level by 0.73 with very little reduction in wages (-0.02): as a matter of fact, consumption taxes are quite indifferent toward saving and investment decisions; they do not distinguish between imports and locally-produced goods and they guarantee a symmetrical treatment of labor, transfer and capital income, thus creating fewer disincentives to work. On the other hand, the shifting from labor to corporate income tax could be still better for the employment level despite the significant fall in wages (-2.10) and in GDP (-0.67). A reduction in labor tax rate equivalent to one percentage point of GDP, and financed by a reduction in government transfer payments, would determine instead a rise of 2.01 in employment, of 0.03 in the level of wages and lastly, of 2.29 in GDP.

When one talks about PIT, the suggestions are as follows: the broadening of the bases by limiting special allowances, the introduction of a suitable tax treatment for the self-employed and the increase of the neutrality of capital income taxation. In France, between 2001 and 2003 the most important interventions concerned the personal income tax focus on tax cuts for low income, the introduction of a refundable tax credit for low-paid workers and gradual reduction of *CSG* (*contribution sociale généralisée*) and *CRDS* (*contribution pour le remboursement de la dette sociale*) for workers earning up to 1.3 times the minimum wage. France has also recently raised the general personal income tax allowances, thus exempting the income of most low-qualified workers from taxation. At last, the Financial Law of 2001 lowered the first four PIT tax rates by 0.75 percent and the last two by 0.5 percent. However, tax rates on personal income will be trimmed once again and the top marginal rate should be lowered to reach 52.5 percent in 2003.

Another important aim of tax reforms should be the reduction of VAT rates and the simplification of this important indirect tax. Reducing the complexity and increasing the modernization of the VAT system would, in turn, cut compliance costs and thus improve the fiscal situation of small businesses and their propensity to exportation. Technology is changing the nature of consumption taxes and these challenges call for renewed and enhanced coordination in VAT and other indirect taxes (Tanzi 1995). For the period 2000–2, for instance, France planned to apply a general cut in the VAT rate (one percentage point: from 20.6 to 19.6) and reduced

VAT rates on labor-intensive services with the objective of stimulating demand for these services, raising the employment level and bringing part of the informal economy to the surface.

A fiscal reform proposal concerns the neutrality of the tax system toward savings vehicles in order to increase economic efficiency and reduce administrative costs. On this subject, France and other EU governments have started an exchange of information, the only way to avoid distortions in the taxation of the income from the invested savings.

Also the increase on the taxation of property at local level, that implies a bringing up to date of land registers and a correct evaluation of land and building, could contribute, as an alternative to the net wealth taxation, to improving the neutrality of the tax system and rebalancing the tax burden on labor. Devolving the expenditure and taxing power (fiscal devolution), optimizing the benefits (local governments are better able to meet local needs and preferences for many public services) and minimizing the disadvantages could help to achieve other important targets.

There are four recommendations concerning corporate income tax: first, the neutrality of funding, that is the reduction of the bias toward debt financing of corporations; second, the broadening of the base; third, the strengthening of the existent special corporate tax regimes for small enterprises, newly-created and information technology companies; and, finally, the introduction of strict anti-fragmentation rules. The incentives and the progressive rates structure may give rise to abuse, with larger companies splitting up into smaller units for tax purposes. As concerns corporate and capital taxes, there is room for the creation and the extension of an environmental-related tax financing the reduction of the working week and for a cut of taxes on dwellings. At last, from 2001 to 2002 the French corporate tax rates have been reduced (Table 5.3): from 26.5 percent to 15.45 percent, from 35.3 percent to 34.3 percent and finally from 20.14 percent to 19.57 percent as concerns PME exempted from social contributions. On the other hand, as regards "other than PME," from 36.43 percent to 35.43 percent and from 20.77 percent to 20.20 percent.

The fiscal reform must also aim at achieving environmental targets in a coordinated way. In fact, coordination efforts have not been very successful in the past and tax breaks for polluting activities exposed to international competition continue to exist. However there is much room for taxes on different kinds of energy to reflect the environmental externalities caused by their use and for exemptions in particular sectors to be cancelled. These interventions, together with the planned progressive rise in the environmental taxes, should improve the efficiency and simplify the achievement of these environmental targets. France has been trying for some years to make its growth environmentally sustainable: however, environmental taxes and charges have been used more with a view to financing expenditure on pollution control than providing adequate microeconomic incentives, thus showing the difficulty of framing a coherent environmental strategy.

Finally, one must improve the tax administration, reducing compliance costs and overlaps among levels of government, reinforcing the relationship with the taxpayers and raising the efficiency of the tax collection: all these interventions would free-up resources for more beneficial uses such as combating tax evasion.

Notes

1 Fiscal rules are assembled in a General Code (*Code Général des Impôts – CGI*) consisting of two books: the first concerns the calculation of the basis of assessment and settlement of the different taxes, and the second concerns the terms of collection.
2 This 10 percent is calculated as follows: 7.5 percent to *CSG* (*Contribution sociale généralisée*), 0.5 percent to *CRDS* (*Contribution pour le remboursement de la dette sociale*) and 2 percent to social withdrawal.

References

Bernardi, L. (2000) "Note sull'evoluzione recente e sulle prospettive future dei sistemi tributari," *Studi e Note di Economia*, 1: 25–50.
Daveri, F. and Tabellini, G. (2000) "Unemployment, growth and taxation in industrial countries," *Economic Policy: A European Forum*, April, 30: 47–8.
Economic Outlook (2001a) *Challenges for Tax Policy in OECD Countries*, 62, ch. V, 169–86, June.
—— (2001b) *France*: 61–4, Organisation for Economic Cooperation and Development, Paris and Washington, DC.
EU Commission (2000) "Public finances in EMU 2000; MSs' update of stability programmes, 1999–2000"; Joint Employment Report 2000 (2000-07-28); *National Action Plans for Employment 1998–2001*.
—— (2001) *Directory of Taxes in the EU: France*, Brussels: EU Commission.
—— (2002) *Statistical Annex of European Economy*, Brussels: EU Commission.
Eurostat (2000) *Structures of the Taxation Systems in the European Union, 1970–1997*, Brussels: EU Commission.
—— (2002) *New Cronos Statistics*, databank CD-ROM.
Giannini, S. and Maggiulli, C. (2001) *The Effective Tax Rates in the EU Commission Study on Corporate Taxation: Methodological Aspects, Main Results and Policy Implications*, CAPP, Università di Modena e Reggio Emilia.
Guy, G. (1991) "Local taxation and intergovernmental fiscal relations in France," in Fossati, A. and Panella, G. (eds) *Fiscal Federalism in the European Union*, London: Routledge.
Joumard, I. (2001) "Tax systems in European Union countries," Economics Department Working Paper 301, Paris: OECD.
Leibfritz, W., Thornton, J. and Bibbee, A. (1997) "Taxation and economic performance," Economics Department Working Paper 176, Paris: OECD.
Liberati, P. (2000) *Il Federalismo Fiscale. Aspetti Teorici e Pratici*, Milano: Editore Ulrico Hoepli.

L'Horty, Y. (2000) "Vertus et limites des allègements de charges sur les bas salaires," University of Evry and CSERC.

Monaco, C. (1999) "L'imposta sulle società nell'ordinamento francese," Università di Pavia, Dipartimento di Economia Pubblica e Territoriale.

OECD (2000) *Economic Survey – France 2000*, Paris: OECD.

—— (2001a) *Economic Survey – France 2001*, Paris: OECD.

—— (2001b) *Revenue Statistics 1965–2000*, Paris: OECD.

—— (2001c) "Tax and the economy: a comparative assessment of OECD countries," *Tax Policy Studies*, 6, Paris: OECD.

—— (2002) "Fiscal decentralisation in EU applicant states and selected EU Member States," Paris: OECD.

Petretto, A. (2002) *Unità europea e Economia pubblica*, Bologna: Il Mulino.

Tanzi, V. (1995) *Taxation in an Integrating World*, Washington, DC: The Brookings Institution.

Wagstaff, A. *et al.* (1999) "Redistributive effect, progressivity and differential tax treatment: personal income taxes in twelve OECD countries," *Journal of Public Economics*, 72: 73–98.

Websites

http://www.bancaditalia.it
http://www.impots.gouv.fr
http://www.minefi.gouv.fr
http://www.oecd.org

6 Germany

Giorgia Chiara Maffini

Introduction

This chapter is devoted to the analysis of the German fiscal system. The study has been completed using data from different sources in order to develop a broad picture of the German fiscal system by analyzing not only existing taxes but also their effective burden, their proceeds, the destination of their revenues and the impact of the recent reform.

Various reasons lead us to investigate the tax system and tax reform in the Federal Republic of Germany. First, it is a key country in the EU as, in 2000, it generated the largest level of GDP, which amounted to 2,040 billion euro. This means that, to a certain extent, Germany could be a benchmark for many other countries. For instance, the tax reform project which is currently under discussion in Italy is, in some elements, inspired by the new German tax system.

Second, and this is the main reason for our investigation, in 2001 an income and business tax reform took place in Germany. The transformation of the German fiscal system was implemented during a period characterized by a complex economic and political environment. It is particularly interesting to investigate how the economy reacted, as we have documented on pages 148–9. On the one hand, the reform was necessary to improve the German political and economic framework: corporations and individuals suffered from a very high tax burden compared to other European countries, a great number of German banks and financial institutions held shares of domestic corporations merely because it would have been too costly to sell them and, finally, the imputation system was not considered to be in line with the European tax law. On the other hand, the substantial loss of revenues implied by the tax reform occurred in a phase of strict budget constraints: in 2001 Germany showed the highest deficit ratio in the EU, as we illustrate on pages 128–9 and 148–9.

The chapter proceeds as follows. In the next paragraph we analyze the structure of the German fiscal system from the 1970s up to the present day, by investigating the composition of different tax revenues. Overall fiscal pressure (as a share of GDP) has been growing. It increased by almost ten percentage points from 1970 to 1997. This is mainly due to the rise of both social security contributions and the personal income tax (PIT). In relation to total fiscal proceeds, income tax is the major source of revenue in 2000 and VAT follows in second position. In relation to GDP, in 2000 social security contributions represent the greatest share. At the end of the section, the German fiscal burden is compared to the European average. Since the 1970s, PIT and social security contributions as a share of GDP have been higher than the EU average, while the opposite is true for indirect and corporate taxes.

Following this, we then describe the features of the main German taxes, giving particular attention to the personal income tax, the corporate tax and VAT. The PIT is highly progressive, its base is characterized by high personal deductions, as we describe on page 134. Besides, weighty allowances are granted to taxpayers. Typical features of the German corporate tax before the reform were a split-rate system, high statutory rates and a narrow base due to high depreciation deductions. The VAT rate is low compared to other EU countries. We also consider social security contributions, business tax, the solidarity surcharge and other minor taxes. The business tax is the exemplification of the German Federal fiscal system: its rate is fixed by municipalities and contributes to increase the corporate tax burden. This is also true for the solidarity surcharge whose rate is, on the contrary, established by central government.

After that, we illustrate the distribution of the fiscal burden using different indicators: implicit tax rates, taxation by economic functions and tax wedges on labor, capital and consumption. Implicit tax rates on labor have been quite high and displayed a growing long-term trend. The opposite is true for implicit tax rates on capital. The same conclusions can be drawn from the analysis of taxation by economic functions: a high share of fiscal pressure is borne by labor, primarily by employed labor. The analysis of the tax wedge on corporate income shows a strong distortion in favor of financing investment by debt. A comparison of German fiscal burden is played out on the European stage: even after the fiscal reform, the Federal Republic displays an elevated tax burden. We also investigate the relations between the different levels of government and taxation by attributing tax revenues to the central government, states and municipalities: intermediate levels of government (*Länder*) receive a great amount of total tax revenues as well as, to a minor extent, municipalities.

In the final part of the chapter, after a brief analysis of the economic and political environment, we describe the fiscal reforms implemented from 1990 until now, and try to give some policy evaluations of the new provisions. This is a key period for Germany: the latest fiscal reform rearranged the whole system by simultaneously broadening the base and lowering the rates. Considering different tax pressure indicators, Germany was one of the countries with the highest fiscal pressure in the EU. It was characterized by high statutory rates together with narrow bases. Direct taxes were high while indirect taxes were lower than the EU average. The 2001 fiscal reform did not much improve the ranking of the Federal Republic within the European Union.

The structure of the system and of its development from the 1970s

The current structure of the tax system and social security contributions

In 2001 the general government deficit reached 2.7 percent of GDP (EU Commission 2002). This was a significant slippage from the originally agreed budgetary targets.[1] However, at the end of 2001 the debt was 57.8 percent of GDP, which means that it decreased from 2000 values.[2] The cyclically adjusted primary balance (CAPB) was 0.7 percent of GDP.

From 2000, the government revenue ratio decreased by 1.5 percent to 46.1 percent, above all owing to the tax reform which came into force at the beginning of the year. In the same year, total expenditures came to 48.9 percent of GDP. As a result, the German fiscal balance moved considerably further away from the requirements of the European Stability and Growth Pact. Germany currently has the highest deficit ratio in the EU. Net borrowing was −1.5 percent of GDP and cyclically adjusted net borrowing was −1.4 percent.

In 2001[3] total public expenditures[4] can be divided into personal expenditures (27.4 percent of total expenditure), other operating expenditure (10.7 percent), current grants (35.7 percent) interests paid (12.9 percent), capital formation (6.8 percent), financial aid[5] (6.4 percent). The 80.1 percent of total public revenues[6] come from taxation and other fiscal charges.

As we could not find any data on 2001 tax revenue composition, we may rely on data from the Federal Office for Statistics (*Statistisches Bundesamt*). They show that general taxes amount to 73.3 percent of total revenues. Among them the wages tax (*Lohnsteuer*) represents 33.2 percent of total tax revenues and, together with income tax, is the major source of revenue from taxation (35.7 percent of total revenues). The second most important tax is VAT (*Umsatzsteuer*): its revenues total is 21.3 percent. Among general taxes, corporate tax corresponds to 4.9 percent of total tax proceeds. Another significant tax is the business tax (*Gewerbesteuer*), whose returns amount to 5.4 percent. Among excises, the great part of revenues is due to the excise on mineral oils (7.5 percent) and excise on tobacco (2.3 percent).

For 2001 we can only report[7] that tax revenues fell by 4.5 percent, mainly because of the tax reform. The turnover tax declined by 1.5 percent and performed even less favorably than the VAT tax base. Corporation taxes, receipts from which were depressed by the cut in tax rates plus the distribution of profits retained in earlier years, showed a negative balance for the first time (-0.5 billion euro), although this was accompanied by additional revenue from non-assessed tax on earnings. The worsened profit situation and smaller payments than in earlier years likewise contributed to the disappointing corporation tax result, as well as depressing trade tax receipts. However, revenues from wage tax and assessed income tax marginally exceeded expectations.

According to the *Statistisches Bundesamt*, in 2000 direct taxes were 54.9 percent of total tax revenues while indirect taxes represented 37.6 percent of total income from taxation. Among the former, income taxes (35.7 percent), corporation tax (4.9 percent) and tax on industry and trade (5.4 percent) were the major source of revenues. Concerning indirect taxes, VAT dominated, with 21.3 percent of total tax revenue. Total excises amounted to 12.6 percent of total tax income.

Concerning the share of different type of taxes on GDP, in 2000 social security contributions represented the main share of GDP (18.7 percent). In 2001 revenues from social security contributions increased by 1.5 percent according to the German Central Bank. Direct taxes totaled 12.5 percent of GDP and indirect taxes 12 percent.

Developments of the system from 1970 to 1999

The Federal Republic of Germany has long been a country characterized by a high fiscal burden, both on individuals and corporations. This feature is linked to German history: during the 1990s the country had to cope with the reunification process[8] and the budget constraints established by the Maastricht Treaty. Until the last reform[9] the two main features of the system were high statutory tax rates and relatively narrow bases.[10]

From 1970 to 1999, the total tax burden as a percentage of GDP increases almost regularly but quite slowly: in 1970 the percentage of total tax revenue on GDP is the lowest (19.2 percent). The share of total tax income increases from 1970 to 1980 (22 percent); it remains almost constant until 1985 (21.6 percent) and then it exhibits a local minimum point in 1990 (19.9 percent). Afterwards, it rises and reaches a global maximum point in 1999 (24.4 percent).

Total direct tax burden on GDP rises almost regularly from 1970 to 1999: it stretches from a minimum of 9.9 percent in 1980 to a maximum of 12.2 percent in 1999.

Total indirect tax revenues linger around an average value of 9.8 percent, with a minimum value of 9.2 percent in 1975 and in 1990 and a maximum value of 12.2 percent in 1999. The greater part of the indirect tax burden is composed of VAT revenues, which alone, on average, amount to 6.3 percent of GDP.

A comparative view against the European average

As shown in Table 6.1, the German total tax revenues as a share of GDP are always lower then the European average. The gap between Germany and the European values seems to become wider and wider until 1995 when it recovers. In 1990, the European average is 6.3 percentage points greater than the German tax share on GDP while, in 1995, it declines to 6.2 percentage points and in 1999 it reaches a value of 3.2 percentage points.

The disparity is mainly due to the share of indirect taxes on GDP. From 1970 to 1999 they run below the European mean. This does not mean that, for example, VAT has been lower than the European average since 1970. In fact it lingers around the European average but, at the same time, is counterbalanced by the course of excise duties. These latter also run close to the European average: the maximum gap between the two values is 1.7 percentage points in 1999. The share of their revenues on GDP from direct taxes is lower (one percentage point) than the European average in 1970. Afterwards the situation is turned upside down: from 1975 to 1999 the German values drop under the European mean. The gap is largest in 1990 and, in 1995, by around two-and-a-half percentage points.

On the other hand, personal income tax revenues on GDP are always higher than the European average (except for 1990 and 1995 when they are equal to, or 0.3 percentage points lower). This is not true for the corporate income tax proceeds, which are, as a share of GDP, always lower than the European mean.

German total social contributions as a share of GDP are well above the European values. The gap between the two ratios ranges from a minimum value of 2.2 percentage points in 1975 to a maximum of 3.5 points in 1995. This is due primarily to the fact that employees' contributions are particularly high compared to the European mean. While employers' contributions run a little below, the self-employed contributions progress with higher values than those of the European average.

Some quantitative and institutional features of main taxes

The personal income tax – PIT (**Einkommensteuer**)

Individuals domiciled or resident in Germany are subject to income tax on their worldwide income falling under one or several of the following categories.

- Income from agriculture and forestry
- Income from trade or business

To compute the taxable income in these two categories the net worth comparison method is used. However, the net income method can be

Table 6.1 Structure and development of fiscal revenues in Germany and European average as a percentage of GDP, 1970–99

	1970		1975		1980		1985		1990		1995		1999	
	Ge	Eu	Ge	Eu	Ge	Eu	Ge	Eu	Ge	Eu	Ge	Eu	Ge	Eu
Direct taxes[1]	9.9	8.9	11.4	11.9	12.2	12.7	12.2	13.1	10.7	13.2	10.9	13.3	12.2	13.7
personal income	8.2	5.5	10.1	8.9	10.4	9.3	9.9	9.0	8.9	8.9	9.3	9.6		9.3
corporation income	1.7	2.2	1.3	1.9	1.8	2.2	2.3	2.8	1.8	2.9	1.6	2.4		3.0
Indirect taxes[2]	9.3	13.0	9.2	12.2	9.8	13.2	9.4	13.0	9.2	13.0	9.8	13.6	12.2	13.9
VAT	5.9	5.1	5.6	5.7	6.6	6.6	6.4	6.1	6.4	6.6	6.8	6.9	7.0	7.0
excise duties	3.4	3.5	3.6	3.5	3.2	3.2	3.0	3.2	2.8	3.1	3.0	3.4		3.5
Total tax revenue	19.2	21.9	20.6	24.1	22.0	25.9	21.6	26.1	19.9	26.2	20.7	26.9	24.4	27.6
Social contributions	11.7	11.7	15.0	12.8	15.7	13.4	16.3	13.8	15.9	13.7	18.5	15.0	18.0	15.0
employers	5.4	7.2	6.9	7.7	7.3	7.8	7.5	7.9	7.3	7.8	8.2	8.0	7.7	8.2
employees	4.9	3.5	5.7	3.8	6.2	4.3	6.4	4.5	6.3	4.5	7.1	5.1	7.0	5.0
self-employed	1.4	1.0	2.4	1.3	2.2	1.3	2.4	1.5	2.3	1.4	3.2	1.8	3.0	1.9
Total fiscal revenue	30.9	33.6	35.6	36.9	37.7	39.3	37.9	39.9	35.8	39.9	39.2	41.9	42.4	42.6
Administrative level														
Central government	21.5	19.7	21.3	21.1	21.8	22.3	21.2	22.1	19.8	22.2	20.8	22.5	20.4	22.9
Local government	2.6	2.2	3.0	2.8	3.3	2.9	3.2	3.1	3.0	3.8	2.7	4.0	3.3	4.0

Sources: 1970–95, Eurostat, 2000; 1999, Eurostat New Cronos databank 2002 (data equalized with Eurostat, 2000).

Notes
Minor items are omitted.
1 For 1999 we could not find split data for personal and corporation income.
2 For 1999 we could not find data for excise duties.

applied if the annual profits do not go above €24,542 and the turnover does not exceed €255,650.[11] Expenses incurred in producing the income are generally deductible. Some restrictions apply for personal expenses (gifts, guest houses, etc.). Dividends and other profit distribution from shares held as business assets are taxed applying the new half-income system (*Halbeinkünfteverfahren*).

- Income from professional services[12]
- Income from employment[13]

Employment income is defined as any sum, in cash or in kind, received by an employee for his or her employment.[14] Expenses for generating and maintaining employment income are deductible, although sometimes only up to a certain limit. If those expenses do not reach €1,002, the taxpayer benefits from a lump-sum deduction of €1,002. Other deductible expenses are: contributions to professional and trade associations; necessary expenses incurred for the maintenance of two households (limited to a two-year period if the physical place of work does not change); expenses for working tools and working clothes and depreciation of income-producing assets. Expenses related to tax-free income are not deductible. Benefits in kind received or enjoyed from an employment in addition to regular salary are categorized as income from employment and normally valued at market price, including VAT. A ruling, which fixes the value of certain benefits, e.g. housing and food, is issued annually.[15]

Pension income derived from the statutory pension scheme is considered as other income. Other types of pension income[16] paid in the form of an annuity (*Leibrente*) are taxable as employment income. A tax-free allowance of 40 percent is granted for an annual maximum of 6,000 DEM (€3,067).

- Income from capital investment (dividends and interests) and
- Rental income from immovable property and certain tangible movable property and income from royalties

Normally, expenses sustained for producing income in these two categories are deductible. For the first category, an allowance of up to €1,533.9 per year (€3,067 for jointly assessed spouses) is granted. According to the imputation credit scheme, the corporate income tax paid on dividends or similar capital income is set off against the resident shareholder's tax liability. The credit is three-sevenths of the dividends.

After the new fiscal reform, the imputation method has been eliminated and the new half-income method (*Halbeinkünfteverfahren*) has been introduced. The shareholder is only taxed on 50 percent of the amount of the dividend or the profit distribution received. Consequentially, only half of the expenses connected with the production of the income are deductible. Dividend distributions of resident companies fall under the new rules if the underlying profits have been derived during 2002. Dividend distributions of non-resident companies fall under the new rules from 1 January 2001.

- Other income (gains from private transactions, alimony, annuities, etc.)

Pension income derived from the statutory pension scheme is taxable. The taxable base is computed as the excess of each payment over a proportionate share of the invested capital spread over the life expectancy of the recipient. The excess is fixed as a percentage of the payments, which depends on the age of the recipient when he first received pension payments. The same treatment is applied to pension payments derived from a direct insurance and pension funds. The payments made by the employer to insurance or to the pension fund are regarded as employee's income from employment and are therefore taxed as such.

In order to form the taxable base, the income resulting from every category is gathered together and personal deductions are subtracted. Allowances and rates are then applied to create the fiscal liability. Negative income from one source of income can be set off against positive income from other sources only within certain limits.[17]

The German fiscal system recognizes the following types of income as exempt: payments from health, accident, disability and old age insurance; some social distribution; lump-sum payments under the statutory pension scheme; scholarship for research activities, scientific or artistic education and training; 50 percent of qualifying dividend and capital gains on alienation of shares.

Capital gains

Capital gains arising in the course of a business are treated as ordinary business income. Gains from the disposal of assets withdrawn from a business are taxable under the rules on private transactions.

Capital gains derived from private transactions are generally free of tax. However, they are taxable if they total more than €511.3 and arise from the disposal of either immovable property within ten years of the date of acquisition or movable property within one year of the date of acquisition and, finally, from the disposal of derivatives. The capital gains are then added to an individual's taxable income. Special rules apply to the taxation of capital gains from the sale of a significant interest in a company, that is, 10 percent of the company's share capital or more (from 1 January 2002 the limit was lowered to 1 percent in resident companies).[18] They are not considered as deriving from a private

transaction but they form business income. This means that they are entitled to the benefits of loss set-off and carry-over. The described discipline
does not apply from 1 January 2002. As a matter of fact the new half-
income method is used: only 50 percent of capital gains are subject to
taxes.[19]

Personal deductions, allowances and credits

Various properly documented expenses are deductible in the German
fiscal system. They can be divided into special expenses (*Sonderausgaben*)
and extraordinary expenses (*aussergewönliche Belastungen*). The former
group includes social security contributions and insurance premiums
(deductible up to a total limit of €1,334 for a single taxpayer and €2,668
for jointly assessed couples). Mortgage interest is deductible only against
income from property. Tax advisers' fees and the church tax are fully
deductible. Contributions to German charities and certain international
charities are deductible up to 5 percent of adjusted gross income. For contributions for scientific purposes, the percentage is increased to 10
percent. Donations to political parties are deductible up to €1,533
(€3,067 for married taxpayers filing jointly). From 2000 there are additional deductions available for donations to public law foundations and
certain non-profit private law foundations. Extraordinary expenses[20] may
be deducted if they are necessarily incurred and if they exceed expenses
borne by comparable taxpayers with a comparable income. These costs
are deductible only in excess of a certain limit, depending on the applicable schedule.

A basic allowance (*Grundfreibetrag*) of €7,205[21] is deducted from the
taxable base. Special allowances for children are granted whenever the
monthly child benefit[22] is not sufficient to cover the minimum subsistence
of a child. The allowance amount to €147 per month for every child
under 18 years who is maintained by the taxpayer. As from 1 January 2000,
a new additional childcare allowance (*Betreuungsfreibetrag*) of €773 per
year was available for children under 16 years and for those who are
handicapped.

Rates

The German income tax is levied at progressive marginal rates using
complex tables. Abbreviated tables are as Table 6.2.

The solidarity surcharge is imposed on the amount of tax computed
according to Table 6.2.

Table 6.2 Personal income tax rates

Single taxpayer Annual taxable income (€)	Rate (%)	Tax payable (€)
up to 7,205.75	0	0
7,205.75–9,248.9	19.96–23.02	8.2–441.2
9,248.9–54,999	23.02–48.50	447.4–16,658.1
over 54,999		16,813.6
Jointly assessed spouses Annual taxable income (€)	Rate (%)	Tax payable (€)
up to 14,412	0	0
14,412–18,498	19.96–23.02	16.4–882.5
18,498–109,998	23.02–48.50	894.8–33,600.6
over 109,998		33,627.2

Social security contributions

The social contributions are computed on the basis of gross salary and up to certain limits. Normally, the employer contributes an equal amount and withholds the employee's part from the salary that it transfers to the healthcare institution, which then distributes the relevant amounts to the other social security institutions. For 2002 the contributions are indicated in Table 6.3.[23]

Social security contributions and insurance premiums are deductible from adjusted gross income up to specified limits.

Table 6.3 Social security contributions

Type of insurance	Rate (%)	Maximum salary[1] €/month	Contribution €/month
Pension insurance (*Rentenversicherung*)	19.1	4,500	859.5
Unemployment insurance (*Arbeitslosenversicherung*)	6.5	4,500	292.5
Health insurance (*Krankenversicherung*)	13.5[2]	3,375	455.63
Insurance for disability and old age (*Pflegeversicherung*)	1.7	3,375	57.38

Notes
1 The maximum applies if the employee is resident in one of the five new *Länder*.
2 The average rate; the contributions depend on the insurance company.

Inheritance and gift taxes (Erbschaft-und Schenkungsteuer)[24]

Each beneficiary or donee is assessed separately according to his or her share in the estate or the gift. For the tax levied on gifts, the donee and the donor are jointly liable. The taxable base is the fair market value.[25] The rates depend on both the category of the beneficiary or donee and on the amount of the taxable base. They vary from 7 percent to 50 percent. The first €255,650 is exempt in case of a business property located in Germany, obtained by inheritances or gifts *mortis causa* and only 60 percent of any excess is taxable. The same applies to shares in a resident company if the deceased/donor held a direct interest of more than 25 percent. Some allowances are granted for inheritance and gifts, varying according to the category of beneficiaries or donees. Up to €51,130 the lower rates are applied, whereas higher rates apply to acquisition in excess of €25.6 million.

Corporation tax – CT (Körperschaftsteuer)

The German Corporate Income Tax Law states that taxable persons have unlimited liability in relation to their worldwide income (unlimited tax liability). The basis of assessment is the total income received by corporation during the fiscal year.[26] Profits are determined according to the net worth comparison method. For financial years ending December 2000, Germany applied a full imputation[27] system for the last time at the following rates: 30 percent (distributed profits) and 40 percent (undistributed profits).

This is a split-rate system, which can result in a reduction in the corporate income tax if retained earnings that had been subjected to the full corporate income tax rate are distributed. On the other hand, distributions can lead to an increase in corporate income tax up to the distribution rate if income that has been subject to reduced rates or certain tax-free income is distributed. This guarantees that all profits are uniformly imposed at the same rate upon distribution.

After the abolition of the imputation system, corporate income tax is no longer included in the taxable base of the shareholder, and there is no imputation of the corporate income tax against the income tax payable by the shareholder. The resulting double taxation is softened by both the reduction of the corporate tax rate at 25 percent with no distinction between retained and distributed profits and the introduction of the half-income system (*Halbeinkünfteverfahren*). This means that only half of the distributed dividend is taxable.

Most company expenses (*Betriebsausgaben*) related to taxable income are deductible. Remunerations (e.g. salary, benefits in kind and social contributions) to employees are fully deductible. The same applies for fees paid to a member of the management board. Interest on loans and other debts are commonly deductible. Some limits apply to interest deductions. Limits on interest paid to affiliates are basically debt/equity ratios of 3:1 (9:1 for German holding companies) on fixed-interest loans and 1:2 on finance provided for a consideration based on profits or similar criteria. The following taxes are deductible: business tax (*Gewerbesteuer*) and real estate tax (*Grundsteuer*). Corporate income tax, real estate transfer tax and VAT on non-deductible items listed are not deductible.

Concerning capital allowance, the applicable methods are the straight-line, declining-balance and production methods. Among immovable properties, land is not depreciable, buildings are depreciable according to different rates. The latter depend on the date of the construction of the building and on how it is used. For plant, machinery and equipment, the straight-line and the declining balance methods apply if the plant does not constitute immovable property. The declining-balance method rate is limited to three times the allowable straight-line rate, with a maximum of 30 percent.[28] Intangible assets may only be depreciated using the straight-line method. Goodwill may only be capitalized if it was acquired.

Capital gains realized by a company are taxable as ordinary income for corporate income tax purposes. The normal tax rates apply both for the corporate income tax and the business tax. After 1 January 2002, the following capital gains are exempt: capital gains realized by companies from the sale of a qualifying investment in a foreign company and capital gains realized from the sale of shares in domestic and foreign companies.

Relating to losses, at the taxpayer's option, ordinary losses for corporation tax purposes may be carried back and offset up to the amount of €511,500 against taxable income of the preceding year. Remaining losses are carried forward without time limit. Capital losses are considered as ordinary losses.

Business tax on income (Gewerbesteuer)

Business tax is a local tax due on any business carried out in Germany, whether by a resident or non-resident. Business income tax rates depend on the municipality in which the business is located.[29] Business tax is deductible from its own base and for corporate income tax purposes.

Taking into account the deductibility, the effective tax rates range from 10 percent and 15 percent. The business tax takes over the taxable base computed for corporate income tax purposes and adjusts it by certain add-backs and deductions.[30]

Value added tax – VAT

The value added tax in Germany is a standard European VAT. The following rates apply: 16 percent to every taxable supply of goods and services not subject to the reduced or zero rate; 7 percent to the supply of essential goods and services, such as food and beverages (but 16 percent if consumed on the spot), pharmaceuticals, newspapers, books, the services of theaters, museums and concert halls; zero to exports and intra-Community supplies. The taxpayer is generally entitled to offset against the value added tax payable the amount of such tax charged by suppliers or paid on imports.

Excise duties

Excise duty on mineral oils[31] (*Mineralölsteuer*) is payable on certain goods, classified and described in a uniform way for the Community, provided that they are used as motor or heating fuels. Rates depend on the type of goods and their use. Duty on tobacco (*Tabaksteuer*) is payable on cigarettes, cigars and cigarillos and smoking tobacco. Rates depend on the type of good. Duty on spirits (*Alkoholsteuer*) is payable on liquid having an alcoholic strength by volume exceeding 22 percent and on alcoholic products. Other excises are duty on sparkling wines (*Scahumweinsteuer*), intermediate products (*Zwischenerzeugnissteuer*), beer (*Biersteuer*), coffee (*Kaffeesteuer*) and beverages (*Getränkesteuer*).

Solidarity surcharge, church tax (Kirchensteuer) and taxes on capital

Resident and non-resident companies, persons with unlimited and extended limited tax liability, associations and funds are subject to a solidarity surcharge of 5.5 percent. The basis of assessment is income tax, corporation tax, wage tax, capital yield tax, income or corporation tax prepayments.

Church members are required to pay a church tax at a rate of 8 percent or 9 percent of their income tax payable, depending on the *Land* in which the taxpayer is resident.

The net wealth tax (*Vermögensteuer*) was abolished effective from 1 January 1997. Individuals are subject to real-estate tax (*Grundsteuer*). For individuals, the real-estate tax is only deductible for income tax purposes if the property is used in the course of a trade or business or if it constitutes a source of income, e.g. in the case of rental income.

The fiscal burden

The distribution of taxation charge

As a consequence of a relatively low VAT standard rate (16 percent) implicit tax rates on consumption stayed below the European average from 1970 to 1997 and they scarcely deviated from their average level of 16 percent. The implicit tax rate on employed labor maintained its rising long-term trend and, in 1997, achieved a level of 44.1 percent, which is

Table 6.4 Implicit tax rates in Germany and Europe, 1970–97

		Consumption	*Labor employed*	*Other factor*
1970	Germany	16.6	30.0	34.8
	EU	17.6	28.9	26.2
1975	Germany	15.7	34.9	46.1
	EU	15.5	32.2	34.7
1980	Germany	15.8	36.5	48.3
	EU	16.0	35.1	36.6
1985	Germany	14.7	39.5	40.3
	EU	15.6	37.1	32.3
1990	Germany	15.6	38.5	34.4
	EU	16.2	37.5	31.5
1995	Germany	16.4	43.9	32.3
	EU	16.7	41.7	29.4
1997	Germany	15.8	44.1	30.0
	EU	16.8	41.9	31.1

Source: Eurostat (2000).

approximately 15 percentage points more than in 1970. Implicit tax rates on labor in Germany have always been higher than in the European Union: the average gap between Germany and the EU is 1.8 percentage points. The implicit tax rate on factors of production other than employed labor[32] has progressively dropped since 1980, starting from 50 percent and reaching 30 percent in 1997.

With regards to the aggregate implicit tax rate on labor and other factors, Germany displayed an upwards trend until to 1980. Afterwards, the total implicit tax rate declined in 1990, rising again five years later before dropping to 74.1 percent in 1997. The value of 1997 is approximately ten percentage points higher than that of 1970. German values are significantly higher if compared to the European mean. Above all, this is due to elevated implicit tax rates on other factors (i.e. capital and self-employed labor) in comparison with the European average.

The same results can be derived from the analysis of the structure of taxation according to economic function as a percentage of GDP.

From 1970 to 1997 the taxation on consumption as a percentage of GDP does not deviate much from its average value of 10.2 percent. On the contrary, taxation on labor displayed a long-term upward trend, rising from 20 percent in 1970 to 27.8 percent in 1995. Only in 1997 did it decrease, to 26.9 percent. The share of tax on GDP paid by both employees and employers grew from 1970 to 1997. In contrast, taxation on the self-employed fell slightly, starting from 4 percent in 1970 to 3.6 percent in 1997. From 1970 to 1997 the taxation on capital did not diverge much from its average value of 4.8 percent, with the greater share of tax on capital being levied on income.

As regards the redistributive effects of the German fiscal system, we can

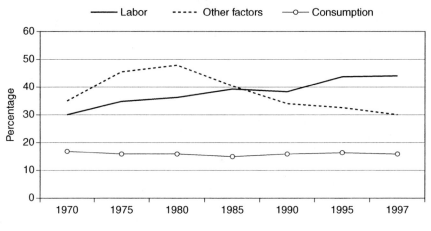

Figure 6.1 Germany: implicit rates 1970–97.

Source: Eurostat (2000).

Table 6.5 Structure according to the economic function as a percentage of GDP

	1970	1975	1980	1985	1990	1995	1997
Consumption	10.6	9.8	10.3	10.0	9.8	10.8	10.4
Labor	20.0	25.4	26.1	26.2	24.7	27.8	26.9
employed	16.0	20.1	21.4	22.1	20.9	24.0	23.2
paid by employers	5.6	7.2	7.4	7.5	7.3	8.2	8.2
paid by employees	10.4	12.9	14.0	14.6	13.6	15.9	15.0
self-employed	4.0	5.3	4.7	4.1	3.8	3.7	3.6
Capital, of which	5.1	4.6	5.2	5.4	4.9	4.3	4.5
real estate	0.6	0.6	0.6	0.6	0.5	0.6	0.7
real capital	0.5	0.5	0.5	0.4	0.4	0.4	0.4
monetary capital	0.3	0.3	0.3	0.4	0.5	0.9	0.9
income	2.7	2.6	3.1	3.4	2.7	1.7	2.2
wealth	0.7	0.5	0.4	0.3	0.4	0.3	0.2
others	0.2	0.3	0.3	0.3	0.4	0.4	0.2
Total	35.7	39.8	41.6	41.6	39.4	42.9	41.8

Source: Eurostat (2000).

Note
1997 is the last data available.

only rely on data for 1988.[33] These data can approximate the situation until 1999, since no change in the system was implemented until the general fiscal reform of 2000, implemented in 2001. In 1988 Germany displayed a very low Gini index both for pre-tax income and post-tax income (0.2591 and 0.2312). It is the country with the most equal distribution of pre-tax and post-tax income according to Wagstaff *et al.* (1999). The average tax rate is 0.1108, one of the lowest among the countries analyzed in this book.

As regards the vertical distribution, Germany has a low vertical distribution in comparison with other countries. It is achieved through a combination of low average tax rate and relatively high level of progressivity (measured with the Kakwani index). The discrepancies between redistributive effect, RE and vertical redistribution, caused by non-zero values of the measures of horizontal inequity and/or re-ranking, are minor in Germany. This means that the impact of differential tax treatment on the distribution of income is far less important than progressivity. The gap between redistributive effect and vertical redistribution is small.

The Kakwani index is quite high for Germany (0.2433), which means that the income tax levied is fairly progressive. Positive values of H (measures the extent of classical horizontal inequality) and $e R$ (measures the extent of re-ranking in the move from the pre-tax distribution to the post-tax distribution) reflect the presence of differential tax treatment which reduces the redistributive effect of the tax.

After the fiscal reform, the tax schedule of personal income tax may be less progressive than before: average rates will fall significantly throughout the income range but the cut will be larger at the two extremes of the distribution. At intermediate income levels, in which many taxpayers are likely to be located, the cut is less significant.

The fact that capital income both from dividends and capital gains is taxed according to the half-income method can have a negative effect on income distribution.[34] Moreover, ceilings on social security contributions are reflected in a slight decline in net tax rates when the income rises.

Tax wedges on labor and corporate taxation

The total average tax wedge on labor increased by 5 percent from 1991 to 2000. Only in the last two years has the tax burden on labor decreased. Since 1998 Germany has cut social security contributions to the pension system by one percentage point[35] in order to enhance the demand for labor. The cut in marginal rates on labor income had the same aim. These provisions reduced the tax wedge on labor and contributed, together with the lowering of depreciation allowances of equipment, to rebalancing the relative cost of capital and labor. According to OECD data,[36] in 2000 the total[37] average tax wedge on labor was approximately 51 percent. It may be reduced to about 18 percent if considering only personal income tax and, to around 32 percent if also taking into account employee's social security contributions. In 2000 the marginal tax wedge on labor was around 65 percent, according to calculations by OECD.[38]

One of the purposes of this section is to investigate the effective tax burden borne by German companies. Table 6.6 presents German data on

Table 6.6 Cost of capital and EMTR

Corporate tax rates[1]	52.35
Overall mean	
cost of capital	7.3
EMTR	31.0
Cost of capital	
intangibles	5.4
industrial buildings	7.2
machinery	5.8
financial assets	10.0
inventories	7.9
retained earnings	9.7
new equity	7.6
debt	3.2
EMTR	
retained earnings	48.4
new equity	35.5
debt	−56.2

Source: EEC (2001).

Note
1 Including surcharges and local taxes.

the cost of capital and the EMTR obtained considering only corporate taxation (i.e. statutory tax rates, the surcharges and local taxes).

In Germany the average cost of capital is 7.3 percent and the most tax-efficient way of financing is debt. This is due to deductions of nominal interest payments from the corporation tax base. Normally, this effect is higher in countries where the corporation tax rates are higher. This is the case of Germany, as Table 6.7 shows: in 1999 the Federal Republic of Germany had the highest statutory tax rate on profit within the EU (52.35 percent).

Financing through new equity and retained earnings is unfavorable, since no deduction from the taxable base for the corresponding payments (dividend) is allowed. The German effective tax burden for both forms of financing approximately equals the tax rate on profit: the EMTR for retained earnings is higher since the associated statutory corporate tax rate was higher than that for distributed dividends (40 percent versus 30 percent) until the fiscal reform in 2001. The EMTR is negative when the investment is debt financed. This is due to the relations between interest payments deductibility and tax allowances for depreciation in excess of economic depreciation. The higher the statutory tax rate and the more accelerated the depreciation, the greater the subsidy. Intangibles and machinery are taxed quite generously.

The German effective average tax rate (EATR) (39.1 percent) is higher than the effective marginal tax rate (EMTR, 31 percent) but is still lower than the overall nominal profit tax rate. The effective average tax rate for

Table 6.7 Effective average tax rate (a)

Corporate tax rates[1]	52.35
Overall mean	39.1
Intangibles	33.9
Industrial buildings	39.0
Machinery	34.9
Financial assets	46.8
Inventories	40.8
Retained earnings	46.1
New equity	40.1
Debt	27.7

Source: EEC (2001).

Note
1 Including surcharges and local taxes. Here the pre-tax real
  rate of return is 20 percent.

debt is positive. The gap with the EMTR for debt is particularly high due to the fact that Germany is a "narrow base country."

In order to have a clearer picture of the German effective fiscal burden, personal taxation is included in the analysis (see Table 6.8). If the personal taxation[39] is introduced in the case of marginal investment, the effective tax burden increases appreciably, as shown in Table 6.9. The personal taxation involves a reduction in the cost of capital and an extensive increase in the effective marginal tax rates. This is due to the investment backflows in the hand of the shareholder. Debt remains the most favored form of finance and retained earnings remains the least favored.

The investigation thus far has been based on the tax regimes which were in place in 1999. However, the German tax reform[40] changed the effective tax burden on corporation and it is thus important to investigate its effects on the cost of capital, EATR and EMTR. Table 6.9 reviews the

Table 6.8 Effective average tax rate (b)

	Average cost of capital
Cost of capital	5.4
EMTR	79.5
Intangibles	4.0
Industrial buildings	5.3
Machinery	4.3
Financial assets	7.7
Inventories	5.6
Retained earnings	6.8
New equity	4.1
Debt	3.5

Source: EEC (2001).

Table 6.9 Cost of capital EMTR EATR

	Intangibles	Industrial buildings	Machinery	Financial assets	Inventories	Mean
Retained earnings	6.6	8.4	7.4	9.5	8.2	8.0
	24.6	40.7	32.1	47.4	39.3	37.8
	34.4	39.9	36.6	43.2	39.3	38.7
New equity	6.6	8.4	7.4	9.5	8.2	8.0
	24.6	40.7	32.1	47.4	39.3	37.8
	34.4	39.9	36.6	43.2	39.3	38.7
Debt	3.2	4.7	3.9	5.7	4.5	4.4
	−58.0	−6.5	−28.6	12.9	−11.8	−13.8
	23.9	28.6	26.1	31.7	27.9	27.6
Mean	5.4	7.1	6.1	8.2	6.9	6.8
	7.8	29.8	18.6	38.9	27.7	26.0
	30.8	35.9	32.9	39.2	35.3	34.8

Source: EEC (2001).

effects of reform on the cost of capital, the EATR and the EATR for domestic investments in the case in which there are no personal taxes.

The lower rate on retained earnings reduces the cost of capital for investment financed in that way. Moreover, as the split rate system is eliminated,[41] and with no personal taxes, the cost of capital for retained earnings is the same as that of new equity. The cost of capital for new equity increases due to a certain extent to the enlargement of the tax base, and in part due to the elimination of the effective subsidy in paying dividends.

The cost of capital for debt finance increases considerably as well. This is due to the decrease in the tax rate, which denotes that the value of interest deductibility will drop.

All types of investment benefit from the tax rate decline. Nevertheless, only investment in buildings and machinery suffers from the reduction in depreciation allowances. Generally, the average cost of capital across assets is cut; however, it grows for investment in machinery. The new provisions of the German fiscal reforms reduce EMTR. This is mainly due to the lower nominal tax rates. According to Table 6.10, debt is still the most convenient way of financing, even though it is far less favored than before. EATR depends more directly on the statutory tax rather than the cost of capital, EATR on retained earnings decreases significantly (on average, from 46.1 percent to 38.7 percent). The EATR on investment financed by new equity also drops (contrasting with the evolution of the cost of capital) imitating the lower statutory corporation tax rate for distributions. To conclude, on average the EATR for investment financed by debt is roughly unchanged, even if there are discrepancies across assets.

Table 6.10 Tax revenues across different levels of government

Taxes	Amount	% on revenues
Customs	3,394	15.5
VAT	9,496	43.5
Revenues of Federal Government	198,793	100.0
of which: wage tax and income tax (42.5%)	62,883	31.6
corporation tax (50%)	18,545	9.3
withholding tax on interests (44%)	3,227	1.6
VAT (52%)	75,990	38.2
States revenues	189,495	100.0
of which: wage tax and income tax (42.5%)	62,883	33.2
corporation tax (50%)	18,545	9.8
withholding tax on interests (44%)	3,227	1.7
VAT	61,958	32.7
business tax on income (26/45)	1,815	1.0
Increased business tax on income	2,378	1.3
Municipalities revenues	57,297	100.0
of which: municipal rate of income tax	23,234	40.6
municipal rate of VAT	2,927	5.1
business tax on income	5,523	9.6

Source: Statistisches Bundesamt, Stat. Jahrbuch, 2001, million euro.

Taxation by levels of government and fiscal federalism

The Federal Republic of Germany is a federation composed of five different levels of government:[42] the national government (*Bund*), the administrative departments (*Regierungbezirke*), the provinces (*Landkriese*), 16 states
(*Länder*) and the municipalities (*Gemeinde*). We will only analyze inter-
actions among the *Bund*, the *Länder* and the *Gemeinden*, which share tax
revenues.

Länder budgets predominantly depend on tax revenue from shared
taxes. Normally more than 80 percent of the taxes of all levels is in shared
taxes and, more importantly, all of these shared taxes are federally determined: all tax laws are federal.[43] With reference to the vertical allocation
of revenues, a great part of tax proceeds are distributed to regions and
communities according to the derivation principle; that is, they follow the
regional origin of the tax revenue. A region receives the percentage of the
tax collected in its particular area. It is worth noting that regions have no
entitlement to fix the rates for their own taxes. Local governments
(*Gemeinden*) can establish the rates on the real estate tax (*Grundsteuer A*[44]
and *Grundsteuer B*[45]) and the business tax (*Gewerbesteuer*) and only have to
devolve part of the proceeds base of the business tax to regional and
central budgets. Their biggest tax revenue consists of an income tax share,
for which they cannot fix rates (even if the constitution clearly allows a law
that could provide for it). The federal constitution itself states that 42.5
percent of the income tax revenue must be retained by the national

government, 42.5 percent by *Länder* and 15 percent by municipalities.[46] The horizontal allocation of tax revenues is made throughout a system of transfers among *Länder*. The horizontal apportionment of the income tax revenue strictly follows the residence principle. On the other hand, the horizontal sharing of other tax revenues (e.g. VAT) is also carried out both in proportion to population and to "financial weakness."[47] In the German fiscal system, resources are also transferred from a *Land* to its *Gemeinden*. Every *Land* has its own particular system. Moreover, the state government assigns some federal transfers to municipalities, according to their "fiscal weakness."

Table 6.10 displays the rate of each tax perceived by each level of government in 2000.

As shown by Table 6.10 the federal government, *Länder* (42.5 percent) and the municipalities (15 percent) are the beneficiaries of the income and wages tax. In 2000 revenues from income tax correspond to the main tax revenue both for municipalities (40.5 percent of total municipal income) and for states (33.1 percent). It is the second largest source of tax revenues for the federal government (31.6 percent).

VAT revenues are the major income for central government (38 percent) and the second greatest income from taxation for the *Länder* (32.7 percent of their total revenues in 2000).

Table 6.11 also shows that in 2000 the federal government collected 46.8 percent of total tax revenues, state governments (*Länder*) 43.9 percent and municipalities 9.3 percent.

Using OECD data we can observe the evolution (from 1975 to 1999) of the main central government taxes as a percentage of total tax revenues of central government. The trend revealed in the data for 2000 is the same as that in the OECD data: the state governments receive the greater part of tax proceeds from taxes on individual income (an average of 36.1 percent of total tax revenues). The second largest source of income is general taxes and then tax on goods and services. Percentages do not vary greatly from 1975 to 1999.

Data for the tax revenue of the main state and local taxes as a percentage of GDP or as a percentage of total tax revenues for these levels of government give a similar picture. State and local governments both

Table 6.11 Attribution of tax revenues to sub-sectors of general government as a percentage of total tax revenues

	1975	1985	1999
Federal or central government	33.9	32.0	30.4
State or *Länder* government	22.5	22.2	22.1
Local government	9.3	9.0	7.9
Social security funds	34.2	36.9	39.5

Source: OECD (2000).

receive the greatest part of resources from taxes on income and profits. The proceeds from these latter total the largest share of the fiscal revenues of the states, though their amount is lower for local than for state government. Actually, the share of income and profits taxes on GDP is lower for local than for state governments.

Two other types of taxes play an important role in the *Länder* and municipalities budget: the share of general taxes on states' budgets increased from 1975 (21.8 percent) to 1999 (38.1 percent). The municipalities' budget is particularly influenced by taxes on property, even though the share decreased from 1975 (20.3 percent) to 1999 (15 percent).

According to the 2000 OECD data (see Table 6.11), the share of tax revenues obtained by central government has fallen from 1975 (33.9 percent) to 1999 (30.4 percent). The share of taxes on total fiscal proceeds collected by the state government has remained mainly constant (around 22 percent), while the share of local government has decreased from 9.3 percent in 1975 to 7.9 percent in 1999.

German reunification was an opportunity to redefine these shares. The automatic application of the horizontal system to the new *Länder* had implied a growth in transfers from rich to poor from approximately 1.8 billion euro to nearly ten billion euro. This means that all old *Länder* (except Bremen and Saarland) would have become net payers.

The solution to this problem was found by transferring more than two-thirds of the equalizing transfers to the federal government. Moreover, the share of VAT proceeds to *Länder* was increased first to 37 percent, then to 44 percent and finally, at the end of 1996, to 49.5 percent. The Table 6.12 shows how resources were divided between new and old *Länder*.

New *Länder* receive far fewer resources than the old ones. This is certainly due to the lower development level of the former East German regions. However, it is worth noting that the new *Länder* are far less numerous than the old ones (5 versus 11).

Table 6.12 Allocation of tax revenues between old and new *Länder*

Taxes	*Old* Länder	*New* Länder	*New/old* Länder (%)
States revenues	146,560	42,935	29.3
corporation tax	18,157	388	2.1
withholding tax on interests	3,149	78	2.5
business tax on income	1,671	144	8.6
increased business tax on income	2,378	–	
Municipalities revenues	52,402	4,895	9.3
municipal rate of income tax	21,802	1,432	6.6
municipal rate of VAT	2,480	447	18.0
business tax on income	10,339	264	4.5

Source: Statistisches Bundesamt, Stat. Jahrbuch, 2001, million euro.

A comparative view against the European average

The German fiscal burden on companies has always been very high compared to other European countries. Germany shows a very high average cost of capital (7.3 percent) and EMTR (31 percent): both indicators display the second highest values in Europe after France (7.5 percent and 33.2 percent). This is related to the fact that, in 1999, Germany had the highest statutory tax rate on profits.

All around Europe the most tax-efficient way of financing is debt. This is particularly true in Germany, especially when considering the EMTR. The effective marginal tax rate in the case of debt financing is the lowest in Europe (−56.2 percent).

As regards infra-marginal investments, Germany displayed the highest EATR in 1999, with an overall mean of 39.1 percent. The German value for debt financing is the second highest in Europe, after France. The same can be observed if considering new equity. However, when taking into account EATR for retained earnings, the German value is by far the highest in Europe (46.1 percent). Moreover, when profitability is set at 20 percent, the German EATR for industrial buildings, intangibles and machinery is the second highest in Europe, while inventories and financial assets are the highest, with the latter being far more expensive than in other European countries.

Germany is also characterized by a high tax wedge on labor. In 2000 the German average tax wedge was above the European average and it displayed the second highest value in the EU. This value is influenced by three different elements: a personal income tax, which is only lower than the Nordic countries,[48] employee's social security contributions, which exhibit the top rate in the EU, and finally employer's social security contributions.[49]

Furthermore, the German tax wedge on labor was the one which increased the most in Europe from 1991 to 2000. According to the marginal tax wedge, in 2000, Germany was above the European mean and displayed the second highest value after Belgium.

Tax reforms in the 1990s and those currently planned

A quick glance at the budget and the general economic environment

In 2001 the general government deficit reached 2.7 percent of GDP (according to an estimate by the statistical office of the European Commission): slowdown in growth,[50] revenue shortfalls (amounting to 1 percent of GDP) caused by the tax reform, expenditure overruns in the healthcare sector and in some *Länder*[51] led to the deterioration of the government budget.[52] In 2002, the public accounts' deterioration was even sharper, with the general government deficit reaching 3.6 percent of GDP, breaching the 3 percent threshold defined by the Stability and

Growth Pact. Thus, Germany incurred in the Excessive Deficit Procedure by the ECOFIN in January 2003.

Looking back to 2001, we see that the previous year's oil price hike resulted in the worst economic performance since 1993 for Germany: the GDP growth rate was only 0.6 percent. Only the first quarter recorded temporally positive growth thanks to the fiscal reform, which stimulated private consumption. However, the effects of the reform were disappointing: a much more robust rise in demand had been expected from the tax relief provided. Finally, households' nominal disposable income rose by 3.5 percent in 2001, which was the fastest rate of growth for quite some time. Real consumer spending could not keep pace with the intense rise in income since important losses in purchasing power had to be taken into account, and the household savings ratio grew for the first time since the early 1990s. In the second quarter, growth stopped because of a huge fall in investment volumes. Construction, which had been falling from the middle of the 1990s, fell again by 5.8 percent in 2001. Equipment investment dropped by 5 percent. In the second part of the year, the growth rate became negative and the events of 11 September intensified the economic slowdown, by lowering consumer and business confidence. Demand was progressively satisfied more through reducing inventories than by increasing production. The consequential stock depletation reduced GDP growth in 2001 by 0.9 percent.

As for 2002, German economic activity was even more depressed. German GDP increased only by 0.2 percent in 2002 that led to the worsening conditions for public finance.

Tax reforms in the 1990s

Tax reforms in the 1990s were not substantial in Germany: while others embarked on rate cutting and base-broadening reforms along the lines of the 1986 US reform, the Federal Republic became an outlaw in international tax comparisons. Its fiscal system was characterized by high statutory tax rates and narrow bases. The introduction of the tax on industry and trade in 1991, and the solidarity surcharge in 1993, in order to finance the reunification process, follows the same path.

Between 1998 and 2000, reductions of 1 percent of social security contributions to the pension system were implemented. The reductions were financed by the introduction of ecological taxes in 1999, which will gradually increase until 2003. However the fiscal system was not changed significantly until the Tax Relief Act of 1999–2000–2002.

The fiscal reform

The act on the reduction of tax rates and on the reform of corporate taxation (*SteuerSenkungsGesetzt*) obtained final parliamentary approval on

14 July 2000. The tax reform provisions were planned to enter into force on 1 January 2001 and were described by the government as the "most far-reaching tax reduction program in the history of the Federal Republic of Germany." However, the government presented a supplementary bill to reflect a compromise between the two Houses of Parliament calling for a further reduction of 1 percent in the top marginal rate of income tax for the year 2005 onwards and for further relief for middle-market business.

The primary goal of the tax reduction act is to permanently lighten the tax burden by sinking the rates and by changing the corporation tax system. The basic tax rate fell from 25.9 percent in 1998 to 19.9 percent in 2001. The top rate was cut (step-by-step) from 53 percent in 1998 to 48.5 percent by as soon as 2001. Over the same period the basic allowances increased from approximately €6,322 to €7,206 (in 2002 it will be €7,235).

From 2003 the basic personal allowance will be increased to €7,426.[53] The basic tax rate will be cut to 17 percent while the top rate will be brought down to 47 percent. From January 2005, the basic personal allowance will be increased to €7,664. The basic tax rate will be reduced to 15 percent while the top rate will fall to 42 percent. The top rate will be applied only to taxable income in excess of €52,152. This will help to alleviate the progressive increase in the tax rate for middle-income earners and in addition there will again, as in 2001, be a general lowering of tax rates.

The rate cuts will reduce the tax charge on all payers of income tax, affording the greatest relief to employees and families with low and medium incomes as well as to small and medium-sized unincorporated businesses.

Corporation tax is levied at a uniform rate of 25 percent[54] for all business years beginning on or after 1 January 2001. As regards the taxation of dividends, the full imputation system is replaced by the so-called half-income system to make cross-border investment within Europe more attractive. Under this system, only half of the distributed profits of a corporation are included in the shareholder's personal income tax base. In return, it is no longer necessary to credit the corporation tax paid by the company against the shareholder's income tax.

As for capital gains, the original plan defined by the Tax Relief Act of 1999–2000–2002 has been partially scrapped by the medium-term fiscal plan signed by the Red–Green government late in 2002, aimed at driving budget deficit into line. According to the original fiscal reform plan, capital gains from the sale of cross-corporation shareholdings were generally exempt from tax. In order to prevent abuse, however, various restrictions were imposed. Furthermore, under certain conditions, this provision would not have applied to credit institutions and financial services. The new rules entered into effect from the 2002 tax year.

Private shareholders could sell their stakes in corporations after a minimum holding period of one year without paying tax as before, unless they have a substantial interest. However, the threshold for what constitutes a substantial interest is reduced from 10 percent to 1 percent as from 2002. If the sale was subject to tax, i.e. when shares were sold within the one-year holding period or represent a substantial interest, the half-income method applies. The medium-term fiscal plan reintroduces a tax on capital gains for individuals, starting from 2003. At the same time, capital losses can be set against capital gains, acting as a cushion for retail investors against the high volatility in asset prices.

Unincorporated business benefits from the considerable cuts in income tax rates. Unincorporated companies deriving their income from trade or business and subject to local trade tax have an additional reduction in their tax burden as the trade tax is credited against their income tax liability in a standardized form. Their income tax is reduced by an amount corresponding to 1.8 times the assessment basis for trade tax. The trade tax is still deductible as operating expenditure. As a result of the mediation procedure, these provisions have been readjusted with respect to their precise objective in order to limit over-compensation. Below the line, however, the majority of companies are still granted full relief from trade tax.

The tax relief for the sale or closure of a business is raised from approximately €30,680 to €51,130 (from 2002 it is €51,200).

Company transfers and corporations involving unincorporated SMEs are facilitated by reintroducing the co-partner tax remission. This provision allows for tax-neutral transfers of assets with undisclosed reserves and it helps, in particular, unincorporated SMEs to cope with intergenerational succession. Advance depreciation provisions for the new investment undertaken by SMEs, adjusted to the new depreciation conditions, are retained.

The tax relief is financed principally by restricting tax depreciation arrangements. The declining-balance tax depreciation rate for movable assets is reduced from 30 percent to 20 percent. The depreciation rate for company buildings falls from 4 percent to 3 percent. From 2001, the official depreciation rate tables are based on the more realistic "useful life" periods. The rules on shareholder debt financing are reinforced with the aim of limiting abuse.

According to the government, the taxpayers are receiving lasting tax relief in an annual amount of about 56 billion euro a year. This is due to the tax measures adopted by Germany's Social Democratic Government since 1999, namely the Tax Reform 2000, the Tax Relief Act 1999–2000–2002, the Family Benefits Act (Stages one and two) and other reform measures, including the Pension Reform Law. The tax reform in 2000 alone will provide tax relief of 32 billion euro. Families, wage and salary earners and small and medium-sized business will be the main beneficiaries of the reform. As a result, according to the government, the tax reform will stimulate private consumption and ease new investment, two essential requirements for promoting growth and employment.

According to the Ministry of Finance, the revenue loss coming from the full implementation of the fiscal reform will be 31.9 billion euro, equivalent to 1.5 percent of current GDP. The personal income tax will generate the greater part of revenue losses. The net cost of the business tax provision reproduces the balanced effects of huge gross changes from the reduction in rates and expansion of the base.

Table 6.13 displays the full revenue effects of the reform.

The new corporate income tax system seems to conform to EU law, because equal tax status is provided to dividends and gains on the disposal of both domestic and foreign shares. However, an imputation system is also compatible with EU law when the corporate tax credit is extended to foreign dividends. A full imputation system has the advantage of being closer to capital export neutrality when international differences in corporate tax rates exist.

The imputation system was abolished on the grounds that it was not suitable for application within Europe, since it is open to abuse because its application may be obtained surreptitiously (dividend stripping) and, additionally, it is extremely complicated. It is questionable, however, whether these problems were actually solved by the implementation of the half-income system. In the absence of the German right to tax, the non-resident taxpayer does not benefit from the half-income system; conversely, the resident taxpayer has to include only half the dividends in his assessment basis, even in the case of foreign dividends. Looking at pages 130–7, it would appear that it does not make any difference whether the dividend is derived from a domestic or a foreign source. This unequal treatment of resident and non-resident taxpayers results in a discrimination of the latter and, therefore, it is extremely questionable with regard to European law. However, domestic taxation is the responsibility of the respective national legislator.

Since the corporate tax rate remains at a persistently high level in Germany, the reform has only a minor impact on the ranking of Germany

Table 6.13 Full revenue effects of the reform

Billion DM	*Billion euro*
Overall revenue effect	−31.9
Of which	
business tax	−5.4
Comprising	
cuts in corporate tax rates	−10.4
cuts in rates on unincorporated enterprises	−3.1
tighter depreciation rules	8.7
other measures	−0.51
personal taxes	−26.5

Source: Ministry of Finance (2000).

as an investment location.[55] However, the lower corporate and income tax rates and, the extension of the dividend income exemption from capital gains taxation on the sale of domestic as well as foreign investments are factors, may lead foreign corporations to review their group structures and bring at least some of their German and foreign subsidiaries under the roof of a German holding company.

Moreover, since foreign dividends are no longer at a comparative disadvantage, the reform makes it easier for German investors to exploit international differences in corporate tax rates. The reduction of the German corporate income tax rate may attract additional foreign equity financed investment. However, other EU-investment locations still exhibit lower corporate tax rates. The tax reform sharpens restrictions on debt-financed inbound investment by tightening up thin-capitalization rules; this higher taxed equity capital displaces lower tax debt capital. Moreover, the debt-financed acquisition of German corporations by foreign-controlled German holdings may be restrained by non-deductible interest payments. The tax reform discourages post-acquisition reorganization of the share deals but facilitates restructuring of German investment.

The inbound investor will probably wish to seriously consider the use of a partnership. In contrast to a German corporation, a partnership suffers no thin-capitalization restrictions, would repatriate its profits freely abroad without deduction of withholding tax, might offer possibilities for obtaining an interest deduction both in Germany and abroad and can in some circumstances increase the scope for loss utilization.

Some other changes from the 2002 medium-term fiscal plan

Besides the introduction of taxation on capital gains for individuals, the medium-term fiscal plan agreed late in 2002 includes some other proposals.

The most striking piece of news for German companies is the introduction of new limits to their ability to consolidate losses against profits. So far, there were no limits to the amount or the timeframe over which corporations could carry forward past losses. From 2003, past losses can be used to compensate profits only for 50 percent of profits in any given year for a limited time period of seven years.

Another proposal concerns group of companies that won't be allowed to compensate losses incurred at one company with profits made at another under the trade income tax. Furthermore, the government has planned to restrict rules on transfer prices and retroactive profit-transfer.

Last but not least, the scrapping of some other tax breaks are on the cards (that is, the exemption from energy taxes for German industry and VAT exemptions for some agricultural products).

Notes

1 In the German stability program the target for 2004 was at −1 percent of GDP but in February at the ECOFIN council the German government committed itself to a budget close to balance by 2004.
2 In 2000, the debt at the end of the period was 60 percent of GDP. In 2002 the debt ratio is expected to rise again to 60.8 percent as a consequence of high nominal deficit and weak nominal GDP growth.
3 For further details see *Deutsche Bank Monthly Report,* January 2002.
4 Including discrepancies in clearing transactions between central, regional and local authorities.
5 Expenditure on investment grants, loans and acquisition of participating interests.
6 We could not find a better description of 2001 public revenues. We only have data for 2000, which report that total revenues come from taxation and other fiscal charges (84.7 percent), benefit taxes (2.7 percent), economic activity (1.8 percent) capital revenues (7.7 percent) and other revenues (3.1 percent).
7 For further details see Deutsche Bundesbank's *Annual Report,* 2001.
8 The reunification process led to a huge financial effort, which ended up in redistributing to the eastern *Länder* almost 6 percent of GDP each year.
9 The latest fiscal reform was realized during the Schröder government. It started with the Tax Relief Act 1999–2000–2002 and ended with the Tax Reduction Act (*Steuersenkungsgesetzt*) approved by the German Parliament (*Bundesrat*) on July 14, 2000. It has been implemented over 2001 and 2002. See also pp. 143–53.
10 It is important to note that, since the US tax reform in 1986, many countries reformed their fiscal system by broadening tax bases and reducing statutory tax rates. This means that until 2000 Germany moved along a different path in fiscal reforms.
11 This method determines the taxable base as the gross income less related expenses in accordance with the cash receipts and disbursement method.
12 The net income method is used for this category, unless the taxpayer elects to employ the net worth comparison method.
13 In the German fiscal system there is a special method of collecting income tax chargeable on income from paid employment. It is the so-called wages tax (*Lohnsteuer*). It has the same characteristics as income tax but it is withheld by the employer on the basis of a wages-tax card and wages-tax tables for daily, weekly or monthly wage payments.
14 The income tax plus the solidarity surcharge and the social security contributions must be withheld and transferred by the employer to the authorities.
15 The benefit arising from non-marketable stock options is taxable only when the option is exercised. In this case the taxable benefit is equal to the fair market value of the shares at the time the option is exercised, less any amount paid by the employee when the option was granted. If the stock options are freely marketable, the income is realized when the employee receives the option. The taxable income is the market price of the stock option on the stock exchange at the date the option was received, less any amount the employee actually paid for the option.
16 In Germany there are different pension schemes (in addition to the statutory scheme) funded on a contract between the employee and the employer. They can be paid in the form of a lump-sum (*Kapitalabfindung*) or in the form of an annuity (*Leibrente*).
17 In 1999 the off-set of negative income was possible until €51,130 or €102,260 for jointly assessed married couples.

18 For non-resident companies, the new rules applied from 1 January 2001.

19 This discipline does not discriminate between dividends and capital gains.

20 They include expenses for the occupational training of children and expenses for domestic help for the elderly or the sick.

21 The allowance was applicable from 1 January 2001 and is €14,412 for jointly assessed spouses.

22 The child benefit is a monthly payment of €138 for the first and the second children, €153 for the third child and €179 for the fourth and any further children.

23 The values are comprehensive of the employer's and employee's part.

24 Inheritance and gift tax is imposed on acquisitions by way of inheritance or gift, on donations made for a particular purpose and once every 30 years on the property of a family foundation.

25 Debts of the deceased, funeral and administrative expenses are deductible.

26 All types of income realized by the company are deemed business income.

27 This means that the corporate income levied at company level is fully credited against the income tax charge of a resident shareholder. If the imputation credit exceeds the shareholder's tax charge, the excess is refunded.

28 The new rates, after the fiscal reform, were effective after 1 January 2001. They vary from 6 percent to 10 percent for machinery, 12.5 percent for office equipment, from 8 percent to 10 percent for office furniture, 33.3 percent for computers and from 11 percent to 16 percent for cars, trucks, etc.

29 The beneficiaries of this tax are the municipalities (80 percent), the *Länder* governments (about 15 percent) and federal government (about 5 percent).

30 See Sections eight and nine of *Gewerbesteuersgesetzt* (Law on business tax).

31 On 1 April 1999, the federal government introduced the ecological tax reform. The aim of this reform was to gradually increase energy prices and to use the additional energy tax receipts to reduce pension insurance contributions.

32 That is, capital and self-employed labor.

33 See Wagstaff *et al.* (1999).

34 A taxpayer who earns 100 DM as capital gains has a lower tax burden than a taxpayer who only has wage income.

35 This cut was financed by ecological taxes introduced in 1999. They will increase gradually until 2003.

36 See Joumard (2001).

37 Total tax wedge includes personal income tax, employee's social security contributions and employer's social security contributions.

38 See Joumard (2001).

39 Here a qualified shareholder taxed at the highest personal tax rate is considered.

40 It came into effect on 1 January 2001.

41 This means that Germany progresses toward greater tax neutrality on investment financing.

42 The German Constitution of 1949 leaves all functions to the *Länder* unless otherwise specified. This "unless" goes a very long way. Some largely restricted local functions are reserved. Local governments in general are poorly represented in the Constitution. Moreover, quite a lot of federal functions are openly cited like foreign affairs, currency, defense, etc. Finally, articles 73 and 74 of the Constitution record several functions as the subject of the "current legislation." This means "the *Länder* shall have the power to legislate as long as, and to the extent that, the federation does not exercise its right to legislate."

43 Recently there has been a great debate in Germany about whether the *Länder* should be granted more autonomy in their tax law. However, recent studies by

the ZEW (Center for Economic Research) demonstrate that, without a reform of the fiscal equalization system, the introduction of partial tax autonomy of the *Länder* would lead to undesirable harmful incentives for fiscal policy. Regardless of the tax competition among *Länder*, an increase in the tax burden may emerge.

44 *Grundsteuer A* is levied on agricultural real estate. The base rate is six per thousand in the entire Federal Republic.

45 *Grundsteuer B* is imposed on all other real estates and buildings (private and used for an economic activity). Base rates are 2.6 per thousand and 3.5 per thousand for West Germany and 5 percent and 10 percent in East Germany. The difference is due to the fact that the cadastral values in East Germany are those of 1934.

46 It is worth noting that the municipalities only have a consultative role in the formation of fiscal law.

47 Not only income tax revenue but also the VAT are split. At the first level, three-quarters of it is apportioned to the states according to their population. Another quarter is reserved for those states considered "financially weak." They receive supplementary transfers from VAT in order to bring their fiscal potential up to at least 92 percent of the average of total regional taxes per capita. In real terms this means that Eastern states acquire roughly twice as much VAT revenue per capita than their Western counterparts. At a second level, there is a redistribution of resources among states in accordance to a special mechanism based on the differentials in tax capacities. The benchmark is compared with the effective financial situation of each state, and the gap is subsequently equalized according to a formula. States below the average receive a compensation that is to be financed, in progressive steps, by the states below the average. At a third level, there is a final corrective of the distribution of public resources in the form of asymmetrical vertical grants by the federal government: so-called supplementary federal grants.

48 Finland, Denmark, Norway.

49 The share of the latter is low in comparison to many other European countries, but they cannot compensate for the other two factors described here.

50 The slowdown in growth had two main effects on the German government budget. On the one hand, the deficit increase was due to the working of the automatic stabilizers. On the other hand, when growth stops, enterprises and households pay less taxes.

51 Most of the deterioration in the German deficit resulted from an increase in the deficit of the *Länder*, whereas the federal level (*Bund*) kept its deficit under control. The 2001 fiscal cut in corporate income tax mainly deprived the *Länder* of revenues. However they continued to spend as before and, since they spent as much as the *Bund*, they increased the deficit by about 1 percent of German GDP.

52 In 2000 the general government balance swung into a surplus of 1.5 percent of GDP. The result is sharply influenced by the revenues from the auctioning of UMTS mobile phone licenses, which amounted to 2.5 percent of GDP. Net of these receipts, the deficit recovered by 0.4 percent of GDP, less than in 1999. As a matter of fact the structural balance remained almost unaffected: cyclically-adjusted net borrowing reached 0.7 percent of GDP in 2000. In 2002, according to estimates by the European Commission, general government deficit is projected to rise to 2.8 percent of GDP. This is due to both more benefits and rising payments for growing unemployment and slow growth, which is itself not tax-friendly. Government consumption is forecast to increase by 2 percent. This will be due to high spending on internal and external security, rising public sector salaries and health expenditures. In 2000, net govern-

ment interests payments amounted to 2.8 percent of GDP and the primary surplus to 3.99 percent of GDP.

53 The increase in the basic allowances scarcely compensate for inflation: if the inflation is 2 percent, the real growth between 2000 and 2005 is less than 1 percent.

54 The situation is complex because there are two other taxes. The first is the solidarity surcharge of 5.5 percent and the second is the local trading tax. They bring the combined marginal rate to an average of around 39 percent, shifting between 36 percent and 42 percent. This contrasts with a combined rate on retained earnings under the pre-reform system of about 52 percent (Keen 2001).

55 See pages 141–4.

References and Bibliography

Atripaldi, V. and Bifulco, R. (2001) *Federalismi Fiscali e Costituzioni*, Torino: Giappichelli Editore.

Banca d'Italia (2001) *Supplementi al Bollettino Statistico, Statistiche di Finanza Pubblica nei Paesi dell'Unione Europea*, anno XI, 62.

Berger, H. and Quack, J.S. (2001) "Aspects of the German tax reduction act with regard to the treatment of dividends and capital gains," *Intertax*, 29, 3: 76–86.

Büttner, T. and Schwager, R. (2002) "Tax autonomy of the *Länder*, EU Commission presents study on corporate taxation in Europe," *Zew News English Edition*, 2.

Carey, D. and Tchilinguirian, H. (2000) "Average effective tax rates on capital, labour and consumption," Economic Department, Working Paper 258, Paris: OECD.

Deutsche Bundesbank (2001) *Annual Report*.

—— (2002) *Monthly Report*, 54, 1, January.

—— (2002) *Monthly Report*, 54, 2, February.

—— (2002) *Monthly Report*, 54, 4, April.

EU Commission (2000) *Directory of Taxes in the EU: Germany*, Brussels: EU Commission.

—— (2001) *Company Taxation in the Internal Market*, SEC(2001) 1681, Brussels: EU Commission.

—— (2002) *Statistical Annex of European Economy*, Brussels: EU Commission.

Eurostat (2000) *Structure of the Taxation Systems in the European Union, 1970–1997*, Brussels: EU Commission.

—— (2002) *New Cronos Statistics*, databank CD-ROM.

Fausto, D. and Pica, F. (2000) *Teoria e fatti del federalismo fiscale*, Bologna: Il Mulino.

Giannini, S. and Maggiulli, C. (2001) *The Effective Tax Rates in the EU Commission Study on Corporate Taxation: Methodological Aspects, Main Results and Policy Implications*, CAPP, Università di Modena e Reggio Emilia.

Jacobs, O.H. *et al.* (2000) "Stellungnahme zum Steuersenkungsgesetz," Dokumentation, 00-04, *Zew*.

Jacobs, O.H. (2002) *Unternehmensbesteurung und Rechtsform, 3, völlig neubearbeitete Auflage*, Verlag C.H. Beck.

Joumard, I. (2001) "Tax system in European Union countries," Economics Department Working Paper 301, Paris: OECD.

Keen, M. (2001) *Tax Reform in Germany*, Fiscal Affairs Department, Washington: IMF.

Lammersen, L. and Spengel, C. (2001) "EU Commission presents study on corporate taxation in Europe," *ZEW News English Edition*, 4.

Liberati, P. (2000) *Il Federalismo Fiscale. Aspetti Teorici e Pratici*, Milano: Editore Ulrico Hoepli.

Martinez-Mongay, C. (2000) "The ECFIN effective taxation databank. Properties and comparisons with other databanks," European Commission Economic Paper 146, Brussels: EU Commission.

OECD (2000) *Revenue Statistics 1965–2000*, Paris: OECD.

Raedler, A.J. (2000) "Germany: changing the corporate tax system," *Algemeen Fiscaal Tijdschrift*, 8: 345–9.

Schreiber, U. (2000) "German tax reform: an international perspective," *Finanz-Archiv*, 57, 4: 525–41.

Spengel, C. (1995) *Europäische Steuerbelastungsvergleiche, Deutschland, Frankreich, Grossbritanien*, IDW–Verlag.

Statistisches Bundesamt (2001) "Statisctisches Jahrbuch 2001," *Journal of Applied Social Science Studies*.

Wagstaff, A. *et al.* (1999) "Redistributive effect, progressivity and differential tax treatment: personal income taxes in twelve OECD countries," *Journal of Public Economics*, 72: 73–98.

7 Ireland

Alessandro Sommacal

Introduction

The aim of this chapter is to analyze the Irish tax system and its evolution from an economic policy point of view. Due to the reform of the last decade, this small country is now characterized by an interesting combination of good economic growth and strong budgetary situation, along with a low fiscal pressure, in particular on corporations and labor.

On pages 161–5 we give some quantitative information on the taxes levied and on the evolution of the tax system between 1970 and 1999, comparing it with the EU average. Irish fiscal burden, measured as the ratio between taxes and GDP, shows in this period a "hump" path, increasing until 1985 and then decreasing to the current value, the lowest in Europe. To better understand this issue, it is important to look at the composition of fiscal revenue, stressing the fact that, compared to other EU countries, Ireland has a low fraction of GDP absorbed by social contributions, while the quota absorbed by taxes is almost the same in Ireland and in the rest of the EU. Concerning the composition of taxes, direct and indirect taxes have the same importance. Among the first category the major role is played by income tax, even if during the last 30 years corporate tax has become also important while, among the second, VAT is the most relevant. Fiscal receipts are strongly centralized, since the amount of them received by the local authorities is far below the EU average.

Then, on pages 165–9, we analyze some institutional features of the Irish taxation system, focusing on the main taxes. One of the main features of income tax is the strong degree of individualization, in the sense that it is designed in order to take into account personal characteristics of the taxpayer, such as marital status, age and number of dependent children. This is true not only for tax relief and exemptions, but also for tax bands. Concerning tax relief, it must also be noticed that most of them are in the form of tax credits rather than tax deductions. In this way fiscal saving is equal for all taxpayers. Tax rates are characterized by only two values: a lower one of 20 percent and a higher one of 42 percent. With regard to tax units, some elements of family taxation are present.

Corporate tax has been characterized for a long time by many special regimes, of which the most important is the facilitated rate of 10 percent. This special rate is to be progressively phased out over the next few years (until 2005 or 2010, depending on the specific activity carried out). However, it must be noticed that, at the same time, the standard rate has been reduced and it is 16 percent in 2002 and in the 2003 it will be 12.5 percent; thus the statutory rate on corporations remains very low. A separate tax is charged on capital gains, whose value is computed taking into account inflation and the interests on deposit. Dividends are charged at 20 percent, but the tax withheld can be used as a tax credit against the recipient's income tax liability. The main indirect taxes, as in other EU countries, are value added tax (VAT) and excise duties, and do not present specific features. Taxes on (the transfer of) property are also present: capital acquisition tax (CAT), stump duties and rates. Concerning the latter, it must be noticed that they are the only relevant local taxes.

This institutional description represents the necessary background for the analysis that will be carried out later on. First we consider the evaluation of the distribution of fiscal burden. Both functional classification and implicit tax rates show that the burden is first of all charged on labor, and then on consumption and other factors. Nevertheless, compared to other European countries, Ireland has a large amount of taxes on consumption and a low level of taxes on labor. However, the marginal tax wedge shows a remarkable (even if declining during the 1990s) distortion on labor supply: this disincentive effect of the tax system is one of the most relevant constraints to the further growth of the Irish economy. Regarding the effect of corporate taxation, it must be stressed its very low level, in accordance with the statutory rate and the effective (marginal and average) rate. This can explain the fact that Ireland strongly attracts foreign investments. An important shortcoming is, however, represented by the discrimination between equity and debt, in favor of the latter, that is still present.

Finally, we describe and examine the main reforms of the 1990s, trying to give an evaluation of the system. Since the second half of the 1980s, Ireland has seen a considerable fiscal consolidation, achieved through expenditure cuts rather than a rise in taxes (that have instead been reduced); at the same time, the Irish economy has grown at a very fast pace. Despite this positive situation, some important policy focus remains, such as binding labor constraints. On this point taxation plays an important role, owing to its distortion effect on labor supply; the reforms carried out are a move in the right direction, since they have tried to enhance work incentives, but further efforts are probably required. Concerning corporate tax, the phasing out of special regimes (under pressure from the EU) and the contemporaneous reduction of general corporate rate also prove to be positive measures. Further reforms are still needed to eliminate fiscal discrimination between equity and debt finance and VAT would probably benefit, from an efficiency point of view, from more uniform rates, even if such a reform would increase distributive problems.

The structure of the system and its development from the 1970s

The current structure of the tax system and social security contributions

In 2001 the Irish general government balance was in surplus for an amount equal to 1.4 percent of GDP (with a primary balance of 3 percent of GDP) and public debt reached the level of 35.8 percent of GDP. This remarkable result is due to the dramatic changes in fiscal policy that took place in the 1990s, and caused total expenditure and total receipts to achieve, respectively, the values of 33.4 percent and 34.8 percent of GDP. Concerning the composition of total expenditure, both collective consumption and gross fixed capital formation constitute 14 percent, while social transfers (in kind and monetary) represent 27 percent, interest payments 5 percent, subsidies 4 percent and other expenditures 37 percent. Total receipts can instead be divided into three items: taxes, social contributions and other revenues whose percentage relative to total receipts are respectively 72 percent, 12 percent and 15 percent (see Department of Finance 2001).

The main source of receipts by far are fiscal revenues (i.e. taxes plus social contributions), whose structure as a percentage of GDP is described in Table 7.1, for the years 1970–99. In 1999 the total fiscal pressure, measured as the ratio between total fiscal revenue and GDP, was 33.5 percent. As we will see in more detail later in the chapter (pp. 164–5), this value was the lowest in Europe, where average fiscal pressure amounted to 43.1 percent. Focusing on the composition of Irish fiscal burden, direct and indirect taxes were both 14.5 percent of GDP and social contributions 4.5 percent. In the composition of direct taxation, personal income tax is without doubt the most important part. Corporate income taxation also plays an important, but quantitatively less considerable, role. Among indirect taxes, the main role is played by Value Added Tax (VAT), that represents 50.3 percent of indirect taxation. Another important category of indirect taxes is the excise duty, that amounts to 32.4 percent of indirect taxation. Finally, social contributions are mainly paid by employers and by employees: the first finance 62.2 percent of social contributions and the latter 33.3 percent. The remaining is due from the self-employed, whose contributions represent 4.4 percent of social contributions. This composition of revenue has not remained the same over the last 30 years, but is the result of changes, often of remarkable import, that we will examine in detail in the next section.

Fiscal receipts in the Irish system are strongly centralized: 84 percent go to central government and only 3 percent to local government

Table 7.1 Structure and development of fiscal revenues in Ireland and European average as a percentage of GDP, 1970–99

	1970		1975		1980		1985		1990		1995		1999	
	Ireland	Europe	Ireland	Europe	Ireland	Europe	Ireland	Europe	Ireland	Europe	Ireland	Europe	Ireland	Europe
Direct taxes	9.4	8.9	10.3	11.9	12.7	12.7	14.5	13.1	13.9	13.2	13.9	13.3	14.5	14.5
personal income	7.0	5.5	8.8	8.9	10.9	9.3	12.3	9.0	11.1	8.9	10.2	9.6	9.3	9.9
corporation income	1.3	2.2	0.7	1.9	1.5	2.2	1.7	2.8	2.2	2.9	3.2	2.4	4.4	2.8
Indirect taxes	19.4	13.0	17.0	12.2	16.8	13.2	18.4	13.0	16.2	13.0	14.8	13.6	14.5	14.6
VAT	0.0	5.1	4.6	5.7	5.0	6.6	8.0	6.1	7.2	6.6	7.1	6.9	7.3	7.3
excise duties	10.2	3.5	8.8	3.5	9.4	3.2	8.0	3.2	6.5	3.1	5.5	3.4	4.7	2.5
Total tax revenue	28.8	21.9	27.3	24.1	29.5	25.9	32.9	26.1	30.1	26.2	28.7	26.9	29.0	29.1
Social contributions	2.8	11.7	4.7	12.8	5.2	13.4	6.0	13.8	5.5	13.7	5.1	15.0	4.5	14.0
employers	1.4	7.2	2.6	7.7	3.2	7.8	3.6	7.9	3.1	7.8	2.9	8.0	2.8	7.8
employees	1.3	3.5	2.1	3.8	2.0	4.3	2.4	4.5	2.1	4.5	1.9	5.1	1.5	4.5
self-employed	0.0	1.0	0.0	1.3	0.0	1.3	0.0	1.5	0.2	1.4	0.2	1.8	0.2	1.7
Total fiscal revenue	31.6	33.6	32.0	36.9	34.7	39.3	38.9	39.9	35.6	39.9	33.8	41.9	33.5	43.1
Administrative level														
Central government	25.7	19.7	24.7	21.1	28.0	22.3	31.3	22.1	28.7	22.2	27.5	22.5	28.0	23.7
Local government	3.3	2.2	2.4	2.8	1.3	2.9	1.0	3.1	1.0	3.8	0.9	4.0	0.9	4.3

Sources: 1970–95, Eurostat; 1999 Eurostat New Cronos databank 2002 (data equalized with Eurostat).

Note
Minor items are omitted.

(the remaining fraction is absorbed by the social security system and by EC institutions).

Developments of the system from 1970 to 1999

The evolution of fiscal pressure shows a "hump" path: the fraction of GDP absorbed by fiscal revenues has increased since 1970, reaching its highest level in 1985; it then fell and it is now fixed at a value differing from that of 1970 by 1.9 percent of GDP. We will now examine the structural evolution of the fiscal system in more detail.

A first general feature is a slight reduction in the weight of taxation relative to total fiscal revenue. The ratio between social contributions and total fiscal revenue increased from 8.9 percent in 1970 to 13.4 percent in 1999; conversely, taxation passed from 91.9 percent in 1970 to 86.6 percent in 1999. This change in the structure of the system is not due to a reduction of the GDP fraction absorbed by direct taxation (which shifted from 28.8 percent of GDP in 1970 to 29 percent of GDP in 1999), but to a sharp increase in the social contributions paid (whose value shifted from 2.8 percent of GDP in 1970 to 4.5 percent of GDP in 1999). However the structural change described above took place for the most part in the first half of the 1970s, when the ratio between taxation and total revenue fell from 91.1 percent to 85.3 percent and social contributions rose from 8.9 percent to 14.7 percent. In the following years the composition of the fiscal system remained substantially unchanged, but in the second half of the 1990s we notice a decrease of almost 2 percent in the weight of social contributions relative to total revenue. Social contributions are also lower (as fraction of GDP absorbed and as percentage of total fiscal revenues) in Ireland than in other European countries, as we will see on pages 164–5.

A second important feature concerns the evolution of the role of direct versus indirect taxation. The relative importance of the first has strongly increased: in 1970 the ratio between direct taxation and total taxation amounted only to 29.7 percent and the ratio between indirect taxation and total taxation was 61.4 percent; in 1999 these two ratios were both 43.3 percent. The key period of this change is from the 1970s to the first year of the 1990s; since then the situation has been more or less stable. This development is due to an increase (reduction) in the percentage of GDP absorbed by direct (indirect) taxation.

It is also important to explore the evolution of the composition of indirect and direct taxation. In the structure of direct taxes there is a trend toward the greater importance of corporate income taxation, whose share, relative to direct taxation, has increased from 13.8 percent in 1970 to 30.3 percent in 1999; conversely, personal income tax has reduced in importance. The structure of indirect taxation has drastically changed from 1970 to 1999. In particular, the importance of VAT grew quickly in the 1970s and 1980s: in 1975 it represented 27.1 percent of indirect tax and in 1985

43.5 percent; in the last 12 years the share of indirect taxes represented by VAT increased at a slower pace, reaching the value of 50.3 percent in 1999. At the same time, excise duties have fallen progressively from 52.6 percent of indirect taxes in 1970 to 32.4 percent in 1999 (this path shows a "hump" in the second half of the 1970s where the ratio between excise duties and indirect taxation reached 56 percent, that is the highest value in the last 40 years). Even more remarkable is the decline in importance of the other indirect taxes.

Finally, concerning the sorting of fiscal revenues according to the level of government receiving them, we can observe a growing centralization of fiscal receipts, with the fraction pertaining to central government increasing by 9 percent.

A comparative view against the European average

The situation of Irish public finance is in general very good, even in comparative terms. As we have already seen in this chapter, the general government balance in Ireland is in surplus, and this positive result will not change over the next years, even if a reduction in the surplus is forecasted. Moreover, government debt is very low, especially if we consider that in the EU there are countries such as Italy, Belgium and Greece that have ratios between public debt and GDP around 100 percent.

A similar situation characterizes the burden of taxation: Ireland has the lowest ratio between total taxation and GDP. This is due in particular to the relatively low quota of GDP absorbed by social contributions: this quota was 4.5 percent in Ireland in 1999 versus the 14 percent European average. If we exclude social contributions, we can see instead that the burden of taxation in Ireland is similar to the European average. In fact one of the main peculiarities of the Irish system (from a quantitative point of view) is the small role played by social contributions compared to other European countries. Social contributions in Ireland represents only 13.4 percent of total taxation, while the European average is 32.5 percent; conversely the share of total revenues due to taxation is 86.6 percent in Ireland while the European average is 67.5 percent. However, if we look at the composition of taxes, the Irish mix of direct and indirect revenue is similar to the European average: about 50 percent of taxes are indirect and the remaining 50 percent are direct.

The resources used for pension purposes in Ireland do not only derive from compulsory social contributions. In fact, besides the compulsory PAYG pillar, there exists a second pillar financed through voluntary contributions, while in other EMU countries, where social contributions are higher, these complementary pension schemes could be less developed. One of the most debated topics in Ireland over the last few years has been the low coverage of the pensions system, as revealed by a study of the Economic and Social Research Institute in 1995 and remarked upon by the

National Pension Board in 1998. In order to try to solve this problem and enlarge the coverage of the second pillar, in 2002 the government introduced a new personal retirement saving account (PRSA) (though the aging problem is less worrying in Ireland than in other European countries, in 2001 the government also introduced a funded component, the so-called National Reserve Fund, in the first PAYG pillar).

Some quantitative and institutional features of main taxes

The personal income tax – PIT

Income tax is the main source of direct revenue in Ireland. The beneficiary is the state and it is payable by all (individuals and unincorporated bodies) residents (in general on their total income from all sources) and non-residents (for Irish-sourced income). The basis of assessment is total income; deductions and exemptions can be applied. Total income includes pension, income earned as an employee together with benefits in kind given by the employer (there are some exemptions) and self-employed income. Losses which the self-employed may incur in a year can be set against total income in the same year and can also be carried forward without any limit of time, but only used against profits arising from the same activity. The self-employed can deduct all the expenses wholly and exclusively for the purpose of their business. More restrictive conditions are instead effective for employees, though they may have some allowances for expenses wholly, exclusively and necessarily required for their employment. Concerning financial activities, dividends are inserted in the tax base with a tax credit, since they are also subject to a withholding tax. Interests on deposits and capital gains are subject to separate taxation (for more information, see also the sections on corporate tax and taxation of financial activities, pp. 167–8).

In computing taxable income, the taxpayer, in addition to the deductions quoted above, can claim some other relief: for example s/he can deduct, within certain limits, permanent health contributions and medical expenses; previously long-term unemployed persons enjoyed other deductions. Moreover, in order to encourage the second pillar of the Irish pension system, a deduction on contributions to complementary pension schemes is also granted, within certain limits. After recent reforms, the majority of tax reliefs is in the form of tax credits, as we will see later in this section and on pages 174–8, analyzing the reforms carried out over these years.

Regarding the tax unit, a married couple can decide to be taxed as if they were single (the so-called "assessment as a single person"), or choose some form of family taxation, i.e. Joint Assessment or Separate Assessment. In Joint Assessment the incomes of the two spouses are treated as belonging to only one of them. In Separate Assessment, the spouses are taxed separately, but allowances are given in such a way that the result, from a tax point of view, is equal to Joint Assessment. This feature is important in order to understand the income bands to which the tax rates apply, as described in Table 7.2. Income bands are in fact individualized, as they depend on the status of the taxpayer: single (or treated as single by his or her own choice), with or without children, or married, taking into account if both spouses work (the standard rate is applied to unincorporated bodies).

The system of exemptions is quite complex, as summarized in Table 7.3, and it depends on individualized parameters too: the exemption limits change with marital status, with age and with the number of dependent children.

If total gross income is below these values, the taxpayer is exempted from income tax and no other tax relief is granted. If total gross income is higher than the exemption values, tax rates described in Table 7.2 generally apply, after some deductions; but if the gross income is only slightly above the values of Table 7.3, the so-called "marginal relief system" can be called into operation, under which the tax to be paid is given by 40 percent of the income in excess of exemption limits. This system is

Table 7.2 PIT tax rates

Status	Tax rates (%)	Tax band (in €)
Single/widowed (without dependent children)	20	0–28,000
	42	28,000–
Single/widowed (with dependent children)	20	0–32,000
	42	32,000–
Married couple (one spouse with income)	20	0–37,000
	42	37,000–
Married couple (both spouses with income)	20	0–37,000
	42	37,000–

Notes
In the case of a married couple where both spouses have an income, the threshold value of 37,000 may be increased with the lower of:
1 the income of the second spouse.
2 €19,000.

Table 7.3 Exemptions (in €)

	Single	Married
Aged under 65	5,210	10,420
Aged 65 and over	13,000	26,000

Notes
Exemption levels are increased: for the first and the second dependent child by €575; for the later child by €830.

applicable only when the benefits that the taxpayer can get are higher than that achievable under the tax rate system of Table 7.2.

In order to reach net tax liability once the gross tax is computed, we must subtract some tax credits; among them, the most important are those linked to the specific status of the taxpayer. For example, we have a basic personal tax credit (that is €1,520 for singles and €3,000 for couples), a tax credit for widowed persons and for widowed parents (in this case the tax credit changes with the number of years after bereavement), a tax credit for persons aged 65 or more, a tax credit for incapacitated children (that is €500 per child), a tax credit for a dependent relative (that is €60 per relative) and others. For the employees, there are specific tax credits of €660. Up until the tax year 2001, there was a tax credit for mortgage interests; but from 1 January 2002, this relief is granted directly at source, the individuals paying net mortgage interest, an interest from which tax relief has been deducted.

Corporation tax – CT

Corporation tax is payable on all profit (income plus capital gains) of every Irish company; non-Irish companies are taxed on the fraction of profits that is attributable to the branch located in Ireland. The most remarkable feature of Irish corporation tax concerns the system of tax rates on income, which has changed in recent years. There are three tax rates on income: the standard rate, the higher rate and the facilitated rate.

The standard rate applies in general to trading income; for the year 2002 this rate was 16 percent and from 2003 it is 12.5 percent. However, for small companies, that is companies with a trading income not exceeding €254,000, the rate was already 12.5 percent; a marginal relief system is used if the trading income is between €254,000 and €317,500. This 12.5 percent rate also applies to some shipping activities. A higher rate of 25 percent is applied to other activities. This, for example, concerns foreign income (unless its source is an Irish trade), income from mining and petroleum and income from dealing in land (the sale of residential land is taxed at a rate of 20 percent). Finally there is a reduced rate of 10 percent, that has represented the main facilities given to manufacturing companies by the Irish taxation system for years. Under the pressure of the EU and the planned reduction of the standard rate, the 10 percent rate will be ruled out until 2005 or 2010, depending on the kind of activity carried out.

Capital gains are also charged under corporation tax, but with a different rate that is, with some exceptions, around 20 percent. In computing capital gains, inflation is taken into account using an indexing system.

Concerning the computation of trading income, it can be noted that, in evaluating stocks, only FIFO (first in, first out) or its approximation can be used, while the application of LIFO (last in, first out) is forbidden.

Moreover only some specific provisions and reserves are deductible (for example, reserves for specific bad debts). Capital allowances, that is fiscal depreciation, depend on the kind of asset used: for machinery and plants there is, for example, an allowance of 20 percent. Trading losses can balance other income or gains in the current year, or can be carried back (against profit of any kind, in the preceding year) or carried forward (against trading income, without any limit of time). Finally dividends and distributions are charged, with a remarkable number of exemptions (such as an exemption for dividends and distributions given to an Irish company), to a withholding tax with a rate of 20 percent; this withholding tax can then be used as a tax credit against the recipient's income tax liability, computed using the gross dividend.

Taxation of income from financial capital

Capital gains from the disposal of an asset by an individual or by a company are in general charged at a tax rate of 20 percent. The capital gain is computed as the difference between the sale value and the acquisition cost, where the second is defined taking into account inflation with an indexing device (called indexation relief). The first €1,270 of capital gains is exempted from tax. Capital losses are generally deductible from gains and the excess can be carried forward.

Interests from Irish deposits are subject to a withholding tax (DIRT), deducted at source by financial institutions, whose rate is 20 percent if interests are payable annually or more frequently, and 23 percent if interests are payable less frequently. Other specific interests are also subject to withholding taxation.

Capital income may be subject to preferential tax treatment. For instance, Special Saving Incentive Accounts (SSIAs) are savings schemes that enjoy a concessionary tax regime. These financial instruments (introduced on 1 May 2001) are five-year saving schemes, in which the government takes part, making an extra investment of 25 percent of the sum deposited monthly; the return, achieved at the end of the five years, is taxed at a rate of 23 percent.

Value added tax – VAT – and excise duties

Value added tax (VAT) represents the main indirect revenue on which the government can rely. It is charged on the supply of goods and services in Ireland and on imports, provided that these activities are carried out by a taxable person, that is someone that supplies goods/services or make imports above some minimum limits; exports are chargeable at zero percent rate. The computation of VAT is made with the application of the tax-to-tax method, i.e. the tax liability is the difference between the sales VAT and the purchase VAT.

Tax rates depend on the goods to which they apply; some relevant cases are:

1   zero percent: exported goods, goods imported from outside the EU transferred to another EU state, books, food and drink for human consumption, oral medicine, children's clothing and footwear, printed books and booklets;
2   4.3 percent: the sale of greyhounds, horses, pigs;
3   12.5 percent: newspapers, magazines, chocolate, biscuits, snacks, energy for heating and light;
4   21 percent (the standard rate): applicable to other good and services.

The main exemption are: human blood, milk and organs; goods supplied to members by a non-profit organization.

Finally, among indirect taxes, there exists a consistent number of excise duties, such as excise duty on hydrocarbons, on tobacco products, on ethyl alcohol, on wine and on beer.

Capital acquisition tax, stamp duties and rates

In Ireland there are three main kinds of taxes on property: capital acquisition tax (CAT) stamp duties and rates. CAT is levied on gift and inheritance, with a rate of 20 percent above the amount of the exemption (the exemption increases the closer the relationship is between the donator (the testor) and the recipient (heir) and goes from a minimum of €21,108 to a maximum of €422,148). There are also many other partial or total exemptions, among which the most relevant is the transfer, in the form of gift or inheritance, from a married person to their spouse.

Stamp duties are charged on certain documents, relative for example to transfer of property, transfer of stocks and marketable securities, mortgages and leases. The tax rate depends on the specific kind of deeds: for example, for residential property it ranges from 3 percent to 9 percent according to the value of the transfer and the status of the purchaser, while for the transfer of stocks it is 1 percent. Rates are taxes levied by local authorities to finance expenditure in excess of the transfers made to them by the state. The basis of assessment is represented by immovable property such as buildings, factories, shops, railways, canals, mines, woods, right of fishery, right of easement over land and so on. Important exemptions are constituted by domestic property, farm buildings and land used for agriculture, horticulture, forestry and sport.

The fiscal burden

The distribution of taxation charge

In order to understand how revenues are distributed among economic activities and factors of production and the way in which the system discriminates between them, it is useful to analyze the so-called functional classification of the fiscal receipts. Table 7.4 shows the taxes levied on consumption, labor and capital as a percentage of GDP for the years between 1970 and 1997. Taxes on labor and capital are divided into subgroups.

Taxes on labor play a major role, since they absorb 14.4 percent of GDP (that is, 42.4 percent of total fiscal revenues); taxes on consumption also represent a considerable fraction of GDP, 12.9 percent (that is, 37.9 percent of total fiscal revenues), while this percentage is only 6.7 percent (that is, 19.7 percent of total fiscal revenues) for taxes on capital.

If we look at the evolution of this structure in the last 30 years the main change concerns the reallocation of taxation between consumption and labor. In 1970 taxes on consumption (that are fundamentally VAT and excise duties) were 16 percent of GDP while taxes on labor (i.e. social contributions plus fraction of income tax levied on labor income) amounted to 9.2 percent of GDP; that is, respectively 50.6 percent and 29.1 percent of total fiscal revenues. Thus, taxes on consumption have fallen progressively over the years, with the exception of 1985; however, the reason for this temporary inversion of the trend can be found in the growth of the overall fiscal burden that increased from 34.7 percent in 1980, to 38.9 percent in 1985 and then again to 35.5 percent in 1990. Instead taxes on labor show a "hump" path with a maximum in 1985, for the reason given above.

If we look at the composition of taxes on labor, the main feature con-

Table 7.4 Structure according to the economic function as a percentage of GDP

	1970	1975	1980	1985	1990	1995	1997
Consumption	16.0	14.4	14.8	16.7	14.4	13.2	12.9
Labor	9.2	12.8	15.3	17.9	16.1	14.8	14.4
employed	8.4	11.8	14.4	16.3	14.6	13.3	12.9
• paid by employers	1.4	2.6	3.2	3.6	3.1	2.9	2.8
• paid by employees	7.0	9.2	10.8	12.7	11.4	10.4	10.1
self-employed	0.8	1.1	1.3	1.5	1.6	1.5	1.5
Capital, of which	6.4	4.8	4.7	4.4	5.0	5.8	6.7
real estate and capital	0.8	0.3	0.4	0.4	0.6	1.4	1.3
monetary capital	0.0	0.0	0.1	0.1	0.1	0.1	0.1
Total	31.6	32.0	34.7	38.9	35.6	33.8	34.0

Source: Eurostat.

Note
1997 is the last data available.

cerns the importance of employees, who pay 70 percent of labor taxes, while the remaining is paid by employers (19.4 percent) and by the self-employed (10.4 percent). Observing the evolution of this composition, there has been no drastic structural change in the split between employers, employees and the self-employed, although there was a slight reduction in the percentage of revenues levied on employees and an increase of those charged to the self-employed and employers.

Capital taxes in Table 7.4 are heterogeneous and derive from the aggregation of taxes levied on many sources, such as real estate, real capital and monetary capital; they also include taxes on income and wealth of difficult allocation. Capital taxes play a small role and their percentage of GDP has been substantially stable from 6.4 percent in 1970 to 6.7 percent in 1997. Looking at the composition, the main trend is the reduction of real estate taxes as a percentage of GDP (from 3.4 percent of GDP in 1970 to 1.1 percent in 1997) and the symmetric increase of taxes on unallocable income and wealth (from 2 percent of GDP in 1970 to 4.1 percent in 1997).

We can now examine implicit tax rates. They are indicators complementary to the functional classification described above, and they are useful to measure the fiscal burden charged on the inputs and the activity of an economy. Table 7.5 and Figure 7.1 show the evolution of the implicit tax rates on labor employed, consumption and other factors (i.e. on the net operating surplus of the economy plus consolidated government interest payments). According to these indicators, the burden of taxation is distributed first of all on labor employed (with an implicit tax rate of 29.8 percent in 1997) and then on consumption (with an implicit tax rate of 23.7 percent in 1997) and on other factors (with an implicit tax

Table 7.5 Implicit tax rates in Ireland and Europe, 1970–97

		Consumption	*Labor employed*	*Other factor*
1970	Ireland	21.1	16.1	25.1
	EU	17.6	28.9	26.2
1975	Ireland	20.2	20.7	20.2
	EU	15.5	32.2	34.7
1980	Ireland	20.2	23.4	22.3
	EU	16.0	35.1	36.6
1985	Ireland	25.1	30.3	16.3
	EU	15.6	37.1	32.3
1990	Ireland	22.5	30.8	16.1
	EU	16.2	37.5	31.5
1995	Ireland	22.5	29.6	18.3
	EU	16.7	41.7	29.4
1997	Ireland	23.7	29.8	20.5
	EU	16.8	41.9	31.1

Source: Eurostat.

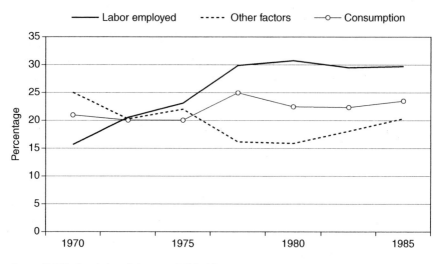

Figure 7.1 Ireland: implicit rates 1970–97.

Source: Eurostat.

rate of 20.5 percent in 1997). Though the implicit tax rate in Ireland is below the European average, recent reforms have further reduced the burden of taxation on labor and will very likely continue to reduce it in the coming years.

The distribution of the implicit tax rate has not always been the same; in 1970 the burden was mainly charged on other factors and consumption, while the implicit tax rate on labor employed was very low. In the following years the situation changed progressively. The implicit tax rate on labor employed has increased from 1970 to 1997 by 13.7 points, showing a "hump" path with a maximum value (31.3 percent) in 1993 and 1994. A slightly different pattern characterizes the implicit tax rate on consumption, that starts from a value of 21.1 percent in 1970, reaching the higher value of 25.1 percent in 1985, decreasing to 21 percent in 1993, and then increasing again to 23.7 percent in 1997. Finally, the evolution of implicit tax rates on other factors has a less regular movement, but on the whole it fell between 1970 and 1997 by 3.6 percent.

We will now briefly discuss the effect of personal income tax (PIT) on income distribution. In a comparative analysis of 12 OECD countries (Wagstaff *et al.* 1999), the pre-tax income distribution in Ireland in 1987 was one of the most unequal in the EU, as shown by the Gini coefficient, whose value was 38.7 percent; this result does not change if we consider the post-tax income distribution, that shows a Gini coefficient of 34.18 percent. However, even if PIT cannot greatly change the inequality ranking of Ireland with respect to other countries, its distributive effects, measured by the difference of the Gini index on gross and net income, were strong even in comparative terms and amounted to 0.0452 (this is the highest value among the 12 countries considered in this analysis).

However notice that, though Wagstaff's paper dates from 1999, Irish data used refers to 1987. After that date, income tax changed. The tax rate structure in 1987 was a step function with three different rates (35 percent, 48 percent, 58 percent), and now shows only two rates (20 percent and 42 percent). At first glance, this reform may have reduced the distributive effect of PIT, but a careful analysis should also take into account income bands and tax relief, using more recent data.

Tax wedges on labor and corporate taxation

The marginal tax wedge on labor provides a measure of the effect of taxation on the supply of labor. Though Ireland does not have a high level of taxes on labor (according to functional classification and to implicit tax rate), work incentives do not seem to be very strong, since the marginal tax wedge is around 55 percent (Joumard 2001).

The statutory rate on corporation is the lowest in the EMU; although this is an important indicator, to better assess the effects of taxation on corporation, it is useful to analyze the so-called "effective rates," both marginal (EMR) and average (EAR). Ireland, considering average values between equity and debt, has the lowest EAR; EMR is also very low, although Italy (that has a remarkably high EAR) do better with a negative EMR. These results prove the importance of the statutory rate, that has more incidence on EAR than on EMR, in determining the location of business. In fact Ireland seems to attract foreign investments (especially from outside the EU) more than Italy. This confirms the thesis of Devereux and Griffith (1999) that US multinational firms, once having taken the decision of investing in the EU, decide the specific location with careful attention to the EAR. If we look at corporate funding, equity is discriminated relative to debt, since the effective rates of the former are higher than those of the latter (Giannini and Maggiulli 2001).

Finally, another feature of Ireland is the relation between EMR, EAR and statutory rate in the case of equity finance. The most common relation in European countries shows an effective average rate growing with profitability up to the statutory rate, while in Ireland (and in other countries such as Great Britain and France) this relation is reversed, since the statutory rate is the lowest and EMR is higher than EAR. This is probably due to the higher level of real-estate tax in Ireland when compared to other countries (Giannini and Maggiulli 2001).

A comparative view against the European average

On pages 164–5, we noted that the overall Irish fiscal burden, measured as the fraction of GDP absorbed by fiscal revenues, is the lowest in the EU.

Now we make a more detailed comparison, using the economic indicators analyzed above, in order to find possible differences between Ireland and the EU average in the distribution of this burden.

A prominent feature of Irish taxation seems to be the importance of taxes on consumption; according to functional classification, in 1997 taxes on consumption in Ireland were above the EU average by 1.5 percent of GDP. This finding is strengthened if we consider the implicit rate of 23.7 percent in Ireland versus the 16.8 percent of the EU average. On the contrary, the burden charged on labor seems to be exceptionally low; considering functional classification, taxes on labor in Ireland are below the EU average of 7.1 percent of GDP and the implicit rate is 29.8 percent for Ireland and 41.9 percent for the EU average. Nevertheless the Irish marginal tax wedge on labor is slightly above the European average (which is very high and far greater than the OECD average) and one of the main topics of debate in reforming the taxation system in Ireland concerns this problem and searching out its most pertinent solution. This apparent contradiction can be explained by remarking that, concerning the labor supply incentive, not only the amount of taxes matters but also the specific way in which they are designed.

Taxes on capital are not very dissimilar from the EU average if based on functional classification (they differ only by 0.8 percent of GDP). However this result changes remarkably if based on implicit rates: in 1997 the Irish value was 20.5 percent, while the EU average is 31.1 percent. In particular, corporations receive a favorable treatment, due, as already noted, to the low statutory and effective rates.

Finally Ireland is one of the European countries with the lowest fraction of revenues destined to local government and has very reduced intermediate levels of government; for this reason we have decided not to discuss this topic in more detail.

Tax reforms in the 1990s and those currently planned

A quick glance at the budget and general economic environment

In Ireland an impressive episode of fiscal consolidation took place from the second half of the 1980s to the end of the 1990s. This process can be divided into three phases (Lund 1998). The first, until 1989, is characterized by a reduction of expenditure and of revenue, both relative to GDP and in real terms. The second, from 1990 to 1995, represents a halt in fiscal consolidation. Revenue continued to decrease, while expenditure strongly increased: nevertheless the balance worsened only by 0.2 percent of GDP, due to reduced interest payments. Government balance started to improve again between 1996 and 1999 (the third phase of the restoration of public finance), achieving a surplus in 1997. This process has some similarity with that of the first phase, because it was carried out through a reduction in expenditure; but ultimately differs, since, in real terms, expenditure was increased. On the whole, the balance has shifted from a deficit above 8 percent in 1987, to a surplus above 2 percent in 1999, and public debt has also fallen in the same period from a value above 110 percent to 49.3 percent.

This improvement in public finance has been accompanied by the outstanding performance of the Irish economy; in particular between 1994 and 1999 the growth rate was always above 7 percent, with a peak of 11.1 percent in 1995 and 10.4 percent in 1998. Causal relations between such high growth rates and fiscal consolidation have been widely explored, but a unique position does not emerge (Bernasconi 1999).

It could be suggested that fiscal consolidation has caused high economic performance. Alesina and Ardagna (1998) stress the fact that fiscal consolidation has been carried out through a reduction of expenditure rather than a rise in taxation and think that this "composition effect" is the reason why consolidation has caused the high performance of the Irish economy. Though based on different arguments, the interpretation of Giavazzi and Pagano (1996) also underlines the important role that the restoration of public finance played in Ireland's positive economic performance.

Nevertheless, other explanations single out the international economic situation as the key element for Irish growth and the competitive advantage that characterizes a small economy such as Ireland. Even if the composition effect and other non-Keynesian effects of fiscal policy may have played a role, it's probably growth itself, driven by factors other than improvement in public balance, that has allowed the achievement of this exceptional restoration of public finance.

With regard to the current situation, although government balance has slightly worsened between 2000 and 2002, shifting from 4.5 percent of GDP in 2000 to 0.7 percent in 2002 (estimated value), the good performance that Irish public finance has achieved in the last decade seems to be sound and stable. Public debt, with a value of 35.8 percent of GDP in 2001 is low, particularly compared to other EMU countries like Italy. GDP growth has slowed down from 11.5 percent in 2000 to an estimated 3.9 percent in 2002, but it would average the remarkable level of 5 percent over the whole period 2002–4; unemployment seems to be stable below 5 percent (it has dropped from 11.9 percent in 1996).

However there are additional policy problems, upon which the future performance of the Irish economy would seem to depend. The most important problem is probably represented by the supply constraints on infrastructure and especially on labor (a problem typical of a full-employment economy). These constraints should be relaxed not only in order to avoid inflationist pressure (Irish inflation in 2002 is estimated at around 4 percent, not high but above the standard in the EMU) but above all to not threaten growth. In fact, an increase in labor force has been an important element in the Irish growth of the last decade, but it is now expected to slow down: the reasons concern the small unemployment rate achieved and a reduction in population growth and migration. This explains, as we will see in more detail in the following section, why one of the key points in reforming the tax system is the reduction in the distortion on labor supply.

Tax reforms in the 1990s

Concerning income tax, the attempt to improve labor market performance has represented the main motivation for reforms during the last decade. In line with this goal, tax rates were reduced in number and level (in 1987 there were three tax rates, while in 2002 there were only two: 20 percent and 40 percent), the tax band was widened (also to avoid fiscal drag), and the exemption level was raised. In particular the reduction of taxpayers belonging to the higher band can be noted and the increase of those exempt to income tax according to the 2001 budget, as shown in Table 7.6 (in which taxpayers exempt, and subject marginal relief system, standard band and higher band are shown).

In recent years, another reform has concerned the substitution of tax deductions with tax credits; the introduction of the tax credit system has been preceded by a standardization of tax deductions. This reform has been intentionally made leaving "the position of higher-rate taxpayers generally unchanged" and improving "the position of those at the standard rate," with the goal of making the fiscal saving equal for all taxpayers; in fact the saving from a deduction, unlike that of a tax credit, depends on the individual marginal tax rate (and so on the individual income).

The corporation tax has also been remarkably reformed, with the goal of making taxation friendly to corporations in order to not damage growth and to attract foreign investors. According to these objectives, the standard tax rate has been reduced from 43 percent in 1991 to 16 percent in 2002, with the objective of a further reduction to 12.5 percent in 2003. On the other side, in 1998 Ireland committed itself, under pressure from the Euro-

Table 7.6 Distribution of income-taxpayers by tax band

Tax year	Exempt cases		Marginal band		Standard band		Higher band	
	No.	%	No.	%	No.	%	No.	%
1997/1998	380,000	25.5	108,000	7.25	580,000	38.75	424,000	28.5
1998/1999	394,000	25.0	82,000	5.25	643,000	40.5	463,000	29.25
1999/2000	474,000	28.5	25,000	1.5	655,000	39.25	510,000	30.75
2000/2001	535,000	29.5	7,000	0.5	718,000	41.0	509,000	29.0
2001/2002	668,000	37.75	4,500	0.25	695,000	39.0	402,000	23.0

Source: Ireland – Stability Programme 2000.

pean Union, to phase out the facilitated tax rate that, up to then, had characterized Irish corporate tax. Following this agreement, the reduced rate for small business, introduced in 1996, was set at 12.5 percent in 2002 and it is 12.5 percent in 2003. Finally, the rate of 10 percent applied to manufacturing will be eliminated until 31 December 2005 for activities carried out in the area of the Shannon Airport and the International Finance Service Centre (IFSC) in Dublin, and until 2010 for other manufacturing activity.

Priorities for future tax reforms

In recent years, there has been some progress toward a reduction of distortion on labor. Nevertheless, at the end of the 1990s the problem of low incentives to work still remained, as we have already said on pages 170–4, where we showed that the marginal tax wedge on labor was high even in comparative terms (Joumard 2001). In particular, as in other European countries, distortion is higher for individuals with low income and education (Koliadina 1999b).

However, the measures taken in the 2001 budget analyzed above (pp. 174–6) seem to go in the right direction: the simultaneous reduction of the standard tax rate and the increase in the number of taxpayers exempt from tax can be interpreted as a positive measure for incentives of low-income individuals. The reduction of the higher tax rate, and the taxpayers subject to it, is a measure enhancing the reward from work. The policy toward social contributions is also inspired by the attempt to further increase the performance of the labor market, since the already low social contributions rates have been reduced from 1996 by more than 1 percent on average, both for employer and employees.[1]

Another important key point of the reforms previously analyzed concerns the standardization of corporate tax regimes. According to EU prescriptions, the phasing out of the special regimes, that characterized Ireland all through the 1990s, is positive and valuable. However this elimination has been accompanied by a general reduction of the corporate rate, that as we have said, is 12.5 percent in 2003 for all companies. Therefore, the attempt by the EU to reduce fiscal competition by phasing out special regimes seems to have caused an extension of the competition from some activities and geographical areas to the entire system of corporate taxation.

It is also important to note that, since 2003, no reduced rate for small companies will be in force. This measure should prevent the "threshold effect," that could discourage the growth of firms, and represents a problem in many EU countries (Joumard 2001). On the other side, it should be stressed that special regimes for small companies could be a useful way of compensating them for the disadvantages they have, relative to larger firms, in obtaining access to the credit market.

A major shortcoming of the current system, concerning corporate financing, is the discrimination between equity and debt finance, analyzed on pages 170–4. The elimination of the negative fiscal treatment of equity finance would be an important measure to strengthen the financial structure of firms and would especially benefit new, small and more innovative companies, that are more likely to use equity because they have problems borrowing funds (Joumard 2001).

Another controversial argument, common to many EU countries, concerns the reform of VAT (Joumard 2001). During the first half of the 1990s, a slight standardization of the rates was achieved, with the decrease of the higher rate and the increase of the middle rate. On the grounds of efficiency, further standardization seems to be required; nevertheless, the elimination of privileged rates on some goods could cause equity problems (IMF 2001).

Note

1 Nevertheless, even if an analysis of the social welfare system is beyond the scope of this chapter, we must stress that in evaluating social contributions, not only the disincentive effect on labor matters.

References

Alesina, A. and Ardagna, S. (1998) "Tales of fiscal adjustments," *Economic Policy*, 27: 489–517.

Bernasconi, M. (1999) "Eurosclerosi e disciplina fiscale," in Bernardi, L. (ed.) *La Finanza pubblica italiana. Rapporto 1999*, Bologna: Il Mulino, pp. 97–120.

Department of Finance (2001) *Ireland – Stability Programme 2001*.

Devereux, M. and Griffith, R. (1999) "The taxation of discrete investment choices," Working Paper W98/16, London: The Institute for Fiscal Studies.

Giannini, S. and Maggiulli, C. (2001) *The Effective Tax Rates in the EU Commission Study on Corporate Taxation: Methodological Aspects, Main Results and Policy Implications*, Università di Modena e Reggio Emilia: CAPP.

Giavazzi, F. and Pagano, M. (1996) "Can severe fiscal contractions be expansionary? Tales of two small open European countries," *Nber Macroeconomics Annual*, 5: 75–111.

Joumard, I. (2001) "Tax systems in European Union countries," Economic Department Working Paper 301, Paris: OECD.

Koliadina, N. (1999) *Work Incentives and Recent Labour Market Policies*, Ireland: Selected Issue, Washington, IMF Staff Country Report.

Lund, A.J. (1998) *Fiscal Consolidation in Ireland and Challenges Ahead*, Ireland: Selected Issue, Washington, IMF Staff Country Report.

Wagstaff, A. *et al.* (1999) "Redistributive effect, progressivity and differential tax treatment: personal income tax in twelve OECD countries," *Journal of Public Economics*, 72: 73–98.

Website

www.revenue.ie

8 Italy

Luigi Bernardi[1]

Introduction

Out of all European Member States, the economic history of Italy over the last few decades has certainly been the most affected by the complex ups and downs of the fiscal system. This does not go unnoticed by eminent national (Pedone, various years) and international observers (Tanzi 1996). In 1972 the tax system was completely reformed to make it suitable to the new economic environment of a developed industrial country. The initial stages of reform were not at all easy. The lack of expected revenues gave rise to the ensuing long saga of Italian budget deficit and debt. But during the 1990s four points of increase in fiscal pressure were crucial to fulfill Maastricht requirements.

Tax avoidance and exemptions in Italy are higher than in any developed countries: this reflects the widespread structure of the economy and also the persistent high level of inefficiency (and corruption) of tax administration. Thus the need to raise revenues to pay for a growing public expenditure has been covered for a long time by the very inefficient rule of "reducing the basis and increasing the rates (or the number of taxes)." Only at the end of the 1990s did the long-due reforms begin to take place, on the initiative of two Ministers of Finance, Mr. Visco and Mr. Tremonti, both eminent but members of conflicting political parties.

Following this introduction, this chapter goes on to reconstruct the development of the system from the time of the fundamental reform of the early 1970s up to the late 1990s. Overall fiscal pressure has increased by almost 15 points and the extra space has been assumed by the great personal and general consumption taxes. The Italian tax system is close to the European average. It shows a departure from the most consolidate models (Nordic, Rhine, Anglo-Saxon and Mediterranean). It looks like a mix of Rhine and Mediterranean models, further characterized by many signs of a diffused presence of taxes with restricted basis and high rates.

The main taxes are about the same in Italy as in other European countries. On pages 186–94 we review their most specific features. The tax basis of income tax is mostly restricted to labor income and formal progressivity is high. The tax unit is the individual, the allowances for dependent parents and single-earner households are low. Corporation tax is slow in catching up with the international progress of reducing and converging "all-in" rates. The field of capital income taxes has been smoothed only recently and generally taxation is carried out by final withholdings (or similar sources taxation). VAT has a low productivity, while excise duties on energy products are particularly high. The main local taxes are a business tax for the regions and a property tax for the municipalities, both introduced during the 1990s, as part of the process of decentralization, but the revenues cover only a part of local expenditures.

The analysis of the distribution of fiscal burden (pp. 194–9) emphasizes the high share suffered by labor, a charge on consumption lower than European average, the weak participation of other factors to total taxation, and the absence of environmental taxes. From the beginning of the 1970s to the late 1990s the overall fiscal pressure has increased almost solely as an effect of the progressive growth of burden on labor (increasing by nearly 30 points over this period). The tax wedge on labor became one of the highest in the EU and OECD. The high statutory rates of corporate taxation have also raised the wedge on corporate capital, although alleviated by a widespread avoidance and elusion, and by generous tax relief.

The reform of the 1970s created a highly centralized revenue system, increasingly criticized from the 1980s. Now the regions are almost self-sufficient, but the level of their effective fiscal autonomy is not high. This is also true for the municipalities. A dramatic devolution of the state's functions to the regions is now planned but it is difficult to imagine other sources of financing than not autonomous sharing of great national taxes.

Finally, we describe the more recent reforms and the current debate. The long stagnation of Italian economic growth from the beginning of the 1990s, and the risk of a decline of the country's economy, required that priority should be given to interventions enhancing growth, by detaxing production factors and creating some impulses from the side of demand. This has been done (or planned) only very partially. Obviously equity should not have losses, remembering the Pigouvian relationship between welfare and the "national dividend."

In 1997 the "Visco reform" started with reference to the Nordic dual income tax system. The "all-in" statutory rate of corporations was reduced by more than ten points even if it still remains well above the European average. An allowance for "ordinary" income from internal sources was introduced, in order to make the choice of financing more neutral and progressively reduce the effective average rate. The attainment of greater neutrality was strengthened by the new wide-base regional tax on business which substituted previous taxes on firms with a more restricted basis. On the whole, the wedge on capital has been reduced but the wedge on labor has not. The redistribution of the burden may have penalized small firms, which are very important for the Italian economy. Changes were also introduced in the domain of capital incomes from different sources which, up to a few years ago, were confusingly taxed (particularly rents) or not taxed at all (capital gains). The different sources were well defined and unified in a homogenous taxation at two final withholding rates. The reform had to be continued, by extending the dual income tax approach and progressively reducing the burden and perhaps also the progressivity of income tax. Many innovations of "Visco reform" were undoubtedly welcome, particularly as to the reduction of the corporation tax "all-in" rate and the new regimes of taxation of capital income. Other interventions on firms' taxation and regional financing were more controversial.

Mr. Tremonti, the Minister of Finance of the new government came into office in spring 2001, and proposed his own bill of reform for the fiscal system in December of that year, which has been passed by Parliament in April 2003. Many changes introduced by Mr. Visco have already been or should be repealed. The structure of the reform is not very far from those adopted recently by many European countries, but its figures are more radical. Income tax should drastically change in its structure, with the result of attributing significant advantages to the low-middle and the highest incomes. The loss of revenue (and the demand impulse) is estimated at about 20 billion euro, above 1.5 percent of GDP. The taxation of capital incomes should be further simplified and, with few exceptions, realized with a final withholding at the low rate of 12.5 percent. Finally, corporate taxation should be thoroughly amended in many respects. Mr. Visco's allowance for internal capital has been frozen, while the regional business tax should be progressively repealed. Statutory "all-in rate" should decrease, but to a level which is still not competitive in the European context. The recent German reform should be imitated to change to participation and dividends exemption and abolish the imputation system. An opportunity should be given to opt for a consolidate balance, even with foreign controlled companies. On the whole, the proposal has been well accepted, but it has also raised considerable debate: the most controversial points are the tax cut for the rich, the low level of capital income rate and the conversely high rate for corporations.

The attempts to improve the Italian tax system, set up by Mr. Visco and Mr. Tremonti, may be evaluated in various ways, including in accordance to one's political preferences. But one has to ask if reforms of this kind (such as those recently adopted in other European countries) are enough to contribute significantly to the priority target of enhancing growth. Given the recent conclusions drawn by a diversified but converging literature (supply and demand of labor; endogenous growth models; more standard demand side econometric estimations; statistical inferences; empirical evidence), a larger and far more radical intervention seems to be required. It should be able to cope with the present main tax constraints on economic development, i.e. the wedges on labor and corporate capital. The following lack of revenue might, in principle, be covered by expenditure cost cuts, not a "rolling back" of the welfare state, a reasonable departure from balanced budget European targets, and increasing taxes on environment externalities, on immovable properties and on consumption. Those on capital should not be reduced too much. This is only a preliminary sketch, which requires to be elaborated in relation to its economic effect and is not easy at all, particularly on political grounds, but at least it seems more relevant to discuss than other minor issues which have been endlessly debated in recent years. In fact, it is broadly in line with recent OECD suggestions concerning tax reforms in European Union countries, but it is far more radical than what is implicit in these suggestions, and further from the marginal kind of the reforms in this direction which have already been adopted or are underway in almost all European countries.

The structure of the system and its development from the 1970s

The current structure of the tax system and social security contributions

In Italy in 2001 the general government net borrowing was 2.6 percent of GDP and it was reduced to just 2.3 percent in 2002. A large primary surplus is still needed (5 percent of GDP) to compensate for the burden of interests, due to the great amount of public debt (currently 107 percent of GDP). Primary expenditure is made up of the high values of collective consumption (43.9 percent) and monetary transfers (41.4 percent, almost all pensions) while capital (7.6 percent) and other minor expenditures are at a low level. Remember that in Italy the welfare system (education, health, pensions and other social transfers) is almost totally in the hands of the public sector.

In Italy the total 1999 government revenues (the most recent data comparable with Europe) may be divided into three headings (Banca d'Italia 2002; Ministero dell'Economia 2002): taxes (30.1 percent of GNP), social contributions (12.8 percent), other non-fiscal revenues (3.3 percent). The basic structure of the taxation system remains the one introduced with the overall tax reform of 1971–4. The previously existing system was completely inappropriate to the new status of industrialized country, which Italy gained after the sustained development of the 1950s and the 1960s. It was still schedular, indirect taxes were prevailing, the relationships among different levels of government were confused, the administration was inefficient and largely corrupt. The goals of the reform (Cosciani 1964), in accordance with prevailing ideas at that time (Keynesian economics and redistributive aptitudes) were:

i to give more room to direct taxation, by introducing a Comprehensive Income Tax, with a large basis and a highly progressive and personalized nature (*Imposta sul Reddito delle Persone Fisiche* – IRPEF), a personal tax on corporation profits and non-business bodies (*Imposta sul Reddito delle Persone Giuridiche* – IRPEG).

ii rationalizing indirect taxes, by replacing the existing turnover tax with a value added tax (*Imposta sul Valore Aggiunto* – IVA), in accordance to EEC rules, and further eliminating customs and toll duties plus a large number of small taxes on goods and services and on operating a business.

iii to centralize tax revenues at the level of central government, in order to reduce administrative costs and to have at hand more powerful tools for fiscal and redistributive policies.

The impact of the 1971–4 reform (see below, pages 185–6, for subsequent developments) can still be seen by looking at the present status of the system, as it is depicted in Table 8.1. Up until 1999 the total fiscal pressure is nearly 43 percent. Taxes make up nearly two-thirds of the total burden and the remaining part is made up of social contributions. The effects of the 1970s reform are clearly demonstrated by the fact that direct and indirect taxes now come to about the same amount. Despite the fact that, in Italy, a large number of taxes survive, a great amount of revenue is yielded from a relatively small number of headings, a feature that Italy shares with almost all European countries: personal income tax, corporate tax, value added tax and main excise duties add up to 23.2 points of GDP, nearly 80 percent of all taxes. Furthermore, direct taxes are dominated by income tax (66.6 percent) and indirect taxes by VAT (55.2 percent).

Italy's social contributions have always been near the European average, but with a larger share for the component due by employers. The pensions system pushes up contributions, it is almost entirely public, PAYG, with high substitution rates and dependence ratios (due to low average age at which workers retire). Note that, from 1998, contributions don't include payments for healthcare, although in Italy the National Health Service supplies a dominant share of medical treatments. The service is financed mainly from a regional tax on business activities (p. 193) and from regional sharing of the revenues of VAT (p. 198).

The share for central government of total tax revenues (i.e. excluding social contributions) is largely higher than the share of local authorities (regions, counties–provinces, municipalities). We will see in the next section that something has changed on this point in recent years. For the moment we should note that the figures reported in Table 8.1 underestimate the fiscal revenues of local government, due to their various sharing of national taxes (income tax, VAT, taxation of energy).

Table 8.1 Structure and development of fiscal revenue in Italy and European average as a percentage of GDP, 1970–99

	1970		1975		1980		1985		1990		1995		1999	
	Italy	Europe	Italy	Europe	Italy	Europe	Italy	Europe	Italy	Europe	Italy	Europe	Italy	Europe
Direct taxes, of which	5.3	8.9	6.1	11.9	9.8	12.7	13.2	13.1	14.6	13.2	15.6	13.3	15.0	14.5
personal income	0.1	5.5	3.0	8.9	6.1	9.3	8.2	9.0	8.6	8.9	9.3	9.6	10.2	9.9
corporation income	3.0	2.2	2.1	1.9	2.4	2.2	3.1	2.8	3.7	2.9	3.6	2.4	2.6	2.8
Indirect taxes, of which	10.5	13.0	8.2	12.2	9.3	13.2	9.6	13.0	11.4	13.0	12.5	15.1	15.1	14.6
VAT	0.0	5.1	3.6	5.7	4.8	6.6	5.2	6.1	5.8	6.6	5.7	6.9	5.6	7.3
excise duties	4.9	3.5	3.7	3.5	2.9	3.2	2.8	3.2	4.0	3.1	3.9	3.4	3.1	3.5
Total tax revenue	15.8	21.9	14.3	24.1	19.1	25.9	22.8	26.1	26.0	26.2	28.1	26.9	30.1	29.1
Social contributions	10.0	11.7	11.7	12.8	11.5	13.4	12	13.8	12.9	13.7	13.1	15.0	12.8	14.0
employers	7.9	7.2	9.7	7.7	8.6	7.8	9.2	7.9	9.2	7.8	8.6	8.0	9.0	7.8
employees	1.7	3.5	1.6	3.8	2.1	4.3	2.3	4.5	2.5	4.5	2.8	5.1	2.4	4.5
self-employed	0.4	1.0	0.4	1.3	0.8	1.3	1.2	1.5	1.2	1.4	1.7	1.8	1.4	1.7
Total fiscal revenue	25.8	33.6	26.0	36.9	30.6	39.3	34.8	39.9	38.9	39.9	41.2	41.9	42.9	43.1
Administrative level														
Central government	13.7	19.7	13.4	21.1	17.9	22.3	21.2	22.1	23.7	22.2	24.6	22.5	23.9	22.9
Local government	2.2	2.2	0.8	2.8	0.8	2.9	3.2	3.1	1.8	3.8	2.9	4.0	6.2	4.0

Sources: 1970–95, Eurostat, 2000; 1999, Ministero dell'economia (2002) for Italy and Eurostat New Cronos databank 2002 (data equalized with Eurostat, 2000).

Note
Minor items are omitted.

Developments of the system from 1970 to 1999

The start up of reform in the 1970s was not at all easy. The number of tax returns increased dramatically, from 3.5 million up to 30 million for PIT and up five million for VAT (the last is about the sum of returns of both Germany and France, due to the wide dispersion of Italian productive structure into many small units). The new taxes were too sophisticated for the average culture of taxpayers and administration officers, as well as being due to a heavy system of accounting that was also imposed upon small businesses to fight avoidance. Thus we can see in Table 8.1 that, in the early 1970s, the level of total taxes was very low in Italy, just at the moment when welfare expenditures were growing at a strong rate. The resulting tax gap unbalanced the budget: the subsequent long story of high Italian public deficit and debt began here.

The change arrived at the middle-to-late 1970s. A general withholding at the source was introduced for all dependent workers and the self-employed were required to self-assess their income and pay tax annually. For lower incomes presumptive coefficients of assessment were introduced together with quick checks, while accounting requirements were reduced. Fiscal drag pushed up the revenue of income tax: from 1974 to the mid-1980s the inflation rate was around 15 percent. At the beginning of the 1980s the main taxes were finally almost working well, but the recovery of revenues up to the European average arrived only a decade later. The way in which this result was obtained was, however, not at all ideal. Tax policy was not made by enlarging the basis of the main taxes and strengthening assessment from the administration, in both cases acting to reduce avoidance and exemptions. Instead new taxes were introduced and the rates of those already existing were raised: the fiscal drag was only partially compensated.[2] The worst part of this irrational tax policy, motivated mainly on political grounds, was a long series of temporary surcharges, of amnesties and anticipations of payments (see Gerelli 1986; Pedone 1989; Galeotti and Marrelli 1992). During the 1990s (Bernardi 2000a) tax policy was an important factor in the fulfillment of Monetary Union requirements: the incidence of total taxes increased by about four points from 1990 to 1997.

The distribution of taxes among different levels of government shows that the share of local authorities, which had decreased after the 1970s reform, recovered slightly in the 1980s, to realize a sharp increase at the end of the 1990s, due to the introduction of the mentioned regional tax on business (p. 193) and of the municipalities' tax on immovable property (pp. 193–4).

A comparative view against the European average

When comparing fiscal systems of different countries one must be very careful, even if these countries are alike in economic and basic fiscal structure and have similar institutions. The need to proceed with caution, particularly with reference to European countries basically originates from the fact that, inside Europe, four models of tax system have historically emerged (Bernardi 2000b). First, the system of Nordic countries that is now changing toward the so-called "dual income taxation – DIT" system, then the British model, the Rhine model at the very center of Europe and finally the Mediterranean model.

As a consequence, levels and composition of taxes may vary considerably among European countries. The average overall pressure is estimated at 43.1 percent in 1999, but this value is the mean of a range which spans from the 34.3 percent of Portugal to the 52.2 percent of Sweden. Indirect taxes are by far the most uniform, due to the harmonization which has been induced over the last few years by the European Commission. The average rate of indirect taxes is around 15 percent, but ranges from 9.9 percent in Spain and rising to 29.6 percent in Denmark. As for social contributions, the average of 11.4 percent is made up, amongst others, of Ireland's 2.7 percent and 16.6 percent for France. These differences come basically through the relative shares of public and private supplies of healthcare, education and pensions. Institutional arrangements may also be relevant as the taxation or non-taxation of pensions, or of other social benefits, or including the reimbursement, or not, of VAT in the yield and so on.

With all of these factors in mind, the case of Italy looks quite particular. For almost all the items, aggregate or specific, Italy is always very near to the European average and consequently not close to any of the typical European models of taxation. One might ask if this closeness to the European average is only a historical causality, or rather the consequence of the middle position occupied by the Italian economy among different groups of countries belonging to the various tax models that we have just seen, particularly between the Rhine and Mediterranean models. Taking further into account the large extension of the informal Italian economy (Tanzi 1996; Bovi 2002), we have an indication that the closeness to the European average may also mean that the main taxes have high rates and restricted basis.

Some quantitative and institutional features of main taxes

The personal income tax – PIT (IRPEF)

IRPEF was introduced in 1974, substituting a large number of previous taxes on income, generally real, both at the national and local level. The beneficiary is the state but some additional rates may be imposed by regions (0.9–1.4 percent) and municipalities (up to 0.5 percent). The basis is the total net income, but the high degree of avoidance and exemptions strongly reduce the coverage of the tax, as one can see in Table 8.2,

Table 8.2 The basis of income tax in Italy, 1999 – absolute values in billion euro

	Absolute values	Percent of the total	Estimated percent avoidance	Estimated percent exemptions
Incomes				
Agriculture	2.0	0.4	2.1	85.4
Buildings	19.0	4.2	33.3	36.7
Dependent labor and pensions	344.0	74.0	8.5	12.9
Self-employed and unincorporated firms	93.0	20.0	59.5	9.4
Capital	3.5	0.8	0.0	94.2
Others	3.0	0.6		
Total	465.0	100.0	22.8	22.9

Source: Figures on basis, our projections from Ministero delle finanze (1997). Estimation of avoidance and exemptions, our evaluation, see Bernardi (1996). The figures concerning buildings are not completely updated to most recent changes of tax code.

bearing in mind that this kind of estimation is inevitably subjected to a high degree of uncertainty. The data on the extension of the informal economy in Italy seem however to confirm what emerges from our (and from other similar, Bordignon and Zanardi 1997) estimates. Agricultural and buildings rents are partially under-valued, both for some persistence of assessments according to the cadastral system (agriculture) and the exemption of the income from the house of residence. Dependent labor and pension incomes are nearly all assessed and cover 74.0 percent of the basis. Tax avoidance is very high for the self-employed and unincorporated firms. Capital rents are only dividends with a generally full tax credit, due to the imputation system in force. All interests are subject to a proportional withholding tax and capital gains were in fact exempt until very recently.

In Table 8.3 we can look at the structure of the tax. It is progressive across five income brackets with increasing marginal rates. The mean declared income (about €15,000) pays a gross average rate of about 23 percent, however, mitigated by allowances in favor of both employed and self-employed persons. The taxing unit is the individual, but allowances are given for the dependent spouse and children. Many estimations show that the correction of the household rate of taxation according to the number of incomes and of dependants is in fact quite poor.

Due to the allowances, the level of exemption is about €6,000 for the single labor worker and €3,000 for the self-employed. In the case of a household with a non-working spouse and two children, the level of exemption is around €9,000. Notice that in Italy the poverty line is estimated at around €6,000 for the single, and double this for a four-component household. Social contributions are deductible from the basis,

Table 8.3 Structure and parameters of income tax in Italy – *IRPEF* 2002 – values in euro

Brackets	Marginal rates[1]	Mean rates[2]	Allowance			
			Dependent worker	Self-employment	Spouse	Two sons
Up to 10,329	18.0	18.0	1,146	413	546	1,032
10,330–15,494	24.0	20.0	542	103	546	1,032
15,495–30,987	32.0	26.0	439	52	496	1,032
30,988–69,722	39.0	33.2	77	–	440	639
Over 69,722	45.0	45.0	52	–	422	570

Notes
1 Marginal rates don't include the surcharges of regions (0.9–1.4 percent) and municipalities (up to 0.5 percent).
2 Mean rates and allowances are calculated around the middle of any bracket.

while tax expenditures can be subtracted directly from the gross tax, to a percentage near to the value of the first rate. The main items are health expenses, life and accident insurance payments, charitable contributions and interests on house mortgage loans.

Corporation tax – CT (IRPEG)

Corporation tax was also introduced in the 1970s' reform. It applies also to non-commercial bodies, but its coverage in Italy is lower than in other countries, due to the prevailing share of small unincorporated firms. It doesn't differ too much from the standard corporation tax adopted in other developed countries, thus the basis is given by net profits, assessed in the ways shown in Table 8.4.

The basis is restricted by many factors: capital gains in some cases are taxed at a rate lower than the standard one: in fact, biggest corporations usually realize them in countries (as the Netherlands) where they are exempt. Stocks can be evaluated up to LIFO. Capital losses are fully deductible. The same in fact is true for interest payments. The acceleration of depreciation can reach a factor of two for the first three years. It should be added that there also exists a relevant level of avoidance that we estimated to be about 25 percent (Bernardi and Bernasconi 1996). A large amount of specific tax relief, incentives and allowances further characterizes the Italian CT, as in other countries. The more relevant incentives are subject to approval from the EU. We should at least mention the "Legge Visco" which, for the years 1999–2000 (and extended to 2001), has given an allowance to investments financed with internal resources. A powerful tax credit has also been adopted for firms which make investments during the years 2001–6 in the south or other disadvantaged regions of the

Table 8.4 The basis of corporation tax in Italy – *IRPEG* – 2002

Profits	
Items	*Assessment*
Revenues	Sale of goods, services, corporation shares, bonds
Capital gains	At realizing
Dividends and interests perceived	Nominal value
Stocks	Up to LIFO

Losses	
Items	*Assessment*
Costs	Labor and goods and services
Capital losses	At realizing
Interests paid	According to taxable incomes
Depreciation	Constant installments and acceleration
Current losses	Up to five years

country. Finally, in 2001 the "Legge Tremonti" was passed, which allows 50 percent of the investments made in 2001–2 to be deducted from the profits for the part which exceeds the average of 1996–2000.

The basic rate of CT in Italy is now at the level of 36 percent (34 percent since 2003) to which the regional tax on business should be added, which hits the net value added to enterprises at a normal rate of 4.25 percent. This "all-in" rate is high with respect to the present European average (Giannini 1999). Also, as we see below it was reduced by the "Visco reform" of 1997 from the level of more than 53 points it reached in the mid-1990s (p. 196 and p. 201). The same reform to alleviate further fiscal burden and to increase incentives for corporate capitalization introduced a preferential taxation for financing with internal sources: the so-called "ordinary revenue" of new capital is taxed at 19 percent. From time to time, the share of assets and profits subjected to the lower rate had to be increased and thus the effective average rate should fall beneath the statutory rate. This regime has, however, been frozen by Minister Tremonti in 2001.

The taxation of dividends may follow two separate paths. First the imputation system, with a tax credit corresponding to the tax already paid by the corporation. Otherwise, one may choose to pay a withholding of 12.5 percent, but without the tax credit. The second system is heavier for taxpayers who have an income up to about €70,000, but it is easier to administrate. In both cases the taxation of dividends stays at a much higher level in respect to interests, a distortion which has not been corrected by the more recent reforms.

Taxation of income from financial capital

This field of taxation gives rise to relevant questions regarding efficiency and equity, and poses further difficulties of assessment in an increasingly integrated world (Tanzi 1995). We saw that the 1970s reform in fact included only dividends on the basis of the personal income tax. Interests perceived by the individual were instead subject to withholdings at a various but generally moderate rate. Capital gains were in fact exempted.[3] These regimes were confused and distorted, with many opportunities of arbitrage and elusion (Giannini and Guerra 2000; Alworth *et al.* 2001).

After the "Visco reform," the returns originating from financial assets are divided into two components: the traditional "capital incomes" (dividends, interests and so on) and the reviewed category of "other incomes" (capital gains from the sale of shares, bonds, currencies, precious metals and receipts from "innovative" financial activities). The present outline of taxation of financial returns in Italy is depicted in Table 8.5. Notice that the number of rates has been reduced to only two. Both capital incomes and "other incomes" are subject to these rates in a coordinated way.

To avoid "lock-in" effects, elusive activities and differences in the burden imposed on the two type of incomes, all capital gains should be taxed at accruals. Non-residents are exempted provided that they don't live in countries classified as tax havens whereas residents who invest outside may choose between a withholding from the intermediary or self-assessment.

Finally the new regime has strengthened the favored treatment of savings devoted to funded pensions that in Italy are still underdeveloped. The model is the EET and avoids double taxation. Then it exempts contributions to pension funds from taxation, within the limits of 12 percent of the income of the saver. Interests gained during the time of accumulation are taxed at 11 percent. If the pension is paid as a rent, it is taxed under the normal PIT as the component originated from contributions. This,

Table 8.5 Taxation of financial returns in Italy by types and rates

Rate of 12.5%	*Rate of 27%*
Capital incomes	Capital incomes
Any kind of public bonds	Bank and Post Office deposits
Private long-term bonds[1]	Bank and private short-term bonds[1]
Dividends without tax credit	Derivative and atypical bonds
"Other incomes"	"Other incomes"
All incomes except capital gains "qualified"[2]	Capital gains "qualified"[2]

Notes
1 Short-term bonds are those which have a duration under 18 months; long-term are those longer.
2 Qualified capital gains are given by more than 5% of total capital for securities traded in regular markets and 25% otherwise.

coming from the interests cumulated during the working life is exempt, whereas the last part corresponding to the interests of the years of pension are taxed at 12.5 percent. The same regime applies if the pension is paid as a lump sum of capital, to which, in this case, applies the average rate of PIT during the five years before drawing the pension to the component due to contributions.

Value added tax – VAT (**IVA**)

The valued added tax (*Imposta sul Valore Aggiunto – IVA*) was introduced by the 1970s reform and follows EU standards. Thus, the tax is payable to the state (but 38.55 percent is now devolved to the regions). As usual in the EU, the basis is the total business value added minus investment expenses. Thus the basis corresponds to final consumption.[4] The due tax is calculated by the method tax-to-tax. Data and parameters of VAT are shown in Table 8.6.

VAT is the second source of taxation in Italy, after the income tax, and its basis is mainly made up of internal sales, after the abolition of customs inside the European Union. Refunds are somewhat high and their reimbursements were paid after a long delay, before that the "Visco reform" allowed their compensation with other fiscal liabilities. After the EU process of harmonization, there remain three statutory rates: at 4 percent for basic food products and essentials (and for books and newspapers), 10 percent for other food products, water, gas and electricity, sport and entertainment. The standard rate is 20 percent for all other goods and services. The weighted rate is about 16.0 percent, the effective rate is 9.5 percent, about 40 percent lower. This value is very low for the European standards, whose mean is about 15–20 percent.

The low productivity of VAT in Italy is a consequence of a high level of both exemptions and avoidance (the latter estimated to be very high, not in industry – about 15 percent – but in the vast domain of services – more than 50 percent): the point is relevant. Avoidance relating to personal income taxes (individuals and corporations) necessarily originates from that on VAT. The exemptions benefit financial transactions, public services and health, education and welfare. A favorable regime is finally granted to agriculture.

Excise duties on energy and other minor taxes

In Italy the total yield of excise duties on energy had been more than three points of GNP during 2000, the highest value in Europe. The tax particularly hits oil products, especially petrol and diesel oil. VAT is charged making the prices to consumers very high – both for households and for firms.

The other area of specific indirect taxes is made up, first, of taxes on

Table 8.6 Data and parameters on value tax in Italy – *IVA* – recent years

Revenues 2000		Rates		Exclusion	
Gross	€91 billion	4%	Basic foods, necessities, drugs, books and newspapers	Exemptions	Financial transactions; public transport; postal services; health; education; welfare
Internal sales	€79 billion				
Imports	€12 billion				
EU and other corrections	€6.5 billion	10%	Other foods; water; energy; sport and entertainments	Not taxable	Exports, some intra-EU sales
Tax refunds	€13.5 billion			Allowances	Agriculture and small units
Net revenues	€71 billion	20%	Standard rate	Total exemptions	12.6%
				Total avoidance	38.2%
% of GDP	6.1	9.6%	Effective rate	• industry	14.6%
% of total taxes	20.6	50.4%	Productivity	• services	55.2%

Sources: Revenues 2000, Ministero dell'economia (2002); Rates, tax code; productivity, OECD; exemptions, not taxable and allowances, tax code, avoidance: Bernardi and Bernasconi (1996).

starting a business, the highest is the tax on registration of legal acts (0.6 percent of GDP). Other taxes are imposed on insurance, mortgages, stamp duties and motor vehicles. Instead, succession and gift tax was completely abolished during 2001: it was largely avoided anyway. Italians like to play and so the state taxes any kind of game, gambling, lotteries, entertainments and the resultant yield is not irrelevant (0.8 percent of GDP).

Finally, at regional and local level, a lot of smaller taxes are applied – for example on authorization of business activity or occupation of public areas, use of public water and the disposal of solid wastes.

Regional tax on business – IRAP

The model pursued by governments in the 1990s to give the greater fiscal autonomy required by regional and local authorities consisted in creating an important local resource, integrating it by sharing national taxes (PIT, VAT, petrol tax) and finally reducing state transfers to specific targets, as investments and, above all, to equalize the local resources of regions with very different levels of wealth.[5]

Thus, in 1998, a new regional tax was adopted, the *Imposta Regionale sulle Attività Produttive – IRAP* which provides about half of the financing for regions. It gives a relevant yield (2.6 percent of GDP) and it is largely (but not exclusively) devoted to financing the health system, the main function of regions. We saw that the aim of the new tax was not only to strengthen fiscal federalism, but also to comply with the overall strategy of the "Visco reform" to innovate enterprise taxation (Giannini and Guerra 2000).

The tax is imposed on all those engaged in commercial business (companies, firms, private services, agricultural producers) and on public administrations. *IRAP* is charged on net value added resulting from the business pursued within the region. The basic rate is 4.25 percent, but it may be changed up a percentage point by regions and different treatments are provided for the various sectors of activity.

Municipalities tax on immovable properties – ICI

According to the same strategy adopted for regions, a specific tax was also introduced in 1993 for municipalities, which hits upon immovable properties, the *Imposta Comunale sugli Immobili – ICI*. The revenue is not very high, slightly less than 1 percent of GDP, a value well below that of taxes on property in countries like the UK (3.3 percent of GDP). There is the suspicion of widespread avoidance, particularly in the south of the country. The revenue is further limited by the fact that a patrimonial basis is given by capitalizing cadastral rents, which are largely underestimated with respect to their effective values. The tax is charged on owners of the property at a rate fixed by municipalities not less than four per thousand and not more than seven per thousand. A deduction is given to residents in their houses and some exemptions are given for particular types of properties or owners.

The fiscal burden

The distribution of taxation charge

The main general indicator of the distribution of fiscal burden is by economic functions, as depicted in Table 8.7. It shows the ratios between the overall tax burden on different factors and a common large basis, given by GDP.

First we find the evidence of the relatively stable, and currently relatively low, role of consumption taxes. Instead taxes (and social contributions) on labor have made a big jump and more than doubled from the beginning of the 1970s to the late 1990s. At present they provide about half of the total revenue. This involves almost all employees, while the charge on the self-employed increased, but is still at a very low level. Notice in particular that in Italy the legal rate for social contributions on the self-employed is, in effect, nearly half of what is charged on dependent workers, but PIT rates are the same and the self-employed account for one-third of total employment (standard labor units). Thus a rough estimation gives the result that the fiscal charge on self-employment is avoided by at least 30 percent of the self-employed.

Taxation on capital also grew over time, but it is lower than the burden on labor and made up primarily by income and wealth not allocable. The

Table 8.7 Structure according to the economic function as a percentage of GDP

	1970	*1975*	*1980*	*1985*	*1990*	*1995*	*1997*
Consumption	9.9	8.0	8.1	8.6	10.3	10.5	10.6
Labor	10.3	14.4	17.4	19.7	21.3	22.4	23.6
employed	9.8	13.7	16.0	17.8	19.2	18.8	20.9
self-employed	0.5	0.7	1.4	1.9	2.1	2.6	2.6
Capital, of which	5.6	3.6	5.2	6.5	7.3	9.0	10.0
real estate and capital	0.8	0.3	0.4	0.4	0.6	1.4	1.3
monetary capital	0.1	0.8	1.7	1.9	2.4	2.2	2.6
Environment	2.8	2.7	2.1	2.2	3.3	3.6	3.7
energy	2.5	2.5	1.9	1.9	2.8	3.2	3.2
transport	0.3	0.2	0.2	0.3	0.5	0.5	0.5
pollution	0.0	0.0	0.0	0.0	0.0	0.0	0.0
Total	27.4	28.2	32.3	36.0	42.4	44.5	45.7

Source: Eurostat (2000).

Note
1997 is the last data available.

typical tax on capital, real and monetary, provides a small contribution to total taxes, particularly through the real capital whose taxation is not more than 1 percent of GDP, due mainly to the municipalities tax on immovable properties. Taxation of monetary capital is also low. At a rate of withholdings of 12.5 percent, the most commonly charged in Italy, it is somewhat lower with respect to European standards, even if it is compared to countries which have a final withholding tax (Joumard 2001). Finally pollution and transport taxes are virtually absent, while the taxation of energy is at a high level, as we had already seen.

This first evidence suggests we should have a closer look at the main headings of distribution of fiscal burdens, i.e. labor, consumption and other factors (gross operating surplus), as are given by implicit rates depicted in Figure 8.1[6] from 1979 to 1997. It is confirmed that the observed time increase in cumulate value should be due mainly to the rate on labor, up to a really very high current value. This trend was impressive (30 points), pushed up from 1975 to the beginning of the 1990s by an ever-greater burden of income tax. Social contributions were already high at the beginning of the period. It is also confirmed that the contribution of consumption and other factors to fiscal effort has been far more limited. The choice of leaving low consumption taxation has been due mainly to anti-inflationary goals and, further, to the high avoidance of VAT. The implicit rate on other factors has increased far less than that on labor, also because of the soft regimes for financial activities and the avoidance in taxes on profits of firms and on the self-employed (Giannini and Guerra 2000). One is forced to conclude that, during the last 30 years, tax policy in Italy has been neither efficient nor equitable.

To end this subsection, we look now at the personal redistributive effects of the tax system and particularly of income tax. In a comparative

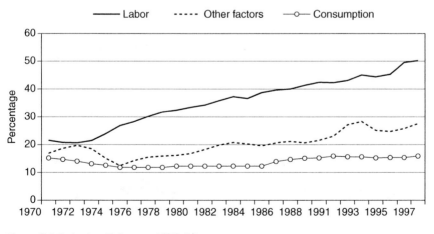

Figure 8.1 Italy: implicit rates 1970–97.

analysis of 12 OECD countries, the distributive effect of income tax for Italy has been estimated in 2.4 percent of difference between the Gini coefficients on gross and net incomes (Wagstaff *et al.* 1999). It was at the lower bound of estimations for countries selected, but it was also below Italian estimates at the same time. To mention only our result (Bernardi 1995), we obtained 4.7 percent of redistributive effect, while the last available estimate gives, for the year 2000, a redistributive effect of 5.1 points: the average rate is at 23.5 percent, the Kakwani at 22.0 percent, both high values if compared with the European average (Bosi and Guerra 2002).

If we instead consider the structure of the whole system and assume the conventional hypotheses of tax-incidence, partial equilibrium and single generation, looking back at Table 8.1 we have to observe that direct taxes, by and large regarded as progressive, are only half of the sum of indirect taxes and social contributions, usually considered regressive, at least as far as they are passed on prices. The traditional result, of an overall pro-portionality of tax system of industrialized countries, first obtained by J. Pechman during the 1960s, would then not be confirmed for Italy whose system at first glance seems to be generally regressive.[7]

Tax wedges on labor and corporate taxation

The charge that we have just seen on labor, and to a lesser amount, on other factors has not only consequences on equity, but also on efficiency. Looking at the tax wedge on labor, we find the confirmation of what we have already observed considering the distribution of tax burden. The average wedge is currently estimated (average) at nearly 50 percent[8] of total labor costs in industry, both by national (Giannini and Guerra 2000) and international sources (Joumard 2001). Its present value increased by almost 20 points from the beginning of the 1970s, nearly 12 points during the 1980s, and finally stabilized during the 1990s. It is worth breaking the wedge into its constituent parts, that due from the employers and that from the employees, considering possible differences in shifting. Employ-ers contribute two-thirds (almost all social contributions) and employees the rest (income tax and social contributions). In the whole of Europe the wedge has, for many years, been one of the main problems of the fiscal systems,[9] due to the evidence that it depresses employment and growth, both from the point of view of supply and that of labor demand (see, for a survey, Petretto 2002): once more the Italian case is one of the worst. We will return to this point when examining tax reforms.

In Italy at the beginning of the 1990s, the "all-in" statutory rate on cor-porations was at the level of 46.4 percent, ten points above the figure of ten years before, and about six points higher than the European average (Giannini and Guerra 2000). Despite a general movement to further reductions, generated by international tax competition, the rate increased up to 53.2 percent in 1997. This rate surely disadvantaged Italian corporations and the location of productive activity in Italy. The spread was, however, mitigated by the generous criteria concerning allowances granted from fiscal legislation[10] and by the level of avoidance (see page 188). Joumard (2001) reports an estimate according to which, in the mid-1990s, the backward effective rate of corporate taxation in Italy was nearly 15 points under the "all-in" statutory rate.

For the same period (Giannini and Guerra 2000), it has been estimated (following the Devereux–Griffith (1999) methodology) that the marginal effective forward rates in Italy were −85.5 percent[11] in the case of debt financing, and 40.3 percent in the case of financing with new equities. The corresponding average rates were 34.5 percent and 47.8 percent, at a profitability rate of 20 percent.[12] Notice the jump between marginal and average rates, which is a signal of a tax with high rate and narrow basis (Giannini and Maggiulli 2001), and makes the country less attractive for most profitable investments. Furthermore the large spread for both the rates between debt and equity financing should be emphasized. Its consequence is the thin-capitalization of corporations.

This picture was changed by the "Visco reform" of 1997. The "all-in" statutory rate decreased to 41.2 percent. The rate had to be reduced further by the new preferential taxation of ordinary income from internal sources, which, however, was frozen in August 2001. After the "Visco reform" (Giannini and Guerra 2000), the marginal effective rate increased to −27 percent, in the case of debt financing, but decreased by about 30 points in the case of financing with equity (10 percent). Average rates decreased both in the case of financing with debt (27.8 percent) and equities (31.7 percent). Thus a relevant result of the reform has been to reduce the statutory and average effective rates as well as the difference between marginal and average effective rates and, moreover, to bring rates closer in the cases of equity and debt financing.

Taxation by levels of government and fiscal federalism

International sources (Eurostat 2000; OECD 2001) apportion total taxes (excluding social contributions) collected in Italy at the end of the 1990s between slightly less than 90 percent to central government and slightly more than 10 percent to local governments (regions, provinces, municipalities). National estimates (Ministero dell'Economia 2002) give a somewhat different picture, by attributing 17.5 percent of total taxes in 1999 to local governments.[13] This percentage rapidly grew from the beginning of the 1990s: it was 12.5 percent in 1994 and it was projected to reach 21.4 percent in 2001.[14] The increase in local resources might also become far more dramatic, if projects under way to substantially enlarge the role of the regions and give rise to a federal state are accomplished.

Currently regions are, on the whole, self-financing and an equalizing system was activated, taking into account the differences in per-capita resources, healthcare needs and other minor factors.[15] Notice that in 1990 own taxes of regions were only 1.6 point of the total revenues, while state transfers covered almost all total expenditure (Arachi and Zanardi 2000). In 1998 the regional tax on business was introduced. At the same time a sharing to national income tax was added at a current rate of 0.5–1.4 percent. Small taxes were also started, particularly on energy, motor vehicles and disposal of solid wastes. The last reform arrived in 2000, when a new sharing plan was adopted to VAT (now 38.55 percent of regional revenue).

However we have already said that this seems to not be the end of the story. An act of constitutional reform, passed by the Parliament in 2001, and the projects of the present government provide a huge devolution of functions from the state to the regions, most notably in the domains of health, education and local police. This change will be dramatic from an institutional point of view and in relation to the sharing of resources. The shifting of financing is currently evaluated around 50 billion euro, which could be covered by raising the regional share of income tax and/or VAT to very high levels. The idea of more autonomous taxes is often invoked, but up to now nobody has been able to show what they should be.

In the 1990s, a similar story could be seen in the provinces and municipalities: the second case being the more relevant. At the end of the 1990s, state transfers and own taxes had about the same value (Cavaliere and Osculati 2000), while one decade before the own taxes were less than one-third of state transfers. The change was mainly due to the introduction, in 1993, of the tax on immovable property and by the subsequent adoption of new taxes or revision of those already existing, particularly in the fields of energy, advertising, occupancy of public areas, waste disposal and registration fees.

Finally it should be mentioned that, from 1997, in view of the requirements of the Maastricht Treaty and the Stability Pact, strict limits were imposed upon the budgetary independence of local authorities, somewhat at odds with the process underway to give them more financial autonomy. The so-called "Internal Stability Pact" (Fraschini 2002) essentially consists of ceilings to budget deficits or to total expenditures, supported by a system of bonuses and penalties. Healthcare expenditure is not constrained by the ceilings of the pact because its increase is very difficult to foresee: it accounts for nearly 90 percent of total expenditure for the regions.

A comparative view against the European average

The indicators of fiscal burden of Italy may now be compared with the correspondent figures of the European average, taking into account that this average derives from a wide cross-section of national data. The general result is that, from many points of view, the Italian case looks worse than the European average and deeper reforms seem to be needed.

In 1997, Italian values of implicit rates were very high for labor (about ten points over), not very different for consumption and slightly less for other factors with respect to the European average. Lower taxation of labor characterizes not only countries with restricted social protection (such as the UK and Ireland) but also those which raised other taxes, for example on consumption (Denmark) or on other factors (France). High taxes on labor create a tax wedge in Italy which, in 2000, occupied seventh place in the OECD list (Joumard 2001), some points over the European average and twenty points over the OECD average.

The "Visco reform" has improved the taxation of corporations, making it lighter and more neutral, but more remains to be done to enhance competitiveness in a country where many non-tax wedge costs are at work. The statutory "all-in" rate is still over the European average of about eight points. Marginal effective rates are lower than the average by the countries considered in this research,[16] particularly in the case of debt financing, while the average rates are in the same order of magnitude.[17]

We are not able to arrive at a firm conclusion concerning the comparison of the redistributive impact of income tax (and of the whole fiscal system) between Italy and the European average. Only some contrasting conjectures may be put forward. As we saw, the mean rate of income tax is rather high now in Italy, and the level of progressivity has increased during the 1990s, without being reduced by reforms similar to the ones adopted in many other countries. Both the share of direct taxes and income tax in Italy are somewhat higher than the European average, while that of the sum of VAT and excise duties is slightly lower,[18] but the share of social contributions due from the employers is also higher and the distribution of their burden would be regressive if they are shifted onto prices.

The available data both from the EU and the OECD do not allow an accurate comparison of the apportionment of taxes by levels of government between Italy and other European countries. But some countries stand out particularly. Revenues of central government are, for instance, low in Germany and very high in the United Kingdom, while the revenues of local governments are particularly high in Nordic countries. We know that now in Italy the main sources of local authorities are the business tax and the share of VAT at the regional level, and the tax on immovable property at the municipalities level. OECD data (2001) seem to indicate that the share of taxes on incomes is larger for the whole area than for Italy, as is also the case for property tax and excise duties: thus, traditional prescriptions of theory should be applied in the last two cases elsewhere but not in Italy.

Tax reforms in the 1990s and those currently planned

A quick glance at the budget and the general economic environment

After the fast development of the 1950s and the 1960s, and the slower and more unbalanced development of the 1970s and the 1980s (Graziani 1979), during the 1990s the average yearly rate of growth in the Italian economy fell to around 1.2 percent, half of the European average and one-third of the US rate. There was more than one reason for this break-down: ten years of tight monetary and fiscal policy to reach the requirements of the Maastricht Treaty and of the Stability Pact, a long period of political crisis during the first part of the decade, general rigidity of the markets, privatization which was not backed up by any suitable industrial policy (Fausto 2002), the instability of the worldwide economy, a prevailing industrial structure of small firms not inducing technical progress (De Cecco 2000). Thus the vintage of capital became older, decoupling the increase of total factor productivity from the possible advances of technological progress (Basu and Fernald 2002).

The government's *Document of Economic and Financial Programming* of July 2002 set the target of increasing the yearly growth rate to 2.9–3.0 percent from 2003 (however, the 2002 forecast is 0.9 percent, while the forecast for 2003 made by the REF of Milan, our reference economic research center is 2.1 percent and similar figures are given by other Italian research centers and international organizations, like the EU, the OECD and the IMF).[19] Potential growth of the Italian economy seems to be dropped to not more than 2 percent.

The government plans to reduce net borrowing to about 0.8 percent of GDP in 2003 and to 0.5 percent in 2004, which are the present EU requirements. These figures should allow room for maneuver (0.5 percent of GDP in 2003) and to start the program of tax cuts that the government aims to carry on. Once more, REF and the other mentioned centers and organizations are far more cautious. In their opinion, net borrowing will decrease much more slowly than envisaged by the government and the room for tax cuts should be still found, alternatively by reducing expenditures or substituting the planned tax cuts with increases in other taxes. In fact, on the basis of the more pessimistic outlook that emerged at the end of 2002, the government has presented a plan of 12 billion euro to improve the budget trend and reach 2003 targets (lately revised upward from 0.8 percent to 1.5 percent of GDP).

Tax reforms in the 1990s and the "Visco reform"

Innovations introduced into the Italian tax system up to 1997 ("the Maastricht year") were considerable in number, but they were in fact almost exclusively devoted to the pressing need of raising more funds in one way or another. Increases affected almost all main taxes, in various ways.[20] A comprehensive reform of the tax system was proposed in 1994 by the Minister, Mr. Tremonti, also then in office, but it was not seen through to the end, due to the fall of the government. Problems in the tax system were, however, evident (Bernardi 2000b with bibliography; Giannini and Guerra 2000; Pedone 2000). The traditional shortcomings were still at large: the high levels of avoidance and exemptions of income tax and VAT, the complexity of the system, the persistent inefficiency of the centralization of revenues. Other problems accumulated and became even more pressing during the 1990s: the excess burden on labor, fears for fiscal competitions, lack of neutrality and efficiency in corporate taxation, and then there were changes in the economic environment to be dealt with, which come under pressure from both the internalization of economies (Tanzi 1995) and from the diffusion of small firms and services (Pedone 2000).

The "Visco reform," launched in 1997, coped with some, but not all of these issues. We now try to provide a summary of the reform's aims, tools and results. The main targets of the reform were to make the system simpler and more neutral; to give more autonomy to local authorities; to reduce fiscal pressure as much as possible, within budgetary constraints, without jeopardizing social expenditure, but trying to limit avoidance and exemptions. The general reference model of taxation has been indicated in the so-called "dual income tax – DIT" (Soerensen 1994), which was developed by the Nordic countries during the 1990s, to find a compromise between equity and the need to avoid capital flights.

As we have seen, the taxation of corporations (and subsequently also of unincorporated firms) has been changed mainly in two ways. First through the introduction of the large basis regional business tax which substituted previous, more restricted basis taxes on profits and net assets, and further by the adoption of the allowance on "ordinary returns" of the increases in capital. There is more than one reason why fiscal burden should have been redistributed in favor of the most profitable and most capitalized firms (Giannini 1999). These might be the largest ones or those operating in the financial sector. This possible outcome has been largely discussed with reference to the multitude of small firms which characterize the Italian industrial structure (Vitaletti 2002a), but up to now a final judgment is still not possible because of a lack of the necessary information.

The new features of corporate taxation, however, significantly reduced the statutory "all-in" rate, and consequently the average effective rate, particularly for the most productive projects.[21] The level of statutory rate remained well over the European average, due to budget constraints, and this has contained the improvement of the Italian tax competitiveness and of the reduction of the previous disincentive to locate activities in Italy.

Furthermore the reform has made the financing of firms among different sources far more neutral (a target also suggested by the OECD and Joumard 2001), by reducing the tax wedge in the case of capital financing. This would favor the capitalization of firms, the undertaking of new initiatives and the efficiency of capital markets (Giannini and Guerra 2000). Unfortunately, in this case we also don't have enough information to appraise how these expected targets have really been reached. Far less satisfactory results were obtained for the labor wedge.[22] It remained at a very high level, with respect to the European average, or even increased. This may influence marginal production costs and technological choices by further disadvantaging labor.

Maybe the achievements of capital taxation reform are less complex and questionable than those of corporate taxation. A clear and general identification of all taxation incomes has been attained. Capital gains are now subject to taxation, in accordance with the taxation of capital rents. The number of rates has also been reduced, though not to only one, in order to avoid any increase in the cost of public debt. The role of financial intermediaries has been expanded, with positive consequences on the level of elusion (Guerra 1998). A debated issue was instead the introduction of taxation of capital gains at accruals and not at the moment of realizing, both from a theoretical and practical point of view (Alworth *et al.* 2001; Giannini and Guerra 2001).

The road of decentralization of state revenues has been covered mainly by means of the introduction of the business tax and of the large devolution of VAT, both of which favor the regions. As an autonomous tax, devoted mainly to financing healthcare, the business tax has been criticized (Bordignon 1997) for its lack of accountability and its poor correspondence to the benefit principle. The basis is furthermore unequally distributed by regions, whose autonomy to manage the tax is limited. Considering that the devolution of VAT is not more than a transfer, that the regional surcharge on income tax is very limited and, finally, that the decentralization of functions has also been very limited up to now, the final conclusion is that the steps which have been made toward fiscal federalism had the prevailing aim of introducing a cautious financial responsibility to the regions.

"Visco reform" had still to be completed (Guerra 2000). The DIT system should have been extended to all capital or mixed incomes. The statutory rate on corporations was planned to decrease and the preferential regime for internal sources to grow as time passed. The rate on capital rents and gains had to be unified around an average of about 19 percent. The tax reform should finally be completed by evaluating a reform of the role and structure of income tax.

Planned tax reforms: the "Tremonti reform" and the debate on fiscal system

Despite the recent "Visco reform" (whose innovations are now largely planned to be repealed), Mr. Tremonti, the Minister of Finance of the new government elected in the spring of 2001, launched his own widespread project for new fiscal reform. The delegation bill was approved by the Cabinet in December and was approved by Parliament in April 2003. The reform is based on a four-year plan (2003–6), to make its cost (about 25 billion euro, two points of GNP, in the government's estimation) compatible with the strict budget constraints imposed by the Stability Pact. The reform is presented as a step in the direction already taken by other European countries, but in fact it is more radical than elsewhere and two weighty specific aims are added to more common goals (simplification, neutralization, international standardization and competitiveness).

The first aim is political–ideological in nature (Bernardi 2002). The proposal is based upon a pro-market view of the social economy. The ideal of a natural right to have a "just taxation" corresponding to more freedom is affirmed. The roots of this principle could be found in many views on social justice (Granaglia 1991), but the proponents (Vitaletti 2002a) appear instead to be closer to the Wicksellian and Italian tradition of the voluntary state. Obviously this point is open to question in the light of Beveridgean, Welfarist and Rawlsian traditions, the diffused market failures of the real world and the fact that income distribution can be conceived as a matter of collective choices and not a naturally occurring right.

The second and not debatable aim is to enhance growth but it draws substantially on an expectation–supply-side view. The beginning of a credible path of decreasing taxes should trigger a "virtuous circle": "less taxes– more growth," only as an effect of gentle, across-the-board cuts of the rates (Pedone 2002). An additional Keynesian effect on consumption (Vitaletti 2002a) should also be welcome. Unfortunately this optimistic view is not easily supported with recourse to more recent literature. The low size of the effects of tax cuts on factors' supply is a well-known fact, from US debate in the 1980s (Bosworth and Burtless 1992), that has been fully confirmed by recent analyses (Leibfritz *et al.* 1997).[23] Labor demand models (see Petretto 2002, for a survey) show that elasticity of demand is also low. The previous contrasting results of endogenous growth models (Petretto 2002) seem to be solved by the most recently updated and sophisticated estimates (Cassou and Lansing 2000), which show a very low effect on growth of reducing income tax progressivity. The EU estimated with traditional demand models (Leibrfritz *et al.* 1997) that a point of GDP cut would deviate growth from a base line of an average of two points in the case of corporate tax and 1.25 in that of labor's taxation. The already-quoted Italian *Document of Economic and Financial Programming* indicates an

0.25 percent (not necessarily permanent) increase in growth to be attributed to a tax cut of one point of GDP. Notice that we are speaking of points of GDP: two points is the total tax cut of "Tremonti reform." We would not conclude that an inverse relationship between taxation and growth doesn't exist at all, but the empirical evidence for this is neither high nor robust (Tanzi and Zee 1996). Taxes should then be cut by relevant amounts and in order to reach carefully selected targets. The simple across-the-board filing of rates would not be enough.

Bearing all that in mind, we now come to the other major items of "Tremonti reform." An important aim is the building of a unified and coherent tax code, by filtering the present dispersive and, at times, contradictory legislation. Other main areas of interventions are listed below.

i) *The reform of income tax and the new* IRE. A deep reform concerns income tax and builds upon similar changes already adopted by other European countries during recent years (EU Commission 2000): even the name of the tax should be changed to *Imposta sui Redditi – IRE*. The basis and the subjects should not be changed substantially, while the present structure (pp. 186–8) should be amended radically. The brackets should be reduced to two, the first up to the high level of €100,000, the second one over and above. The corresponding rates had to be set low, at 23 percent and 33 percent respectively.[24] The present tax allowances should be transformed from tax credits into deductions from the taxable income and integrated with a "new" deduction, to exempt, for instance, an income of about €7,500 in case of a single person and of about €12,000 earned by a dependent worker in a household supporting a dependent spouse and a child (Vitaletti 2002b). Following the bill's provisions, deductions should be "concentrated" on low and middle incomes and decrease as income increases and disappear at about €40,000–50,000 (Vitaletti 2002a). The lack of revenue is quantified by the government at about 20 billion euro.[25] The consequent reduction of the average fiscal pressure and labor cost has been estimated by REF at a level of about −3 percent (REF 2002). Such a level is not irrelevant but also not very high, particularly because the projected distribution of gains is in favor of the bottom and top incomes and not that of the average productive worker.[26]

In fact, according to the government's estimates (Vitaletti 2002b), once fully accomplished, the reform will raise the level of exemption and give substantial gains to households with incomes from about €12,000 up to about €20,000. The "no-tax area" would be widened, particularly for the low-income households. Over this threshold the reform becomes progressively neutral, but from about €40,000 advantages increase once more and reach high figures up to over 12 points of the average rate for a low number of the upper incomes.[27] REF has calculated very rough figures of the distribution of overall gains. About half would benefit nearly 14 million taxpayers, with about 40 percent of the total income, situated over the present level of exemption and below €20,000. The other half would benefit the highest decile of taxpayers: about three million, with a mean per capita income close to €50,000. The remaining 13 million taxpayers would have no substantial gains and losses, because they are already exempt or situated in the wide "neutral" area.

Such a radical change proposed for the distribution of the income tax burden has obviously been widely debated. The proponents argue that progressivity (and also personalization) is not justified on the grounds of efficiency, or equity (Patrizii 2002; Vitaletti 2002a). The main argument is that the basis of the tax is substantially restricted to only labor incomes. Further, redistributive goals are better performed through public expenditure in a non-minimal Nozik state. These points are not new, but well established in the debate on dual income tax or expenditure taxation. The answers might be (Bernardi 2000; Guiannini and Guerra 2000) that, in any case, all efforts should be focused on making the whole system more equitable, by reducing avoidance and preferential tax treatments and by taxing all incomes (those from capital in particular) at an even rate. Furthermore, one should be cautious in removing the only evidence of progressivity present in the tax system and which concerns nearly 60 percent of net GDP (Bosi and Guerra 2002). Finally it has been noted that the advantages given by the reform to the rich are very significant (Baldini, Bosi and Matteuzzi 2002). A minimal suggestion would be to reduce the upper limit of the first bracket to €40,000 and leave the rate of 33 percent unchanged, it being a political commitment of the government. A more ambitious suggestion should be to introduce a tax similar to the French tax on large fortunes (see Chapter 5).[28]

Focusing the debate on vertical equity has distracted general attention from horizontal equity by presuming that this would be a minor problem, due to the adoption of such a long basic bracket. Instead, the strengthening of decreasing deductions raises again the traditional distortion of household taxation in the presence of a different number of earners. For example, if we are right to quantify a government's indications, a household with an income of €40,000 received by a single earner will be taxed at an average rate at least double the rate to which a family with two earners of €20,000 each would be subjected. A proposal would be to devote some part of the deductions also to correcting this serious distortion.

ii) *The taxation of capital incomes.* The government tax reform also aims to innovate the taxation of capital incomes, even though it was recently modified by the "Visco reform." The proposed changes are as follows. All capital incomes (for example, rents and capital gains) should be unified in a single class and converge to the taxation regime of state bonds, i.e. final withholdings at the single rate of 12.5 percent. "Unqualified" dividends should also only be taxed with an at-source rate of 12.5 percent, without tax credit.[29] The same rate should apply to capital gains realized by mutual funds and taxation should be deferred to the time of sale or redemption of shares. Finally, incentives provided for private pension savings should be further strengthened, by eliminating taxation on the interests accrued during capital accumulation. The loss of revenue is estimated at 1.7 billion–1.8 billion euro.

The general target of the reform is to try to make financial capital taxation still more neutral, fair and simple, in order to improve its international uniformity and competitiveness. This would come from the common treatment of all financial incomes and also from the repeal of the at-accrual regimes which would be too complex and without precedents in other countries (Panzeri 2002). The low rate should favor the containment of the cost of public debt, investment activities and higher net revenues on financial assets, while discouraging capital flights from residents (Vitaletti 2002a).

The uniform taxation regimes at a single rate has been generally well accepted in principle,[30] but the proposal raised also various criticisms (Guerra 2002; REF 2002). In fact some disparities of treatment of income from different sources remain or increase, particularly between interests and dividends and those due to the different timing of taxation that the at-accrual system tried to overcome. The proponents' reasons supporting the adoption of a low rate appear to be questionable. Most of all, the fiscal burden on financial capital should still drop at a rate which would be the lowest among European countries (Joumard 2001).[31] Finally the gains in competitiveness relate only to residents (non-residents are exempt, as we have seen) and may contrast with EU attempts to strengthen capital income taxation of non-residents. A progressive converging to the European average of final withholdings (20 percent) seems to be cautious and more equitable.

iii) *The taxation of corporations.* The delegation bill gives much room to the reform of corporate taxation and its relating proposals radically amend the innovations introduced by the "Visco reform." The main aim of the reform is once more to simplify the present system and to bring it closer to the European norm (the German system in particular), in order to achieve more efficiency and neutrality. This should be achieved as follows. Both the preferential taxation on ordinary income from internal financing and regional business tax should be repealed. Broadly speaking (Vitaletti 2002a), they would have been unfair, giving a comparative advantage to the largest and financial corporations and penalizing small exporting and labor-intensive firms. Furthermore, the allowance on internal sources would be too complex, without similar schemes in other European countries, and not welcome by firms which don't like to increase their capitalization. The cost of labor should be the first part of the basis of business tax to be eliminated. The statutory rate for corporate taxation should decrease from the present 36 percent to 33 percent.

The bill further suggests the adoption of the system of participation exemption, to give a more European and advanced solution to the problem of intra-corporate taxation. Tax credit on dividends should be substituted by an exemption at 95 percent. Capital gains from the sale of shares should not be subject to more taxation, with the obvious consequence of eliminating the deductibility of capital losses: this system would also help to avoid elusive practices (Vitaletti 2002a). Further, within certain limits, the option should be given to the corporations to have a consolidated budget, by adding their taxable basis to those of the controlled companies. Finally the reform intends to contrast thin-capitalization in the case of debt financing coming from or guaranteed by shareholders or inducing a too-high level of leverage. The sum of all the parts of the reform should not change tax revenue. These structural changes have generally been well received. They follow and in some cases anticipate European tendencies, and are more suitable for the new international environment and allow a better organization of companies. All these factors may favor the location of corporations in Italy.

The gains coming from the reform on the level of fiscal burden suffered by corporation and on its distribution and effects have, however, been considered contrasting or small (Giannini 2002; REF 2002). At least in principle, the reduction to 33 percent of the corporate statutory tax rate would not be more favorable than keeping the allowance for internal sources in force with its expected effect of progressively reducing effective average tax rate. The "all-in" statutory rate remains far higher in Italy than the European average.[32] This seems the main drawback of the reform. The rate is also far over those of income tax and of interests, and thus it increases opportunity for arbitrages and elusion. The progressive repeal of regional business tax planned by the government might reduce these spreads, but it is not easy to be compensated (also to finance the regions) without further charges on enterprises. Finally the just mentioned proposals of the abolishing of the business tax and the allowance on internal sources would reduce neutrality of investments financing, while raising the capital marginal effective rate.

We tried to discuss at length both the "Visco reform" and the "Tremonti reform," by pointing out the main pros and cons, as emerged from a wide debate, without avoiding giving our judgments and suggestions. But our fundamental argument is that both reforms do not do enough to afford the true priority of reforming Italian (and European) fiscal systems, i.e. the need to reduce the burden on production factors, labor first of all. An obvious difficulty arises from the liability to the budget constraints imposed by the Stability Pact. Further, a significant reduction of social expenditure (which needs however to be restructured) would be quite questionable and, furthermore, it is almost unfeasible politically. Other possible cuts of primary expenditure also seem possible if not very large, by considering that its level in Italy has already been compressed by the huge amount of interests.

Overall resources which can be collected from expenditure cuts and a reasonable departure from the most strict implementation of balanced budget European rule can, however, contribute by a significant amount. Some further funding could be raised in the middle term, by augmenting taxes on externalities (transport and environment) and on immovable properties up to the European average, while not pulling down capital income taxation and reducing avoidance and exemptions, particularly in the case of VAT and income tax. All these resources can reach the amount needed, first to lighten the burden of income tax, but without giving too many advantages to the rich and with more horizontal equity, second to cut down the corporation tax "all-in rate" below the European average, and finally but most of all to abate markedly the social contributions paid by private employers. A proportion of pensions should be funded by means of general fiscal revenues (and paid only at statutory age of pension) while contributions should only cover the remaining part in accordance with the contributing history of the pensioner.[33]

These suggestions are obviously only a first sketch, which require many deep checks on their economic effects as well as on their practical implementation and, above all, on their political feasibility, particularly as to regards the radical and non-marginal shifting of taxes proposed, the non-parametric changes of the pension system (Galasso and Profeta 2002). However, at least some steps have to be done according to the directions proposed here which are also in line with (but far wider than) recent OECD suggestions (Joumard 2001).

Notes

1 Thanks are due to M. Bernasconi, A. Fraschini, C. Guerra, F. Osculati and P. Profeta for their careful reading, their comments and suggestions. C. Bronchi and I. Joumard at OECD and L. Pench at the EU Commission gave invaluable help in finding the needed data and information. The English text has been carefully reviewed by L. Sweet.

2 The rate of CT increased from 25 percent to 36 percent, the standard rate of VAT from 12 percent to 20 percent. The exemption of interests on public bonds was eliminated in 1986 and the rates on capital incomes were augmented.

3 Interests and capital gains were instead included in the taxable basis of corporate and unincorporated firms.

4 Note the difference with regional business tax (p. 193) whose basis is made up by a different definition of value added, i.e. the sum of labor costs, interests paid and profits, net from depreciation.

5 If we fix the income per capita at 100 in Lombardia (the richest region), the correspondent value for Calabria (the poorest) is about 60.

6 Implicit rates are given by the ratios of taxes on various factors and their own potential basis. Their estimated values are somewhat controversial. The order of their magnitude and trends presented here are, however, out of discussion. Obviously estimations don't consider possible tax shifting.

7 We are completely aware of how this result is (poor) hypotheses dependent, but have also to note that the hypotheses here mentioned are those commonly used in standard models of micro-simulations of income-tax burdens.

8 The marginal rate should be at least five points over the average rate (Joumard 2001).

9 In the US, the wedge is currently estimated at about 30 percent, a value which has not changed during the last 30 years. Due caution, however, is needed in comparing European and US data: the last don't comprise the contributions to private health systems and pensions plans.

10 Particularly concerning the regimes of depreciation, interests deductions and other incentives.

11 This value might well be negative, due to favorable regimes for depreciation and interests and to the high level of statutory rates.

12 Remember, however, that forward-looking rates are not influenced by avoidance.

13 Two-thirds are due to regions, the remaining to provinces and municipalities.

14 This value does not comprise the recent and large sharing of VAT among regions that we cover on pages 197–8.

15 We remember that the main and growing function of regions is public healthcare (more than 90 percent of the budget), plus other functions relating mainly to land management (agriculture, transports, public works, tourism and so on). Further other minor tasks were recently assigned by the state to regions (and thus to provinces and municipalities) in order to realize so-called "administrative decentralization."

16 About −21 percent in the case of debt and about 33 percent in the case of equity (Giannini and Maggiulli 2001).

17 About 33 percent in the case of both debt and equity financing (Giannini and Maggiulli 2001).

18 It is not easy to qualify for the regional business tax (2.5 points of GNP), included among indirect taxes by National Accounts.

19 Both private estimates and government programs were drastically revisited in the second half of 2002. GDP has grown to 0.4 percent in 2002 and is not expected to grow much faster in 2003.

20 Income tax was de-indexed to inflation, corporations suffered from a raise in the "all-in" rate and from a new tax on net assets, VAT rates were augmented. Many temporary taxes, advances of collections and delays in reimbursement were also adopted.

21 For a critical view, particularly concerning the reference to effective rates, see Alworth *et al.* 1997.

22 As a result the government was forced to reduce social contributions and raise energy taxes.

23 Labor supply elasticity is currently estimated in 0.15 for men and 0.3 for women in the US. These figures may be slightly higher in more unionized European labor markets. Elasticity of demand is estimated around the double of the supply average figure (Leibfritz *et al.* 1997).

24 Note that the country where the "long" bracket has been invented, i.e. the UK, the basic bracket ends at a value of about €50,000, and the subsequent rate is fixed at 40 percent.

25 The first step of the reform is planned for 2003 and its lack of revenue is estimated in 5 billion–10 billion euro. It should be made up of a mix of the structures of the new and the present income tax, only to concern low-middle incomes.

26 This distribution might recall some prescriptions of the optimal taxation theory, but the proponents of the reform explicitly indicate that this theory is completely useless for concrete reforming of the tax system (Patrizii 2002).

27 Some recent indications by the government, however, seem to be oriented to also distribute more gains to middle incomes.

28 A discussion of different arrangements of brackets and rates may be found in Baldini and Bosi (2002). The rejoinder is in Vitaletti (2002a).
29 The only exceptions would be "qualified" capital gains and dividends. They should be included in the income tax only for a quota but without tax credit for dividends.
30 This is also a recommendation from OECD, which, however, is not in favor of excessive incentives to pension savings (Joumard 2001).
31 The rate of final withholdings on interest in Europe is comprised from 15 percent (France and others) to 30 percent (Sweden). In seven countries interests of the residents are still included in income tax (Joumard 2001).
32 37.2 percent in Italy and 32.4 percent as the European average are expected for 2003 (Giannini 2002).
33 A similar proposal has been advanced recently by REF (2002).

References

Alworth, J., Hamaui, R. and Violi, R. (1997) "Ancora sulla tassazione dei redditi da capitale," in Bernardi L. (ed.) *La Finanza pubblica italiana. Rapporto 1997,* Bologna: Il Mulino: 187–214.
—— (2001) *The Taxation of Income from Capital in Italy: 1990–2001,* mimeo.
Arachi, G. and Zanardi, A. (2000) "Il Federalismo fiscale regionale: opportunità e limiti," in Bernardi, L. (ed.) *La Finanza pubblica italiana, Rapporto 2000,* Bologna: Il Mulino: 157–94.
Baldini, M. and Bosi, P. (2002) *L'imposta sul reddito della legge delega della riforma fiscale: prime interpretazioni e analisi degli effetti di gettito e distributivi,* Università di Modena e Reggio Emilia: CAPP.
Baldini, M., Bosi, P. and Matteuzzi, M. (2002) *Effetti Distributivi della Proposta di Riforma dell'Irpef: Prime Valutazioni "in Corso d'Opera,"* Università di Modena e Reggio Emilia: CAPP.
Banca d'Italia (2002) *Relazione del Governatore,* Roma, May.
Basu, S. and Fernald, J.G. (2002) "Aggregate productivity and aggregate technology," *European Economic Review,* 963–92.
Bernardi, L. (1995) "L'IRPEG: ragioni di una riforma e analisi di una proposta," *Rivista di diritto finanziario e scienza delle finanze,* LIV: 436–84.
—— (2000a) "Note sull'evoluzione recente e sulle prospettive future dei sistemi tributari," *Studi e Note di Economia,* 1: 25–50.
—— (2000b) "Stabilizzazione ed evoluzione strutturale della finanza pubblica italiana," *Rivista di Diritto Finanziario e Scienza delle Finanze,* 1: 3–36.
—— (2002) "Imposte giuste, giuste giustizie e riforme impossibili," *Politica economica,* 3: 585–96.
Bernardi, L. and Bernasconi, M. (1996) "L'evasione fiscale in Italia: evidenze empiriche," *Il Fisco,* 38, October: 19–36.
Bordignon, M. (1997) "L'Irap e la riforma della finanze regionali," in Bernardi, L. (ed.) *La Finanza pubblica italiana. Rapporto 1997,* Bologna: Il Mulino: 137–60.
Bordignon, M. and Zanardi, A. (1997) "Tax evasion in Italy," *Giornale degli Economisti e Annali di Economia,* 3–4: 169–210.
Bosi, P. and Guerra, M.C. (2002) *I Tributi nell'Economia Italiana,* Bologna: Il Mulino.
Bosworth, B. and Burtless, G. (1992) "Effects of tax reforms on labour supply, investments and savings," *Journal of Economic Perspectives,* 6: 3–25.

Bovi, M. (2002) "The nature of underground economy, some evidence from OECD countries," Documento di lavoro, 26/02, Roma: ISAE.

Cassou, S.P. and Lansing, R.J. (2000) *Growth Effect of a Flat Tax*, Manhattan, KS: Kansas State University.

Cavaliere, A. and Osculati, F. (2000) "Finanza e servizi pubblici loculi: autonomia e apertura al mercato," in Bernardi, L. (ed.) *La Finanza pubblica italiana. Rapporto 2000*, Bologna: Il Mulino: 195–230.

Cosciani, C. (1964) *Stato dei Lavori della Commissione per lo Studio della Riforma Tributaria*, Milano: Giuffrè.

De Cecco, M. (2000) *L'economia di Lucignolo*, Roma: Donzelli Editore.

Devereux, M. and Griffith, R. (1999) "The taxation of discrete investment choices," Working Paper W98/16, London: The Institute for Fiscal Studies.

EU Commission (2000) "Public finances in EMU," *European Economy*, 3: 69–92.

Eurostat (2000) *Structures of the Taxation Systems in the European Union, 1970–1997*, Brussels: EU Commission.

Fausto, D. "Privatizzazioni e interesse pubblico," in Fausto, D., Jossa, B. and Panico, C. (eds) *Teoria Economica e Riformismo Politico*, Milano: Franco Angeli.

Fraschini, A. (2002) "Local borrowing: the Italian case," in Dafflon, B. (ed.) *Local Public Finance in Europe. Balancing the Budget and Controlling the Debt*, Cheltenham: Edward Elgar.

Galasso, V. and Profeta, P. (2002) "The political economy of social security: a survey," *European Journal of Political Economy*, 18: 1–29.

Galeotti, G. and Marrelli, M. (eds) (1992) *Design and Reform of Taxation Policy*, Dordrecht: Kluwer Academic Press.

Gerelli, E. (ed.) (1986) *Il Sistema Tributario oggi e domani*, Milano: Franco Angeli.

Giannini, S. (1999) "Dit e Irap e loro impatto sulla competitività internazionale delle imprese italiane," lecture given to the Conference Fiscalità d'impresa e concorrenza internazionale, Venezia.

—— (2002) *La Nuova Tassazione dei Redditi di Impresa nel Progetto di Legge Governativo n. 2144 (d. d. l. delega fiscale)*, Università di Modena e Reggio Emilia: CAPP.

Giannini, S. and Guerra, M.C. (2000) "Dove eravamo e dove siamo: il sistema tributario dal 1990 al 2000," in Bernardi, L. (ed.) *La Fnanza pubblica italiana. Rapporto 2000*, Bologna: Il Mulino: 231–66.

—— (2001) "Requiem per la riforma Visco?," in Bernardi, L. and Zanardi, A. (eds) *La Finanza pubblica italiana. Rapporto 2001*, Bologna: Il Mulino: 103–30.

Giannini, S. and Maggiulli, C. (2001) *The Effective Tax Rates in EU Commission Study on Corporate Taxation: Methodological Aspects, Main Results and Policy Implications*, Università di Modena e Reggio Emilia: CAPP.

Granaglia, E. (1991) *Efficienza ed Equità nelle Politiche Pubbliche*, Milano: Franco Angeli.

Graziani, A. (1979) *L'Economia italiana dal 1945 ad oggi*, Bologna: Il Mulino.

Guerra, M.C. (1998) "La riforma tributaria: attuazione e prospettive," in Bernardi, L. (ed.) *La Finanza pubblica italiana. Rapporto 1998*, Bologna: Il Mulino: 159–82.

—— (2002) *La Tassazione dei redditi finanziari nel disegno di legge delega proposto dal Governo*, Università di Modena e Reggio Emilia: CAPP.

Joumard, I. (2001) "Tax systems in European Union countries," Economic Department Working Paper 301, Paris: OECD.

Leibfritz, W., Thornton, J. and Bibbee, A. (1997) "Taxation and economic performance," Economic Department Working Paper 136, Paris: OECD.

Longobardi, E. (ed.) (2002) *I cento giorni e oltre: verso una rifondazione del rapporto fisco-economia*, Roma: De Agostini professionale.

Ministero dell'Economia (2002) *Relazione trimestrale di cassa al 31 dicembre 2001*, Roma: Dipartimento della Ragioneria generale dello Stato.

OECD (2001) *Revenue Statistics 1965–2000*, Paris: OECD.

Panzeri, M.C. (2002) "La tassazione del risparmio: prospettive di riforma," in Longobardi, E. (ed.) *I cento giorni e oltre: verso una rifondazione del rapporto fisco-economia*, Roma: De Agostini professionale: 257–84.

Patrizii, V. (2002) "Equità verticale e orizzontale: i problemi dell'Irpef," in Longobardi, E. (ed.) *I cento giorni e oltre: verso una rifondazione del rapporto fisco-economia*, Roma: De Agostini professionale: 363–80.

Pedone, A. (ed.) (1989) *La questione tributaria. Analisi e proposte*, Bologna: Il Mulino.

—— (2000) "Il sistema tributario italiano tra le due riforme," *Economia Italiana*, 4: 583–602.

—— (2002) "La sfida di un Fisco per la crescita e la riduzione degli squilibri," in Longobardi, E. (ed.) *I cento giorni e oltre: verso una rifondazione del rapporto fisco-economia*, Roma: De Agostini professionale: 52–70.

Petretto, A. (2002) *Unità Europea e Economia Pubblica*, Bologna: Il Mulino.

REF (2002) "La delega fiscale: un confronto con i sostenitori della riforma," *Congiuntura IRS*, anno IX, 3, 30 giugno.

Soerensen, P.B. (1994) "From the global income tax to the dual income tax: recent tax reforms in Nordic countries," *International Tax and Public Finance*, 1: 57–80.

Tanzi, V. (1995) *Taxation in an Integrating World*, Washington, DC: The Brookings Institution.

—— (1996) "Il sistema tributario italiano: una prospettiva internazionale," in Monorchio, A. (ed.) *La Finanza pubblica italiana dopo la Svolta del 1992*, Bologna: Il Mulino: 19–68.

Tanzi, V. and Zee, H.H. (1996) "Fiscal policy and long run growth," IMF Working Paper, WP/96/19, Washington, DC: IMF.

Vitaletti, G. (2002a) "Una prospettiva di analisi della riforma fiscale," *Congiuntura IRS*.

—— (2002b) "Studi di settore e riforma fiscale," *Il Fisco*, October, 26: 56–61.

Wagstaff, A. *et al.* (1999) "Redistributive effect, progressivity and differential tax treatment: personal income tax in twelve OECD countries," *Journal of Public Economics*, 72: 73–98.

9 Spain

Davide Tondani

Introduction

In this chapter we analyze the fiscal system in Spain and its recent evolution. We start half-way through the 1970s using a historical viewpoint. In these years, Spain, compared with the other European countries under consideration in this book, was somewhat backward, with an economic and a social situation similar to other Mediterranean countries (such as Portugal and Greece). Since 1975, when Spain shifted to democracy, the country has experienced a period of strong reforms. Initially, the aim of reforms was to modernize the economic structure of the country and to guarantee an expenditure level higher than in the past. During the 1980s, reforms concerned the adaptation of the revenues and expenditures to the European standard, in view of Spain's entrance into the European Community. Finally, in the 1990s, Spanish policy makers' choices have been concentrated on the aim of the Monetary Union (EMU) and on improving the employment rate.

We then analyze the main features of the Spanish tax system and the composition of revenues, in comparison with other European countries. Finally, we discuss the economic impact of the more recent reforms of the tax system.

On pages 215–19, we include an analysis of the tax system, showing the behavior over the last two decades of the most important variables, related to the performance of GDP, underlining the main characteristics of the revenue structure, direct taxes, indirect taxes and social contributions and comparing the performance with the European average. In this section we examine how the shift to democracy and entry into the European Community contributed to raise, particularly during the 1980s, expenditure and, in so doing, revenue. Total revenue, in fact, grew from 1980 to 1999 by 11 percent, but the growth rate of expenditure decreased in the 1990s, caused by efforts to respect the Maastricht Treaty. At the same time, the composition of revenue has also been modified, aimed at a greater convergence with European standards. Harmonization of VAT caused a strong increase in revenue for this tax, while, on the side of direct taxation, a constant growth of corporate and personal taxation has been observed. Social contribution has increased, particularly the amount charged to employees, with the aim of increasing the social protection system.

On pages 219–25, we give an overview of the main taxes of the Spanish system, such as corporate and personal income tax, VAT and excise duties. For each of these, the analysis summarizes economic characteristics and tax rates. It can be observed how some characteristics distinguish the Spanish tax system from the European standards. Interestingly, for example, the taxation of savings and financial activities are included in personal taxation (with a starting account, whose rate depends on the type of financial activity). Moreover, some autonomous communities have a special regime that allows them to collect an additional personal income revenue. These autonomous communities, due to various special laws caused by ethnic tensions, also collect some other taxes, such as VAT or excise duties. With regard to corporate taxation, it is important to underline that, over the rate of 35 percent of taxation, a lot of special laws come in to play, in order to make corporate tax more user-friendly, causing large deductions in some cases or tax rates to be lower than the statutory rate.

The consequence of this, as explained on pages 228–9, is an effective corporate tax rate 11 percent lower than the statutory rate. This is close to the average tax relief provided in the European Union. Pages 225–33 shows the economic impact of the tax system, analyzing implicit tax rates, the tax wedge and the division of the tax burden by economic or territorial criteria. From this, we provide an overview of tax effects on labor supply, wages, investment and production choice and it is necessary to understand the guidelines of recent reforms in Spain and the aim of more recent policies. This analysis uncovers what is the lowest tax wedge on labor in the European Union (the EU average is 51.3 percent) although it is still higher than the OECD average. However, there is an obvious trend toward lower taxation of capital and the implicit tax rate on labor, which usually increased in the past, but remained constant in 2001–2.

The reduction of progressivity in the 1990s caused a reduction of the redistributive effect of the tax system. In fact, in the European context, Spain shows a higher degree of inequality in income distribution pre- and post-taxation.

Concerning decentralization, it must be emphasized how the Spanish system devolves 29 percent of revenues to local governments, against a European average of 18 percent.

A historical view of the reform process of the tax system is included on pages 233–9. There, the main reforms in the 1990s are explored, in conjunction with the main macroeconomic indicators (i.e. public balance and unemployment) observing the general process of convergence toward the EMU and the constraints of the Growth and Stability Pact.

From this analysis the more important guidelines of the reform become apparent. Convergence with the EMU and the constraints of the Maastricht Treaty obliged Spanish policy makers to reduce net borrowing and public debt. Although the high growth rate of GDP, and a lower level of public expenditure than in other countries, could help Spain to stay within the parameters requested by the EU, high rates of unemployment (although implicit rates and tax wedge are lower than European average) have driven the government toward strong taxation reform. The aim of the reform was to increase the neutrality of the system, reducing the distortion of taxation, and to build a less progressive personal income taxation system, thus increasing labor supply and investments. In the same way the taxation of some unemployment benefits was linked to major labor market reform.

In 1991 and 1998, a reform of the brackets and the tax rates strongly reduced the progressivity of the system. The cost of the reforms is secondary to the redistributive effect of taxation. These reforms were balanced by an increase of the taxation on consumption, caused by harmonization with European laws on VAT, and an increase in some excise duties.

In the same years the process of decentralization continued, increasing the revenues and the fiscal accountability of local governments.

Future reforms will have the same aim of those carried out in the 1990s. The economic and demographic data indicate the need for further reform of the social security system, in order to take account of the aging of the population. This implies a set of policies aimed at improving the labor supply and which are able to insure a sustainability of the social security system. So, next, reforms must work toward further neutrality of the system, a reduction of taxation on labor, financed by a growth of taxation on consumption. A reduction of social contributions of low-paid employment will be necessary to improve the supply of low-skilled jobs, and, consequently, move resources from unemployment assistance to the aging population. Income tax should be drastically changed in its structure, with the result of attributing relevant advantages to the low-middle and the highest incomes.

Moreover, the decentralization process must be further pushed in order to achieve higher accountability of local government in the expenditure process.

The structure of the system and its development from the 1970s

The current structure of the tax system and social security contributions

In 2000, the general government expenditure (Banca d'Italia 2001) reached the level of 40 percent of GDP, decreasing by 5 percent from

1995. From this aggregate, we can extract the current expenditure, which is 35.2 percent of GDP. It may be divided in four parts: final consumption (17.1 percent of GDP and 48.5 percent of total current expenditure), transfer and subsidies (14.8 percent of GDP and 42 percent total current expenditure), interest and, finally, investment (3.3 percent and 9.4 percent respectively).

Spanish expenditure decreased, during the second half of the 1990s, according to a general European trend, caused by the constraints imposed by the Maastricht Treaty. However, current expenditure is lower than the EU average. The largest difference concerns lower interest expenditure and social transfer, compensated by higher expenditure in investment.

Using the time series of Banca d'Italia, fiscal pressure, excluding capital taxes is 35.5 percent of GDP. Including capital tax, this number grows to 35.9 percent.

Comparing details of expenditure and current revenue (38.6 percent of GDP), we can observe, over recent years, a growth in balance surplus. From 1995 to 2000, huge primary surplus increased from a deficit of 1.4 percent of GDP to a lending of 2.9 percent (Banca d'Italia 2001). This growth used to modify the national balance. In fact, the net borrowing, reached the level of 0.4 percent of the GDP in 2000 (in 1995, this data was 6.6 percent of GDP).

The current Spanish tax system provides the following main taxes: a personal income tax, called *Impuesto sobre la renta de las personas físicas* (*IRPF*), a tax on the income of non-residents (*Impuesto sobre la renta de No Residentes*), a corporation tax (*Impuesto sobre sociedades*), a wealth tax (*Impuesto sobre el patrimonio*), succession and gift duty (*Impuesto sobre sucesiones y donaciones*) and, in addition to VAT, some taxes on special goods (tobacco, beer, alcoholic beverages) and other less important taxes. On pages 219–25, we analyze some of these taxes making up the Spanish tax system.

European statistics (Eurostat 2000) show how, in 1999, direct taxes (11.7 percent), indirect taxes (12 percent) and social contribution (12.8 percent) contribute to total revenue by about one-third each. The taxation of income (personal and corporate) and VAT are the main ways to finance expenditure. In 1999, these categories constituted 10.1 percent and 6.5 percent respectively of GDP.

Looking at the internal composition of the three loudest voices in revenue, the main source is VAT, which provides more than half of the indirect taxes, while, with regards to direct taxes, the main source is the tax on income, with a majority of revenue due to personal income taxation.

Developments of the system from 1970 to 1999

As shown in Table 9.1, according to a trend common to all industrialized countries, since 1980 total tax revenue rose strongly (from 13.7 percent to

Table 9.1 Structure and development of fiscal revenue in Spain and European average as a percentage of GDP, 1980–99

	1980		1985		1990		1995		1999	
	Spain	*Europe*	*Spain*	*Europe*	*Spain*	*Europe*	*Spain*	*Europe*	*Spain*	*Europe*
Direct taxes, of which	7.1	12.7	8.6	13.1	11.9	13.2	11.4	13.3	11.7	14.5
personal income	4.8	9.3	5.8	9.0	7.6	8.9	8.1	9.6	10.1[1]	9.9
corporation income	1.2	2.2	1.6	2.8	3.1	2.9	2.0	2.4		2.8
Indirect taxes, of which	6.6	13.2	9.4	13.0	10.4	13.0	10.5	13.6	12.0	14.6
VAT	0.0	6.6	0.0	6.1	5.4	6.6	5.4	6.9	6.5	7.3
excise duties	1.5	3.2	1.7	3.2	2.0	3.1	2.9	3.4	5.5[1]	2.5
Total tax revenue	13.7	25.9	18.0	26.1	22.3	26.2	21.9	26.9	23.7	29.1
Social contributions	11.8	13.4	11.9	13.8	12.2	13.7	12.4	15.0	12.8	14.0
employers	9.3	7.8	8.4	7.9	8.8	7.8	8.6	8.0	8.9	7.8
employees	1.9	4.3	2.0	4.5	1.9	4.5	2.1	5.1	2.1	4.5
self-employed	0.7	1.3	1.5	1.5	1.4	1.4	1.7	1.8	1.8	1.7
Total fiscal revenue	25.5	39.3	29.9	39.9	34.5	39.9	34.3	41.9	36.5	43.1
Administrative level										
Central government	11.3	22.3	13.9	22.1	17.3	22.2	16.7	22.5	17.0	23.7
Local government	2.4	2.9	4.1	3.1	4.4	3.8	4.6	4.0	5.7	4.3

Sources: 1970–95, Eurostat, 2000; 1999, Eurostat New Cronos databank 2002 (data equalized with Eurostat, 2000).

Notes
Minor items are omitted.
1 Aggregate data caused by the lack of further disaggregation in New Cronos databank.

the current 23.7 percent). In Spain this is due to the shift to democracy after 1975. In fact, after this, government expenditure in Spain was fairly low by international standards, keeping tax pressure considerably below the OECD average.

The social contributions have also increased according to the aim of improving the social protection system. However, the trend shows a growth in the percentage of contributions charged to employers, with the aim of reducing the labor cost and unemployment.

In Spain, the harmonization of VAT in the European Union caused a strong increase in the revenue of this tax, until recently valued at 6.5 percent of GDP. In the field of indirect taxes, we can also notice a growth in excise duties.

Regarding direct taxes, the constant growth of revenue was due to the constant growth of the principal taxes (corporation and income tax). However, in the 1990s, there was a decrease in the revenue of corporation tax, caused by a more helpful policy for enterprises, and a slower growth of increase in personal income tax than in the 1980s.

To sum up, during the last 20 years, the Spanish tax system has aimed at catching up with European standards. This is due mainly to two reasons: the shift to democracy and the entry, in 1986, into the European Community. More recently, the policies implemented aimed at reducing the fiscal burden and supporting economic growth.

A comparative view against the European average

In 1999, the estimated aggregate level of taxation in Spain was 36.5 percent of GDP, 6.6 percent less than the EU average. This lower value was constant during the 1980s and 1990s. However, during the 1980s, the differential between European and Spanish average decreased from 13.8 percent in 1980 to 10 percent in 1985 and then to 5.4 percent in 1990, while, from 1995 the value of the differential has increased to 7.6 percent (1995). This is a consequence of new policies implemented in recent years, as mentioned at the end of the previous section.

A natural consequence of this trend is lower revenue for the single items of Table 9.1, except for the social contribution charged to employers that are always higher than the European average. This means a lower charge for employees that pay a lower sum than in other countries.

However, during the last 20 years, there has been a general adjustment of the composition of the revenue, which is now more similar to the European structure than in the early 1980s. In 1980 the weight of social contributions on the total fiscal revenue was very high, while in Europe a more balanced fiscal revenue composition existed (with direct taxes, indirect taxes and social contributions each making up one-third). In 1999 the composition of fiscal revenues was similar to the European average. The weight of social contribution (although this is 3 percent higher than in the EU) decreased by more than 11 percentage points, compensated by a strong growth in indirect taxes (7 percent of the total) and direct taxes (4.3 percent of the total).

To summarize, although the fiscal revenues of Spain are always lower than the average of EU countries, the current structure of the tax burden is similar in its composition (direct/indirect taxes and social contributions).

Another point of interest is the distribution of tax revenues across levels of government. While in other EU countries about 55 percent of the fiscal revenue is managed by central government, in Spain this percentage is only 46.5 percent. In 1980 this was 56.7 percent for the EU and 44.3 percent for Spain. This means that, in Spain, like in the rest of the EU, there has been an increase of resources devolved to local government. However, a high rate of fiscal centralization is still present in Spain only partially compensated for by more favorable treatments reserved to some local communities, as the Basque Country and Navarra (OECD 2002).

Some quantitative and institutional features of main taxes

Personal income tax – PIT and the taxation of financial capital

The last reform of personal income tax in Spain goes back to 1998. An important characteristic of the Spanish system is that the beneficiaries of the tax are not only central government but also two autonomous communities: the Basque Country and Navarra. In these communities, to calculate the amount of the tax due, citizens must consider the specific autonomous community tax rate plan.

The tax unit, by decree of the Constitutional Court of 1989, is not the family but the individual. The basis of assessment is the amount of the taxpayer's disposable income. This includes income from employment, capital, business, capital gain and losses and imputed income as laid down by law.

In particular, the composition of the single income item is as follows:

- employment income: job wage, fringe benefits, compensations, travel expenses, if higher than the sum provided for by law, pensions and supplementary pension received by the consort, insurance premium and social security contributions paid by the employer;
- land rent: rent by real properties and 2 percent of the cadastal income of the properties;
- capital gains or losses: interests, capital gains, dividends.

The law on personal income taxation allows certain deductions. The most important concerns the salary. In fact people who have a yearly wage lower than €8,113.6 have a deduction of €3,005, while people who earn between €8,113.6 and €12,020.2 can have a deduction of €3,005 less the difference between the income earned and €8,113.6, multiplied by 0.1923. So, if the income is higher than €12,020.2, the annual deduction is €2,253.8.

The deduction increases in case of invalidity, while the system allows deduction of a percentage of medical care expenses.

Other deductions concern insurance premiums against death or invalidity, the purchase or the building of a house, the purchase of cultural goods and the gift for non-profit association.

Family deductions are structured as follows:

- €601 for each parent in charge aged over 65;
- €1,202 for each son aged under 25 living with the taxpayer;
- €1,803 for the third and other sons under 25 living with the taxpayer.

There exists a personal deduction of €3,305, increased to €3,906 for people aged over 65, and €5,108 in the case of a percentage of invalidity from 33 percent to 65 percent. If this percentage is over 65 percent, the amount of the personal deduction is €6,911.

This sum is increased by €300 if the son is less than three years old or by €150 if he is less than 16.

Other forms of deduction are provided for invalidity and for contribution to pension plans. No deduction for the spouse is provided for by the law. Table 9.2 summarizes the list of deductions.

There is a long list of incomes exempt from personal taxation. The most important are public scholarships, child allowance and unemployment benefit.

The rates given in Table 9.3 are applied to the net general taxable basis. This is obtained by making deductions from the general taxable basis for contributions to pension plans or provident mutual societies. Table 9.4, instead, presents the additional rates adopted in the autonomous communities.

Concerning capital income, the Spanish tax system provides for a withholding rate of 18 percent or 20 percent for some financial activities (see Table 9.4) or for an exemption in other cases, plus taxation based on the marginal personal income tax rate of any taxpayer. It must be underlined that some financial products held for more than two years offer a more favorable personal income rate than the tax rates provided for the normal brackets of income.

Corporation tax – CT

The *Impuesto sobre sociedades* is regulated by a law in force since 1 January 1996. As for the personal income tax, the beneficiary of the revenue is central government and the autonomous communities of Navarra and the Basque Country.

Table 9.2 Deduction on personal income tax

	Quantities	Limit (€)
Descendants		
First and second (each one)	1,202	
Third and other	1,803	
Physically and mentally handicapped (33%–65%), blind	1,803	
Physically and mentally handicapped (over 65%), blind	3,606	
Passive subject aged over 65	601	
Physically and mentally handicapped (33%–65%), blind	1,803	
Physically and mentally handicapped (over 65%), blind	3,606	
Insurance		
Life, death, incapacity	10%	601
Mixed, contract over 10 years	10%	300
Housing loans		
For the first 2 years		
Under €4,508	25%	4,508
From €4,508 to €9,016	15%	9,016
Following years		
Under €4,508	20%	4,508
From €4,508 to €9,016	15%	9,016
Gift		
For non-profit associations	20%	
Other associations of public interests	10%	
Professional activities		
Dividends (in general)	40%	
Dividends from general insurance company, social security institutes, etc.	25%	
Tax on the increase of the land value	75%	
Dependent work	162	
Other		
House purchasing or modernization	15%	9,015
Medical expenditure	15%	
Child care	20%	

Table 9.3 General rates for personal income tax, year 2000

Net taxable basis (€)	Rate applicable (%)	Basque Country and Navarra (%)
Less than 3,678.19	15.00	3.00
From 3,678.19 to 12,873.68	20.17	3.83
From 12,873.68 to 25,134.32	23.57	4.73
From 25,134.32 to 40,460.13	31.48	5.72
From 40,460.13 to 67,433.55	38.07	6.93
Over 67,433.55	39.60	8.40

Source: Agencia Estatal de Administracion Tributaria.

Table 9.4 Withholding rate on financial savings, year 2000

Financial products/income	Withholding rate			
	Held for less than 2 years	Held for more than 2 years	Held for more than 5 years	Held for more than 8 years
Bank account, life insurance contracts, dividends	18			
Capital gains on mutual funds	20	20		
Treasury bill, private bonds, capital gains on shares	0	0		
Bank account, housing savings schemes, pension funds (lump-sum payments), life insurance contracts (lump-sum payments)	18			
Life insurance contracts (lump-sum payments)			18	
Life insurance contracts (lump-sum payments)				18

The taxpayers of this tax are all resident legal persons except for partnership and other entities without legal status, such as investment funds, joint ventures, risk capital funds, etc.

The basis of assessment is the amount of income generated during the tax year, less any negative tax bases carried over from previous years. The basis of assessment is calculated by making certain tax adjustments to the results reported in the accounts.

There are two cases of automatic exemptions:

- a complete exemption for central government, the autonomous communities, certain public bodies and the Bank of Spain;
- a partial exemption for some incomes accruing to political parties, trade unions, associations and common agricultural policy subsidies.

Moreover, company-restructuring operations (merger, divisions and transfer of assets and exchange of shares) enjoy tax neutrality.

The deductions are as follows:

- to avoid domestic double taxation, dividends or shares of profits received from other business resident in Spain qualify for a 50 percent deduction or for a 100 percent deduction if the receiving company has owned, directly or indirectly, 5 percent of the capital of the distributing company for at least one year prior to distribution;
- to avoid direct or indirect double taxation at international level, an exemption system based on a 100 percent deduction for income received from abroad was introduced in 1996;

- to provide permanent incentives for certain activities such as research and development, exporting (for 25 percent of foreign investment), investment in cultural goods, film production and book publishing, investments for environmental improvement and pollution control, employment of disabled workers.

All these deductions may not exceed 35 percent of the full tax liability less the deduction allowed to avoid domestic and international double taxation and any applicable allowances.

The standard rate is 35 percent, but the law provides reduced rates for small businesses (30 percent for profit, up to €90,152) and for mutual insurance companies, social welfare organizations, mutual guarantee schemes, credit cooperatives and non-profit-making organizations (all these categories pay a rate of 25 percent).

Other reduced rates are provided for cooperatives (20 percent for the result of their activities), foundations and public associations (10 percent), pension funds (zero percent), enterprises extracting hydrocarbons and related activities (40 percent).

Negative tax bases may be carried forward to offset positive tax bases generated over the following ten tax years. Newly founded companies may begin counting the carry-over period from the tax year in which their tax base first became positive.

Value added tax – VAT

The legal base of *Impuesto sobre al valor anadido* was approved in 1992, but has been frequently amended. The beneficiary is central government and the autonomous communities of the Basque Country and Navarra, where tax is collected in accordance with central government legislation, except using different tax declaration forms. Part of the revenue accrues to the communities.

The tax is payable by:

- natural or legal persons who exercise business or professional activities and make taxable supplies of goods or services;
- traders or professional persons for whom taxable transactions are carried out by persons or entities not established in Spain;
- importers, whether or not traders or members of the professions;
- undivided estates, persons owning goods in community and other economic units without legal status carrying out taxable transactions.

The tax is payable on supplies of goods made by traders or professional persons, habitually or occasionally, in the course of their business or professional activity. People that import goods, irrespective of the destination of the goods imported and the status of the importer, are also subject to

VAT, and the same rule applies to intra-Community acquisitions[1] and for the supplies of goods and services made by traders or professional persons in the course of business in mainland Spain or the Balearic Islands.

The exemptions concern several categories. The most important of these are the exports and the transaction of goods sent definitively to the Canary Islands, Ceuta or Mellila, the supplies of goods intended for another Member State, if the purchaser is an entrepreneur and some transactions in accordance with international treaties regarding Spain.

The basis of the assessment consists of the total value in consideration for the taxable transactions, excluding discounts allowed after the transaction. The amount of VAT paid on the acquisition of goods or services directly linked to the business or professional activity of the taxable person is generally deductible from the amount due in respect of that person's activity. The exemptions also concern some domestic transactions, such as healthcare, social security, education, welfare work, insurance and reinsurance, finance, supplies of non-building land and the public postal service, etc.

There are three tax rates:

- 4 percent, applicable to certain basic necessities (i.e. bread, milk, medicines);
- 7 percent, applicable to certain goods and services regarded as basic necessities such as food for human consumption, water, medical equipment, air and sea transport of passengers;
- 16 percent, applicable to all other transactions.

Excise duties

The Spanish tax system includes several excise duties. The most important concerns hydrocarbons, tobacco, beer, wine and certain means of transport. For all excise duties, the beneficiary is central government, the Basque Country and Navarra.

The *Impuesto sobre hidrocarburos* is payable on the manufacture and import of hydrocarbons. The basis of assessment is the volume of dutiable product or, in some cases, the unit of weight or gigajoules (GJ). Table 9.5 explains the tax rate for hydrocarbons.

The excise duty on tobacco (*Impuesto sobre las labores del tabacco*) concerns the manufacture and import of several tobacco products such as cigar and cigarillos, cigarettes, cut tobacco for rolling and other tobacco for smoking.

The basis of assessment could be *ad valorem* or in number of units; the tax rates for this tax are in Table 9.6.

The *Impuesto sobre la cerveza* is paid by the manufacturer and importer of dutiable products. The basis of assessment is the volume of dutiable products, and the tax is payable when the goods leave the brewery or authorized warehouse. The tax rate is calculated by dividing the type of

Table 9.5 Tax rate for hydrocarbons

Leaded motor fuels	€404.7/1,000 litres
Unleaded motor fuels	€402.9/1,000 litres (97 octane and above)
Other	€371.7/1,000 litres
Diesel oil for general use	€269.8/1,000 litres
Diesel oil for use as motor fuel	€8.6/1,000 litres
Fuels oil	€13.4/tonne
LPG for general use	€795.2/tonne
LPG for PSVs	€57.5/tonne
LPG not used as fuel	€7.4/tonne
Methane for general use	€16.8/GJ
Methane not used as fuel	€0.16/GJ
Kerosene for general use	€404.7/1,000 litres
Kerosene not used as fuel	€404.7/1,000 litres

Source: Directory of taxes, EU Commission 2001.

Table 9.6 Excise duty on manufactured tobacco

Cigar and cigarillos	12.5% on the maximum retail price
Cigarettes *ad valorem*	54% on the maximum retail price
Cigarettes (specific)	€3 per 1,000 units
Cut tobacco for rolling	37.5%
Other tobacco products	22.5%

Source: Directory of taxes, EU Commission 2001.

goods into classes of alcoholic strength and calculating tax per hectolitre. Other excise duties similar to this one concern wine (*Impuesto sobre el vino y bebidas fermentadas*), other spirits and alcoholic beverages. In the last case, the rate is calculated according to the quantities of pure alcohol.

The excise duties on certain means of transport concern the first definitive registration or entry into Spain of new or used self-propelled vehicles powered by an engine, for use on the road or on public land, small vessels, boats for pleasure or water sports, mechanically powered aircraft and light aircraft. The tax is payable by the person or entity in whose name the means of transport is initially and definitively registered.

The tax rate depends on the capacity of the vehicle and if the vehicle is powered by a petrol or diesel engine. Special tax rates, cheaper than in the rest of Spain, concern the Canary Islands, while there's no taxation in Ceuta and Melilla.

The fiscal burden

The distribution of taxation charge

The statistical sources (Eurostat 2000) show that, in 1997, more than 54 percent of the total fiscal revenue originated from labor, while slightly less than 18 percent originated from capital. The residual quota of revenues is imputable to the consumption (Table 9.7).

The structure of total revenues according to the economic function shows how, during the 1980s and 1990s, the fiscal burden rose in all sectors, although a rising weight of the taxation of consumption and the aim, in the 1990s, to decrease the burden on capital are acceptable. This has been compensated by an increase in the pressure on labor. From Table 9.7 the recent deceleration of labor revenues growth, caused by the intentions of employment policy, can be observed.

The implicit tax rate on consumption (13.8 percent) is very low, because of the low overall level of taxation. Taxes on consumption produce about 27 percent of total tax revenue. The trend indicates a strong growth of this implicit rate during 1980s and then stabilization above 13 percent.

The implicit tax rate on labor is 34.7 percent and it shows a constant increase.

In the second half of the 1980s and in the early 1990s the implicit tax rate on other factors of production (i.e. self-employed labor and capital)

Table 9.7 Structure according to the economic function as a percentage of GDP

	1980	*1985*	*1990*	*1995*	*1997*
Consumption	5.3	8.4	9.2	9.3	9.8
Labor	15.5	16.4	17.8	18.9	19.2
employed	14.7	14.7	16.1	16.8	17.2
self-employed	0.8	1.7	1.8	2.1	2.0
Capital	4.8	5.1	7.5	6.1	6.5
Total	25.6	29.9	34.5	34.2	35.5

Source: Eurostat (2000).

Note
1997 is an estimated datum.

Table 9.8 Implicit tax rate in Spain and Europe from 1980 to 1997

		Consumption	*Labor employed*	*Other factor*
1980	Spain	7.3	28.8	16.6
	EU-15	16.0	35.1	36.6
1985	Spain	11.6	31.8	18.4
	EU-15	15.6	37.1	32.3
1990	Spain	13.3	32.2	27.3
	EU-15	16.2	37.5	31.5
1995	Spain	13.2	34.1	22.3
	EU-15	16.7	41.7	29.4
1997	Spain	13.8	34.7	24.9
	EU-15	16.8	41.9	31.1

Source: Eurostat (2000).

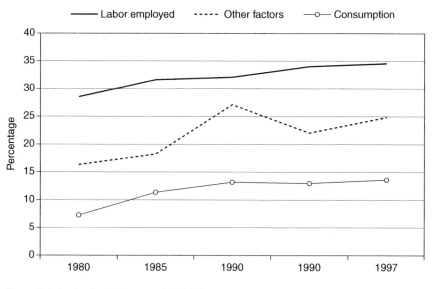

Figure 9.1 Spain: implicit rates 1980–97.
Source: Eurostat (2000).

increased significantly and then fell again by several percentage points. In 1997 it stood at 24.9 percent. The main factor behind these evolutions may be found in the development of corporation tax revenues, which account for a third of taxes on capital.

The standard approach to measuring the impact of a tax on the distribution of income is to take the difference between pre-tax and post-tax Gini coefficients. The factors that influence the redistribution so measured are summarized in a short index, proposed by Aronson, Johnson and Lambert (1994). Using this approach, Wagstaff *et al.* (1999) calculated the redistributive effect of income tax for 12 countries.[2] Spain has a strongly unequal pre-tax income distribution (Gini index pre-tax is 40.83 percent). The post-tax Gini index is 39.64 percent, thus the redistributive effort of taxation is 0.0329. This figure is very high, but insufficient to converge to European inequality standard levels. The average tax rate is 13.97 percent, while Kakwani's progressivity index assumes the value of 0.2545, underlining a high value of progressivity. However, this calculation dates back too many years. Many reforms have since taken place, like that concerning personal tax rates, which imply a lower progressivity, and can thus strongly modify these figures. However, the European statistics on redistribution indicate that Spain and the Mediterranean countries have, over recent years, a high degree of inequality.

Tax wedges on labor and corporate taxation

The tax wedge is an indicator to measure the distortion caused by taxation on the factors and production choices of economic agents. Taxes on labor income account for almost 60 percent of general government revenues. The tax wedge is currently estimated at about 43 percent of total labor costs in industry in 2000 (Joumard 2001). A decomposition of the wedge into the three main "voices" of personal taxation explains how the highest percentage of the Spanish wedge is imputable to employers' and employees' social security contributions, that together accounted for three-quarters of the tax wedge.

Although in the early 1980s and 1990s the Spanish tax wedge rose strongly, affected by an increase of total fiscal revenues in this period, over recent years the growth of the tax wedge has diminished. In the same period employment policies have contributed to reduce the wedge on labor in the rest of Europe.

The regressivity of tax wedge on labor[3] and the provision for a minimum social security contribution cause the high tax wedge rates that low-paid workers must face. This is likely to adversely affect employment of the low-skilled.

The marginal tax wedge on labor, which is an important indicator for work incentives,[4] is significantly below the EU average, with data for an average production worker of 44 percent in 1998 (Joumard and Varoudakis 2000).

The 1994 labor market reform largely redressed tax distortions related to unemployment benefits because most of them became taxed and severance payments, received in connection with employment security provisions, and still enjoy a partial tax relief.[5]

While Spain has a relatively low tax wedge by European standards, some studies (Joumard and Varoudakis 2000) indicate that its adverse impact on employment may have been exacerbated by some rigidities that reduced firms' incentives to resist upward pressure on wages, and thereby facilitated forward shifting of taxation into labor cost.

Statutory corporate tax in Spain is 35 percent. In the period 1990–6, the effective corporate tax was 11 percentage points lower than the statutory rate. Major corporate tax incentives are economy wide and take the form of investment tax credits. Moreover, a number of special sector-based and geographic corporate tax regimes exist. In 1996 (see Table 9.9) total tax expenditures amounted to 24 percent of total gross corporate income tax liabilities (0.7 percent of GDP), with half of them accounted for by the various tax incentives to investment.

The analysis of effective taxation on corporate profits (Giannini and Maggiulli 2001) shows that the effective marginal tax rate (less than 25 percent) is lower than both the statutory rate and the effective average tax rate (about 30 percent, at a real return equal to 20 percent). The gap

Table 9.9 Breakdown of gross corporate income tax liabilities, 1996

The gross tax liabilities	
Net corporate income tax liabilities	76%
Tax allowance for double taxation of dividends	12%
Tax relief	
Tax incentives to investment	2%
Other corporate income tax exemptions	
The structure of tax relief	
Carry over of tax exemptions	34%
Transitory 1995 5% tax credit on investment	29%
General tax incentives to investment	14%
Canary Island special regime	7%
Transitory 3-years tax relief for business start-ups in 1994 and 1997	6%
Tax relief for exporters of educational and cultural goods	3%
Other corporate tax incentives	3%
Tax relief for employment creation	2%
Cooperative societies	1%
Tax credit applying in Ceuta and Melilla	1%

Source: Spanish Ministry of Economy and Finance.

between marginal and average effective rate is higher when considering debt financing of an investment. In this case the effective marginal tax rate is negative. This depends on the interaction between interest payments deductibility and tax allowances for depreciation in excess of economic depreciation.

Taxation by levels of government and fiscal federalism

Over the last two decades, Spain has undertaken an important decentralization process involving large areas of the public sector. Until 1978 (when the new Constitution was approved), the Spanish public sector was essentially characterized by centralism, with central government assuming control of practically all public expenditure. The 1978 Constitution introduced a second level of government (17 autonomous communities or regions, two of which benefit from a special regime) and a third level (50 county councils or local governments) providing for a division of competencies over the three levels (OECD 2002).

International sources (Eurostat 2000) explain that, in the early 1980s, revenues to central government were a little more than 82 percent (86 percent in the European Union). At the end of the 1990s, the same indicators were something more than 71 percent to central government and a little less than 29 percent to local government. From 1980 the process of decentralization of levels of expenditure has grown. This is due to an important process of devolution of function and expenditure to the 17 regional governments, each with significant differences between them.

At one extreme are the Basque Country and Navarra regions. These two regions have their own personal and corporate income tax systems and collect most taxes. Most power of expenditure has been devolved, excluding social security transfers, which are implemented by Spain's unitary social security system. For other spending programs, carried out exclusively at the state level, these two regions pay a share to the state, the *cupo*.

The revenue-raising powers of the other regional governments are more limited. In 1997, these so-called *common regime* regions were granted revenue-raising power on a share of the personal income tax and on the "cede taxes" (mainly on property). Taxes over which the common regime regions have revenue-raising powers account, respectively, for about one-fifth and one-half of their total and unconditional resources. The remaining tax receipts are pooled at central government level and redistributed across the regions in order to guarantee to each region the ability to provide a given standard of public services.

Through this redistribution of tax receipts, rich regions contribute to finance the poorest ones.

The implementation of the 1997–2001 financing system for the common regime regions implies that a large proportion of a region's financial resource depends directly upon that region's economic performance. Specifically, for the regions that accepted the agreement, the share of unconditional financial resources that depends on its own personal income tax doubled. However, Table 9.10 shows that it varies significantly from one region to another.

The participation to the state revenues from personal income tax (PIT), which correspond to the additional share (for most regions, 15 percent) of PIT revenues collected in their jurisdiction, is 26 percent of unconditional resources in Cataluña but only 11 percent in Andalucia. On the other side, the state transfers are 16 percent of unconditional resources in Cataluña and 61 percent in Andalucia and Galicia.

Moreover, Table 9.11 shows the difference between regions under the common regime and the Basque Country and Navarra, with respect to the financing of their regional government. The unconditional resources,

Table 9.10 Unconditional resources in some regions under the common regime, percentage, 1996

	Cataluña	Andalucia	Galicia	Castilla–La Mancha
State transfer	16	61	61	32
Ceded taxes and fees	32	16	15	25
PIT regional part	26	11	12	21
PIT participation in state revenues	26	11	12	21

Source: Bank of Spain, Agencia Tributaria.

Table 9.11 The financing of the regional governments, percentages for 1996

	Regions under the common regime	Basque Country and Navarra
Borrowing	16	12
Conditional transfer	43	30
Unconditional resources	41	58

Source: Bank of Spain, Agencia Tributaria.

i.e. the sum of the regional part of PIT, ceded taxes and fees and other transfers, in the common regions are 41 percent of total financial resources, while in the autonomous community this percentage is 58 percent.

The implicit tax competition across regions allowed by the new financing system could also induce a further increase in the variability of the regions' resources. However, to prevent tax-induced migration flows across regions, measures were introduced to limit the taxing powers of regional governments (imposing bands of tax rates) and a stricter definition of tax residence was implemented.

To protect the regions against temporary revenue shortfalls, a guarantee scheme was designed in 1996 and modified in 1998. Regional governments no longer face any downside risk on their core financial resources: actually the state is committed to granting matching transfers to each individual region if the 30 percent share of personal income tax revenues collected in its jurisdiction grows less than nominal GDP.

This guarantee scheme poses three big problems:

- it is asymmetric since the central government has to pay in the event of bad outcomes while regional governments do not fund an insurance system in the event of good outcomes. It may thus imply a significant cost for the state budget;
- guarantees do not provide regional governments with the right incentives to contain expenditures;
- the guarantee scheme also constrains efforts to reduce the overall tax burden since the cost would have to be borne exclusively by central government.

A comparative view against the European average

The most general indicators of the incidence of the fiscal burden are certainly the implicit rates (see Table 9.8). During the 1980s, the Spanish trends of implicit tax rates on consumption converged to the European average, but now the Spanish figure (13.8 percent in 1997) is still lower than the European figure (16.8 percent). The gap between the Spanish and the European implicit rates on labor employed remained constant during the 1980s. Since 1995 this gap has increased and in 1997 the Spanish average was 7.2 percent lower than the European average. The third kind of implicit tax rate, that is on other factors, is 6 percent lower than the European average: in 1997 it was 24.9 percent in Spain and 31 percent at the EU level.

From the point of view of efficiency, taxes on labor create a tax wedge in Spain which in 2000 occupies fourteenth place in the OECD list (Joumard 2001). The tax wedge is close to the OECD average, and thus well below the European average. During the 1990s, the tax wedge increased by two-and-a-half percentage points, nearly as much as the European Union average. Concerning marginal tax rates, Spain is significantly below the EU average, with a marginal tax wedge for an average production worker of 44 percent in 1998 (Joumard and Varoudakis 2000).

As observed in many OECD countries, the rising tax wedges on labor income may partly account for the increase in structural unemployment because a higher tax wedge raises labor costs and can lead to a reduced demand for labor.

Spain has a statutory corporate tax rate (35 percent) very close to the EU average, though, as elsewhere in Europe, it displays a lower effective rate of corporate taxation, also as a result of a number of tax incentives.

The effective corporate tax (11 percent lower than the statutory rate) is close to the average tax relief provided in the European Union (Buijink, Janssen and Schols 1999).

Due to relatively high marginal tax rates for higher-income taxpayers, the overall tax wedge on physical investment is rather high by international standards. This is due to the taxation of dividends that is added to the overall tax wedge on investment and to the more favorable tax treatment of capital gains on assets held for at least two years (see pp. 220–3). For these reasons, the overall tax wedge on investment falls by a third. It stands close to the average for the OECD countries.

Concerning the division of fiscal burden by economic function criteria, a comparison with the European average indicates that Spanish figures are a bit lower than the EU concerning work and, consequently, higher concerning capital.

The redistributive effects of taxation indicate that together with Ireland, the UK and the USA, Spain has the most unequal pre-tax income distribution. These four countries also have the same ranking in post-tax income distribution. For Spain, the redistributive effort of the taxation (RE is 0.0329), is lower than in Ireland, Sweden and Finland. Kakwani's progressivity index assumes the value of 0.2545, underlining a higher value of progressivity compared with the majority of the other countries examined, although the reduction of the brackets in the 1990s has lowed this value. Although Kakwani's progressivity index indicates a high progressivity, the re-ranking effect and horizontal inequality assume low values, insuring high levels of redistribution, but they are not sufficient to obtain a degree of post-tax inequality similar to the European average.

The degree of decentralization in Spain is higher than the European average, being that 29 percent of revenue is devolved to local government against about 18 percent of the European average.

To sum up, in Spain the implicit tax rates and the tax wedge are lower than the European average. Moreover, like in other countries, taxation is more favorable, according to the capital and the degree of decentralization, which is higher than in other countries, caused in part by ethnic tensions. However, this structure is not sufficient to prevent two important characteristics of the Spanish economic system. The first is inequality in the primary distribution of income: high rates of progressivity (although limited by reforms) appears insufficient to reduce the post-tax inequality to EU standards. The second is the high structural unemployment rate: a taxation more favorable than in other countries is not efficient enough in improving the employment rate.

Tax reforms in the 1990s and those currently planned

A quick glance at the budget and general economic environment

Spanish public finance during the 1990s was not particularly negative. In 1996, when many European countries started big financial adjustments of public finance to converge with EMU, the ratio of public debt/GDP was 68.1 percent, against a European guideline of 60 percent and a European average of 72.3 percent. In the same year, net borrowing was more worrying, being 7.8 percent of GDP, with a European average of 4.2 percent and a catch-up parameter of 3 percent. However, the moderate level of interest expenditure compared with other countries (5.2 percent in the same year), added to a high rate of GDP (more than 4 percent per year) and a low level of public expenditure, allowed entry into the EMU with the first group of countries and the plan of reforms in order to respect the Stability and Growth Pact.

In 2001, the Spanish economy grew by 2.8 percent after four consecutive years at little more than 4 percent. This slowdown was due to the more muted expansion of domestic demand and weakening exports, under pressure of an adverse international climate.

GDP growth in Spain stood at 1.3 percent higher than the Euro zone average, while its employment growth lead was around 1.5 points. This conduct marks a significant break with the pattern of the past, when the Spanish economy paid a higher downcycle toll in production and job losses because of lags in adjusting to external and supply shocks, the rigidity of markets and the use of policies to bolster income and demand, which ended up raising prices and undermining international competitiveness.

The progressive slowdown in Spanish and international economic growth was echoed in the year-long performance of labor markets. Employment and unemployment figures both continued to improve, but at an appreciably slower pace than in previous years. This loss of steam was not met by a similar moderation trend in labor-cost indicators.

Labor Force Survey (LFS) estimates put the year-on-year increase in the employed population at 1.8 percent in the last three quarters of 2001, while the year-on-year rise in social security enrolments was 3.4 percent in January 2002, close to the outcome of the two preceding quarters. Conversely, unemployment indicators showed further deterioration. LFS estimates an unemployment rate at 13 percent at the end of 2001.

On the side of public finance indicators, in 2000, the net borrowing of general government in Spain (Banca d'Italia 2001) reached the level of 0.4 percent of GDP. In 1995, this was 6.6 percent of GDP. The decrease was due to the effort to conform to the constraints of the Maastricht Treaty and the Stability and Growth Pact.

In the same period, primary surplus increased from a deficit of 1.4 percent of GDP to a lending of 2.9 percent, while the current account balance reached a lending of 3.4 percent of GDP. The low level of public debt (60.9 percent of GDP in 2000) produced interest payments of 3.3 percent.

Tax reforms in the 1990s

Tax reforms during the 1990s aimed at raising potential output by improving labor market performance and raising capital formation. In 1991, the income tax reform included provisions to raise incentives for women to join the labor force by assessing taxes individually rather than as a family unit. The main objectives of the 1991 personal income tax reform can be summarized in three points (Joumard and Varoudakis 2000):

1   the tax treatment of families became more neutral: married couples were given the option of filing separate returns, while the previous system aggregated incomes. The reform reduces disincentives to labor-force participation of household partners;
2   the tax base was broadened, including new sources of income;
3   long-term savings were given tax incentives. The taxation of undistributed profits of private investment funds was brought more into line with tax regimes existing in other EU countries.

Moreover, the structure of the brackets of income, that, since 1987, provided for 37 brackets with tax rates from 8 percent to 65.13 percent, was simplified during the 1990s through several new laws.

A small shift in the tax mix, away from labor income, was carried out in 1995 to improve labor market performance by reducing labor cost; social security contributions were reduced by one percentage point, in tandem with an offset increase in VAT rates. In addition, targeted temporary reductions in social security contributions were implemented as part of the 1997 labor market reform, with the aim of improving employment prospects of workers at the margin of the labor market. Finally, in order to rebalance the tax mix from direct to indirect taxes and to better reflect the costs and benefits of government-provided services, substantial increases in excise taxes and user fees were introduced in 1997.

The more recent far-reaching reform dates back to 1998. The importance of this law can be summarized in the following points:

1 marginal rates of income tax were lowered, from 56 percent to 48 percent for the top income bracket and from 20 percent to 18 percent for the lowest. Moreover, the number of brackets was reduced from ten to six, with the tax rates shown in Table 9.3;
2 neutrality across various types of incomes has been improved. Labor and capital income have been put on a more equal footing. Capital income, except long-term capital gains, has been integrated into the tax base. Most partial exemptions on capital gains and income have been removed;
3 the reform also made progress in harmonizing tax rates and withholding rates on income from different financial assets held during the same period;
4 an exempted living standard minimum has replaced a vast range of tax relief. Before reform, personal income tax included a large amount of tax relief, which reduced its productivity, created horizontal inequities and provided broad scope for tax avoidance. In 1998, the reform introduced a tax-exempt living standard minimum which takes into account the characteristics of the tax unit;
5 compliance and collection costs have been lowered, thus freeing resources to fight tax evasion. Withholding payments were redesigned to take into account individuals' characteristics, and thus fit better with effective tax liabilities. In 1998, the threshold below which individuals are not required to fill a tax return was raised to €21,035.

Reforms have also aimed to ease constraints on corporate financing and investment, to promote risk-taking, and to enhance firms' competitiveness. In 1995 the corporate income-tax reform improved the neutrality of the tax system toward different financing instruments and investments, and reduced discrimination against foreign direct investments by Spanish firms.

In fact, the 1995 reform abandoned the distinction between types of income (operating income, net capital gains and net increases in assets), identifying the balance of the profit and loss account as the unique tax base. Concerning discrimination against foreign investments, the correction for international double taxation of dividends and capital gains was applied to corporations owning 5 percent of the capital of foreign companies instead of the previous limit, 25 percent, for at least two years (one year from June 1996). In addition, in June 1996, a set of tax measures was adopted to facilitate firms' access to capital markets. These measures included a change in the taxation of capital gains through personal income tax[6] and the period during which firms can carry forward losses and offset them against future profits was raised (from five to seven years). The maximum period was raised to ten years by the 1999 budget law.

Moreover, distortions on investment decisions were reduced: the reform of corporate income tax (1995) allowed firms to value inventories adopting the LIFO method, as in many other OECD countries, avoiding the taxation of changes in values reflecting inflation developments. The same reform gave more freedom to small and medium-sized enterprises in spreading capital depreciation expenses over time and also introduced tax incentives for investment. Finally, the 1997 budget law introduced a lower tax rate that applies to them, from 35 percent to 30 percent up to the first €90,152 of taxable income.

During the 1990s a decentralization process took place, characterized since 1997 by an imbalance between tax assignments and expenditure functions. Until 1997, in fact, fiscal devolution to the regions was confined to the so-called "ceded taxes," mainly on property.[7] Since 1997, regional governments are able to modify the base and the rates of the ceded taxes, though with some limitation. Limited powers to set marginal personal income tax rates and tax credits have also been granted. In addition, the principles of financial solidarity across regions and of resource sufficiency for the provision of public services act as a limit to a rapid and more ambitious devolution of tax competition (OECD 2002).

Planned tax reforms and the debate on fiscal systems

The tax system has been designed to achieve a large number of objectives, which may conflict with each other. Reforming the tax system thus requires the decision of which objectives are most important and how far they should be pursued by the tax system or by other policies.

The main tax reforms options follow four fundamental guidelines (Joumard and Varoudakis 2000):

a   a further reducing of the tax burden on labor, with priority given to the low-paid, by shifting toward taxation of consumption;
b   a promotion of tax neutrality across saving instruments and corporate tax regimes, and enhancing the effectiveness of tax incentives to investment;
c   an improvement of decentralization tax, in order to effectively comply

with the Stability and Growth Pact, with a reinforcement of incentives to match regional spending by locally raised tax revenues and provision of the right incentives for sound management of public finance at regional and central level;

d   an improving of efficiency standards concerning tax collection and administration.

The reduction of the tax burden on labor, aimed at improving labor market outcomes, would need to be carried out in tandem with labor market reforms. A priority in this field is the cutting of social security contributions at the low-end of the pay scale, improving employment prospects of low-skilled workers. These measures could be implemented together with cash transfer to active workers whose earnings are below a certain threshold, in order to prevent an increase in the number of the *working-poor*. Reduction of the tax burden on labor can be implemented (although Spain was already working in this direction during 1990s reform) as well as reduction of the marginal tax rate of top-income earners, who are more disposed to income mobility toward countries where top-income taxation is lower. High marginal tax rates, under such conditions, frustrate the efficiency of the system without any gain in terms of equity. Raising the employment rate by reducing the tax rate is also needed to enhance the sustainability of the social security system in view of aging population prospects.

The reduction of the tax burden can be financed by a reduction in primary expenditure and a rise in consumption-based taxes, that are now lower than the European and OECD average. So, this is a solution that may harmonize the Spanish VAT system with European standards.

Macroeconomic simulations (Leibfritz, Thornton and Bibbee 1997) broadly assess the relative pay-off, in terms of growth and employment, of changes in tax mix.

A reduction in labor taxes, financed by a cut in unemployment benefits, has a much stronger employment and output impact than cuts in labor taxes offset by an increase in other taxes (especially consumption taxes), while the big increase in GDP and in employment rate concerns a hypothetical reduction of the corporate tax.

Table 9.12 also shows the financial consequence of the aging of the population, to 2030, that must be addressed to avoid a big decrease of output and employment consequent to the rise of costs to finance bigger social security programs.

Moreover, to remove tax-induced distortions in the labor market and enhance incentives to workers on replacement income, severance payments should be included in taxable income, as in the case of unemployment benefits in 1994.

Further improving neutrality of taxation on financial assets would increase the liquidity of the Spanish stock market and the efficiency of

Table 9.12 Long-term effects of tax changes: model-based estimates

		GDP	Employment
1 percent of GDP reduction in[1]			
labor taxes	Spain	0.91	0.76
	EU	2.08	1.83
corporate income taxes	Spain	2.02	0.39
	EU	3.09	1.06
consumption-based taxes	Spain	0.66	0.54
	EU	1.46	1.28
1 percent of GDP shift from			
labor to consumption-based taxes	Spain	0.26	0.23
	EU	0.64	0.57
labor to corporate income taxes	Spain	−1.12	0.38
	EU	−1.04	0.76
corporate income to consumption-based taxes	Spain	1.35	−0.15
	EU	1.60	0.22
Tax changes to match projected rise in social security cost resulting from aging[2]			
increase in labor taxes	Spain	−2.84	−2.48
	EU	−6.89	−6.00
increase in consumption-based taxes	Spain	−0.90	−0.73
	EU	−2.03	−1.72

Source: European Commission, DG II and OECD Secretariat.

Notes
1 offset by a reduction in government transfer payments to household.
2 projected social security expenditures over the period up to 2030.

resource allocation. In this direction, it is maybe opportune to reduce preferential tax rates for some types of investments (i.e. pension funds) in order to reduce the distortion of taxation in investment choice.

Progress to remove the preferential tax treatment on long-term capital gains, by taxing all capital gains at the current flat rate, placing the taxation of dividends and retained earning on a more equal footing, would work in the same direction. At the same time, this would lessen the need to rely on overgenerous tax incentives for business start-ups.

Aiming to improve the neutrality of corporate taxation and further enhance business investment would involve removing the reduction of the corporate tax rate for smaller companies. Typically these reductions are intended to target market failure, or to contribute to social policy or equity objectives. Effective targeting is often undermined by arbitrage opportunities, which erode the tax base and cause distortions in the allocation of resources.[8] Non-tax measures that lower the overall cost of doing business in a certain region, such as infrastructure development, or the provision of training facilities are more transparent and may create more durable positive effects.

Moreover, it suggests further extension of the provision of inheritance tax, aiming to prevent the break-up of family businesses, to a wider range of descendants. Streamlining inheritance tax and associated exemptions would help to improve horizontal equity in the transmission of small business.

The 1997–2001 financing agreement is a step in the direction of progress toward balanced and efficient fiscal decentralization and closing the gap between sub-national government spending and revenue-raising powers, providing them with the ability to tailor taxes devolved to them to locally, specific conditions.

Additional reforms are necessary to improve the degree of decentralization. Thus, in granting tax powers to the regions, it would be important to avoid a rise in collection and compliance costs and in tax avoidance. Further devolution of taxes that are also designed to achieve redistributive objectives is difficult since different rates could entail incentives for migration, and virtuous or vicious cycles. Additional resources for the regions could come from consumption taxes that have the advantage of generating less volatile revenues than income taxes.

A particular problem is the efficiency of the tax system in reducing administrative cost and preventing illegal tax abuse. The resources absorbed by tax administrators for the collection and filling of a tax reform are yet another element of the cost of taxation. Measures that could be envisaged to improve cost-effectiveness include the reduction of overlap between local and central government tax administrations, with regard to collection and processing, and the introduction or extension of information technology. In this field there are also all the problems concerning cross-border taxation of the operations, i.e. consumption tax regimes. In fact, in some circumstances, the basic principle of taxation in the place of consumption can prove either problematic or give rise to some complexities.[9] In the absence of frontier-based fiscal controls since the completion of the single market in 1993, the VAT regime for transactions within the European Union necessitates specific rules for transactions between the Member States, in order to prevent complicated procedures that generate additional compliance costs to business.

Notes

1 That is, supplies of goods and similar transactions carried out in accordance with the communities' transitional arrangements for VAT, between operators in two or more Member States of the European Union.

2 In the case of Spain, they used a sample of 21,233 families drawn from income tax files of the Institute for Fiscal Studies (IEF) for the year 1990.

3 This is due to minimum payments and contribution ceilings, which apply to both employees' and employers' social security contributions.

4 If the system contains some elements of family taxation (either because income

taxes are levied on households rather than individuals or because there are family-related tax allowances or credits), high marginal tax wedges on labor may discourage a potential second earner from taking on a job.

5 The *marginal effective tax rates* (METRs = 1 − (net income in work + net income out work)/gross income of household). Income out work takes into account the influence of both the social benefit and tax system. They indicate the share of extra-earned income of the family that is "taxed away" because of withdrawal of unemployment benefits, cancellation of means tested social benefits or higher income taxes. In 1997, METRs ranged from 78 percent in case of a household with a single full-time earner and a non-working member, not entitled to benefits based on previous earnings, to 19 percent in case of household with an unemployed person and a person employed part-time, without benefit entitlements. In the case of a single-earner household where part-time work is taken up after a long period of unemployment, the METR is 159 percent, with a high probability of these workers falling into the unemployment trap.

6 Moreover, in 1997, the corporate income tax was cut from 35 percent to 30 percent for small enterprises.

7 Tax revenues retained by the regions accounted for only 7 percent of the central government total tax revenues (excluding social security contributions) in 1995.

8 For example, special tax regimes designed to lower taxes paid by certain companies alone can lead to a serious distortion of competition.

9 Is the case of some elements of VAT regimes applicable within the European Union.

References

Aronson, J.R., Johnson, P. and Lambert, P.J. (1994) "Redistributive effect and unequal tax treatment," *Economic Journal*, 104: 262–70.

Banca d'Italia (2001) *Public Finance Statistics in the European Union*, Supplements to the Statistical Bulletin – Monetary and Financial Indicator, XI, 62 – November 15, Rome.

Buijink, W., Janssen, B. and Schols, Y. (1999) *Corporate Effective Tax Rates in the European Union*, Maastricht Accounting and Auditing Research and Education Centre, April.

Eurostat (2000) *Structures of the Taxation Systems in the European Union, 1970–1997*, Brussels: EU Commission.

Giannini, S. and Maggiulli, C. (2001) *The Effective Tax Rates in the EU Commission Study on Corporate Taxation: Methodological Aspects, Main Result and Policy Implications*, Università di Modena e Reggio Emilia: CAPP.

Joumard, I. (2001) "Tax systems in European Union countries," Economics Department Working Paper 301, Paris: OECD.

Joumard, I. and Varoudakis, A. (2000) "Options for reforming the Spanish tax system," Economics Department Working Paper 249, Paris: OECD.

Leibfritz, W., Thornton, J. and Bibbee, A. (1997) "Taxation and economic performance," Economics Department Working Paper 176, Paris: OECD.

OECD (2002) *Fiscal Decentralization in EU Applicant States and EU Selected Member States*, Paris: OECD.

Wagstaff, A. *et al.* (1999) "Redistributive effect, progressivity and differential tax treatment: personal income taxes in twelve OECD Countries," *Journal of Public Economics*, 72: 73–98.

10 The Netherlands

Graziano Abrate

Introduction

This chapter analyzes the tax system of the Netherlands and its recent evolution. The Netherlands has a relatively small-scale, but very open
economy. At the end of the 1990s, the financial health of the government
sector, in terms of the Maastricht parameters, allowed a substantial reduction of the tax burden, together with a structural modification of the fiscal
system. The reforms currently in progress aim at stimulating employment
opportunities and strengthening the Netherlands' economic structure
and international competitive edge. The social security system is under
substantial revision and the sources of financing for the government have
been radically changed since the 1970s. The taxation of capital has some
features that differentiate the Dutch system with respect to the other
industrialized countries, and make the Netherlands an attractive location
for businesses operating on an international scale.

The chapter is organized as follows. On pages 243–6, we analyze the
evolution of the fiscal revenue structure and compare it with other European countries. The overall tax burden was one of the highest in the
Union in the early 1990s, but more recently this trend was reversed. The
high share of social contributions, in particular the ones charged to
employees, has always been a characteristic of the system, but recently a
substantial revision of social security has been implemented. This probably means a re-classification of the Dutch model, from the classical
Rhineland model toward a system with many features typical of the Anglo-
Saxon model. Revenues from direct taxation, which were the main
sources of tax revenues in the 1970s and 1980s, progressively shifted to
indirect taxation.

On pages 246–54, we look at the explanation of the main taxes. The
personal income tax (PIT) was revised in 2001 with the new Income Tax
Act, which lowered the tax rates and involved many changes in the assessment base. We will explore details of the personal tax allowances and the
favorable conditions for the self-employed. Both social security contributions and taxation of financial activities are collected within the PIT.

However, returns from savings and investments are no longer taxed with progressive rates, and are now taxed with a 30 percent flat rate on the base of assumed yield of 4 percent on personally held assets. The classical system of taxation of dividends (double taxation, at corporate and personal level) provides a complex framework for the taxation of different activities. As concerns the corporation tax (CT), the participation exemption ensures that CT is levied only once on the profit obtained within a group.

After this description of the structure of the fiscal system, we will move on to an analysis of its economic implication. Therefore, pages 254–60 provide some useful indicators to understand the consequences in terms of equity and efficiency of the tax burden distribution among the different factors (labor, consumption and capital). Labor was heavily taxed, and shifting away from this charge was one of the goals of the reform process that began in the 1990s. The data on the implicit tax rate on labor relative to 1997 was still five percentage points above the European average, but the difference has been significantly reduced, considering that it was 12 percent in 1993, and that the more recently taken measures should further reduce this value. On the contrary, the tax burden on consumption is increasing. A peculiarity of the Dutch system stems from the weight given to environmental levies, and the attention given to the issues of pollution and road traffic regulation.

Perhaps the main difference between the Netherlands and the other European countries lies in the taxation of capital. The implicit tax rate is five percentage points lower than the average and the taxation at the level of corporation is one of the lowest in the Union. This data confirms the Netherlands' power of attracting business. Moreover, the new system of taxation of financial activities has many effects in terms of neutrality between the investment choices.

Finally, on pages 260–6 we focus on reforms, their economic goals, and their coherence to the suggestions of the OECD and the EU. In particular, the reduction of the tax wedge on labor and the reform of social security with the attempt to favor new opportunities of work are the answers to the policy problems related to the low participation rates of older workers and workers with few marketable skills. The goal of the government is also that of ensuring that the Netherlands remains attractive to businesses, through the indication of the OECD concerning the harmonization of the international taxation on corporations. Moreover, the reduction of the overall tax burden is still in progress and only in the next few years will an evaluation of its effects on the economic activities be possible.

The structure of the system and its development from the 1970s

The current structure of the tax system and social security contributions

During the second half of the 1990s, the government balance showed a continuous reduction of net borrowing (4.2 percent of GDP in 1995), and this indicator finally turned to a net lending in 1999 (0.4 percent). This result was achieved mainly because of a lower level of expenditure. The most important components of the latter are final consumption expenditure (23 percent), social transfer not in kind (12.5 percent) and interest payments (4.5 percent). Indeed, the overall tax burden in the Netherlands amounted to 46.7 percent of GDP in 1999 (data by Eurostat, see Table 10.1) and it is characterized by a high amount of social contributions. In fact, more than 40 percent of total fiscal revenues are raised via social contributions (only Germany and France rely to a greater extent on this source of financing). Social contributions are collected as a share of the first two brackets of the personal income tax[1] and they are mainly charged to employees (9.5 percent of GDP, against 6.4 percent paid by employers). A relevant share is also collected from the self-employed (3.5 percent).

Within the tax revenues, the greater source of financing is represented by indirect taxes, which constantly increased their weighting during the 1990s and now they account for more than 14 percent of GDP. More than half of these revenues are financed by value added tax (VAT), but environmental taxes also play an important role. Direct taxes represent less than 30 percent of total revenues, and they are characterized by a low share charged to the individual or household income and a relatively high share collected through corporation tax. More specifically, revenues from PIT represent only 6.5 percent of GDP, while those from CT amount to 4.6 percent of GDP, a high value compared to other industrialized countries. This is probably a consequence of the power of the Netherlands in attracting investments, and to the high share of corporate business in enterprises.

At the administrative level, local government raises only 2 percent of total fiscal revenues, perhaps because the Netherlands is a relatively small and homogeneous country (OECD 2002b). Within the municipal taxes, the most important is property tax, which is paid by both users and owners on the value of that property.

However, as we will see in more detail in the rest of the chapter, the new tax system introduced from January 2001 involves many changes both in the level and the structure of taxation. In fact, the wide-ranging fiscal reform which entered into force on 1 January 2001 is leading to a significant decrease in revenues from income tax and social security contributions that is only partly offset by the increase in indirect taxes, such as VAT

Table 10.1 Structure and development of fiscal revenues in the Netherlands and European average as a percentage of GDP, 1970–99

	1970		1975		1980		1985		1990		1995		1999	
	NL	Europe	NL	Europe	NL	Europe	NL	Europe	NL	Europe	NL	Europe	NL	Europe
Direct taxes	12.9	8.9	15.5	11.9	15.9	12.7	12.9	13.1	15.8	13.2	13.3	13.3	13.2	14.5
personal income	9.7	5.5	11.5	8.9	11.6	9.3	8.4	9.0	10.8	8.9	8.2	9.6	6.5	9.9
corporation income	2.5	2.2	3.3	1.9	3.0	2.2	3.1	2.8	3.4	2.9	3.3	2.4	4.6	2.8
Indirect taxes	10.9	13.0	10.8	12.2	12.1	13.2	12.1	13.0	12.4	13.0	12.8	13.6	14.1	14.6
VAT	5.4	5.1	6.1	5.7	7.1	6.6	7.3	6.1	7.2	6.6	6.7	6.9	7.3	7.0
excise duties	3.0	3.5	3.3	3.5	3.0	3.2	3.0	3.2	3.0	3.1	3.5	3.4	3.4	3.5
Total taxes revenue	23.8	21.9	26.3	24.1	28.0	25.9	25.0	26.1	28.2	26.2	26.1	26.9	27.3	29.1
Social contributions	13.5	11.7	17.2	12.8	17.9	13.4	20.5	13.8	17.1	13.7	19.0	15.0	19.4	14.0
employers	6.1	7.2	7.6	7.7	8.0	7.8	7.9	7.9	3.6	7.8	3.5	8.0	6.4	7.8
employees	5.7	3.5	7.1	3.8	7.2	4.3	8.8	4.5	10.3	4.5	11.7	5.1	9.5	4.5
self-employed	1.7	1.0	2.5	1.3	2.7	1.3	3.8	1.5	3.1	1.4	3.8	1.8	3.5	1.7
Total fiscal revenue	37.3	33.6	43.5	36.9	45.9	39.3	45.5	39.9	45.3	39.9	45.1	41.9	46.7	43.1
Administrative level														
Central government	23.3	19.7	25.1	21.1	25.8	22.3	22.6	22.1	25.6	22.2	23.3	22.5	24.5	23.7
Local government	0.6	2.2	0.5	2.8	1.2	2.9	1.3	3.1	1.4	3.8	1.7	4.0	1.9	4.3

Sources: 1970–95, Eurostat; 1999, Eurostat New Cronos databank 2002 (all data equalized with Eurostat).

Note
Minor items are omitted.

and environmental levies. The reform lowered the basic rates of income taxation, in order to stimulate the economy and employment opportunities. The lower taxation on income from employment, together with a shift from direct to indirect taxation, strengthens the Netherlands' economic structure and its international competitive edge. In fact, the Dutch tax system has many features which make the Netherlands an attractive location for businesses operating on an international scale.

Developments of the system from 1970 to 1999

The total fiscal burden grew quickly in the 1970s, as in many other European countries, boosted by a large increase in direct taxes and social contributions. In the 1980s and 1990s the level of total revenues stabilized, though they showed a slight tendency to rise, reaching a maximum of 48.6 percent of GDP in 1993. Recently, the trend was reversed.

In particular, the weight of direct taxes significantly decreased between 1993 and 1995 owing to the so-called "AAW-schuif." Looking at Table 10.1, it can be noted that it is mainly due to the reduction in the share of the personal income tax.

It accounted for 11.6 percent in 1980, very high if compared with the European mean, where now it has slowed down to 6.5 percent. On the contrary, the indirect taxes, which accounted for less than one-quarter of total taxation in 1975, constantly increased their share. In more recent years, the shift from direct to indirect taxation is evident, and clearly it has many implications in terms of losses of the redistribution effects of taxation.

Social contributions have always represented a high share of revenues, but what has changed most dramatically over the years is their distribution between employees and employers. Until 1989 the division was roughly equal. Then, with the "Oort operation," contributions for exceptional medial expenses and disability were levied on the employees instead of the employers (employees are awarded a compensation payment on top of the gross wage). For this reason, the employees' contributions reached 11.7 percent of GDP in 1995. In 1998 a new rescaling occurred, and so a quota of employees' contributions shifted to the employer, even if the former remain very high if compared to the Union's average. The substantial changes in social security system, which occurred in the last 15 years, will be analyzed in more detail on pages 261–4.

Local governments, even if collecting only a small share of revenues, constantly obtained an increasing share of funds through the year (now about 2 percent of GDP).

A comparative view against the European average

In the early 1990s the tax burden in the Netherlands was one of the highest in the Union. In recent years it has become closer to the middle range of the Member States. However the 1999 level is still three-percentage points above the Union's average.[2] This is mainly the result of a high amount of social contributions. If one only considers the tax revenues, they are clearly below the middle range of European countries.

Analyzing the structure of tax revenues, PIT gives a particularly low contribution if compared to other countries, accounting for only 15 percent of total taxation. On the contrary, the level of revenues from corporate income tax is relatively high and reaches 10 percent of total taxation, partly as a consequence of the high share of corporate business in enterprises. The Dutch Tax Department has always recognized that the tax system should not hinder the international expansion of business, and recent international studies have confirmed that the Netherlands scores well as an investment location.

Another peculiarity of the Netherlands' system concerns the weight of environmental taxes, from which the government raises almost 10 percent of its tax revenues. The level of pollution taxes (numerous special levies in connection with water pollution, waste disposal, sewerage charges) is the highest in the Union.

As concerns the four models of tax system historically developed in Europe (Bernardi 2000), the Netherlands' system is not easily accommodated. Perhaps we could say that, with the reform in progress involving a reduction of the overall tax burden and social contributions, it is moving away from the Rhineland model, assuming some characteristics that place the system nearer to the British model.

Some quantitative and institutional features of main taxes[3]

The personal income tax – PIT

Under the present Income Tax Act, resident individuals are liable for income tax on their worldwide income, while non-residents are only taxed on the income deriving from a limited number of sources in the Netherlands. The beneficiary is the state. The basis of assessment is composed of three categories, so-called "boxes" of taxable income:

- box I: taxable income from work and home. They consist of business profits with a number of additions or deductions plus net income from work, certain periodical payments, home and personal liabilities, which are received back. Taxation is levied at a progressive rate (see Table 10.2). As we have already seen, the first two brackets consist of both tax and social contribution, whilst the other two rates consist solely of taxes;[4]
- box II: taxable income from substantial interests. They consist of dividends and capital gains when the taxpayer holds, solely or with his or her partner, directly or indirectly, at least 5 percent of the capital of the company.[5] The relevant tax rate is 25 percent;

Table 10.2 Structure and parameters of **PIT** in the Netherlands – 2001 – Values in € – box I

Brackets	Marginal rates	Mean rates	Dependent labor	Self-employment	Partner	Sons
Up to 14,870	32.35 (29.4)[1]	32.35	Tax credit of €920	Tax credit of €920	Assisting spouse deduction	Expenses for the care of each child up to 13 years old are deductible up to €8,800
14,870–27,009	37.6 (29.4)[1]	33.9		Relief of €5,993 for profits up to €11,775 that falls progressively to €2,893 for profits up to €50,065	Increases to other tax credits	Further credits are allowed for children under 27 living at home
27,009–46,309	42	36.6		12% of profits may be deducted and added to the old-age reserve		Further credits are conditional to the status of partner or employed
More than 46,309	52					

Notes
Mean rates are calculated at the middle of any brackets.
1 Quota of social contributions.

- box III: taxable income from savings and investments, e.g. bank savings, second home, stock, bonds, based on the assumption that the taxpayer has an (annual) return of 4 percent on his or her capital. The rate applied is 30 percent.

In this section we focus on the general principles of PIT and on revenues from box I, whereas the details on the taxation of financial activities (i.e. box II and III) will be described on pages 251–3. Personal circumstances are taken into account when making the assessment of the amount of tax to be paid. As a result, taxable income is the income less the deductible losses. Personal deductions are set off primarily against taxable income from box I. They will be set off against taxable income respectively from boxes III and II if there is still a portion left. The tax-free annual allowance amounts to €3,800.

For PIT purposes, the taxable unit is the individual. Therefore partners pay tax on their own income and can only use their own deductible items. Some income and deductible items are joint (for example, the ones relating to the living expenses for children up to 27 years old). As a peculiarity of the system, there is not a "wife deduction," but the *partner* status offers a series of advantages. First, there is the eligibility for a number of business-related facilities. For example, when one spouse assists the other in the latter's business, the entrepreneur qualifies for a deduction from income (assisting-spouse deduction), the amount of which depends on the extent to which the entrepreneur is assisted in this way.[6] Second, they have the option of allocating the yield assessment base for the investment yield tax (box III) and the joint elements of income to both partners at their discretion. Furthermore, there are possibilities to increase the other tax credits depending on the total joint incomes of the partners (e.g. supplementary child rebate) (Meussen 2000).

The amount of tax owed is calculated by applying the appropriate tax rate. The result is reduced by one or more tax credits. Everyone benefits from a general tax credit, which amounts to €1,576. Additional credits are available depending on personal circumstances. For individuals with income from current employment, the credit is increased by a minimum of €920. For taxpayers with children under 27 living at home, single parents and elderly persons, there are further credits. Table 10.2 summarizes the main circumstances that allow special fiscal treatment, which often have to be considered together.

The profits (box I) should be determined according to sound business practice and consistent accounting methods. The concept of sound business practice has been developed mainly in case law. For example, unrealized losses may be taken into account, while unrealized profits may be ignored. Losses may be offset against the taxable income of the three preceding years (carry back) and against taxable income of the following eight years (carry forward). There are many different forms of tax relief concerning investment, research and development (which means qualified work) and self-employed persons. In particular, there is an investment allowance with respect to investments in business assets of up to €261,000,[7] with particular attention to investments in energy saving projects and so-called "environmental investments." Self-employed resident taxpayers are allowed to offset a certain percentage of their profits toward the provision of a pension scheme (old-age reserve).

Income tax has two advance levies, which are the tax on wages (deducted at source by the employer) and the dividend tax (deducted at source by the paying company).

Corporation tax – CT

Corporation tax is levied on companies established in the Netherlands (resident taxpayers) and on companies not established in the Netherlands, which receive income from the Netherlands (non-resident taxpayers). The main types of companies referred to in the Corporation Tax Act are the public companies (NV) and the private companies with limited liabilities (BV). The beneficiary is the state and there are two tax rates: 30 percent for the first €22,689, and 35 percent for the reminder.

CT is levied on the taxable amount, which is the taxable profit made by the company less the deductible losses. The determination of company taxable profits corresponds largely to the one subject to the personal income tax (sound business practice). Rules concerning investment and their promotion are similar to the ones for the PIT. Table 10.3 summarizes the basis of assessment for the CT in the Netherlands. The basic principle is that all expenses associated with business operations are tax-deductible. Some restrictions concern mixed expenses, which are business expenses with a private element.[8]

An important feature of corporation tax is the participation exemption, applicable to both domestic and foreign shareholding, which ensures that corporation tax is levied only once on the profit obtained within a group. This means that a company receiving dividends does not have to pay corporation tax on these dividends since the company distributing the dividends has already paid the tax. The main features of this scheme are the following: all gains from shareholdings are exempted, the costs associated with a shareholding are not deductible,[9] and losses arising from liquidation of the company are only deductible under certain conditions. A shareholding is deemed to exist if the taxpayer holds at least 5 percent of the shares in a subsidiary.

Under certain conditions a parent company may form a fiscal unity with one or more subsidiaries. For CT purposes, this means that the subsidiaries are deemed to have been absorbed by the parent company, and as a result, losses of companies belonging to the unit can be set off against profits from another company. This type of consolidation can

Table 10.3 The basis of corporation tax in the Netherlands

Profits item	Assessment	Losses item	Assessment
General principle	Unrealized profit may be ignored	General principle	Unrealized losses may be taken into consideration
Stocks	Valuation based on cost, unless the market value is significantly lower. Value determined using FIFO or LIFO	Depreciation	The linear method is generally used, but accelerated depreciation is permitted for certain fixed assets (e.g. environmentally friendly fixed assets)
Capital gains and dividends	All gains from shareholdings are exempted	Passive interests	Deductible, with some limits concerning interests and other charges on intercompany loans
		Losses	Carry back (3 years) and carry forward (all years to come)

occur only if a parent company holds 100 percent of the shares in its subsidiary.

Another special feature concerns the investment institutions that can be required to pay CT at zero percent. The purpose of this system is to ensure equal treatment for persons investing in investment institutions and persons who invest directly. An investment institution does not qualify for the participation exemption.

Taxation of income from financial capital

The Netherlands represents a classical system of taxation, as dividends are taxed twice, both at the corporate and at the personal level. At the personal level, the dividend tax is collected as an advance levy on PIT. As already seen on pages 246–9, the law makes a great difference between dividends and capital gains earned when the taxpayer has a substantial interest in the company (corresponding to box II) and other financial revenues (box III). In the first case, dividends and capital gains derived from the sales of shares are taxed at a proportional rate of 25 percent within the income tax. In the case of capital losses, 25 percent of those losses may be offset against the tax, which would otherwise be due.

In the second case, taxation on income from savings and investments is based on the assumption that people will have a taxable return of 4 percent on their net capital. This is the main change introduced by the reform on income tax since January 2001. The current level of return (for example, interest, dividend, capital gains or losses) is not relevant at all. Net capital is determined as the average net capital during the calendar year.[10] Only capital available for savings and investment is taken into account. Therefore capital invested in someone's own company or in a substantial interest is not considered here.[11] Each person is entitled to a tax-free capital threshold of €17,600, and for each child under 18, the threshold is raised by €2,349.

Considering the Dutch classical system, Table 10.4 provides a picture of the taxation on the different assets.

The tax on presumptive capital income is levied at 30 percent, and so it is equal to a net wealth tax levied at a rate of 1.2 percent. Expressed as a percentage of the effective return, however, the tax liability differs between assets, depending on the actual return (the higher the actual return becomes, the lower is the tax expressed as a percentage of that return). This tax has replaced the pre-existing system, which involved a tax on net wealth levied at a rate of 0.7 percent and a progressive tax on actual personal capital income. In fact, dividends and other capital income were taxed at the usual progressive rates (those of box I). Only certain earnings were taxed at proportional rates, varying from 10 percent to a maximum of 45 percent, to be applied only where income exceeded the first income band, fixed at €6,800. The most important category was

Table 10.4 Taxation of different type of returns in the Netherlands

Type of return	Tax
Return on equity, including capital gains, invested in proprietorships	Taxation on an *ex-post* basis, at progressive rates (box I of **PIT**).
Return on equity, including capital gains, invested in closely held corporations (income from substantial interests)	Taxation on an *ex-post* basis, at proportional rates: • 35% at the corporate level; • 25% at the personal level (box II of **PIT**).
Return on equity, including capital gains, invested in publicly held corporations	Taxation on an *ex-post* basis at the corporate level (35%) and on an *ex-ante* basis at the personal level (box III of **PIT**, i.e. 30% on an assumed yield of 4%). In this second case, capital gains are not specifically taxed, however, they are included on the assumed yield.
Return on individually held assets, such as deposits, bonds, debt claims and real estate	Taxation on an *ex-ante* basis, at proportional rates (box III of **PIT**).
Owner-occupied property	Taxation on an *ex-ante* basis, at progressive rates (box I of **PIT**). The assumed yield is 0.8% instead of 4%.
Return on savings held in pension funds	Not taxed.[1]

Note

1 Actually, pension payouts are taxable, but pension contributions are deductible, and depending on the different tax rates, the return on pension savings is in fact subsidized through the tax system (Cnossen and Bovenberg 2001).

represented by the incomes from substantial interest in a company, taxed at the same present rate of 25 percent.[12]

Value added tax – VAT

VAT is levied at each stage in the chain of production and distribution of goods and services. Taxable persons are persons conducting a business, who are defined as those who conduct independent business, including natural persons, corporate bodies, associations and partnerships. Every taxable person is liable for VAT on his or her turnover (the output tax), from which the VAT charged on expenses and investments (the input tax) may be deducted. There are four taxable activities:

- supplies of goods in the Netherlands, interpreted in its broader sense (goods are all physical objects, but also include electricity, heating, cooling);
- supplies of services in the Netherlands;
- acquisition of goods by an entrepreneur or legal body in the course of his/her/its businesses;
- importation of goods.

Several types of transaction are exempt from VAT, while prepaid VAT cannot be deducted. Exemptions apply to transactions such as the transfer or rental of immovable property (with certain exceptions), certain supplies of services by banks, insurance companies, postal services and medical services, and the activities of youth organizations, sports clubs, non-profit-making institutions of a social or cultural nature, (most) education, composing and writing. Special arrangements are provided for sole traders and the agricultural sector.

The standard rate is 19 percent. A reduced rate of 6 percent applies to the supply, import and acquisition of goods and services mentioned in Annex 1 to the VAT Act. In general, it refers to goods and services that can be regarded as necessities (mainly foodstuffs and medicines). A rate of zero percent applies to goods exported by an entrepreneur to non-EU countries.

Excise duties and other minor taxes

Excise duties are levied on the ultimate use or consumption of mineral oils, beer, wine, other alcoholic products and tobacco products. Like VAT, the duty is included in the price consumers pay for these goods, and the manufacturers and wholesalers remit the tax. The largest contribution to the treasury comes from the excise duty levied on mineral oils (about 70 percent of revenues from excise duties and 6 percent of total tax revenues in the Netherlands).

Excise duty legislation in the Netherlands is fully in accordance with the EU Council Directives on harmonizing excise duties in the internal market of the European Union. Since the EU excise duty system came into force in the Netherlands on 1 January 1993, indirect taxes on products other than mineral oil, tobacco and alcohol are admissible only insofar as they do not give rise to border formalities in trade between Member States. In this context, consumer taxes on non-alcoholic beverages, and tobacco products for non-smoking purposes, still exist in the Netherlands.

Several taxes in the Netherlands are levied for environmental purposes, as last amended by the law of 14 December 2000 on environmental taxes. The fuel tax is levied on mineral oils (together with excise duty), coal and natural gas. Other taxes are charged on the extraction of fresh groundwater, on the supply of tap water, on the disposal of waste to establishments operating dumps and incinerators. The regulatory energy tax is levied on the consumption of natural gas, electricity and mineral oil products when used as substitutes for gas by domestic users or commercial establishments.

The fiscal burden

The distribution of taxation charge

An initial illustration of the distribution of taxation charge according to economic functions is given in Table 10.5. The labor is the most heavily taxed factor and raises more than 50 percent of the total taxation. In particular, the charge to employed labor is very high, given the minimum

Table 10.5 Structure according to the economic function as a percentage of GDP

	1970	1975	1980	1985	1990	1995	1997
Consumption	9.8	9.8	10.8	10.9	10.9	11.2	11.4
Labor	22.9	28.4	29.2	28.7	27.7	27.0	25.5
employed	18.9	25.1	26.7	26.5	25.8	25.0	23.9
self-employed	4.0	3.4	2.5	2.1	1.8	2.0	1.6
Capital, of which	4.7	5.3	5.9	5.9	6.6	7.0	8.8
real estate and capital	0.8	0.8	1.3	1.4	1.5	1.9	2.1
monetary capital	0.4	0.3	0.3	0.4	0.5	0.3	0.5
Environment	2.5	2.4	2.5	2.6	3.1	4.1	4.3
energy	1.4	1.2	1.0	0.9	1.2	1.8	2.0
transport	0.9	0.9	1.0	1.2	1.3	1.5	1.5
pollution	0.2	0.3	0.5	0.5	0.6	0.8	0.8
Total	37.3	43.5	46.0	45.5	45.2	45.2	45.8

Source: Eurostat (2000).

Note
1997 is the last data available.

burden on self-employed labor also showing a decreasing trend. On the contrary, taxation on capital shows an increasing trend, almost aligned with the European trend. However, it is composed primarily of non-allocable incomes and wealth, whereas the typical kind of capital, real and monetary, gives a small contribution to total taxes, particularly from the returns on monetary capital (only 0.5 percent of GDP). A peculiarity of the Netherlands' system concerns the weight of environmental taxes, from which the government raises almost 10 percent of its tax revenues. The level of pollution taxes (numerous special levies in connection with water pollution, waste disposal and sewerage charges) constantly increases and it is the highest in the Union (almost 1 percent of GDP).

Implicit tax rates well summarize the data on distribution of fiscal burden among factors, permitting a wider analysis and comparison with the international trends. The trends of these indicators in the Netherlands from 1970 to 1997 are shown in Figure 10.1: they relate to labor, consumption and other factors (i.e. gross operating surplus).

The implicit tax rate on employed labor has always been the highest one and it grew significantly during the 1970s, as a consequence of the marked increases in social contributions. It reached 50.9 percent in 1985 and then remained more or less constant until 1993. In 1993, when direct taxes began to decrease, it started to slow down and, in 1997, the level of the labor implicit tax rate was 46.9 percent. If one compares this indicator with the European average, it can be argued that the level of taxation on labor in the Netherlands has always been higher than the European average. However, the difference between the Netherlands and the middle range of the other countries was significantly reduced in recent years, falling from 12 percent in 1993 to only 5 percent in 1997.

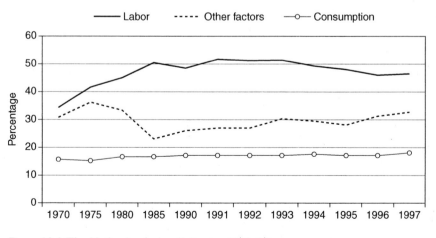

Figure 10.1 The Netherlands: implicit rates 1970–97.

Source: Eurostat (2000).

Regarding consumption, the implicit tax rate has shown a moderate upward trend, increasing by two percentage points. This increase does not correspond to the trend of the other European countries. As a consequence, while in 1970 the implicit tax rate in the Netherlands was only a bit higher than the European mean (16.1 against 15.2), in 1997 the gap reached almost four percentage points (18.2 against 14.5).

The average level of the implicit tax rate of the other factors of production, taxation on capital and self-employed labor, was around 31 percent in 1970, a level higher than the European average. However, after reaching a peak in 1975, it started to go down, following reduction in corporation tax revenues and showing a trend seemingly opposite to the other European countries. From 1985, when the level was at 23.4 percent, the trend was reverted and started to increase up to 33 percent in 1997, but it is still five percentage points lower than the middle range of other European countries.

Another important feature of a fiscal system concerns the goal of reducing inequality among people. This is mainly pursued through the PIT. The redistributive effects of PIT in the Netherlands, estimated as the difference between the Gini index on gross and net incomes, was 3.3 percent in 1992. This is the data shown in a comparative analysis of 12 OECD countries (Wagstaff *et al.* 1999), and it is in line with the other analyzed countries. This value can be decomposed between the effect of average rate (15 percent) and that of progressivity (Kakwani index equal to 19.8 percent): both the values put the Netherlands in a middle position.

Since the weight of revenues from PIT on the total fiscal revenues significantly decreased from 1992 up to now,[13] it may be argued that a recalculation of the redistributive effects with recent data should give a lower result. It is, however, more difficult to make conjectures about the progressivity index. Even if the maximum rate was reduced from 60 percent to 52 percent, the present PIT has one more bracket, and taxation burden on the poorest incomes has been lowered. Moreover, an accurate evaluation of the redistributive effects should also take into account social security contributions and the whole fiscal system.

With the new Income Tax Act, the Netherlands follows the international trend to create a system with a broader base and lower rates. However, an interesting simulation for the Netherlands (Caminada and Goudsward 2001) shows that a flat rate individual income tax has a low impact on the redistributive effects as overall tax progressivity is mainly caused by the fixed personal exemption.

Tax wedges on labor and corporate taxation

Joumard (2001) provides an estimation of the average tax wedge on labor for the year 2000. In the Netherlands the level is around 45 percent, aligned with the European mean. It is characterized by the low impact of the personal income tax, whereas the employee's social security contributions play a fundamental role. The indicator slightly decreased during the last ten years, and it should be expected to drop further due to the recent reduction of social contributions and the shift from direct to indirect taxation. The marginal tax wedge is one of the highest in the union (nearly 60 percent) and despite progressively nominal income tax schedules; the marginal wedge is very high even at the lower end of the wage scale. This is one of the reasons why the Netherlands traditionally shows a low participation rate, though in the 1980–90s, there was a significant increase in the number of persons employed and in the total hours worked. In fact, employment (in person) grew at an annual rate of 1.4 percent, thanks especially to a rapid population growth and the gradual catching up of low female labor-force participation rate to the European average. However, the boom of these years is ahead, and, as underlined by the OECD (2002a), improving the functioning of the labor market should remain a high short- and medium-term priority. In this respect the large pool of "inactives," i.e. working-age benefit recipients not seeking a job, remains a weak point of the Netherlands' economy.

Moving to the tax wedge in corporate taxation, the "all-in" statutory rate on corporations is 35 percent, and it corresponds to the corporate income tax rate,[14] as there are no surcharges and no other taxes are imposed on corporate profits. However, to have a more precise assessment of the tax burden charged on corporations, effective rates should be analyzed. Joumard (2001) reports an estimate of the "backward-looking" effective rate of corporate taxation, which takes into account the allowances granted from fiscal legislation. However, the average level in the Netherlands, from only 1990 to 1996, was a few points under the statutory rate (31.80 percent).

The "forward-looking" approach considers *ex ante* a hypothetical investment project and it is based on the calculation of the EMTR (for the marginal project) and the EATR (effective average tax rate). According to the calculation in Giannini and Maggiulli (2001), in 1999 both marginal and average effective tax rates were at the same level of statutory rate in the case of equity finance (not distinguished between new equity and retained earnings). This is not a surprise, considering the legislative framework where no depreciation is allowed for financial assets, dividends are not deductible and there are no specific allowances for retained earnings. The picture is different when one considers the case of debt finance. In this case, due to the deductibility of interests from the tax base, the EMTR turns out to be a negative result (as in most European countries) and the EATR is just above 20 percent. These results are similar to those shown in the work of Baker and McKenzie (1999), that estimate the weighted average EMTR at the level of 23 percent. The authors also provide an estimate of the impact of the investment incentives (accelerated depreciation), which reduced the EMTR by about 5 percentage points.

In the same work analysis is not only carried out at corporate level, but also takes into account taxation at the level of shareholders. In this case, the weighted average EMTR comes up to 57 percent, and shows the advantage of financing the activity with retained earnings with respect to the other sources of financing. It must be considered that the Dutch tax system provides an example of the "classical system," under which distributed profits are taxed separately at corporation level (under the corporation tax) and at shareholder level (under the income tax). Until the recent reform, carried in the new Income Tax Act of 2001, the statutory combined corporate and personal income tax wedge on distributed profits for resident top earner individuals was at 74 percent, the highest level in the OECD, as shown in Joumard (2001).[15] After the reform, the classical system is maintained, but capital personal income is now taxed at lower proportional rates.[16]

Neutrality considerations and the effect of the new capital income tax are analyzed by Cnossen and Bovenberg (2001). The previous income tax regime encouraged publicly held corporations to finance their investments through profit retention rather than debt. Now the high personal income tax rate on actual nominal interest income is replaced by a low 30 percent rate on a presumptive return of only 4 percent. The calculation in Cnossen and Bovenberg (2001) confirms that the presumptive capital income tax has reversed the privileged position of retained profits versus debt. Another interesting consideration concerns the comparison between retained profits and new shares. While the old regime favored financing through retained profits,[17] the presumptive capital income tax does not depend on the form in which the return on equity is enjoyed (dividend or capital gain), and so the decision to distribute profits is no longer being distorted.

Taxation by levels of government and fiscal federalism

The Netherlands has no strong intermediate levels of government and a small share of total fiscal revenues are collected by local government (1.9 percent of GDP in 1999 according to Eurostat, 1.4 percent according to OECD 2001). However this share is not insignificant, especially if one considers that it has constantly increased over the years (it was just one-third in 1970). According to the OECD classification, in the Netherlands there are two main sources of finance for local government: taxes on property and taxes on use of goods, or on permission to use goods or perform activities (see OECD 2002b).

Property taxes are the most important revenue source for the municipalities and raise more than 60 percent of local revenues. The tax is paid by both users and owners on the market value of that property and municipalities are free to establish the tax rates. Allers *et al.* (2001) carried out a study about the partisan influence on the local tax burden. Using data regarding Dutch local property taxes in 1996, they show that municipalities with a council dominated by left-wing parties have a higher tax burden, whereas larger coalitions have lower levels of taxation.

However the most dynamic source of financing seems to rely on the taxes on use (these revenues recently increased to 0.5 percent of GDP in 1999), which consist mainly of environmental taxes and other levies connected with road and parking utilization. The increasing attention given to upgrading the quality of the physical environment and to the protection of some resources like water can represent a great opportunity for the financing of local bodies.

A comparative view against the European average

The indicators of fiscal burden provide a picture of the features of the Netherlands' taxation system, compared to the EU average.

First, all indicators reveal that labor, and in particular employed labor, is heavily taxed if compared to the other European (and also non-European) systems. As seen on pages 254–6, in 1997 the implicit tax rate was still five percentage points higher than the European average, even if it has slowed down in recent years. Tax wedge on labor (in particular the marginal one) is higher than the mean, mainly because of the high level of employee's social contributions. The major consequence is relatively low participation rates and working hours, though the unemployment rate is one of the lowest in the Union. A peculiarity of the Dutch system, however, relates to the self-employed, who are charged a relatively low share of taxes (1.6 percent of GDP, with respect to the EU average of 2.3 percent, with an opposite trend during the years in the Netherlands and in Europe).

The taxation on consumption shows a slight but constantly increasing trend and its implicit tax rate is now almost four percentage points above the European average. This data reflects the trend in indirect taxation, whose returns now exceed those from direct taxation. The further shift from direct taxes and social contributions to indirect taxation involved by the 2001 reform should result in a further increase of taxation on consumption, whereas it should keep the taxation on labor near (or under) the European average.

Perhaps the most important difference between the Netherlands and other European countries depends upon the taxation of capital. The implicit tax rate is five percentage points lower than the average and taxation at the level of corporation is one of the lowest in the Union. However it should also be remembered that the Dutch have a classical system, and so the distributed profits are taxed twice. The new Income Tax Act of 2001 also involves the introduction of a presumptive capital income tax, which is unique in the industrialized world.

As concerns the redistributive impact of income tax (and of the whole fiscal system), the available data put the Dutch system in a middle range position among European countries. Nevertheless, the data refers to the early 1990s, and as we have seen, in the last ten years fundamental changes have occurred in the system, first of all PIT now provides a lower share of government revenues, one of the lowest in the Union.

Tax reforms in the 1990s and those currently planned

A quick glance at the budget and the general economic environment

After the 1993 recession, the Dutch macroeconomic performance was buoyant, and real GDP grew by at least 3 percent each year from 1995 (with a peak of 4.3 percent in 1998). 2000 was no exception to this trend since growth reached 3.5 percent, supported by buoyant private consumption and, in contrast with 1999, by exports that also proved extremely dynamic.

Private consumption was probably the main engine of growth in the Dutch economy and it was first fueled by the rapid increase in employment. Employment increased by about 2.5 percent a year in the period 1995–2000, whereas unemployment continued to fall, albeit at an increasingly slower pace, from 6.8 percent in 1994 to 2.8 percent in 2000 and 2.4 percent in 2001. Private consumption was also boosted by the tax cuts operated in recent years and by accelerating wage increases (in particular from 1997) which probably brought 15 years of wage moderation to an end.[18]

The government sector fully benefited from the positive economic trend. In 2000, revenue exceeded expenditure generating a surplus of 2.2 percent of the GDP.[19] The government debt ratio fell by more than seven percentage points of GDP in 2000, decreasing from 63.1 percent in 1999 to 56 percent. It fell below 50 percent in 2002, with a further reduction of the expenditure for interests. This context allows a substantial reduction of the tax burden without the necessity of cutting the primary expenditure. In fact, the wide-ranging fiscal reform which entered into force on 1 January 2001 is leading to a significant decrease in revenues from income tax and social security contributions that is only partly offset by the increase in indirect taxes, such as VAT and environmental levies. Accordingly, the general government surplus should decline and vanish in 2002 (European Commission, economic forecasts, spring 2002).

However the peak of the growth cycle is now clearly behind. Investment proved less dynamic than expected and seemed to remain stagnant in the third and fourth quarters of 2000. While GDP growth exceeded 4 percent in annual terms in the first half of 2000, it slowed to about 3 percent in the second, and according to preliminary estimates, it fell down to 1.1 percent in 2001. Exports felt the effects of the slowdown in international trade and the impact of the deterioration of competitiveness in recent years, no longer compensated by the depreciation of the euro. The slowing down of GDP growth is due to the crisis of investments but also to a deceleration of private consumption.

Forecasts for 2002 and 2003 indicate a slight recovery, with the GDP growing by 1.5 percent and 2.7 percent respectively. The main engine of growth in the Dutch economy will probably remain private consumption, boosted by a very solid increase in household disposable income (about 10 percent in nominal terms and 6 percent in real terms) amplified by the effects produced by reduction in income taxes and social security contributions implemented at the beginning of 2001. However, the unemployment rate, now certainly close to a frictional level, should invert the tendency and slightly increase (up to 3.5 percent in 2003). Nevertheless, higher employment is expected to result essentially from a higher activity rate, which, despite climbing significantly in recent years, is still relatively low in international terms.

It can be argued that the recovery of the Dutch economy will also depend on the positive effects on private activity expected from the new tax system. In the meantime, the economic environment will have an influence on the level of tax revenues and consequently on the government surplus or deficit. The situation of the government sector, which in the past has allowed a policy of reduction of the tax burden, will represent either an opportunity or a constraint in deciding future tax policies.

Tax reforms in the 1990s

As already seen, in the early 1990s the tax burden in the Netherlands was one of the highest in the Union. Now the situation has changed, due to a series of reforms, which involve substantial tax reduction, permitted by a favorable economic environment. In this section we try to summarize the main changes of the structure of the Dutch fiscal system.

A first fundamental characteristic concerns the social security model. As noted by Bolkenstein (2000), in the early 1990s the Dutch model (or the so-called "Polder model") clearly fitted like a variant of the Rhineland model, a regulated market economy with a comprehensive system of social security and with harmonious relations between social partners.[20] The symbol of such a system was probably the wage moderation facilitated by the so-called Wassenaar agreement between employers and the union in 1982. However, at a certain point, the Dutch came to the conclusion that their initially strongly centralized model resulted in slow adaptation and low flexibility. That was the time of the Dutch recession in the early 1990s. Therefore, the model was adjusted: there is currently less emphasis on consensus building and much more on the achievement of concrete policy goals. From the 1990s up to now, some distinctive features implied a certain convergence toward the Anglo-Saxon model.[21] The most important reforms focused on disability insurance and on sickness benefits.

The level of social protection benefits was very generous, and the lack of incentives for the low-skilled workers to take a job is evident when one considers that, in 1995, there were 82 social security beneficiaries for each 100 active persons.[22] Officially 13 percent of the working population was disabled and this number is obviously too high, making the Netherlands the unhealthiest place in north-western Europe, whilst having the highest life expectancy.[23] Bovenberg (2000) distinguishes two combined strategies in the welfare state reform:

- the first aimed at fighting moral hazard through a more efficient administration of social benefits, preserving as much as possible the European legacy of solidarity;
- the second, which can be identified with the Anglo-Saxon approach, focused on reducing the level of public insurance and widening the income gap between the working and non-working.

The goal of the progressive reforms made in the 1990s is certainly to increase the activity rate of the population, reducing benefits and tightening the criteria for eligibility. In this sense there is also a reduction of social security contributions for workers aged above 65. The privatization of the sickness insurance contributed to a marked reduction in the problem of sickness absenteeism. The healthcare system has been involved in reforms since 1988, and the goal, not yet achieved, is a universal compulsory insurance within a regulated competition framework (Mapelli 2000).

The stimulation of employment opportunity and the reduction of the tax burden on labor have clearly been pursued during the last ten years, not only through the reduction of social security contributions. From 1993, direct taxation has been progressively shifted toward indirect taxation. Tax rates on personal income have been reduced. With the new Income Tax Act introduced since January 2001, the top rate is now at 52 percent, against the previous 60 percent; the intermediate rate slowed down from 50 percent to 42 percent; the lower rate from 33.9 percent to 32.25 percent. The level of taxation is very low, especially if one considers that at the lower bracket only 2.85 percent consists of taxes (before the reform, it was 4.5 percent), while the remainder are social contributions. With the new tax rates, across the board from high to a very low income, net income after tax increases by 2.1 percent up to 9.7 percent (Meussen 2000). Moreover, the reform introduced an employment tax credit to employees and the self-employed of up to €920, and the minimum level of exempted income was increased. The tax burden has been partially shifted toward consumption, with the increase of the standard VAT rate from 17.5 percent to 19 percent, and with a progressively increasing relevance of the environmental levies. The Netherlands is clearly devoted to promoting sustainable economic development ("greening") and they are one of the most advanced countries in promoting such a policy within the European Union.

A peculiarity of the tax system concerns the taxation of financial activities (see also pages 251–3) that are taxed in box II and III of the PIT. The tax treatment of profits from substantial business interests changed dramatically, with effect from 1 January 1997. As of this date, not only capital gains on shares belonging to a substantial interest are characterized as profits from substantial business interests (gains on disposal), but also the regular income, such as dividend income. The tax rate was raised from 20 percent to 25 percent, in order to fight the phenomenon of the closely-held corporation, set up to avoid the high personal income tax rates.[24] Moreover, a fictitious wage was imputed to manager-shareholders that could previously transform their labor income into capital income without limit. Under the Income Tax Act 2001, this system has been largely left intact in box II.[25]

The most important change concerns the tax levied on income from savings and investments. Under previous legislation, income actually received in a year, such as rental income, dividends from listed shares, interest on savings accounts, etc. were taxed at progressive rates and capital gains were not taxed. Instead, from January 2001, a fixed assumed yield of 4 percent is calculated each year on the value of assets held. This income is taxed at a flat rate of 30 percent. It is clear that, if the effective return exceeds the assumed 4 percent yield, the excess is not taxed at all. As a consequence, in the Corporation Income Tax Act, it has implemented a 20 percent CT surcharge on certain excessive dividends distributed during the period from 2001 through 2005. Another important feature of the new tax system regards the Dutch real estate owned by foreign entities, which will always be considered to be a permanent establishment and so the related capital gains will be subject to tax.

The presumptive capital income tax has several implications in terms of neutrality considerations of investment choices (Cnossen and Bovenberg 2001):

- it reverses the privileged position of retained profits versus debt, the latter becoming a more attractive source of finance;
- it raises the costs of equity finance in owner-occupied housing and proprietorships, and worsens the discrimination of equity with respect to debt, because the tax on equity income at the corporate level is no longer offset by the exemption of capital gains at the personal level;
- it eliminates the distortion in the choice between financing with retained profits and new shares. Issuing new shares is no longer less attractive and this should shift equity capital from mature corporations, which generate retained profits, to new growing corporations, which have to rely on the external capital market to attract equity.

However, though the tax incentive to borrow vanishes, tax arbitrage is still possible considering the different tax rates in the various boxes. By excluding owner-occupied housing, equity in closely held corporations and proprietorships and pension wealth, the presumptive capital income tax features only a relatively small base.

Tax reforms currently planned

Reforms caused substantial changes in the taxation structure. How does the Netherlands fit in the international scenario of reforms with respect to the suggestions of the OECD and the EU? When one considers the demand for harmonization of fiscal systems within the European Union, it mainly concerns the field of indirect taxes, while there is a less pressing need in the domain of personal income tax and social contributions. In fact, substantial differences in indirect taxation can create an immediate obstacle to the free movement of goods and the free supply of services within the internal market. Indeed, a significant degree of harmonization in this direction has already taken place.

The most controversial problem seems to be the tax competition within companies and corporations, particularly the avoidance of harmful competition. The Netherlands has engaged in a fruitful dialogue with other Member States resulting in the adjustment of its ruling practice to internationally accepted OECD standards. Tax reform in 2001 may have an impact on the Netherlands' tax position on foreign companies (Van der Stok and Sunderman 2001). Previously, foreign companies that held Dutch real estate which was no part of the assets of a business were taxed only on income derived from the real estate, while there were no taxes on capital gains realized. Now real estate held by foreign companies is deemed to form part of a Dutch business, and so it is subject to both income and capital gains tax in the Netherlands. However, the most fundamental change in the new Income Tax Act is probably the taxation of income from savings and investments (box III). Especially in an international perspective, the taxation of an assumed investment yield is something of a curiosity, being unique in the industrialized world. In the Netherlands some scholars have argued that this takes the country, as far as taxation is concerned, back to a system familiar in the nineteenth century. On the other hand, although the Netherlands do not have a capital gains tax, some of the specific measures mean that many assets have been taken out of box III and situated in box I (making assets available), thus effectively leading to a partial introduction of a capital gains tax (Meussen 2001). However, the small tax base distorts economic choices and harms efforts to coordinate capital income taxes within the European Union. Cnossen and Bovenberg (2001) evaluate the alternatives to the presumptive capital income tax and they conclude that the effective and neutral taxation of capital income could best be ensured through a combination of the following:

- a mark-to-market tax on the returns from easy-to-value financial products (i.e. the base of taxation for these products should be the annual accretion of wealth measured in real terms); and
- a capital gains tax on the returns from hard to value real estate and small business.

The current fiscal policy in the Netherlands is certainly coherent with the suggestion of shifting tax burden away from labor (Joumard 2001 and OECD 2001). This policy has been pursued, reducing social contributions and increasing indirect taxes like VAT and environmental levies, and it is devoted to reduce the tax wedge and favor new opportunities of work. The main issue of reforming social security is still open, as the major remaining policy problems concern the low participation rates of older workers and of workers with few marketable skills. Benefit recipients still seem to have very limited access to work, and this is reflected in the high share of the long-term unemployed in overall unemployment. The official unemployment figure substantially underestimates the overall level of inactivity in the Netherlands, because of the high share of hidden unemployment. Despite progress over the recent years, more reforms remain necessary, as stressed in the government agenda. In more detail, the 2002 tax plan includes five bills dealing with:[26]

- labor market and incomes policy;
- economic infrastructure;
- nature, environment and transport;
- review of inheritance and gift tax, VAT measures, arrangements for artists and sportsmen and other changes;
- social security legislation.

The bills will result in a total tax cut of 1.3 billion euro (around 0.3 percent of GDP), continuing the policy of reducing the total tax burden. A substantial proportion of this will be used to promote employment, and measures will also be taken to strengthen the economic structure and policy on nature, environment and transport. To tackle current labor market problems, the government will introduce a large number of tax measures to encourage job seekers and promote labor participation. These measures should also increase the acceptance of taxes and social insurance contributions and reduce the number of people on benefit. To promote labor participation, the government will introduce a tax credit for certain benefit claimants who find work and other people re-entering the labor market. The tax credit, a maximum of €2,723, will be paid to taxpayers only once, over a period of three years. In certain conditions, it may be awarded to claimants who find work or to people who have had no income or a very low income for two calendar years. The government intends to grant the employers of people re-entering the labor market a reduction of €700 in tax and social insurance remittances. It also wants to promote labor participation by keeping people in the labor market longer, and is planning to introduce a package of tax incentives for employees over the age of 58.

Tackling the poverty trap has been an essential part of government policy for some time. It is important to make paid work more attractive if the labor market is to function properly, as the poverty trap can deter people from seeking paid work. Proposals to further reduce the poverty trap include increasing the employed person's tax credit and increasing the child tax credit while abolishing child allowances under the Housing Benefit Act.

The government believes that company taxes need to be reduced to ensure that the Netherlands remain attractive to businesses. One proposal is to reduce corporation tax by 0.5 percentage points to 34.5 percent. This structural tax cut will give an extra boost to the business environment in the Netherlands. Though the suggestions of the OECD mainly concern the coordination in the base assessment of CT and not the tax rates, this proposal certainly remains in the field of fair tax competition.

The 2002 tax plan will continue with the "greening." Despite many years of environmental policies, many policy goals have still not been achieved. It appears that in formulating environmental policy goals, policy makers have paid insufficient attention to the issue of how to realize these goals, having a tendency to be too optimistic about the effects of the adopted measures.[27] However, the proposals deal with the continuation of lowering and "greening" of vehicle taxes begun last year. Motor vehicle tax for cars that can use LPG will be reduced by 6.5 percent. In addition, excise duty on low-sulphur petrol and LPG will be temporarily reduced by €1.36 as from 1 October. The government will also encourage people to buy fuel-efficient cars. Depending on how economical a car is, some of the motor vehicle tax paid by the buyer will be refunded.

Alongside marriage, other forms of cohabitation have become commonplace in recent decades. This makes it necessary to modernize inheritance and gift tax. The 2002 tax plan proposes a general exemption from inheritance and gift tax for partners; the definition of "partner" will be broadened.

Changes to the VAT system are also proposed. For instance, VAT on domestic air tickets will be changed to the high rate and that for sports centers will be changed to the low rate.

Notes

1 29.40 percent of the first €27,000. See also pages 246–9, which concern the personal income tax.
2 It should be noted that the Eurostat data concerning the Netherlands seems to be a little high if compared with other sources of data like OECD, which placed the Netherlands closer to the middle range of European countries.

3 The contents of this section are based mainly on works by the EC (2001) and Ministry of Finance (2001).

4 People aged 65 and over are no longer liable for several social security contributions, and so they pay a first rate of 14.45 percent and a second rate of 19.70 percent, which consist solely of taxes.

5 So the shareholder is supposed to have a substantial interest in a company if he or she holds at least 5 percent of it.

6 Income earned by a spouse in assisting the other in his/her business is attributed to the spouse who runs the business, unless both spouses request otherwise, and the income amounts to at least €5,000.

7 Investments are divided into nine bands, with the percentage of the allowance declining as the investment increases. For investments of up to €30,000 the allowance is 25 percent.

8 Limitations are tighter for companies with one or more persons holding a substantial interest in the company who also work for the company. An option consists in treating as non-deductible a fixed amount of €1,500 for each person with a substantial interest working for the company.

9 An exception is made when the taxpayer is able to show that the costs are conducive to making domestic taxable profits. In practice, the main non-deductible costs are those of financing the participation.

10 It is obtained by calculating the mean between the capital owned on 1 January and 31 December.

11 Examples of assets taxed under box III are: bank and saving accounts, a second home, stocks and other shares, endowment insurance policy which is not linked to an owner-occupied dwelling.

12 In more detail, the rates were the following:

- 45 percent in the case of certain types of profit and income, like profits made when a business is sold;
- 25 percent in the case of income from a substantial interest in a company;
- 20 percent in the case of profits deemed to be made on an entrepreneur's death;
- 10 percent in the case of bonus shares obtained when an officially quoted limited company issues new capital.

13 As we saw on pages 243–6, revenues from PIT now represent less than 15 percent of total fiscal revenues. They were 11.5 percent of GDP in 1992, whereas they were less than 7 percent in 2000.

14 Since 2000, profits up to €22,686 are taxed at a lower rate of 30 percent.

15 The top rate of income tax was at 60 percent, so the calculation is as follows: 35 percent + 60 percent (100 − 35).

16 For dividends from participation of at least 5 percent (substantial interest), the rate has not changed, as they were already taxed at the rate of 25 percent, and the calculation is as follows: 35 percent + 25 percent (100 − 35) = 51.25 percent. The other dividends and capital gains are taxed at 30 percent on a presumptive base. See pages 251–3 for more details.

17 The net dividend that shareholders forego, considering the high personal income tax rate to pay, was lower than the cost of new equity.

18 This increase partly reflected the labor productivity growth and partly the higher real unit labor cost, affecting the competitiveness of the Dutch economy.

19 The primary surplus was 6.1 percent of GDP (3.9 percent was the expenditure for interests).

20 Generally speaking, in such a system, the participants in the economic process try to achieve a harmony of interests pursuing a sustainable, stable and continuous economic growth and a high level of employment.

21 Bolkenstein (2000) also underlines that many measures were taken without a harmonious agreement between the different social parts (in contrast with the Rhineland model). For example, one should remember the reduction of the tax burden, the policy to stop matching any increase in wages with an equal increase in minimum social benefits, the decentralization of collective bargaining agreements, the privatization of health insurance and the reduction of benefits for the disabled.

22 Source: CPB (1998).

23 This data can be explained by many features that made the Dutch system of disability insurance unique. For example, only the degree of disablement was relevant and not its origin, whereas in other OECD countries less generous benefits are provided if the impairment is not job related. Another peculiarity was that those persons who were only partly disabled were entitled to full disability benefits if the labor-market situation did not allow them to find a job.

24 In fact business form was greatly favored over proprietorship, because current profits were taxed at the corporation tax rate of 35 percent, while deferred profit distributions attracted 20 percent tax, instead of the progressive income tax rate.

25 The original proposals included an increase of the tax rate for substantial business interests to 30 percent, but at the end the tax rate has been maintained at 25 percent.

26 Press release, 2001 (www.minfin.nl).

27 CPB (2001).

References

Allers, M.A., De Haan, J. and Sterks, C.G.M. (2001) "Partisan influence on the local tax burden in the Netherlands," *Public Choice*, 106: 351–63.

Baker and McKenzie (1999) *Survey of the Effective Tax Burden in the European Union*, Amsterdam.

Bernardi, L. (2000) "Note sull'evoluzione recente e sulle prospettive future dei sistemi tributari," *Studi e Note di Economia*, 1: 25–50.

Bolkenstein, F. (2000) *The Future of the Social Market Economy*, Speech, Brussels, December.

Bovenberg, L. (2000) "Reforming social insurance in the Netherlands," *International Tax and Public Finance*, 7: 345–68.

Caminada, K. and Goudsward, K. (2001) "Does a flat rate individual income tax reduce tax progressivity? A simulation for the Netherlands," *Public Finance and Management*, 1 (4): 471–99.

Cnossen, S. and Bovenberg, L. (2001) "Fundamental tax reform in the Netherlands," *International Tax and Public Finance*, 8: 471–84.

CPB (1998) *CPB Report*, Netherlands Bureau for Economic Policy Analysis, The Hague.

—— (2001) *CPB Report*, Netherlands Bureau for Economic Policy Analysis, The Hague.

EU Commission (2001) *Directory of Taxes in the EU: The Netherlands*, Brussels: EU Commission.

—— (2002) *Statistical Annex of European Economy*, Brussels: EU Commission.

Eurostat (2000) *Structures of the Taxation Systems in the European Union, 1970–1997*, Brussels: EU Commission.

—— (2002) *New Cronos Statistics*, databank CD-ROM.

Giannini, S. and Maggiulli, C. (2001) *The Effective Tax Rates in the EU Commission Study on Corporate Taxation: Methodological Aspects, Main Results and Policy Implications*, Università di Modena e Reggio Emilia: CAPP.

Joumard, I. (2001) "Tax systems in European Union countries," Economics Department Working Paper 301, Paris: OECD.

Mapelli, V. (2000) "Le riforme sanitarie in alcuni Paesi Europei (1990–2000)," in Bernardi, L. (ed.) *La Finanza pubblica italiana, Rapporto 2000*, Bologna: Il Mulino.

Meussen, G.T. (2000) "Netherlands: income tax act 2001," *European Taxation*, 40 (11): 490–8.

Ministry of Finance (2001) *Taxation in the Netherlands 2001*, The Hague: Ministry of Finance.

OECD (2001) *Revenue Statistics 1965–2000*, Paris: OECD.

—— (2001) "Tax and the economy: a comparative assessment of OECD countries," *Tax Policy Studies*, 6, Paris: OECD.

—— (2002a) *Economic Survey – Netherlands*, Paris: OECD.

—— (2002b) *Fiscal Decentralisation in EU Applicant States and EU Selected Member States*, Paris: OECD.

Van Der Stok, E. and Sunderman, M. (2001) "Netherlands finance officials busy in 2000 with tax reform 2001," *Tax Notes International*, 22 (3): 251–8.

Wagstaff, A. *et al.* (1999) "Redistributive effect, progressivity and differential tax treatment: personal income taxes in twelve OECD countries," *Journal of Public Economics*, 72: 73–98.

Websites

http://europa.eu.int.
http://www.cpb.nl/eng/cpbreport.
http://www.minfin.nl.
http://www.oecd.org/.

11 The United Kingdom

Giuseppe Migali

Introduction

This chapter is devoted to an analysis of the United Kingdom's tax system. We consider the present status of the main taxes in the context of a 30-year period, their working and future reforms.

The current tax system was born with the reforms of the 1980s. The pre-reform tax system might have contributed to negative economic performance in the UK during the 1960s and 1970s. It was mainly designed to redistribute income, but in fact achieved little redistribution and weakened work incentives for many people. Since the 1980s, the UK has embarked on a series of structural reform that have changed the institutions and the role of the public sector in product, labor and financial markets. The income tax rate structure has been transformed, savings taxation has been repeatedly adjusted, the national insurance contributions system has been overhauled, VAT doubled and some excise duties changed.

Pages 271–6 describe the public sector's fiscal framework, and focus on direct taxes, indirect taxes and social security contributions. The development of the tax system from 1970 to 1999 is compared with the European average. The shift from direct to indirect taxes started in the 1980s seems not to have reached its objective. In fact the reduction of personal income tax has been offset by the increase in corporation tax, and the rise in VAT offset by the decline of excise duties. However, a cut in social contributions has been realized, and they are now much below the European average.

Pages 276–86 describe the structure of the main taxes: income tax, corporation tax, capital taxes, local taxes, value added tax and other indirect taxes. Personal income tax is analyzed, focusing on the current tax rates, bands and the new system of benefits. Corporation tax has a particular structure with three rates and a system of relief to help companies with small profits. Individual capital gain tax is described, looking at the 1998 reform that introduced a tapering system, with the objective of encouraging longer-term holding of assets. Local taxes have a small impact on total revenue, due to the different reforms, such as the introduction of poll tax and its subsequent substitution with the council tax, which is a property-based tax.

On pages 287–93, we examine the distribution of fiscal burden; the analysis starts by observing the evolution of implicit tax rates from 1970 to 1997. Taxation on labor has decreased sharply over the last 25 years, while implicit tax rates on consumption have remained quite stable, despite the increase of VAT. Taxation on capital and other factors fell deeply, from 55 percent in 1970 to 38 percent in 1997. The analysis goes on to look at the progressivity of the tax system in the UK, and how it has changed over this period. Finally, we describe the tax wedges in corporate and labor taxation. The tax wedge on labor is lower than the EU average, primarily due to the reduction of social contributions.

This is followed with a brief overview of the new macroeconomic framework, showing that the economy has experienced a period of stability and steady growth. We assess the fiscal reforms that have taken place during the 1990s. The new directions for future tax reform are a reduction in the complexity of VAT, the shift of the national insurance structure nearer to that of income tax and greater financial support for low-income working families and those with children. Finally, there is an open debate on the reform of double taxation relief for companies, to replace the credit system with an exemption system for direct investment.

This chapter has tried to show the main features of the UK tax system and to describe major changes. Some reforms have been more successful than others, e.g. the cutting of social contributions and the reduction of the tax wedge on labor. The shift toward indirect taxation has not been achieved, and the reduction of income tax, which was initially in a regressive trend, has been corrected to help low-income earners. The changes in local taxation resulted in a system looking more like the original than the intermediate one. Local revenue is too low, council tax is the only local tax left and local authorities have little control over their budgets. Finally, the taxation of foreign investments is more addressed to defending UK advantages than to converge with EU standards.

The structure of the system and its development from the 1970s

The current structure of the tax system and social security contributions

The surpluses of net borrowing declined from −1.7 percent of GDP in 1999–2000 to −0.6 percent of GDP in 2001–2; a net borrowing deficit of 1 percent of GDP is estimated for 2003–4.

Total managed expenditure declined dramatically from around 44 percent of GDP in 1992–3 to the lowest point over the last 20 years, almost 37.5 percent in 1999–2000. However in 2002–3 one should observe a gradual increase up to 40 percent. The main items are social security and healthcare services, 27 percent and 19 percent of total expenditure respectively. Around 13 percent of government spending is for education, and 5 percent for housing and the environment, slightly more for defense, almost 6 percent; other expenditures amount to less than 5 percent.

In 2001–2, total current receipts are estimated to be 40.5 percent of GDP, over 617 billion euro,[1] this is equivalent to €13,169 for every adult in the UK, or €10,225 per person.

Total revenue can be analyzed focusing on direct taxes, indirect taxes and social security contributions. Direct taxes include income tax, corporation tax, council tax and business rate. They represent the largest source of revenue for the government, around 18 percent of GDP in 2000–1, 46 percent of total taxation.

According to HM Treasury (2002), income tax is the largest source of revenue for the government, around 11.3 percent of GDP and 26 percent of total revenue in 2000–1. Projections up to 2005–6 show a stable pattern. In 2000–1, corporation tax was around 3.4 percent of GPD and 9.5 percent of total taxation, and it should remain constant until 2005–6. Council tax receipts are 4 percent of total taxation and business rate almost 5 percent.

Indirect taxes include VAT, excise duties and other receipts; they account for 15 percent of GDP and 38 percent of total taxation. VAT raises 16 percent of total revenues, and from 2000–1 to 2005–6 it is estimated to remain constant at around 6 percent of GDP. Excise duties are 13 percent of total receipts and around 4 percent of GDP in 2000–1, and they should decrease by 0.5 in percentage points of GDP until 2005–6.

Social security contributions are around 6.5 percent of GDP and 16 percent of total government revenues in 2000–1. Projections show a stable pattern at around 6.2 percent of GDP up to 2005–6.

In practice, payments are placed in a fund that prevents cash-flow problems. In fact the fund should not fall below one-sixth of national insurance expenditure; the system works assuring that current contributions finance current benefits. Two groups pay the vast majority of contributions: employees, as a tax on their earnings; and employers, as contributions on those they employ. Contributions paid by the self-employed are rather low, around 3 percent of the total.

Developments of the system from 1970 to 1999

The total fiscal revenue as a percentage of GDP rose and fell during the 1970s; in 1980 it was less than 36 percent of GDP, then total receipts increased, reaching an absolute peak of 39 percent in 1983. From 1984 there was a sharp decline of revenues that reached the lowest point for the last 20 years at around 33 percent of GDP in 1993. Then, total taxation rose again and, in 2001, it was estimated to be almost 38 percent of GDP (HM Treasury 2002).

Direct taxes were around 18.5 percent of GDP in 1975, the highest value over the last 30 years. Since the end of the 1970s, government strategy has been to shift from direct toward indirect taxes, but we observe a reduction to 16 percent of GDP in 1980 and then an increase to 17 percent in 1985. Direct taxes remained stable until 1990, when there is a small dip to around 16 percent until 1999. Personal income taxes are, on average, 66 percent of direct taxes and corporation taxes almost 21 percent.

Personal income taxes were reduced by the structural reform of the end of the 1970s, and in fact they decreased from 14 percent of GDP in 1975 to 11 percent in 1980, and then they remained stable at around 10.5 percent until 1999. The hoped-for reduction of direct taxes did not happen because the cut in personal income taxes was offset by the increase of corporate taxes: they rose from around 2 percent in 1975 to almost 4.5 percent in 1985. The reform of corporate tax in 1984 provided a small reduction in revenues up to around 3 percent in 1995, but in 1999 the receipts were again around 4 percent.

Indirect taxes show a stable pattern over a 30-year period, varying between 14–15 percent of GDP. The lowest level was 11.4 percent in 1975; then the policy to increase indirect taxes provided a sharp rise of 14 percent in 1980. During the 1980s the pattern was quite stable at around 14 percent; in the 1990s there was a small increase of almost 0.5 percent.

The introduction of VAT in 1973 and the number of small additions to its base during the 1980s and the 1990s represent the main features of the shift toward indirect taxation. VAT is the main source of indirect taxes, on average 48 percent of the total. During the 1970s VAT rose gradually, in 1975 it was around 3 percent of GDP. In 1979 there was the first change: the VAT standard rate was increased to pay for the reduction in income tax. The receipts increased sharply to more than 6 percent of GDP in 1990. The rate was increased again in 1991 to pay for a reduction of the poll tax, and the revenue rose to almost 7 percent in 1995. The most significant widening of the VAT base, since its introduction, was the imposition on domestic fuel of 1995. VAT rose nearly £3 billion per year by 1996–7.

Despite the considerable growth of VAT, we do not observe a big rise of indirect taxes because there is a fall in excise duties. They decrease from 6.6 percent in 1970 to 3.6 percent in 1990, offsetting the VAT rise. There is a small increase in excise duties of up to 4 percent in 1999, but this ratio is expected to decline over the next few years, reflecting the assumption that consumption goods subject to excise duties grow by less than GDP. Social security contributions are, on average, 18 percent of total revenues, and they remain unchanged at around 7 percent of GDP from 1980 to 2000, despite the radical structural changes introduced. Contributions paid by employers are, on average, 54 percent of total, and have varied by

Table 11.1 Structure and development of fiscal revenue in the UK and European average as a percentage of GDP, 1970–99

	1970		1975		1980		1985		1990		1995		1999	
	UK	Europe	UK	Europe	UK	Europe	UK	Europe	UK	Europe	UK	Europe	UK	Europe
Direct taxes, of which	17.4	8.9	18.5	11.9	16.0	12.7	17.3	13.1	17.3	13.2	15.5	13.3	15.8	14.5
personal income	11.1	5.5	14.0	8.9	11.0	9.3	10.5	9.0	10.6	8.9	10.2	9.6	10.9	9.9
corporation income	3.7	2.2	2.3	1.9	2.9	2.2	4.6	2.8	4.1	2.9	3.3	2.4	3.7	2.8
Indirect taxes, of which	14.2	13.0	11.4	12.2	13.9	13.2	13.9	13.0	13.7	13.0	14.5	13.6	14.8	14.6
VAT	0.0	5.1	3.3	5.7	5.1	6.6	5.8	6.1	6.2	6.6	6.9	6.9	6.9	7.3
excise duties	6.6	3.5	4.3	3.5	3.7	3.2	4.2	3.2	3.6	3.1	4.0	3.4	4.1	2.5
Total tax revenue	31.6	21.9	29.9	24.1	29.9	25.9	31.2	26.1	31.0	26.2	30.0	26.9	30.6	29.1
Social contributions	5.6	11.7	7.3	12.8	6.7	13.4	7.5	13.8	6.9	13.7	6.9	15.0	6.8	14.0
employers	2.8	7.2	4.2	7.7	3.9	7.8	3.8	7.9	3.9	7.8	3.7	8.0	3.7	7.8
employees	2.6	3.5	2.9	3.8	2.7	4.3	3.5	4.5	2.8	4.5	3.0	5.1	3.0	4.5
self-employed	0.2	1.0	0.2	1.3	0.1	1.3	0.2	1.5	0.2	1.4	0.2	1.8	0.2	1.7
Total fiscal revenue	37.2	33.6	37.2	36.9	36.6	39.3	38.7	39.9	37.9	39.9	36.9	41.9	37.4	43.1
Administrative level														
Central government	28.1	19.7	25.8	21.1	25.5	22.3	26.4	22.1	27.2	22.2	27.5	22.5	28.1	23.7
Local government	3.6	2.2	3.8	2.8	3.6	2.9	3.9	3.1	2.7	3.8	1.4	4.0	1.4	4.3

Sources: 1970–95, Eurostat; New Cronos databank 2002 (data equalized with Eurostat, 2000).

Note
Minor items are omitted.

around 4 percent of GDP over the last 30 years; instead, contributions paid by employees are, on average, 43 percent of total, and remain stable at around 3 percent of GDP. A residual part of contributions is paid by the self-employed, less than 3 percent of the total and 0.2 percent of GDP. The ratio of social contribution to GDP is projected to fall slightly over the next five years, because higher rates of contracting are assumed out of the state pension scheme, as individuals increasingly make use of stakeholder pensions.

Looking at the administrative distribution of revenues, the majority of taxes raised by central government represent 27–28 percent of GDP, this percentage being less than 26 percent from 1975 to 1980. Local government receipts decreased from 1970 to 2000, from around 3.5 percent of GDP to the more recent 1.4 percent.

A comparative view against the European average

Total fiscal revenue in the UK was only higher than the Europe average during the 1970s, from 1980 to 1999 the trend was the opposite. In 1985, the UK fiscal revenue was around 39 percent of GDP and the Europe average around 40 percent; in 1999 the difference was more than five percentage points: 37.4 percent of GDP in the UK and 43 percent in Europe.

Total tax revenue in the UK has been higher than the European average since 1970; but the difference has reduced from around 10 percent in 1970 to 0.5 percent in 1999. Direct taxes in the UK are higher than the European average, but following a decreasing trend, the opposite of the European one. In particular, personal income tax in the UK reached its maximum in 1975, at 14 percent of GDP against 9 percent in Europe. The difference decreased by just one percentage point in 1999, respectively 11 percent and 10 percent of GDP.

The UK corporate tax revenue is slightly higher than the European average, the range being one to two percentage points from 1970 to 1999.

The introduction of VAT in the UK in 1973, and its increase during the 1990s seemed to not affect the difference in the indirect tax revenues between the UK and Europe. In fact the UK receipts were always (except in 1975) lower than the European ones by around one percentage point. This may be due to the role of excise duties, that decreased from 1970 to 1999, but were always higher than in Europe, while VAT was always lower.

An important difference between the UK and Europe arises looking at the social contribution revenues, which are far less in the UK by at least five percentage points. This is primarily due to the structural changes of social contribution structure during the 1980s. The UK's cut in contributions in 1985 increased this difference from six percentage points to more than seven in 1999.

Finally, central government revenues in the UK were higher than the European average from 1970 to 1999. This is due to the minor role of local taxes in the UK, which accounted for 1.4 percent of GDP in 1999 against 4.3 percent in the rest of Europe.

Some quantitative and institutional features of main taxes

The personal income tax – PIT

In the UK over 27 million individuals pay personal income tax, but not all kinds of income are taxable. Tax may be payable on income from employment and self-employment, profit from business, occupational pensions, building society and bank interest, dividends on shares, and income from property. Tax is payable on some social security benefits such as the state retirement pension, widow's pension, unemployment benefit and incapacity benefit, but not on others such as income support or child benefit.

Income tax is not payable on: incapacity benefit, widow's payment, war disablement pension, interest received from certain national savings products such as national savings certificates, interest, dividends and other income from investments held in a Personal Equity Plan (PEP), or from a Tax Exempt Special Savings Account (TESSA) (unless you closed it before the five years were up), or an Individual Savings Account (ISA), and finally on premium bonds, national lottery winnings or gambling prizes.

The income tax year of assessment runs from 6 April until the following 5 April.

Income tax operates through a system of allowances and bands of income. An individual's taxable income is calculated by adding together all sources of income liable to tax, and then subtracting allowances and reliefs which are available at the taxpayer's marginal rate. Each individual has a personal allowance. Table 11.2 gives details of some of these allowances and shows their values.

In 2001–2 a taxpayer aged under 65 years received a personal allowance of £4,535, an older taxpayer would be entitled to a higher allowance. Over-65s with an income higher than a certain limit are subject to a taper of 50 percent on their allowance, which is gradually reduced to a minimum level equal to the allowance for the people under 65. In the past, married

Table 11.2 Allowances (financial year 2001–2)

	Personal allowance £ p.a.	Married couples £ p.a.	Income limit £ p.a.
aged under 65	4,535	–	–
aged 65–74	5,990	5,365	17,600
aged 75 and over	6,260	5,435	17,600

Source: Inland Revenue statistics (2002).

couples were entitled to a married couple's allowance (MCA), in addition to their personal allowances. From 6 April 2000, the MCA was abolished for couples where the older partner was born after 5 April 1935; this benefit is available at a flat rate of 10 percent (that means 10 percent of £5,365).

A specific allowance is available to blind people, £1,450 a year per person; married couples where both spouses are blind get double this amount. Two other allowances removed recently are the additional personal allowance (APA), which was available for separated and unmarried people with children, and widow's bereavement allowance. The revenue from the abolition of this benefit is allocated to financing a new children's tax credit (CTC), that is payable to all families with children aged under 16 living with them. In 2001–2, the allowance was 10 percent of £5,200, but the credit is gradually reduced for high-rate taxpayers.

From October 1999 the working families' tax credit (WFTC) has been introduced: for families with an adult working 16 hours or more per week there is a basic tax credit, certain tax credits for each child depending on his or her age, and an extra tax credit for working 30 hours or more per week. WFTC is reduced for families with a net income above a specified limit.

When all eligible reliefs and allowances have been deducted from income liable to tax, taxable income is subject to different tax rates depending upon the "tax band" in which the income falls.

In the 2001–2 financial year, taxable income up to £1,880 is taxed at the lower rate of 10 percent;[2] the next £27,520 is subject to the basic rate of 22 percent, and the portion of income above £29,400 is taxed at the higher rate of 40 percent.

The bands and allowances of individual income tax are subject to statutory indexation provisions, the increase is in line with the percentage increase in the retail price index.

According to the Inland Revenue (2002), the number of taxpayers subject to the lower rate is around 3.7 million, 14 percent of the total. A total of 21 million individuals, that is 76 percent of the total, are taxed at the basic rate and less than three million at the higher rate. However, observing the amount paid as a percentage of the total, the richer individuals pay around 50 percent of all income tax revenue, and middle-income taxpayers just under 49 percent.

Table 11.3 Tax rates and bands (financial year 2001–2)

	Rate of tax	*Band of income*
lower	10%	0–£1,880
basic	22%	£1,881–£29,400
higher	40%	over £29,400

Source: Inland Revenue statistics (2002).

Corporation tax – CT

Corporation tax is charged on the profits made by UK resident companies, public corporations and unincorporated associations such as industrial and provident societies, clubs and trade associations; the tax is not levied on partnerships. Profits taxed are the ones made in each accounting period, i.e. the period over which the company draws up its accounts. The rates of tax are set for the financial year – April to March – where an accounting period straddles 31 March the profits are apportioned between the two financial years on a time basis.

The "all-in" statutory corporate tax rate in the UK is 30 percent, and is the result of different reforms that, in the last 22 years, reduced the rate from a maximum of 52 percent to the current one.

In the 2001–2 financial year, there were three rates and a system of relief that produced a smooth progression in the average tax rate from the lower rate to the main rate.

A starting rate of 10 percent is charged on profits below £10,000, earned after 1 April 2000. Between £10,000 and £50,000 (upper limit), taxable profits are charged at the small companies' rate of 20 percent, with marginal relief given, at the fraction of 1/40, on the amount by which the upper profit limit exceeds taxable profits. This relief produces an effective marginal rate of 22.5 percent. For firms with profits between £50,000 and £300,000 the small companies' rate of 20 percent is applied. Between the lower (£300,000) and upper (£1,500,000) limits of the small companies' rate, taxable profits are charged at the main rate of 30 percent with marginal relief given, at the fraction of 1/40, such that an effective marginal rate of 32.5 percent is levied on profits in excess of £300,000. Over £1,500,000 taxable profits are charged at the main rate of 30 percent.

The profit limits are restricted if a company is part of a group and in proportion to the size of that group, to prevent abuse by a large company fragmenting into smaller ones.

More recently, for financial year 2002–3, the 20 percent and 10 percent

Table 11.4 Rates and bands of corporation tax (financial year 2001–2)

Profits	Marginal rate of tax (%)		Marginal tax relief	Effective marginal rate (%)	Average rate (%)
Under £10,000	10.0			10.0	10.0
£10,001–£50,000	20.0	+	1/40	22.5	10.0–20.0
£50,001–£300,000	20.0			22.0	20.0
£300,001–£1,500,000	30.0	+	1/40	32.5	20.0–30.0
Over £1,500,000	30.0			30.0	30.0

Source: Inland Revenue statistics, 2002.

tax rates have been reduced to, respectively, 19 percent and zero percent, in order to stimulate new entrepreneurship and the growth of small businesses.

For corporation tax purposes, a company's profits include its income and capital gains. Income, whether from trading or investments, is calculated in the same way as for income tax purposes, including capital allowances where appropriate.

Business profit must be computed on a profit and loss statement basis, which gives a true and fair view, subject to any adjustment required or authorized by law in computing profits for those purposes.

Among the positive components of a company's profit there are operating revenues and sundry incomes, excepting property values.

Stock-in-trade is a positive component of income and it is evaluated to be the lower between acquisition cost and market value; if it is not possible to know the value of all undelivered goods, the method of evaluation admitted by law is the FIFO.

Among negative components of income there are all operating costs except costs of capital (distinction between circulating capital and capital assets).

In working out the business profit it is not allowed to deduct the cost of buying, altering or improving fixed assets, or depreciation or any losses that arise when they are sold. Instead, it is possible to claim tax allowances called capital allowances. An adjustment, known as a balancing charge, may arise when an item in the business is sold, given away or no longer used.

Capital allowances provide relief, for corporation tax purposes, for the consumption or depreciation of capital assets incurred for the purposes of trade. Different types of assets qualify for different rates of allowances, and two methods of depreciation can be used: declining-balance or straight-line (see Table 11.5).

The declining-balance method means that a fixed percentage of a not amortized cost is written off each year; for example, if investment is £100 and the ratio of depreciation is 20 percent, in the first year it is written off

Table 11.5 Main rates of capital allowance

Type of asset	Rates (%)	Method of depreciation
Plant and machinery	25.0	Declining-balance
Industrial buildings	4.0	Straight-line
Hotels	4.0	Straight-line
Other commercial buildings	4.0	Straight-line
Patents	25.0	Declining-balance
Know-how	25.0	Declining-balance
Research and development	100.0	

Source: Inland Revenue statistics (2002).

by £20, in the second year by £16 (25 percent of the remaining balance of £80), and so on.

The straight-line method writes off the same percentage of the initial investment each year; for example, using the same values as above, £20 per annum is written off for four years.

Capital allowances may be claimed in the year in which they accrue and any unused capital allowances may be carried forward to set off against profits in later years.

For plant and machinery the allowances are known as writing down allowances, and these are worked out at 25 percent of the cost of the item or "pool" of items for each year, using the declining-balance method. In addition, first year allowances are available for expenditure on plant and machinery by small and medium-sized enterprises at 40 percent.

Most plant and machinery can be lumped together in a single "pool" of expenditure with just a single calculation, no matter how many items are included. This is known as "pooling." If something is bought in the period covered by the accounts, the cost is added to the pool. Conversely, if something is sold, the sale proceeds are deducted from the pool. If the sale price is more than the value of the pool, the difference is a balancing charge. Once these adjustments have been made, the writing down allowance for those accounts is calculated.

If a company makes a trading loss, then that loss can be carried back for one year to set against the profits of an earlier accounting period. An unrelieved trading loss can also be carried forward indefinitely to set against income from the same trade in a future accounting period.

Deductions are allowed from a company's total profits for any charges (interest and other payments) it pays and, in the case of an investment company, its management expenses. From April 1996, new "loan relationship" rules have been introduced for the treatment of interest and similar payments. A deduction against tax liability is allowed for income tax deducted at source from interest received (to the extent that it is not used to cover income tax, the company itself deducts on the interest payments it makes). In addition, the royalties paid for the license agreements of patents and trademarks are deductible as charges on incomes; double taxation relief for foreign tax is allowed as a deduction against the tax on profits.

Taxation of income from financial capital

As far as dividends, in 1965 with the introduction of corporation tax, the government added a charge to income tax when profits were distributed. To mitigate this double tax charge, in 1973, a "partial imputation system" was introduced: the twin mechanisms of advance corporation tax (ACT) and tax credits.

A company paid the ACT when it distributed profits to its shareholders in the form of dividends; the ACT rate was linked to the lower rate of income tax at 20 percent. ACT could be deducted, within a limits, from the corporation tax liability of the accounting period; the remaining tax liability was called "mainstream" corporation tax. ACT financed the tax credit, which the Exchequer made available to the shareholder receiving the dividend. The tax credit could be deducted from the shareholder's income tax liability on the dividend.

A company with the whole of the ACT not offset against the corporation tax had a "surplus ACT." This could be carried back for up to six years to reduce tax liability in earlier accounting periods, or it could be carried forward without time limit. In any accounting period the amount of ACT set against corporation tax was limited to the amount that absorbed the whole of the profits of the accounting period. For example, a company with profits of 100 would have had an ACT limit of 20 (a 25 percent rate of ACT is assumed), because a distribution of 80 and ACT of 20 would have absorbed all the profits of 100.

From April 1999 ACT was abolished and a new payment system introduced for larger companies. Under the new scheme a big firm pays its corporation tax in four equal quarterly installments on the basis of its anticipated liabilities for the accounting period; no account for the distribution of profits is due in advance. The first installment is due in month seven of the accounting period with further installments due in months 10, 13, and 16 with any balance to be paid nine months after the end of the period.

Small and medium-sized enterprises pay all of their tax nine months after the end of the accounting period.

For shareholders, when they get their dividend cheque they also get a tax credit voucher; this shows the amount of the dividend payable and the amount of the tax credit that goes with that dividend. The tax credit is not tax deducted on behalf of the individual, but it represents the fact that the company paying the dividend has paid tax on the profits used to pay the dividend.

Before 1999 the tax credit was equal to the ACT paid by the company, and for individuals that meant 20 percent of the received dividend. Actually, tax credit is 10 percent of the individual's dividend income, and for dividends paid up to 5 April 1999 claim payment of the tax is allowed; instead tax credits on dividends paid after 5 April 1999 cannot be claimed.

For income tax purposes taxable income is worked out adding dividend and tax credit; for individuals, dividend income is taxed at 10 percent up to the basic rate limit, which for the financial year 2001–2 is £29,400, and at 32.5 percent above that amount.

Dividends paid by UK authorized unit trusts and open-ended investment companies are treated in the same way as dividends from shares.

With regards to interest, as a general rule, from 6 April 1996 interest paid to investors by building societies, banks and local authorities is credited net of tax at the rate of 20 percent unless the investor is a non-taxpayer and has registered to receive interest without deduction of tax. Only higher-rate taxpayers have to pay more tax on their interest.

Net interest is also paid by UK authorized unit trusts, open-ended investment companies, certain British government securities and securities of foreign governments. For all taxpayers apart from those paying higher tax rate, this ensures that the individual's tax liability on income has been met in full and there is usually no need for the individual to make a return to the Inland Revenue.

For income tax purposes, taxable income is worked out by adding the total "gross" interest; this is done by summing up all the taxable interests received and the taxes taken off.

For example, if interest from a savings account is £160 and £40 tax has already been taken off, the gross interest on the account is £160 + £40 = £200.

If taxable income in a financial year does not exceed the personal allowance or starting rate band, investors can claim to receive any tax overpaid, and, in case of interest, the tax taken off.

Finally, the capital gain tax (CGT) was introduced in 1965 and is charged on gains arising from the disposal of assets, such as: shares in a company, units in a unit trust, land and buildings, higher value jewellery, paintings, antiques and other personal effects, assets used in a business (e.g. goodwill). CGT affects individuals, trustees and personal representatives; corporation tax is instead levied on capital gains made by companies.

Some assets are exempt from CGT:

1   private cars, cash held in sterling, any foreign currency held for personal use;
2   jewellery, paintings, antiques and other personal effects that are individually worth up to £6,000;
3   savings certificates, premium bonds and British savings bonds, UK government stocks;
4   assets held in an Individual Savings Account (ISA) or Personal Equity Plan (PEP);
5   betting, lottery or pools winnings, personal injury compensation;

In 1998, individual capital gains tax was reformed:

1   introducing a taper relief system;
2   removing the previous indexation allowance;
3   charging to CGT gains accruing during a period of temporary residence abroad in the year of return to the UK;
4   simplifying the CGT charges structure for the gains of trustees and personal representatives of deceased persons.

Taper relief reduces the amount of capital gains tax paid according to the number of whole years (up to a maximum of ten) that an asset has been held. The greater the length of the "qualifying holding period," the smaller the percentage of the gain that is chargeable to tax. There are two different percentage tables, one for business assets and one for non-business assets. Business assets are assets used wholly or partly for trading purposes, or shares and securities in a company; the regime allows a greater reduction for business assets than for others. However, in both instances taper relief, no matter how long the asset has been held, will not cover a proportion of the gain. The March 2000 Budget reduced the taper length for business assets from ten years to four.

The relevant period of ownership is generally equal to the shorter time between the qualifying holding period and the last ten years of the qualifying holding period.

To calculate the CGT, the first step is to list all the assets disposed of in the tax year (6 April to 5 April in the following year). Exempt assets and disposals that do not give rise to a CGT charge and the disposal of private homes can be ignored. Then the gain on each asset is worked out.

The second step is to multiply the amount of any gain chargeable to CGT by the appropriate percentage shown by the taper relief table, according to the years in the qualifying holding period and as it applies to business assets or non-business assets, as the case may be.

Losses of the same period and losses brought forward are to be set against untapered gains before the taxable amount is charged to CGT. In this way net gains are tapered after deducting losses and the taxpayer has the greatest benefit from tapering, resulting in the lowest amount chargeable to CGT.

If the total of net gains in a tax year is less than a certain amount, called the annual exemption amount (AEA), CGT is not paid. For the tax year 2002–3 the AEA is £7,700 for individuals, and £3,750 for trusts. If net gains are more than the AEA, capital gains tax is paid on the excess.

It is estimated that in 2001–2 CGT receipts will be £2.5 billion. This is a small proportion of total government revenues, but CGT is important as an anti-avoidance measure, because it discourages richer individuals from converting large parts of their income into capital gains in order to reduce their tax liability. In 1990–2000 about 186,000 individuals and 29,000 trustees paid CGT.

Value added tax – VAT

VAT is payable on the supply of goods and services by way of business in the UK or Isle of Man. It is also charged on goods, and some services, which are imported from places outside the European Community (EC) and on acquisitions, and some services, received from the EC.

There are currently three rates of VAT:

a   17.5 percent – known as standard-rated goods; on most goods and services;
b   5 percent – known as reduced-rate goods; on fuel and power used in the home and by charities;
c   zero percent – known as zero-rated goods, which do not have VAT levied upon the final good or upon inputs used in its creation. Some examples are: most food, books, newspapers, music, medicines and young children's clothing.

There are also "exempt goods" which are business supplies that have no VAT charged on them at either the standard or zero rate. In this case firms cannot reclaim the VAT paid on inputs. Some examples of exempt supplies are: insurance, selling, leasing and letting land and buildings (not garages, parking spaces, hotel or holiday accommodation) and certain education and training.

It is estimated that almost 56 percent of consumer's expenditure is taxable at the standard rates, and 3 percent at the reduced rate.

Other indirect taxes

Excises duties

Excise duties are flat-rate taxes charged on five major goods: beer, wine, spirits, tobacco and petrol/diesel.

From 28 April 2002, beer and spirits are taxed according to their alcoholic content; wine, home-made wine, cider and perry are all subject to specific (i.e. by volume) duties.

Tobacco products are subject to an additional *ad valorem* tax of 22 percent on the retail price, that includes the flat-rate duty and VAT.

Insurance premium tax

Insurance premium tax (IPT) is a tax on general insurance premiums, and applies to most general insurance where risk insured is located in the UK. There is a standard rate of 5 percent of the gross premium, but there is a higher rate of 17.5 percent for travel insurance and some insurance for vehicles and domestic/electrical appliances.

Most long-term insurance, such as life insurance, is exempted from the tax, as is reinsurance, insurance for commercial ships and aircraft and insurance for commercial goods in international transit. Premiums for risks located outside the UK are also exempt, but they may be liable to similar taxes imposed by other countries.

IPT is designed to act as a proxy of VAT, which is not charged on financial services because of difficulties in implementation.

Landfill tax

This an environmental tax that aims to encourage waste producers to produce less waste, recover more value from waste (for example, through recycling or composting) and to use more environmentally friendly methods of waste disposal.

There are two rates:

a   £2 per tonne for inactive waste;
b   £12 per tonne for all other waste.

Petroleum revenue tax

Companies that earn profits from the extraction of oil and gas from the UK and its continental shelf (mainly from the North Sea) are charged petroleum revenue tax (PRT) as well as corporation tax.

Unlike corporation tax, PRT is not assessed on each company's profits for a 12-month accounting period. It is assessed every six months for each separate oil and gas field, and then levied on the company's share of the cash flow arising in each chargeable period.

The rates at which petroleum revenue tax has been charged since 1993 is 50 percent on existing fields, but new fields are exempt since March 1993.

The corporation tax regime for companies that operate in the North Sea allows any Royalty and PRT liability as a deduction against chargeable profits. In addition to PRT and corporation tax there are royalties levied at 12.5 percent of the value of production, less the cost of initial transportation and treatment, for fields approved before 1 April 1982. Royalties payable are deductible against profits chargeable to PRT and corporation tax.

Local taxes

The most important local tax is the council tax, that replaced the system of local taxation in 1993, or poll tax. It is a property-based tax set annually by each local council, to help pay for local services.

Each domestic property is evaluated according to the assessment of its "capital value" and placed on a "valuation list" in one of eight "valuation bands," from A to H.

Valuation is carried out by the Valuation Office Agency, not by the local authority, and valuation lists can be compiled fairly only by assessing values of dwellings on one common date: 1 April 1991 was the date chosen for this exercise.

Capital values estimated the amount of each dwelling as if it had been sold on the open market on 1 April 1991, subject to certain assumptions.

The object is to determine the relative values of properties within a particular area on a particular date.

In a local area, basic council tax bills for each band depend on the proportions laid down by law. For example, in band A the range of value of a property is up to £40,000 and the proportion fixed by law is six. If the council tax for a dwelling in band A is £200:

a   the bill for one in band D will be one and a half times that amount
     (6:9): £300;
b   for one in band H three times that amount (6:18): £600;
c   and for a dwelling in band F, the bill will be (6:13): £433.

There are, however, a range of exemptions and reliefs available: properties with only one resident adult have 25 percent reduction in their bill. If the house is not the main home (e.g. empty, or a second home) the bill is reduced by 50 percent. In addition, properties that are exempt from council tax include student halls of residence and armed forces barracks.

In 2001–2, council tax was estimated to raise almost £14.1 billion, equal to 20 percent of local government revenue.

A second local tax is the business rate that is applied to occupied or unoccupied non-domestic properties, such as shops, offices, warehouses and factories, and any other property that is not classed as domestic property.

If a property is used for domestic and non-domestic use (e.g. a shop with a flat above) both council tax and business rates will be charged.

Some types of properties are exempt from business rates, for example: agricultural land and buildings, fish farms, churches, public parks.

Every non-domestic property, unless exempt, has a ratable value, that is an official estimate of the market rent for the property.

The local council works out the tax by multiplying the ratable value of the property by the multiplier or "poundage," set each year by the central government. In 2001–2 the poundage[3] was set at 43p, for example, if the ratable value was £12,000, the bill for the year would be £5,160.

Properties are normally revalued every five years (the next valuation is in 2005), and the transitional relief scheme introduced in England makes sure that each business rate does not change beyond certain limits because of revaluation.

Furthermore, relief is available for certain types of property: unoccupied buildings, small rural shops, agricultural land and associated buildings, property used for charitable works.

Business rates were estimated to raise almost £17.5 billion in 2001–2. This is a considerable value, greater than the council tax revenue.

The fiscal burden

The distribution of taxation charge

Looking at the evolution of the overall tax system, according to the economic functions, from 1970 to 1997 a stable pattern appears: labor, capital and consumption remain at 32 percent of GDP.

The taxation on labor was 18 percent of GDP in 1975, but over the following ten years it reached 15 percent. At the end of the 1990s taxes on employed labor accounted for 39 percent of total taxation or 14.5 of GDP. Taxes on self-employed labor remained stable at 0.2 percent of GDP, for the entire period considered. In the UK capital taxes are very high, accounting for around 27 percent of total taxation. One-third of taxes on capital are on real estate and more than half on various kinds of income. Over recent years, capital taxes decreased slightly from 12 percent of GDP in 1990 to 10 percent in 1997.

However, one-third of the tax revenue in the UK is levied in the form of consumption taxes (mainly VAT and excise duties). Between 1985 and 1995 there was a shift toward indirect taxation: increasing VAT and extending it to domestic fuel. Environmental taxes accounted for around 3 percent of GDP, they remained almost stable from 1970 to 1997. The main component is the tax on energy that is around 2 percent of GDP.

Implicit tax rates measure the incidence of the tax burden on each factor of production: labor, capital and consumption. Implicit tax rates

Table 11.6 Structure according to the economic function as a percentage of GDP

	1970	1975	1980	1985	1990	1995	1997
Consumption	10.3	8.9	10.1	11.3	11.0	12.2	12.4
Labor	14.9	18.0	16.8	15.0	14.6	15.1	14.7
employed	14.7	17.8	16.7	14.8	14.3	14.9	14.5
self-employed	0.2	0.2	0.1	0.2	0.2	0.2	0.2
Capital, of which	11.8	10.0	9.5	12.1	12.2	9.4	9.9
real estate[1] and capital	4.0	4.1	3.9	4.2	2.9	3.4	3.5
monetary capital[2]	1.0	0.6	0.3	0.4	0.5	0.2	0.2
Environment	3.4	2.2	2.2	2.7	2.7	3.0	3.0
energy	2.6	1.4	1.4	1.8	1.9	2.3	2.3
transport	0.9	0.8	0.8	0.9	0.8	0.6	0.6
pollution[3]	0.0	0.0	0.0	0.0	0.0	0.0	0.0
Total	37.2	37.2	36.6	38.7	38.0	36.9	37.2

Source: Eurostat (2000).

Notes
1997 is the last datum available.
1 Excludes income tax on rent and stamp duty on property transactions due to lack of data.
2 Excludes income tax on savings and stamp duty share due to lack of data.
3 Includes stamp duty on property transactions and shares, windfall tax and community charge (poll tax).

are obtained by relating the broad categories of tax revenue to the corresponding tax bases: labor income (gross wage), capital income (gross operating surplus) and consumption expenditure.

Table 11.7 shows the implicit tax rates in the UK from 1970 to 1997 (Eurostat 2000). We observe a gradual increase in tax rates on labor employed from 25 percent to around 28 percent, in the period from 1970 to 1980. The reform of income tax at the end of the 1970s involved a decrease of 1 percent of implicit tax rates on labor from 1980 to 1985. A further reduction was due to cuts in social contributions in the mid-1980s: the implicit rates on labor employed reached 25 percent in 1990. Then we observe some fluctuation but always over a range of just 2 percent.[4]

Over the last 25 years, the implicit tax rate on labor employed has been quite stable around 26.5 percent; in 1980, there was a peak to 28 percent.

The implicit tax rates on other factors of production, which include capital taxation and the taxation of self-employed, decreased from a peak of nearly 60 percent in 1975 to around 48 percent in 1980. In 1984 there was an important reform that cut the main corporation tax rate; nevertheless the implicit tax rates rose again, up to 53 percent in 1991. The 1984 reform was intended as neutral revenue, but in fact it raised receipts by bringing many more companies into a taxpaying position.

A further reduction of corporation tax rate (1991–2) instead involved a sharp decrease of implicit tax rates, from 53 percent in 1991 to 37 percent in 1997.[5] In the last decade this development has been strongly influenced by the relative decline of the taxes on real estate.

Implicit tax rates on consumption were quite stable from 1970 to 1997:

Table 11.7 Implicit tax rates in the UK and Europe, 1970–97

		Consumption	Labor employed	Other factor
1970	UK	15.2	25.0	55.4
	EU	15.2	28.9	27.5
1975	UK	12.8	27.3	58.0
	EU	13.0	32.2	38.4
1980	UK	14.3	27.9	48.4
	EU	13.5	35.1	42.2
1985	UK	16.2	26.8	50.6
	EU	13.3	37.1	38.7
1990	UK	15.6	24.8	52.8
	EU	37.5	37.5	37.4
1995	UK	16.1	26.3	35.9
	EU	14.2	41.7	35.7
1997	UK	16.5	26.5	37.1
	EU	14.5	41.9	38.2

Source: Eurostat (2000).

the lowest value was 13 percent in 1975, then the rates increased by up to 16 percent in 1985, and they varied around 15.5 percent and 16.5 percent throughout the 1990s.

The shift toward indirect taxation provides a mere 1 percent increase of implicit tax rates on consumption, and a greater reduction of implicit rates on capital, around 18 percent in 27 years. Labor is quite stable: the change of income tax does not involve a decline of implicit tax rate. Nevertheless, despite the reforms, the highest implicit tax rate remains on others factors: 10 percent higher than labor, and 20 percent more than consumption.

The shift away from direct taxation toward indirect taxation since 1985 also affected the progressivity of the tax system. Looking at the proportion of income of each decile taken by direct taxes (Jiles and Johnson 1994), it increased strongly from 7 percent in the bottom decile to 30 percent in the top decile, in 1995. This reflects the progressive nature of direct taxation: the tax allowances involve no taxation in the bottom deciles of income, and the average rate increases as income rises.

Direct tax cuts since 1985 reduced the tax burden in each decile in a regressive way. They reduced the proportion of income taken by direct tax more in the richer deciles than in the poorer ones. In the top decile, direct tax burden fell from 34.2 percent to 30.5 percent between 1985 and 1995, and for the 1 percent of the income distribution the drop is bigger, around 10 percent. This means that richer people benefit from the cutting of the higher marginal rate, from 60 percent to 40 percent. In 1999, the government tried to solve this inequality by cutting the lower rate of income tax from 20 percent to 10 percent. This measure should

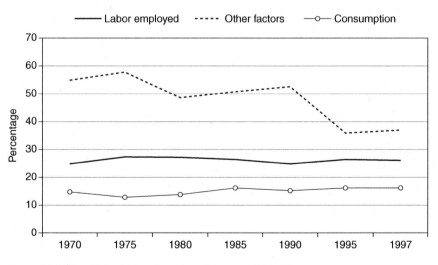

Figure 11.1 The United Kingdom: implicit rates 1970–97.

Source: Eurostat (2000).

increase the progressivity of the tax, reducing the proportion of income taken by tax in the bottom decile.

Since 1985 the increase of indirect taxation has imposed a greater burden in every decile, but by more in the poorer deciles than in the richer ones, thus increasing regressivity. Indirect tax burden rose by 4 percent at the bottom of income distribution and only by 1.5 percent at the top (Jiles and Johnson 1994).

A simple numerical measure of the redistributive effect of the income tax is the difference between the Gini coefficient pre-tax and post tax. According to the calculated Gini coefficient (Jiles and Johnson 1994) for pre-tax equivalent income and for post-tax equivalent income under the 1985 and 1995 tax regimes, the first redistributive effect in the first regime was 0.0468 and in, the second, 0.0338. The 1995 tax system reduced the Gini coefficient by 9 percent, 3.5 percent less than the 1985 system; the RE declines by 0.013 that is around 28 percent. These measures show the regressivity and inequality introduced by the tax changes.

In the study by Wagstaff *et al.* (1999) RE is 0.0352, which means a post-tax reduction of inequality of around 8 percent; the Kakwani's progressivity index is 0.2278. The re-ranking index R, obtained comparing the post-tax Gini coefficient with the post-tax concentration coefficient, is 6.3 percent. In the absence of a marginal tax rate in excess of 100 percent, re-ranking is only due to the differential tax treatment. However, the discrepancy[6] between the redistributive effect and vertical redistribution is very small. This means that, in terms of its impact on redistribution of income, the differential tax treatment is less important than progressivity.

Tax wedges on labor and corporate taxation

The average tax wedge on labor, at the wage level of an average production worker (APW) is less than 28 percent in the UK (Joumard 2001). It can be divided into three components: first, personal income tax, which is the largest, accounting for almost 15 percent, more than 50 percent of the total wedge. The second and the third components of the tax wedge on labor are the employees' and employers' social security contributions: they account for around 6.5 percent each, less than 25 percent of total wedge. At the taxable income level of an average production worker (APW), the marginal tax wedge on labor is around 40 percent. For workers earning 50–60 percent more than the APW, the marginal tax wedge decreases to around 35 percent; for all the remaining higher-income earners, the marginal tax wedge is more than 45 percent (Joumard 2001).

Between 1991 and 2000 the average tax wedge decreased by almost 2.5 percent. The lower tax wedge is due to the policy of reduction of social contributions at the bottom end of the pay scale, and the introduction of tax allowances for workers whose earnings are below certain thresholds (such as the working families' tax credit[7]). All these measures, reducing the average tax rate on the low-income worker, are effective in terms of creating job opportunities for low-skilled workers and may enhance the vertical equity of the tax system.

The impact of corporate taxation on economic activity can be analyzed through the effective corporate tax rates, both average and marginal. The statutory corporate tax rate gives some information, but it is too limited. In the UK there is a negative tax break of around 5 percent: the statutory corporate tax rate is 30 percent, the effective tax rate is almost 25 percent (Joumard 2001).

According to the forward-looking approach, in the case of equity-financed investment (see Giannini and Maggiulli 2001), the marginal effective tax rate is around 35 percent and the average tax rate (computed assuming a 20 percent rate of profitability) is 32 percent. Both the effective tax rates are greater than the statutory rate (30 percent), and the average rate decreases with the increase in profitability.

In most countries, the effective marginal rate is lower than the statutory one and the average rate increases with profitability. The reason for the UK's different situation is due to relatively high real property taxes, such as business rates for companies, which impose a greater effective tax burden on marginal investments than on more profitable ones.

When the source of finance is debt, the effective marginal tax rate is negative, −25 percent, because of interest deductibility and tax allowances for depreciation in excess of economic depreciation. The effective average rate (at 20 percent profitability) is 22 percent and is lower than the statutory rate (30 percent). Effective tax rates in the case of debt finance are always lower than the effective rates in the case of equity finance.

The effective marginal tax rate is 25 percent and the average rate (at 20 percent profitability) is 28 percent; both the rates are lower than the statutory rate (30 percent).

Taxation by levels of government and fiscal federalism

Central government raised around 70 percent of total tax revenues in 1975. The percentage was quite similar in 1985 and increased greatly in 1999, reaching 77.5 percent (OECD 2001).

Local taxation has always been very low in the UK, in 1975 it was around 11 percent of total revenue, and 10 percent in 1985, decreasing dramatically to 4 percent in 1999.

Local taxes have been reformed twice, but the final system is more similar to the original than the intermediate one (OECD 2002). In 1990 there was a big reform in local taxation: the introduction of a poll tax to replace the domestic rates. The taxes on the rental value of a home were substituted by a per capita charge, unrelated to income or property value. The unpopularity of poll tax, due in part to its high level, induced the government in 1991 to introduce a subsidy, paid for by an increase in VAT. This intervention was part of the switch from direct to indirect taxation (Jiles and Johnson 1994).

If it had not been for the poll tax subsidy, there would have been a general increase in the level of local taxes; instead they fell over the period. In the following years, the poll tax was abolished, and the actual system was based on the council tax and business rates.[8]

For these reasons today there are local taxes only on property, accounting for just 1.5 percent of GDP (OECD 2001), although the individual burden of taxation is one of the highest in the EU.

A comparative view against the European average

The implicit tax rates on labor in the UK were significantly below the EU average (Eurostat 2000): in 1970 the difference was only four percentage points, but while in Europe the rate gradually increased, reaching 35 percent in 1980, in the UK the rate was 28 percent. At the end of the 1990s, the EU average was 42 percent, 15 percentage points more than the UK. The main difference was due to the low social securities contributions paid in the UK: in 1999, the effective tax rate on non-wage labor costs (social contributions) accounted for 12 percent in the UK and 25 percent in the EU.

The implicit tax rate on other factors (capital) in the UK is about 28 percentage points higher than the EU average. In 1980 the difference was reduced to only six percentage points; and in 1997 the trend changed; in fact, the EU rate (38 percent) overcame the UK one (37 percent).

The implicit tax rate on consumption in the UK is always higher than the EU average; the difference was around one percentage point until 1980. Since 1985, the increase of indirect taxes (VAT and excises duties) in the UK involved a rise of implicit tax rate, doubling the difference with the EU average.

In the UK, the pre-tax Gini coefficient is the highest among the 12 OECD countries analyzed (Wagstaff *et al.* 1999). Nevertheless, the redistributive effect of the income tax is higher than that of other countries such as Germany, Denmark and USA. The UK is in a cluster of countries, also comprising Ireland, Italy and Spain, which all have average rate values of around 15 percent. This is a middle value, between a minimum of 6.2 percent for France and a maximum of 32 percent for Sweden. The Kakwani's progressivity index in the UK is one of the highest among the 12 countries; this shows that, despite the progressivity-reducing tax reforms during the 1980s, the PIT is still progressive by international standards (Wagstaff *et al.* 1999).

The difference between the effective and the statutory corporate tax rate in the UK (−5 percent) is one of the lowest among the main EU countries: the EU tax break is −10 percent, and more than −15 percent in Belgium, Portugal and Austria (Joumard 2001).

The statutory corporate tax in the UK is one of the lowest in the EU, along with Ireland and the Nordic countries, and far less than Germany, Italy and France (Giannini and Maggiulli 2001).

The average tax wedge on labor (28 percent) is very low: it is slightly less than the OECD average (30 percent), far less than the EU average (around 45 percent) and less than the tax wedges of Germany, Italy, France and the Nordic countries. The marginal tax wedge in the UK (39 percent) is a little less than the OECD average (40 percent), and more than 15 percentage points less than the EU average (Joumard 2001).

Tax reforms in the 1990s and those currently planned

A quick glance at the budget and the general economic environment

The UK economy was successful in 2000. GDP growth increased to 3 percent, significantly above its post-war average of around 2.5 percent; it is expected to increase by between 2.25 percent to 2.75 percent a year over the next three years. Household consumption rose by 3.6 percent. Business investment decelerated in 2000 following rapid growth over previous years, but general government investment increased by an estimated 5 percent. External demand lifted total export volume growth to nearly 7.5 percent in 2000, and goods volumes rose at their fastest rate since 1973. Manufacturing output rose by 1.6 percent, and saw the highest growth since 1994; this contributed to a better net trade performance compared to the previous two years.

Unemployment reached its lowest level since the 1970s: between 1997 and 2000 the International Labour Organisation (ILO) measure of unemployment has fallen by 520,000, with the rate down from 7.2 percent to 5.3 percent, that means just 3.5 percent on a claimant count basis.

The reasons for the unexpected strength of employment growth are the sharp reduction of the non-accelerating inflation rate of unemployment (NAIRU), the containment of wage pressure, caused by reductions in long-term unemployment, the more effective job search and the enhanced product market competition.

Across the public sector, the current budget balance has improved from a deficit of 3 percent of GDP in 1996–7 to a surplus of 2.1 percent in 1999–2000. The current budget surplus in 2000–1 is estimated to have risen to 2.4 percent of GDP: current revenue should be 40.5 percent of GDP and current expenditure 38.1 percent. The surplus is projected to be around 1.7 percent of GDP in 2001–2 and 1.5 percent in 2002–3 (HM Treasury 2002).

The reason for the lower surplus from 2001–2 was the real rise in government expenditure planned at 2.5 percent a year, more than GDP growth estimated at 2.25 percent a year, and the result of some stimulatory taxation measures. Receipt projections were also lower than expected.

The latest outcome of public sector net investment is 0.4 percent of GDP in 1999–2000, and projections show a rise from 0.7 percent of GDP in 2000–1 to 1.5 percent in 2002–3.

Net borrowing is equal to net investment minus the surplus on the current budget. The rapid growth of net investment results in declining surpluses of net borrowing, ranging from −1.7 percent of GDP in 1999–2000 to −0.6 percent of GDP in 2001–2; a net borrowing deficit of 1 percent of GDP was estimated for 2003–4.

The projections of negative net borrowing result in a declining net debt–GDP ratio. It fell from 36.8 percent of GDP in 1999–2000, to 31.8 percent in 2000–1 and to 29.6 percent of GDP in 2002–3. In the coming years there will be small increases of net debt, caused by the modest level of borrowing, but the debt–GDP ratio will remain fairly constant at around 30 percent of GDP.

The primary balance has risen from a deficit of 0.5 percent of GDP in 1996–7, to an estimated surplus of 4 percent in 2000–1. Projections for the future show a decline, but the surplus remains positive up to 2005–6, estimated at around 0.5 percent of GDP.

Tax reforms in the 1990s and before

In 1979 the reform of the rate structure represented the most dramatic change in personal income tax. Until that date there was a lower rate of 25 percent, a basic rate of 33 percent and a higher rate ranging from 40 percent to 83 percent. In addition, a surcharge of 15 percent was applied to high investment incomes, leading to a maximum rate of 89 percent. In 1979, the government abolished the lower rate, reduced the basic rate to 30 percent and the higher to 60 percent; in 1984 the surcharge was abolished. In 1988, the top rate was cut to 40 percent, the basic to 25 percent and lower to zero.

In 1992 the very simple rate structure with two rates (25 and 40 percent) was complicated by the reintroduction of the lower rate at 20 percent, and this was further reduced in 1999 to 10 percent. In 2000 we note that the basic rate was lowered from 23 percent to 22 percent, and in 2001 the bottom tax band was widened.

Other changes concern the allowances system: in 1990, the independent taxation[9] of husbands and wives was introduced with a married couple's allowance (MCA). From 1993, MCA was reduced in value and was finally abolished in 2000; contextually, child benefits have been increased and a means-tested children's tax credit (CTC) has been introduced which provides support for children directly through the tax system.

Since 2000 the more generous working families tax credit (WFTC) has replaced family credit, and two further reforms are planned for 2003. The first is the integrated child credit that will combine the support for families provided in the CTC, in the WFTC and in means-tested benefits for those out of work. Out-of-work families and lower-paid working parents are eligible for this credit.

The second reform is the employment tax credit (ETC), which extends the principle of WFTC to workers without children.

As for social security contributions, since 1975 national insurance contributions have been earnings-related, subject to an income floor.

Prior to 1985 the NI contributions were due on earnings higher than £72 per week, with a jump in liability at rates of 9 percent on all earnings for the employee and of 10.45 percent for the employer. In 1985 there was an important reform that reduced the jump in liability and aligned the rates for employees and employers at 5 percent. In 1989 the entry rate for employers was cut to 2 percent, and then in 1997 the government abolished, for both employees and employers, the jump in liability. Since 2001 employers and employees have started paying for NI contributions when the employee's income reaches the income tax personal allowance. After that limit the employees pay 10 percent of all earnings and employers pay 11.9 percent (with a reduction to 11.8 percent in 2002). In addition, there is an upper income level (UEL) beyond which employees do not pay further contributions. For employers, the UEL was abolished in 1985.

With regards to corporate and capital taxes, companies have been charged corporation tax since 1965, and since 1973 there has been a lower rate for companies with small profits. The "all-in" statutory corporate tax in the UK has been through major reform twice in the last 22 years. The first reduction was in 1984, from 52 percent to 35 percent; in 1992, there was a further cut to 33 percent.

In 1997 the main corporate tax rate was reduced to 30 percent; the government abolished the advanced corporation tax and also changed the taxation on dividend, reducing the tax credit from 20 percent to 10 percent. In 1998 individual capital gains tax was reformed,[10] removing indexation and introducing a tapering system, with the objective of encouraging longer-term holding of assets.

The withholding tax on intra-UK payments of interest and royalties made to companies within the corporation tax charge will be abolished from 2001.

Finally, for consumption taxes, in 1995 the most significant widening of the VAT base since its introduction in 1973 was made. VAT was also imposed on domestic fuel, and the standard rate was increased from 15 percent to 17.5 percent to pay for the reduction of poll tax.

In 1993 there was also an increase on excise duties, notably on petrol and tobacco. Since 2000 the duty on this last commodity has risen by 5 percent. From 2001 a graduated vehicle excise duty for new cars has been introduced, and a climate change levy.

Priorities for future tax reforms

In recent years, in order to improve labor market performance, UK reforms lowered the tax burden on labor. The government's cut the social security contributions at the bottom end of the pay scale, and the trend is a further reduction of NICs for employers. The government's objective is to move the structure of NI nearer to that of income tax, and to change the NI base to match the income tax base more closely. Recent reforms have also reduced the complexity, distortion and horizontal inequity caused by the lack of integration of the two separate systems.

Personal income tax has been reduced, initially for high-income taxpayers involving a regressive redistribution, and, since 1999, cutting the lower tax rate. However, in the UK, 27.6 million individuals, out of an adult population of 45 million, are liable for income tax. This means that attempts to use income tax reductions to help the poorest are likely to fail. The number of lower-rate taxpayers rose after 1992 with the increase of the lower rate band, and fell dramatically in 1999–2000 as the new 10 percent rate was introduced over a narrower range of income than the previous 20 percent rate.

Changes of labor tax and income tax have been accompanied by a reform of the benefit system: the UK has moved from a system that provided financial support to married people, to one that helps poor working families and those with children.

The central strategy of the Conservative government from 1979 to 1997 was the shift from direct to indirect taxes. Nevertheless the balance between direct and indirect taxes changed little: the large growth in VAT was offset by the fall in excise duties, and the reductions in personal income tax were offset by the increase of corporation tax.

The recent debate on VAT concerns two issues: incentives and redistribution (Adam and Frayne 2001). The revenue-neutral shift from direct to indirect taxation was justified by the reduction of tax-induced disincentives to work. But according to the opposite view, the greater number of goods that can be bought with extra work determines the attractiveness of working an extra hour. So a uniform consumption tax and a uniform earnings tax have the same effects. The cut in income tax does not increase the attractiveness of work, if the price of goods rises by an equivalent amount. The shift proposed will reduce the tax burden for one group and increase it for another, affecting in this way the incentives, but the mechanism has little concern for the choice between direct and indirect taxation.

The second argument relates to the justification of zero-rated VAT goods on a distributional basis (Adam and Frayne 2001): low-income earners allocate a large proportion of their expenditure to these items. According to the opposite view, although the better off do not spend much on these goods, they spend a lot of money and are the main beneficiaries of zero rates of VAT. It is unlikely that the best way to help the needy is to identify goods that absorbed a large share of their incomes, then cut indirect taxes for these items.

The direction of new UK reforms, which is consistent with Joumard, is to reduce the complexity of VAT, introducing a package of measures aimed at easing the impact of VAT for small and medium-size enterprises. Moreover, the zero-rating of young children's clothing and footwear will be simplified and modernized.

Enhanced taxation of property should improve the neutrality of the tax system toward different forms of wealth, and can rebalance the tax burden away from labor (Joumard 2001). The UK is the only EU country that adopted this suggestion; in fact there are two forms of taxation on property:

a   national non-domestic rates bearing on productive activities that are property-intensive;
b   council tax based upon property values.

The problem is that the council tax is the only local tax left, because non-domestic rates are set at the national level and it is no longer a local tax in any meaningful sense, but effectively an intermediate tax.

Some suggestions for further reforms arise from the simulations performed by the European Commission for the UK (Leibfritz, Thornton and Bibbee 1997).

A cut in the corporate tax rate by 1 percent of GDP would increase GDP by 4.30 percent, employment by 1.81 percent and wages by 2.54 percent. Nevertheless, if the government aims at increasing employment, it should reduce the labor tax: a cut in the labor tax rate by 1 percent of GDP would increase employment by 2.26 percent.

Another simulation shows that a shift from corporate income tax to consumption tax would increase GDP by 2.32 percent, wages by 2.56 percent and decrease employment by −0.02 percent. If employment were a priority for the government, a shift from labor income tax to consumption tax would increase employment by 0.46 percent. However the shift from labor to corporate tax produces high costs in terms of reductions of GDP and wages

Another important debate concerns double taxation (Inland Revenue 1999). This occurs when income is taxed both by the taxpayer's country of residence and by the country in which the income arises. The credit method[11] is applied in the UK, while other countries use the exemption method.[12] The purpose of double taxation relief is to remove or reduce the disincentive that double taxation represents to outward investment. Credit systems lead in the direction of CEN (capital export neutrality). However, in the UK this is only partially achieved. The main reason is the adoption of the "ordinary credit" method, which involves full neutrality for investment in other countries with tax rates at or below the UK rate and partial neutrality for investment in other countries with tax rates higher than the UK's.

The current discussion is focused on the opportunity to review the UK's system of double taxation relief for companies, with the introduction of an exemption system for direct investment capable to achieve CIN (capital import neutrality) and an optimal allocation of savings. Nevertheless, unilateral adoption of an exemption system for the UK does little to deliver CIN, because it requires a group of countries to collectively adopt this system. Current thinking seems to favor a credit rather than an exemption system: the UK should be more concerned about distortion of allocation of investment than of savings. Moreover, it is not practical to make changes that depend for their effectiveness on the renegotiation of tax treaties.

Notes

1 Assuming €1 = £0.645.
2 Prior to April 1999, the lower rate was 20 percent but applied to a wider band of income.
3 Called uniform business rate or UBR.
4 The average effective tax rates on labor, worked out by Carey and Tchilinguirian (2000) since 1980 to 1997, show a gradual declining trend from 25 percent to 20 percent over the analyzed period. Sometimes there are small increases, but the rates are always in a range of 20–22 percent.
5 The same trend is confirmed by another study (Carey and Tchilinguirian 2000) that calculated average effective tax rates on capital from 1980 to 1997. During the first ten-year period, the rates rose and fell around 45 percent and 50 percent. From 1991 there was a decline to the lowest point of 36 percent in 1994, and then an increase up to 40 percent in the following years.
6 Caused by non-zero-values of horizontal inequity and re-ranking.
7 See pages 276–7 on income tax.
8 See pages 283–4.
9 Prior to 1990, married couples were treated as a single unit for income tax purposes.
10 See pages 284–5.
11 The foreign tax paid on income is deducted from the UK tax payable on the same income.
12 Foreign income is disregarded for tax purposes in the country where the taxpayer is resident.

References

Adam, S. and Frayne, C. (2001) "A survey of the UK tax system," *Briefing Note*, 9, London: The Institute for Fiscal Studies.
Carey, D. and Tchilinguirian, H. (2000) "Average effective tax rates on capital, labour and consumption," Economic Department, Working Paper 258, Paris: OECD.
Eurostat (2000) *Structures of the Taxation Systems in the European Union, 1970–1997*, Brussels: EU Commission.
—— (2002) *New Cronos Statistics*, databank CD-ROM.

Giannini, S. and Maggiulli, C. (2001) *The Effective Tax Rates in the EU Commission Study on Corporate Taxation: Methodological Aspects, Main Results and Policy Implications*, Università di Modena e Reggio Emilia: CAPP.

HM Treasury (2002) *Budget 2001, Investing for the Long Term: Building Opportunity and Prosperity for All*, London.

Inland Revenue (1999) "Double taxation, relief for companies," Discussion paper, London.

Inland Revenue (2002) *Inland Revenue Statistics 2000/2001*, London.

Joumard, I. (2001) "Tax systems in European Union countries," Economics Department Working Paper 301, Paris: OECD.

Leibfritz, W., Thornton, J. and Bibbee, A. (1997) "Taxation and economic performance," Economics Department Working Paper 176, Paris: OECD.

OECD (2001) *Revenue Statistics 1965–2000*, Paris: OECD.

—— (2002) "Fiscal decentralisation in EU applicant states and selected EU Member States," Paris: OECD.

Wagstaff, A. *et al.* (1999) "Redistributive effect, progressivity and differential tax treatment: personal income tax in twelve OECD Countries," *Journal of Public Economics*, 72: 73–98.

Index

References to figures and tables are indicated by *italics*.